Juan Goytisolo and the Poetics of Contagion

Hispanic Studies TRAC
(Textual Research and Criticism)
PUBLICATIONS INSTITUTED BY THE *BULLETIN OF HISPANIC STUDIES*

Textual Research and Criticism (TRAC) publishes Spanish, Portuguese and Latin-American texts of literary, linguistic or historical interest not otherwise available in modern editions. The texts are accompanied by a substantial introductory monograph and full apparatus of critical footnotes. The series, which also publishes literary and critical studies, is aimed at a scholarly readership.

Scholars are invited to apply to the Editors for further information and to submit a brief summary of their projected book. Contributions will be assessed by eminent Hispanists in the appropriate areas, and should not exceed 400 pages of typescript.

Hispanic Studies TRAC (Textual Research and Criticism) Volume 18

Juan Goytisolo and the Poetics of Contagion

The Evolution of a Radical Aesthetic in the Later Novels

STANLEY BLACK

LIVERPOOL UNIVERSITY PRESS

First published 2001 by
Liverpool University Press
4 Cambridge Street
Liverpool, L69 7ZU, UK

British Library Cataloguing-in-Publication Data
A British Library CIP Record is available.

ISBN 0-85323-836-7 cased
     0-85323-846-4 paper

Text set in Monophoto Sabon by
Wilmaset Limited, Birkenhead, Wirral

Printed and bound by
Bell and Bain Ltd, Glasgow

For Chus

Contents

Abbreviations

BL	*El bosque de las letras*
CC	*Contracorrientes*
CI	*Cogitus interruptus*
CS	*Crónicas sarracinas*
D	*Disidencias*
DJ	*Reivindicación del conde don Julián*
ESDS	*El sitio de los sitios*
FC	*El furgón de cola*
Jst	*Juan sin tierra*
LC	*La cuarentena*
LLL	*Libertad, libertad, libertad*
LSDJ	*Las semanas del jardín*
LSDM	*La saga de los Marx*
LVPS	*Las virtudes del pájaro solitario*
M	*Makbara*
PDLB	*Paisajes después de la batalla*
PN	*Problemas de la novela*
SI	*Señas de identidad*

Acknowledgements

This book started life as a doctoral thesis presented at the Queen's University, Belfast. That thesis had quite a long gestation and in the process I was helped and encouraged by many people to whom I owe a great debt of thanks. Michael Gordon took on the initial task of supervision, somewhat reluctantly at first, devoted *galdosista* that he is, but he proved to be a reliably expert guide in those early stages. I was later helped along the way by other tutors at Queen's such as John Kinsella, Trevor Dadson and Paul Russell-Gebbett. In the final stages I was greatly aided by colleagues in the University of Ulster, in particular, Graham Gargett and Richard York, each of whom read and commented on substantial sections of the thesis. In preparing the thesis for publication I was able to benefit from the corrections, suggestions and constructive criticism of my two external examiners, Jo Labanyi and Leo Hickey.

I am also grateful to the University of Ulster for granting me a light teaching semester to enable me to finish work on the last chapter. I would like to thank, too, Robin Bloxsidge, Andrew Kirk and Helen Tookey at Liverpool University Press for their guidance through the publication process and their patience.

I am deeply grateful to Juan Goytisolo for agreeing so readily to meet me during my research, for his generous attention during our meeting and for subsequent contacts, which have always been stimulating. Aside from what I learned through speaking to him, it was pleasing to have one's admiration for the work matched by a profound liking for the man. I thank him and his literary agent for their kind permission to quote from his works.

I would like to give special thanks to my parents for everything. It was a measure of comfort that Dad lived long enough to know that this book was a possibility.

Finally, my greatest debt of gratitude and appreciation must go to my wife, María Jesús, for her patience, tolerance and love throughout.

Introduction

Juan Goytisolo is, in the eyes of many, Spain's foremost contemporary novelist. He came to prominence as a leading member of the group of radical young intellectuals known as the 'Generación del medio siglo', which was the first to contest the prevailing ideology of the Franco regime. This literary generation was the standard-bearer of the type of social realism that characterized the late 1950s and the early 1960s in Spain.[1] Goytisolo himself sums up the characteristics of this group in *El furgón de cola*, describing them as non-conformist, Marxist-orientated, agnostic, and, in terms of literary technique, traditionalist (FC, 82). Of that group, Goytisolo has undoubtedly been the one who made the most radical change in terms of literary theory and practice, with the result that there is a clear distinction between the early period, from *Juegos de manos* (1954) to *Fin de fiesta* (1962), and the period commencing with the publication of *Señas de identidad* (1966). The distinction is such that it is possible to think that the two periods correspond to the work of two different authors. Of course, closer inspection reveals very clear connections between the novels of the early period and those of the later phase.[2]

While Goytisolo does not in any sense disown the works of his previous period, it is undoubtedly the case that he profoundly disagrees with their aesthetic premises, a fact which he makes clear in *El furgón de cola*, a volume of essays published in 1967, which, as well as being a critique of the whole trend of 1950s literature, is also a profound act of self-criticism. Goytisolo firmly believes that he found his literary way with the writing of *Señas de identidad*, and the novels and essays that have ensued from that time, which constitute what he himself recognizes as his 'obra adulta', reveal a writer who, while still constantly exploring new territory and testing the limits of language and the novel form, is doing so from the solid basis of firmly held and carefully pondered aesthetic principles.

It is with these aesthetic principles and their manifestation in the novels and, to a lesser degree, in Goytisolo's non-fiction that this study is concerned. The aim is to look at the way Goytisolo's aesthetic, his approach to his art, has evolved over what throughout this study we will refer to as the post-*Señas* period, that is, the period beginning with the publication of *Señas de identidad* in 1966.[3] For reasons of space it was decided to limit the main part of the study to the novels of the

1

Trilogy (*Señas de identidad*, *Reivindicación del conde don Julián*, *Juan sin tierra*) and *Makbara*, published in 1980. These novels cover the development of Goytisolo's new approach to the novel, from the tentative beginnings in *Señas de identidad* to what I see as the first fully accomplished work, *Makbara*. A concluding chapter examines in less detail the way these aesthetic principles evolve through the most recent novels from *Paisajes después de la batalla* (1982) to *Las semanas del jardín* (1997).

Unsurprisingly, it is the post-*Señas* period in Goytisolo's work which has attracted most critical attention. The novels' technical brilliance and difficulty have prompted a wide range of studies aimed at disentangling the themes, references and influences of the works. Most of the general studies have concentrated on the evolutionary nature of Goytisolo's work, the progression from one novel to the next in terms of development of themes and technical innovation.[4] However, few studies have actually attempted to study in a unified manner the aesthetic theory and practice of the post-*Señas* period.

In many ways this is due to an inattention to the radical nature of the change that Goytisolo's writing underwent at the time of *Señas de identidad*. In his autobiographical sketch 'Cronología', included in *Disidencias*, Goytisolo, writing in the third person, explains the nature of this personal and artistic crisis, experienced in 1963:

> Se entrega a una desgarradora labor de autocrítica—política, literaria, personal—que le aísla paulatinamente de sus amigos y le ayuda a cortar el cordón umbilical que todavía le une a España. (D, 343)

If we remember that *Señas* was written between 1962 and 1966, according to the date line on the final page of the first edition, it can be seen that the crisis occurred during the composition of the novel.[5] The full significance of this will be discussed in the chapter on *Señas*, but it casts light on a general point relevant to my overall approach in this study. Goytisolo's later period is characterized by a reassessment of the nature of artistic commitment. This is summed up in *El furgón de cola* as 'el verdadero compromiso del escritor se sitúa, a mi entender, en un triple plano: social, personal y técnico' (FC, 60 n. 3). This concept of total commitment leads Goytisolo to inject a personal element into his novels. In an interview with Rodríguez Monegal, he explains the beginning of this process in the change from the social realist novel, *La resaca* (1958), to the more subjective (though still realist) approach of the travelogues, *Campos de Níjar* (1959) and *La Chanca* (1962):

> a partir de *La resaca* me di cuenta que, si me proponía reflejar una serie de fenómenos propios de la sociedad española, tenía que hacerlo desde un punto de vista, el mío, que era el único que daba validez a mi testimonio, es decir, aceptar el subjetivismo, escribir en primera persona.[6]

As his ideas develop, the disillusionment with realism, no doubt nourished by the theories circulating in Paris at the time,[7] leads to a commitment to writing, but, unlike Robbe-Grillet, Goytisolo does not lose sight of the explicitly political rationale for this style of commitment. He explains his position as follows:

> He pasado de un compromiso con una determinada ideología política a un comprometerme a mí mismo con mi escritura por una transformación del mundo.[8]

This notion of personal commitment explains the extent of the autobiographical element in the novels and allows us to place it in its proper perspective. The subjectivism of the novels is not their primary purpose. They should not be interpreted as autobiographical. Rather, the personal element is there to give force and authenticity to the social critique. For Goytisolo, it is a means of continuing his aim of criticizing society without incurring the sense of 'impostura' he mentions in relation to La resaca.[9] What this leads to, however, is a literary production which, since it is not written from a dispassionate, 'professional' stance, is susceptible to conflicts, contradictions, internal dislocations that evince the author's deep personal involvement with the writing process. Hence in analysing the novels we must be prepared to recognize such contradictions and ambiguities. In the interview with Rodríguez Monegal he states:

> Si antes podía crear o intentar crear una literatura moral y buscar una armonía dentro de esta creación, a partir de ahora busco una literatura conflictiva, de desgarro, una literatura que sea realmente problemática, que no busque la armonía, que busque la contradicción. [10]

In the post-Señas period he abandons the classic role of the humanist intellectual, characterized, one might say, by a sense of belonging to and forming an integral part of society, while at the same time maintaining a critical eye on its injustices and defects, and espouses a concept of the intellectual as a marginado, an individualist, an anarchic rebel and non-conformist, opposed to everything that is represented by established society and championing the cause of all those groups which are denied a place in that society. This intellectual stance becomes translated into an aesthetic posture of total subversion of all that constitutes conventional society.

This initial experience of crisis and the concomitant posture of transgression find their catalyst in a third aspect of Goytisolo's experience, hinted at earlier, which is fundamental to a proper understanding of the functioning of these later novels, and that is his encounter with the linguistic revolution that swept over literary studies in the late 1950s and throughout the 1960s. Goytisolo's voluntary exile to Paris in 1956 brought him into contact with an important body of linguistic, literary and ideological theory that was to play a major part in shaping his subsequent literary practice.

An important factor, therefore, in the study of the novels will be the general theoretical milieu which forms the background to the works in question and the way this is reflected in Goytisolo's fiction and non-fiction. In *Trilogy of Treason*,[11] Michael Ugarte examines the influence of literary theory on Goytisolo, focusing in particular on Russian Formalism and Structuralism. While admitting that Goytisolo never declares himself a practising structuralist, Ugarte pinpoints a central tenet of structuralist theory, intertextuality (as defined by Kristeva), as having a particular influence on the author, but contends that this 'is at odds with one of the most salient features of his writing: the personal search for cultural (political, religious, sexual, and literary) authenticity' (24). In an otherwise excellent book, Ugarte identifies the extremes of, on the one hand, the novel as expression of the existential concerns of the individual author and, on the other, the structuralist view of the world as 'a series of conventions independent of a perceiving subject' (50), and sees them as mutually exclusive. In their extreme form, they are, but Goytisolo's work is located somewhere between these twin poles. Goytisolo himself has stated on numerous occasions his belief that a work of art contains elements of both.[12] He criticizes novels written 'conforme a ciertos principios clave de la Poética [...] sin conseguir evitar del todo las trampas de lo que podríamos llamar una "estética estructuralista"' (D, 322–23), saying that they sacrifice a number of levels of meaning. Even his intertextual technique, he claims, developed quite independently of the Structuralist movement.[13] The critic, on the other hand, can decide to impose a particular theoretical perspective. However, despite attempting to take account of structuralist theory, Ugarte is unable to refrain from the popular and most unstructuralist tendency to see the text as an expression of the real author's personality (the title of his study in itself is revealing). There is a tension between a traditional and a structuralist mentality in Goytisolo's novels, especially with *Juan sin tierra*, but rather than invalidate the novels, this can be a source of productive readings, often essential to the novels' meaning, and merits treatment as such. As Goytisolo has said: 'la persistencia de determinadas contradicciones a lo largo de la obra de un autor puede ser un índice revelador de su profunda coherencia interna' (CS, 31).

My aim in this study is to trace the manner in which Goytisolo's novels from *Señas de identidad* onwards attempt to translate social concern into aesthetic practice. I have deliberately chosen to employ both the terms 'poetic' and 'aesthetic' while confessing to a certain hesitation over their usage.[14] The study will occupy itself with Goytisolo's 'poetics' in that rather than attempt individually comprehensive studies of the particular works, it will focus on a more general pattern which allows the meaning of the novels to take place. In so far as Goytisolo's novels aim at subversion, they do so by developing a poetics of subversion or transgression which operates within and against an overall poetics of the novel. Therefore, much of our attention, especially in the first chapter, will be concerned with an attempt to pinpoint Goytisolo's general theory of literature as manifested in his numerous essays, particularly in the context of modern literary theory, and so it would be true to say that we are concerned with determining his narrative poetics. The term 'poetics' has an added suitability in that Goytisolo's fiction from *Señas* is much influenced by the whole literary critical movement of structuralism and post-structuralism which led to a heightened interest in the whole issue of narrative poetics.[15] Goytisolo himself in the mid-1970s expressed his preference for a criticism based on poetics while at the same time recognizing its limitations.[16]

However, I use the word 'aesthetic' in the subtitle to refer to Goytisolo's theory and practice of his narrative art in so far as the term 'aesthetic' emphasizes a work's specifically 'artistic' features, such as form and style, as distinct from elements such as themes, ideas, concepts. This highlights the contrast between the 1950s novels' predominant concern with a radical content and deliberate 'down-playing' of aesthetics as inappropriate to a socially conscious narrative, and Goytisolo's writing from *Señas* onwards in which the aesthetic dimension comes to the fore. Moreover, since one of the ideas I will be stressing in this study is the way Goytisolo attempts to bridge that traditional gap between the artistic and the social realm through attention to the role of the reader, the question of aesthetic perception is doubly apt. If etymologically 'aesthetic' refers to the reception of a work of art, derived as it is from the Greek term *aesthesis*, meaning 'sense perception',[17] this is appropriate in that a principal feature of Goytisolo's approach to writing in this period is concerned with an appeal to the reader's senses rather than to his head. In an interview in 1978 he emphasizes 'la función sensual, de fruición estética que distingue el código literario de los restantes lenguajes comunicativos' (CC, 234). In particular, the theme of transgression or contagion which assumes a crucial role in Goytisolo's writing involves not just the act of transgression on the part of the author or the text but, above all, the reader's perception of the transgression as such and accepting the contamination. The role of the reader in activating Goytisolo's radical aesthetic will be one of the aspects this study will concentrate on.

Goytisolo's thinking throughout these novels is dictated by an unflagging utopian vision. His novels aspire to be radical not only in their ceaseless critique of all oppressive features of modern society and their attempts to posit new modes of perception, but also in their aim to rework in a radical way the very premises of the novel.[18] If, at the start, the emphasis was on creating a radically new language, in later writings Goytisolo gave the term a slightly different, but most appropriate nuance in the light of the trend in his writing towards an increasing dialogue with the early classics of Spanish literature. Speaking of this return to the origins of Spanish literature in recent novels, he says:

> En cuanto al regreso del que hablas citaré una frase genial de Gaudí: la originalidad es la vuelta a los orígenes. Lo fundamental es volver a las raíces, radicalizarse, aumentar cada día la relación con el árbol de nuestra literatura.[19]

Goytisolo's early novels won him popularity at an early age, as well as being relatively successful in critical terms. However, according to his own analysis, the radical content of these novels was contradicted by their traditional literary form.[20] These novels, as he himself admits, were characterized by 'su propósito de transformar la palabra en acto, de querer competir con la vida, de hacerse "performativa"' (D, 159), but hampered by the dislocation between revolutionary intent and conventional language and format. A coincidence of several factors in the early 1960s led to the abandonment of this approach, but an important one was the manifest failure of its performative intent. Spain was in fact changing, but in a different way to that expected by the 1950s intellectual (FC, 15), influenced more by neo-capitalism than social realism.

This observable social change, which put in doubt the effectiveness of literature on external reality, was reinforced by the insights offered by Russian Formalism which preached that 'una obra literaria no enlaza tan sólo con el contexto histórico-social en el que surge; responde también, y ante todo, a las leyes evolutivas del género al que pertenece, a las exigencias de su propio arte' (D, 162). This leads in his later, post-*Señas* novels to the burden of subversion being transferred on to the formal level and concentrated in the writing process. Curiously, this opens the way to a new kind of artistic performativeness, of active involvement with reality via the reader. The principal problem posed by these novels, then, is how Goytisolo's shift to what might seem a highly aestheticist approach can be reconciled with the social commitment that continues to lie at the centre of the work. David Herzberger saw a contradiction in Goytisolo's novels, caught between the autonomy of the text and social engagement:

> Goytisolo has maintained in his novels the Sartrian engagement of his early theory while his formalist/structuralist poetics has led him toward the concept of an intransitive language as pure Being.[21]

While it is common to say that in spite of the radical change in Goytisolo's narrative technique, the underlying themes remain the same, the nature of the change as well as the new relationship between form and content need much more detailed examination. What is interesting is the way in which the new aesthetic practice of the later novels responds to and enacts the transgressive and radical themes that it is agreed still underlie the novels, and the degree of success they achieve.

Occasionally, Goytisolo's own comments can cause confusion. In one interview he spoke of radical form being necessary to complement the already radical content:

> Yo reprocho a la literatura de mi primera fase y en general a la literatura de la época, el desajuste entre una escritura lisa, llana y tradicional, puesta al servicio de un propósito de ruptura o provocación social. Había un desajuste entre el fondo y la forma. A partir de *Señas de identidad* mi objetivo fue borrar toda diferencia entre fondo y forma, encontrar un lenguaje tan subversivo como la subversión social o moral que propongo.[22]

In other comments on the relationship between form and content, however, a much greater emphasis is placed on the former, granting it an almost independent function:

> [...] todo un sector—el más consciente—de la novelística actual tiende a abandonar la vieja función del género, de representar el mundo exterior, para fijar su atención en el lenguaje; esto es, a pasar de la copia, del lenguaje transparente, a la escritura, a la autonomía del discurso. (D, 164)

It is quotations such as this that lead critics such as Herzberger to conclude that Goytisolo wished to write 'a book about nothing'.[23] The move towards a self-referential form is considered to militate against the apparent stance of social engagement. However, Goytisolo's move towards a more self-reflexive style has always been conditioned by the trends in contemporary critical and linguistic theory that view language, all language, as being intrinsic to our understanding of and engagement with the world.[24]

Goytisolo's novels from *Señas* onwards operate a move away from realism, a representationalist aesthetic, toward a more self-conscious mode, what Stephen Heath in his study of the *nouveau roman* refers to as a 'practice of writing',[25] that is, a form of writing which seeks continually to draw attention to itself as writing, whose aim is not the 'mirroring of some "Reality" but an attention to the forms of the intelligibility in which the real is produced'.[26] It is my view that a proper reading of Goytisolo's novels must take account of this approach. The novels no longer aim to 'reflect' reality, but rather to engage in an active fashion with the way reality is produced. The process of production of reality is examined at two levels which are interrelated: that of language and that of literature.

Goytisolo subscribes to those contemporary theories that consider language to be the central constituting feature of reality, to the extent that to challenge effectively the social order, it was necessary first to challenge its semantic foundations: 'la crítica y denuncia del edificio semántico en que se apoya [el Régimen] llevaría, no obstante, consigo, la crítica y denuncia de los fundamentos mismos de su existencia' (FC, 32 n.2). He goes on to say that 'la negación de un sistema intelectual-mente opresor comienza necesariamente con la negación de su estruc-tura semántica'. On another occasion Goytisolo commented: 'no se puede descodificar la realidad sin descodificar el lenguaje'.[27]

Goytisolo is not arguing for any direct effect of literature on social reality, but rather recognizing that there is an important level of reality between the individual and what is normally regarded as 'Reality', and that is the linguistic level in which that reality is constituted. From *Señas* onwards, Goytisolo ceases to attempt to engage directly with the world and turns his attention to the linguistic structures of that world, the varieties of discourse that pattern everyday life. Reality gives way to myth - myth in the sense of the various ways society represents itself to itself. As will be seen in the next chapter, Goytisolo's view of myth owes much to Roland Barthes. In *Mythologies*, Barthes claimed that 'myth is experienced as innocent speech: not because its intentions are hidden ... but because they are naturalized'.[28]

Language, then, became a central concern of the novels, but also the novel form itself. Goytisolo's movement towards a more self-conscious form is not, as some commentators have tried to suggest, a flight away from social concerns towards a purely personal, subjective salvation, but rather an attempt at a more authentic type of artistic engagement with the world.[29] Goytisolo in *El furgón de cola* quotes Barthes approvingly:

> Aunque, como dice acertadamente Roland Barthes, 'la obra más "realista" no será la que "pinta" la realidad, sino la que sirviéndose del mundo como contenido [...] explorará lo más profundamente posible la realidad irreal del lenguaje [...]' (FC, 60 n. 4)

According to structuralist theory, the novel, composed of language, not only provides a natural laboratory for its study, it also constitutes one of the main illustrations of the systems of intelligibility to which Stephen Heath referred. In *Structuralist Poetics*, Jonathan Culler claims:

> More than any other literary form, more perhaps than any other type of writing, the novel serves as the model by which society conceives of itself, the discourse in and through which it articulates the world.[30]

Hence, by challenging the novel form, the author is also challenging the way we make sense of the world. One of the principal aims of Goytisolo's fiction is to bring the reader to a critical awareness of the narrative process as a means of producing, or at least encouraging, the same sort of critical attitude to extra-literary reality. In this way, Goytisolo in the post-*Señas* period moves into the wider arena of postmodernism's re-evaluation of the concepts of truth, history and reality. Linda Hutcheon, in her book *A Poetics of Postmodernism*, argues that postmodernist art does not reject these concepts, but rather 'it teaches and enacts the recognition of the fact that the social, historical and existential "reality" of the past is discursive reality when it is used as the referent of art, and so the only "genuine historicity" becomes that which would openly acknowledge its own discursive, contingent reality'.[31]

Fundamental to this process, therefore, is literary self-conciousness. Goytisolo in his theoretical writings attaches considerable importance to both the writers of self-conscious fiction, like Juan Ruiz, Delicado, Cervantes, Sterne, and the theorists of self-consciousness, such as the Russian Formalists and the Structuralists. Self-reflexive fiction is, in his view, the ultimate in artistic honesty,[32] drawing attention to the reality of the text as production. As Julián Ríos suggests in conversation with Goytisolo:

> Mira yo creo que la máxima señal de honestidad de un novelista, como tú haces en la *Reivindicación* [...] y sobre todo en *Juan sin tierra*, consiste precisamente en pasarle por las narices al lector que lo que está leyendo es algo que sucede en la página, está escrito.[33]

The same applies to all fiction in the self-conscious tradition. Goytisolo says something similar:

> Yo hablaría de dos vertientes de la literatura: una es la vertiente típica de la novela del siglo XIX, naturalista, realista, etc., que disimula sus propios signos y quiere convertir la literatura en un trozo de vida, mientras la otra, (que Cervantes representa muy bien y la vanguardia actual es en este aspecto cervantina) no disimula los signos y muestra claramente el proceso de enunciación del autor.[34]

Hence to understand Goytisolo's novels from *Señas de identidad* onwards it is necessary to examine their self-reflexive or metafictional dimension which can be seen to be the central characteristic of the works, and in many ways the key to their interpretation. This study, then, will take as its starting point the way Goytisolo's later novels function as metafictional texts. Metafiction, by drawing attention to the novel as process - a process of writing and of reading - rejects the realist tradition of mimesis, militates against the 'natural attitude' to literature, language and reality and encourages a critical questioning which, Goytisolo makes clear, is his aim and a necessary ingredient of the utopian impulse.[35] It is essential to this project that it be continuously evolving:

> ... el dilema que se plantea al escritor de hoy puede resumirse en estos términos: garrulería o silencio. Avanzar, llevar a cabo el proceso personal a la literatura conduce a una apuesta final que cierra todas las salidas; no avanzar, repetirse, a la garrulería en la que caen el 99 por 100 de los escritores.[36]

Again, parallels with the theory of Barthes can be found. In a 1971 essay, Barthes realized that the battle against myth is unending since every radical demythification will eventually be assimilated into orthodox thinking. The writer needs to progressively extend the scope of his attack:

> The historical field of action is thus widened: no longer the (narrow) sphere of French society but far beyond that, historically and geographically, the whole of Western civilization (Graeco-Judaeo-Islamo-Christian), unified under the one theology (Essence, monotheism) and identified by the regime of meaning it practises—from Plato to *France-Dimanche*.[37]

Allowing for Goytisolo's different treatment of the Christianity-Islam question, such a comment bears a close resemblance to the development of the Spanish author's own work whose targets progressively widen out from a critique of the social realist novel and Spanish historiography to his more recent engagement with the pernicious effects of global capitalism and the New World Order.

In approaching the novels, no specific method of literary analysis has been employed since, as we shall see, a feature of the metafictional nature of the novels treated is that they tend to suggest their own ways of being read. However, in general much use has been made of the findings of structuralist and post-structuralist narratological theory, not least because the novels themselves incorporate a large amount of this theory both implicitly and explicitly. In particular, attention will be given to the process of naturalization, by which is meant the way a reader reduces a text's initial strangeness, renders it intelligible. As Jonathan Culler points out, this is usually done by 'restoring literature to a communicative function'.[38] The novels from *Señas de identidad* onwards seek to foreground this communicative function with a view to disturbing it, and after *Juan sin tierra* Goytisolo comments that he considers that novel 'como una obra última, el finis terrae de mi propia escritura en términos de comunicación, de coloquio' (D, 317). However, as Culler reminds us, 'the strange, the formal, the fictional, must be recuperated or naturalized, brought within our ken, if we do not want to remain gaping before monumental inscriptions'.[39] After *Juan sin tierra*, Goytisolo will continue to exploit this basic need on the reader's part for his subversive purposes.

Since the principal characteristics of these later novels include the focus inward towards their own narrative procedures, the play with their own fictive status, the deliberate attempt to 'lay bare the device' and deconstruct the mechanisms of the traditional novel, the concentration on language as the primary substance not only of the novel but of the world as we experience it, the examination of the problematic relationship between the text and outside reality and, finally, the role of the reader in coming to terms with the text, then it seems logical to use a methodology suited to those aspects of the literary process. Structuralist narrative poetics provides an extremely useful framework for the study of narrative in general, and also, as Culler points out, is especially attuned to the study of the experimental text 'finding in its resistance to the operations of reading confirmation of the fact that literary effects depend on these conventions and that literary evolution proceeds by displacement of old conventions of reading and the development of new'.[40]

One of the main consequences of structuralist theory and metafictional practice has been the emphasis on the reading role. In the post-*Señas* period, the role of the reader is integral to the narrative, frequently mentioned in the text itself. In this sense, the novels approximate to those implied in the semiologist Umberto Eco's concept of 'open' works. Using the example of musical works, Eco defines 'open' works as those which

> reject the definitive concluded message and multiply the formal possibilities of the distribution of their elements [...] they offer themselves not as finite works which prescribe specific repetition along given structural coordinates but as 'open' works which are brought to their conclusion by the performer at the same time as he experiences them on an aesthetic plane.[41]

Above all, what Goytisolo's later novels call for and actively foster is a self-conscious reader, one versed in the rules and conventions of the reading process. Much of their activity is directed at disturbing and playing with our narrative expectations as a means of telling us something or making us think about the world around us. Hence, while avoiding taking a particular theoretical *parti pris* in the interpretation of the novels and instead letting their metafictional dimension guide us in our reading, the study will take special account of structuralist and related theory in so far as it sheds light on the workings of the texts. Structuralist poetics was also, as mentioned earlier, of all the possible approaches, the one favoured by Goytisolo at the time of writing the Trilogy, but he goes on to add an important qualification:

> Tal enfoque crítico no pretende, como suele decirse, que la literatura se baste a sí misma ni postula la llamada teoría del arte por el arte. Al contrario, muestra que la serie literaria es una parte del edificio social, en estrecha vinculación con las otras series del mismo. (LLL, 90)

Thus Goytisolo emphasizes how in these novels the engagement with literary form and language is inextricably bound up with social concern.

Goytisolo's novels of the later period attempt to blend creation and criticism, literature and theory of literature together in the text—this is part of their metafictional nature. In part this was a response to the structuralist theories circulating at the time which Goytisolo felt all serious writers should take into account.[42] As Mark Currie observes, 'one of the major thrusts of structuralist narratology was to demonstrate that the realist novel constructs, rather than reflects, the real world, or, to put it another way, that the outside world is always mediated by language and narrative, however much it is naturalized by the transparency of realistic language'. He goes on to note that 'if narratological criticism insisted this about realistic fiction from the outside, metafiction does so, and always did so, from within'.[43] Currie is right, but the difference with contemporary metafiction is that it often incorporated the insights of theory into the narrative. Hence, it will be useful to look at Goytisolo's theoretical writings as expressed in a series of volumes of essays, and interviews which have appeared concurrently with his creative works in order to identify the principles underpinning his thinking prior to a consideration of their deployment in the novels.

However, the study will mainly seek to determine the reading that the text itself proposes. A characteristic of metafictional writing, according to Linda Hutcheon, is that it 'provides, within itself, a commentary on its own status as fiction and as language, and also on its own processes of production and reception'.[44] Finally, in the analyses of the individual novels which follow, it might seem that considerable areas of the text are ignored. Clearly, in novels as richly layered and semantically dense as those of Goytisolo, no analysis can aspire to be comprehensive. Many of the general studies of Goytisolo by critics such as Lee Six, Levine, Navajas, Ugarte, Lázaro, Romero and Pérez Silvestre have already provided very valuable and competent accounts of the themes, motifs, influences, cultural references and formal features of the novels. Such criticism is largely characterized by the primacy of the thematic approach, and where formal features are studied they tend to be interpreted mimetically, as means of representing the content. This is not to deny the validity of a thematic approach to the novel, essential to a full understanding of the works. However, a result has been a tendency to gloss over certain formal features, especially the role of literary self-consciousness in the author's enterprise of literary subversion. Often this is in the interests of a coherent interpretation of the novels. In this study special attention will be given to precisely those instances of narrative dislocation and aporia that disturb a straightforward reading.[45] The emphasis on form has the further advantage of restoring a balance lost in some of the more recent studies of Goytisolo's work, such as Brad Epps' impressive book *Significant Violence*. While interested primarily in 'charting on both a thematic and a formal level the troubling relations between literary violence and the critique of ideology', Epps is ultimately concerned with Goytisolo's apparent ideological position on specific issues; these make Epps 'sceptical of the liberational trappings of this textual revolution' and result in, for example, a reading of *Don Julián* which sees it as 'denouncing yet reasserting an oppressive morality' because it seems to portray a 'violently misogynistic male homosexuality'.[46] By foregrounding the formal properties of the texts, while at the same time recognizing the ideological ambiguities in Goytisolo's work, this study hopes, though not uncritically, to restore validity to the liberational aspirations of the novels.

NOTES

1 Elías Díaz, *Pensamiento español 1939–1975* (Madrid: EDICUSA, 1978), 122–23. John Butt, *Writers and Politics in Modern Spain* (London: Hodder and Stoughton, 1978), 54–55.

2 See Linda Gould Levine, *Juan Goytisolo: la destrucción creadora* (Mexico: Joaquín Mortiz, 1976); Bernard González, 'The Evolution of Juan Goytisolo's Narrative Technique: Time, Character and Point of View' (PhD thesis, University of California, Berkeley, 1979).

3 Hence, when I use the term 'post-*Señas*' I will be including that novel in the category.

4 Jesús Lázaro (ed.), *La novelística de Juan Goytisolo* (Madrid: Alhambra, 1984); José Carlos Pérez Silvestre, *La trayectoria novelística de Juan Goytisolo (El autor y sus obsesiones)* (Barcelona: Oroel Eds, 1984); Levine, *Juan Goytisolo*; Héctor Romero, *La evolución literaria de Juan Goytisolo* (Miami: Ediciones Universal, 1979).

5 The date line on page 485 of the first edition reads: 'La Habana–París–Saint Tropez–Tánger Otoño 1962–Primavera 1966' (omitted in the amended and definitive second edition). See Mary Ellen Bieder, 'A Case of Altered Identity: Two Editions of Juan Goytisolo's *Señas de identidad*', *Modern Language Notes* LXXXIX (1974), 300.

6 Emir Rodríguez Monegal, 'Destrucción de la España sagrada: Diálogo con Juan Goytisolo', *Mundo Nuevo* 12 (1967), 50.

7 Goytisolo had moved to Paris in 1956. Juan Goytisolo, 'Cronología', *Disidencias* (Barcelona: Seix Barral, 1977), 340.

8 A.C. Isasi Angulo, 'La novelística de Juan Goytisolo (Entrevista con el autor)', *Papeles de Son Armadans* LXXVI(226) (1975), 786.

9 Rodríguez Monegal, 'Destrucción de la España sagrada', 50.

10 Rodríguez Monegal, 'Destrucción de la España sagrada', 52.

11 Michael Ugarte, *Trilogy of Treason: An Intertextual Study of Juan Goytisolo* (Columbia, MO, and London: University of Missouri Press, 1982).

12 'Mirándolo bien, no hay contradicción entre el afán de expresión personal ... y el propósito de construir una textura discursiva que aspire a ser juzgada por sí misma. Como sabes, toda obra literaria propone gran variedad de lecturas: es, a la vez, ilustración de ciertas ideas (políticas, artísticas, filosóficas, etc.), imagen o reflejo de la sociedad en que se produce, expresión del autor que la crea.' *Disidencias*, 307.

13 Goytisolo has said: 'cuando aparecieron el ensayo de Todorov "... Qué es el estructuralismo?" en el que habla del "discurso connotativo" y los textos de Sollers y Kristeva sobre el concepto de "inter-textualidad" había redactado yo la totalidad de mi novela en la que, como he dicho antes, el diálogo inter-textual, connotativo, desempeña un papel primordial'. J. Ríos (ed.), *Juan Goytisolo* (Madrid: Fundamentos, 1975), 120.

14 Robert Escarpit makes a useful distinction: 'While it is perfectly legitimate to call "aesthetic" what relates to artistic perception, we should be more careful when we

speak of literary creation. "Poetic", from the Greek verb poiein (to create), not "aesthetic" is the right word for literary creation. The artist creates according to a poetic pattern; the public perceives the creation according to an aesthetic pattern.' E. and T. Burns (eds), *Sociology of Literature and Drama* (London: Penguin, 1973), 360.

15 Jonathan Culler, in his introduction to Tzvetan Todorov's *The Poetics of Prose* (Oxford: Basil Blackwell, 1977), refers to the 'astonishing revival of poetics' among structuralists in France in the early 1960s (7).

16 'Dicho esto, entre los diferentes métodos de análisis crítico, mis preferencias personales van al de la poética, tal como nos ha sido definida por Jakobson.' 'Escritores, críticos y fiscales' in *Libertad, libertad, libertad* (Barcelona: Anagrama, 1978), 89. But compare: 'Cuando leo un texto, no quiero limitarme a una lectura "poética" o "lingüística"; mi placer de lector aspira a ser ubicuo, total', in 'Entrevista con Juan Goytisolo' by Julio Ortega in Ríos (ed.), *Juan Goytisolo*, 133 (originally in *Revista de Occidente*, April 1974).

17 See also Raymond Williams, *Keywords: A Vocabulary of Culture and Society* (London: Fontana, 1976), 27.

18 In an essay in *Disidencias*, Goytisolo refers to two currents in the contemporary Latin American novel that he admires: one the work of Sarduy and Cabrera Infante, which he terms 'la indagación radical de nuestra actual vanguardia literaria', as opposed to the work of García Márquez, Vargas Llosa and Lezama Lima, which is characterized more by its 'ambición totalizadora' (D, 224). Goytisolo himself, in so far as his novels do not attempt to provide a total world-picture but rather seek to locate themselves at the 'cutting edge' of fiction, out on a limb, exploring the boundaries of the novel, clearly aligns himself more with Sarduy than with García Márquez.

19 Miguel Riera, 'Regreso al origen', *Quimera* LXXIII (1988), 39.

20 David Herzberger in *Narrating the Past: Fiction and Historiography in Postwar Spain* (Durham, NC, and London: Duke University Press, 1995), while recognizing that the 'social realists display scant linguistic self-consciousness' (62), makes a good defence of this literature's thematic and linguistic contestation of Francoist historiography.

21 David Herzberger, 'Toward the Word/World Conflict: The Evolution of Juan Goytisolo's Novelistic Theory', in *Perspectivas de la novela* (ensayos sobre la novela española de los ss. XIX y XX de distintos autores y con una nota introductoria de Alva V. Ebersole) (Madrid: Ediciones Albatros Hispanófila, 1979), 104.

22 Pilar Trenas, 'Juan Goytisolo, ahora sin amargura ni rencor', *ABC*, 7 June 1981, 37.

23 Herzberger, 'Toward the Word/World Conflict', 109.

24 Jorge Larrain, *The Concept of Ideology* (London: Hutchinson, 1979), 130.

25 Stephen Heath, *The Nouveau Roman: A Study in the Practice of Writing* (London: Elek, 1972), 22.

26 Heath, *The Nouveau Roman*, 22.

27 Trenas, 'Juan Goytisolo', 37. Critics such as Brad Epps, while recognizing this facet of Goytisolo's work, doubt its effectiveness in practice: '*Conde Julián*'s textual ire is so extreme that there appears little hope for any sort of positive (extra)textual change'. Brad Epps, *Significant Violence: Oppression and Resistance in the Novels of Juan Goytisolo, 1970–1990* (Oxford: Clarendon Press, 1996), 4.

28 Roland Barthes, *Mythologies* (London: Paladin, 1973), 131.

29 Claudia Schaeffer-Rodriguez, *Juan Goytisolo: del 'realismo crítico' a la utopía* (Madrid: Porrúa Turanzas, 1984), 3, 6. Note Hernandez's interview where Goytisolo admits that, in *Don Julián*, a desire for evasion does exist, but that it co-exists with, rather than replaces, a social function: 'Yo creo que en *Don Julián*, como en mis novelas anteriores, el ansia de evasión y el deseo de cambiar el mundo actúan simultáneamente'. J. Hernández, 'Juan Goytisolo—1975', *Modern Language Notes* XCI (1976), 350–51.

30 Jonathan Culler, *Structuralist Poetics: Structuralism, Linguistics and the Study of Literature* (London: Routledge, 1975), 189.

31 Linda Hutcheon, *A Poetics of Postmodernism: History, Theory, Fiction* (London: Routledge, 1988), 24.

32 Terry Eagleton speaks in similar terms of modernist texts: 'Many modernist texts ... make the "act of enunciating", the process of their own production, part of their actual "content". They do not try to pass themselves off as unquestionable, like Barthes's "natural" sign, but as the Formalists would say "lay bare the device" of their own composition. They do this so that they will not be mistaken for absolute truth—so that the reader will be encouraged to reflect critically on the partial, particular ways they construct reality, and so to recognize how it might all have happened differently.' Terry Eagleton, *Literary Theory: An Introduction* (London: Blackwell, 1983), 170.

33 J. Ríos (ed.), *Juan sin tierra* (Madrid: Editorial Fundamentos, 1978), 21. See also Linda Hutcheon, *Narcissistic Narrative: The Metafictional Paradox* (London: Methuen, 1984), 49: 'the most authentic and honest fiction might well be that which most freely acknowledges its fictionality'.

34 Hernández, 'Juan Goytisolo—1975', 348–49.

35 *Libertad, libertad, libertad*, 43, 93–94.

36 Ríos (ed.), *Juan Goytisolo*, 129.

37 Roland Barthes, 'Change the Object Itself. Mythology Today', in *Image–Music–Text*, ed. Stephen Heath (London: Fontana, 1984), 167.

38 Culler, *Structuralist Poetics*, 134.

39 Culler, *Structuralist Poetics*, 134.

40 Culler, *Structuralist Poetics*, 130.

41 Umberto Eco, *The Open Work*, trans. Anna Cancogni, introd. David Robey (London: Hutchinson Radius, 1989), 3.

42 'Cualquier escritor contemporáneo que ignore, por ejemplo, las nociones básicas de la poética o la lingüística es una figura anacrónica'. *Libertad, libertad, libertad*, 91–92.

43 Mark Currie, *Postmodern Narrative Theory* (London: Macmillan, 1998), 62.

44 Hutcheon, *Narcissistic Narrative*, xii.

45 Frank Kermode, in the essay 'Recognition and Deception' in his *Essays on Fiction: 1971–82* (London: Routledge, 1983), contrasts the 'reading of a consumer' which 'consists of excluding from consideration all that is not relevant to a simple grammar of story' and that of a 'competent producer' which 'consists of the opposite exclusion, namely the neglect of such simplicities in favour of the more difficult possibilities contained in the elements the consumer fails to consider' (107). Brian McHale also talks of this approach to Robbe-Grillet, which he calls 'an "expensive" reading, in the sense that it requires us to smooth over a good many difficulties and to repress the text's own resistance to being read that way'. Brian McHale, *Postmodernist Fiction* (London: Methuen, 1987), 14.

46 Epps, *Significant Violence*, 9, 13.

CHAPTER ONE

Goytisolo and Literary Theory

With the publication of *Señas de identidad* in 1966, Goytisolo turns his back on the explicitly political approach that had characterized his writing in the late 1950s and early 1960s. This change in the concept of commitment was succinctly summed up by the author himself in an interview when he said:

> He pasado de un compromiso con una determinada ideología política a un comprometerme a mí mismo con mi escritura por una transformación del mundo.[1]

The quotation is an important one as it confirms all the vital aspects of his mature writing. Goytisolo's commitment is primarily to literature, but the ultimate aim of social improvement remains. The key to understanding the novels of the later period is to see how they try to reconcile their self-consciously literary status with the urge for social transformation. The durability of this idea is seen in a quotation from one of his most recent books of essays, *El bosque de las letras*, published in 1995, in which he refers to a constant dilemma which he faces as an artist:

> ¿Cómo compaginar, en efecto, la voluntad de defensa de causas cívicas y valores universalmente válidos amenazados por la barbarie, con una escritura personal de acceso difícil e incomprensible para muchos lectores? (BL, 9)

Although stressing that in his non-fictional writing, among other things, he can freely denounce injustices and express his political and moral views, while his fictional production is characterized by more personal and specifically literary concerns, there is no clear demarcation between the two facets of Goytisolo's output, the artistic and the political. It can clearly be seen from many of Goytisolo's comments that literature, while limited in its power of direct action, has a privileged position with respect to transforming society, principally via the consciousness of the reader:

> Creo que el papel de la literatura es a la vez importante y modesto. Modesto a corto plazo porque la literatura no tiene una incidencia real, directa, en la vida política de un país. Pero es al mismo tiempo importante porque sin duda contribuye a crear y configurar la conciencia de la gente y, a largo plazo, a transformar esta conciencia.[2]

Exactly twenty years later, in one of his most recent novels, *El sitio de los sitios* (1995), the obsession with, on the one hand, the power of literature and, on the other, its limitations is given explicit expression.[3]

A closer look at Goytisolo's non-fictional writing from the late 1950s onwards will aid our study of the novels in two ways.[4] First, it will allow us to explore Goytisolo's literary principles as expressed in comments on literary theory and in analyses of his own and others' writing. Second, since it is in the essays where he states more explicitly his political-moral concerns, it will help us set his literary practice in its political context. It must be remembered, however, that Goytisolo is much more important as an artist than as a critic. His role as a 'crítico practicante de la ficción' is much more important than his alter ego the 'novelista que teoriza' (CC, 52), and his essays, while interesting for the light they shed on his literary practice, are not intended as expressions of a literary manifesto against which his novels must be judged.[5] Therefore, it will help us to go beyond the author's own analyses and present alternative readings of the novels.

A study of the non-fiction will also show how Goytisolo's theory, like his practice, while characterized by constant change and renewal, the result of the continual encounter with new ideas and writers, is not, as some would have it, merely dictated to by the latest theoretical fashion.[6] While the essays reveal the breadth and extent of influences on Goytisolo, there is a consistency, as we have already seen, in his views and opinions from the early 1960s onwards which proves that such influences were far from superficial. The radical change that his writing and thinking underwent in the early 1960s was the result of a profound re-evaluation of the role of the writer and the nature of art. The fundamental principles that underlay that new thinking have remained largely unchanged, to the extent that in the 1980s and 1990s we see him reiterate ideas that were first expressed, in almost identical terms, in the 1960s.[7] The encounter with new thinkers and the apparent new directions in Goytisolo's thought prove, on closer examination, to be variations on the same constant theme.

The Realist Phase

All of Goytisolo's thought and literary practice from the early 1960s must be understood in the context of the change of direction brought about by the encounter with post-Saussurean linguistics.[8] It is from this moment, too, that there emerges a greater coherence in Goytisolo's approach to writing and a greater harmony between his theoretical pronouncements and his literary practice. Prior to that period, both his fiction and his theory were dominated by the principle of literary realism. Goytisolo's first published novel *Juegos de manos* appeared in 1954, and it was followed by *Duelo en el Paraíso* in 1955, *El circo* in 1957, *Fiestas* and *La resaca* in 1958. The following year saw the publication of two controversial theoretical pieces: the article 'Para una literatura nacional popular'[9] and the volume of articles *Problemas de la novela*.[10]

The latter coincides with the second stage of Goytisolo's pre-*Señas de identidad* production, that of the three novels—*El circo*, *Fiestas* and *La resaca*—which together constitute the 'El mañana efímero' trilogy.[11] This trilogy, in particular *La resaca*, is characterized by social realism, with a much more marked political content than the previous novels. *Problemas* and 'Para una literatura nacional popular' come to be, in a way, the manifestos of his social realism. In *Problemas* Goytisolo reacts against the hitherto prevailing literary theory in Spain inherited from Ortega y Gasset, and, along with Castellet, whose *La hora del lector* was published in 1957, tries to establish the principles underpinning the novels of the 1950s. In one of the most important articles in *Problemas*, entitled 'Ortega y la novela', Goytisolo sets out his main points of disagreement with Ortega. The latter had argued for a literature that was elitist, one where the emphasis was on the aesthetic rather than the social, and in which the artist, instead of trying to 'represent' reality, 'added' to that reality, invented a new reality.[12] The result for Goytisolo is 'una literatura esteticista y egocéntrica, ajena por completo a la realidad contemporánea' (PN, 84). For Goytisolo a novel must be intimately related to the historical moment and national context in which it is produced.[13]

This emphasis on the social role of the novel—unlike the chauvi-nistic calls for the 'españolización' of the novel (PN, 86)—is a feature of Goytisolo's theory which endures throughout his career even into the post-*Señas* period. Goytisolo argues strenuously for the novel's social purpose and defends the emerging literary current of behaviourism. The novel must concern itself with reality and, above all, the reality of the country in which it is produced. It should become once again a 'national' literature. Rather than directed at a select few, it must be aimed at a wide public. Goytisolo is careful to avoid the excesses of 'socialist' realism with its implicit aim of writing for the masses, saying: 'Siempre me ha parecido absurda la pretensión de algunos colegas, de escribir "para el pueblo". Hoy por hoy, el pueblo no lee los libros de poesía' (PN, 104). Yet he still believes firmly that the writer must write with the widest possible reading public in mind (PN, 104).

The deficiencies of Goytisolo's articles in *Problemas* need not be reiterated, and Goytisolo himself has forbidden its republication.[14] Goytisolo's ambivalence, on the one hand advocating objectivism while, on the other, recognizing the necessary limits on the authorial point of view, is characteristic of the confusion of this early period in which his natural instincts led him to subjectivism, whereas his political allegiances pushed him in the direction of the prevailing trend of objectivism. This ambivalence is present in the early novels too, and accounts for the blend of lyricism and realism in the novels like *Juegos de manos* and *Duelo en el Paraíso*.

What is interesting about *Problemas* is Goytisolo's concern with the novel's social purpose[15] and his rejection of any kind of formalism that would detract from that purpose:

> la novela no puede perder su contacto con la realidad en nombre de una abstracción superior, so pena de convertirse a largo plazo en algo formal y muerto (PN, 37)

Given that the primary characteristic of Goytisolo's post-*Señas* novels is precisely their formalist quality, the challenge for the writer will be how to combine literary experimentation with a profound social concern.

Goytisolo's theoretical stance after *Problemas de la novela* is not so radically different. In these early essays Goytisolo defends the social role of the novelist against the gratuitous and elitist intellectual game theory of Ortega and argues that the novel should treat authentically the reality of the individual and society. He advocates realism but in the form of behaviourism, as a means of offering undogmatically authentic insights into reality, and shies away from an absolute and omniscient approach. This defence of behaviourism can be read as a variation of the subjectivism of the post-*Señas* period. The latter is an extension of the rejection in *Problemas* of the 'impersonalidad de la tercera persona gramatical', which implies 'un valor absoluto e inmutable frente al que no cabe apelación' (PN, 40). What does change is the fundamental attitude to the nature of the relation of the text to reality and the role of language. The relativism that permeates these early essays is extended to language itself. The social concern remains unchanged.

The Break with Realism

The process of change is charted in the essays which make up *El furgón de cola* (published 1967). These were written between 1960 and 1966 and thus coincide with the preparation and writing of *Señas de identidad* (published 1966). Like *Señas*, *El furgón* charts Goytisolo's transition away from social realism and disillusionment with the Official Spanish Left, towards a new definition of the role of the committed artist which takes account of both the relative failure and outmodedness of social realism and the need to concentrate on the aesthetic dimension.

El furgón de cola targets those intellectuals on the left who continued to harbour the same revolutionary ideals in the neo-capitalist, consumer-oriented Spain of the 1960s as they had in the autocratic, isolationist Spain of the 1950s. In his view, the social realist novel was not only passé, it could be seen to have failed in its aim to transform reality and could not even stand on its artistic merits because it had none to speak of, the aesthetic dimension having been disdained and subordinated to the political. Furthermore, the supposed 'pueblo' in whose cause the committed artist wrote no longer existed.[16] If in *Problemas* the predominant influences were those of Sartre and Lukács,[17] *El furgón* reveals the influence of Roland Barthes. In *Qu'est-ce que la littérature?*, published in 1948, Sartre had condemned aestheticism and linguistic play in prose fiction as 'sick language'.[18] The artist is ethically bound to the role of liberation, of giving consciousness to society, and the medium of the novelist, prose, is a transparent vehicle, specifically suited to communication of his message. Lukács, who according to Goytisolo's own admission had exerted a strong influence over him in the second half of the 1950s,[19] had propounded a similar theory of the commitment of the artist through realism and aversion to modernism and literary experimentation as being decadent. Goytisolo was clearly deeply influenced by Barthes' reassessment of Sartre in *Le Degré zéro de l'écriture*. In this work, Barthes emphasized that language was profoundly ideological and that, far from being able to relegate it to a subordinate position in one's concern to reach reality, it was in language that the author engaged with reality at its most relevant level. Barthes also rehabilitated the subversive function of those whom Sartre had considered uncommitted authors: Flaubert, Mallarmé, the Surrealists.

In *El furgón* Goytisolo quotes Barthes to justify this change from naive realism towards a concentration on language and writing (FC, 60 n. 4) and Barthes' ideas are visible throughout *El furgón* in Goytisolo's attempt to reconcile a concern with the specifically literary and the social role of the artist. Barthes in *Le Degré* emphasizes that the artist's duty always had a dual dimension: both to society and the nature of literature itself. It is from Barthes that Goytisolo learns a way to reconcile formalism with social concern.[20] For Goytisolo, in *El furgón* the failure of the *novela social* resided in its neglect of the duty to literature.[21] He goes on to point out the illusory faith the young Spanish novelists (himself included) had in the performative nature of their art, in its practical effect on society. Their concept of commitment consisted of simply siding with the 'fuerzas que hoy combaten por la necesaria transformación del hombre' (FC, 87)—an allusion to the group's left-wing sympathies. Goytisolo justifies the new subjectivism that is to characterize his novels as a more authentic way of channelling his social concern, and he quotes Leiris in *L'Age d'homme*:

> Il s'agissait moins là de ce qu'il est convenu d'appeler 'littérature engagée' que d'une littérature dans laquelle j'essayais de m'engager tout entier. (FC, 87 n. 6)

It is in this essay that Goytisolo advances the idea of a necessary 'visión doble del hombre y del mundo' that is 'una visión juntamente dramática e irónica, cuya existencia responde en mi opinión, a una exigencia específica del arte novelesco' (FC, 88). This introduction of an ironic perspective marks the beginning of an approach to literature which locates the function of the novel, not in the representation of reality, but in the play with the ways that reality is represented. Hence, later in the same essay, Goytisolo advocates the need to explore the possibilities of language and break away from conformity to a conventional literary form. Ideological non-conformism must be matched by aesthetic non-conformity.

However, the ideal of performativeness is not entirely absent from Goytisolo's thinking at this stage. El furgón at times appears to point to something more radical than making form match content. There are signs of a distinct shift of emphasis towards a critique of language as a means to, or preliminary to, social transformation:

> La destrucción de los viejos mitos de la derecha tendría que partir de un análisis y denuncia del lenguaje. Impugnando las palabras sagradas impugnaría simultáneamente los valores que se expresan en ellas. La tarea de minar los fundamentos de la metafísica española exige la crítica implacable de esa rancia prosa castellanista que es a la vez santuario y banco de valores sublimes del Buen Decir. (FC, 258–59 n. 4)

The tone of El furgón matches the indecision that we will detect in its artistic counterpart, Señas de identidad, in that Goytisolo is clearly in a transitional phase and unsure of the way forward. In the face of growing materialism and capitalism, Goytisolo sees the intellectual as faced with a choice between either retreating or escaping into a purely personal quest for self-liberation, an approach he associates, in differing ways, with Rimbaud and Cernuda,[22] or continuing his commitment to the official Left. Both these alternatives are unsatisfactory:

> El intelectual inconformista de hoy se ve en el dilema de escoger entre la rebeldía romántica o convertirse en funcionario organizador; aceptando el primer término de la antítesis, se condena a ser estéril; inclinándose por el segundo, renuncia a su libertad. (FC, 14)

The idea of sterility emphasizes Goytisolo's urge for his writing to be 'productive' in some way, to effect an impact on society. Hence El furgón shows Goytisolo tempted by the idea of art as a personal quest for self-redemption—and the novels from Señas onwards undoubtedly do contain that element[23]—but still clinging to the belief in the social responsibility of the artist. Goytisolo still retains the belief that in certain social situations, such as those pertaining in Franco's Spain, the artist can do no other than put his art at the service of politics.

What the essays do contain are the signs of a way forward in the two ideas mentioned of the Leirisian commitment through subjectivism and the Barthesian critique of language. The former allows Goytisolo a more authentic form of commitment identified less with particular groups in society than with the dilemmas and problems that afflict him as an individual and which have application to society in general.[24] The critique of society through the critique of language allows him to invest the novel's linguistic play with a social significance. The theoretical framework inspiring this approach is, of course, structuralism with its emphasis on the overall interrelatedness, or intertextuality, of social and literary language.

Language and the Body

By the early 1970s Goytisolo appears to have reached a clearer idea of his artistic purpose. The essays included in *Disidencias*, published in 1977, reveal the extent to which the moral and aesthetic dilemma of *El furgón* has been resolved. Not only does he seem to have found his literary identity and his direction, he has even achieved a measure of reconciliation with Spain in the sense that he has found a kindred native tradition with which he can identify and empathize.[25] Authors such as Góngora, Cervantes, Juan Ruiz and Rojas, whose work constitutes a reaction against the prevailing orthodoxy, or those contemporary South American writers whose writing connects with this radical classical tradition, elicit his admiration. On a political and social front, *Disidencias* confirms Goytisolo's shift towards a more libertarian stance.[26] This is unsurprising given that the essays date from the early 1970s, when the libertarian movement was in full flow. It can also be explained by Goytisolo's experience of America from 1969 onwards.[27] One of the principal influences in this aspect was the social philosopher Herbert Marcuse.[28] The interest in the theme of eroticism throughout the essays in *Disidencias* is derived from the principle attributed by Goytisolo to, among others, Marcuse, that 'la sumisión a las normas sexuales de una sociedad dada conduce inevitablemente a la sumisión general a los valores consagrados de aquélla' (D, 92).

However, other, more autochthonous influences have contributed to Goytisolo's libertarianism. His exploration of Spanish history under the influence of Américo Castro led him to an awareness of an important feature of Spanish culture prior to the expulsion of the Arabs and the Reconquest: on the one hand, the relatively tolerant atmosphere that reigned in society during the period of Christian, Islamic and Jewish coexistence[29] and, on the other, more importantly for Goytisolo, the relatively healthy balance inherent in Moslem culture between the demands of the body and those of the spirit, which exerted an influence on literary works like the *Libro de Buen Amor*.[30] After the Reconquest, a sexual repression sets in as a defensive reaction against the 'sensualidad que encarnaban los musulmanes' (D, 91) and as a preventive measure against any future invasion, since 'la mayor "tragedia" histórica de la península (la invasión sarracena y subsiguiente "destrucción de la España Sagrada") fue atribuida por nuestros cronistas a un delito sexual (el amor adúltero del rey don Rodrigo por la hija del conde don Julián)' (D, 91). Goytisolo links these ideas with those of contemporary libertarianism, in particular as expressed by Marcuse in *Eros and Civilization*:

> España es la ilustración viva del hecho de que reprimir la inteligencia equivale a reprimir el sexo y vice versa [. . .] Una sociedad cuyos miembros aprenden a disponer libremente de sus cuerpos es una sociedad que tolerará difícilmente formas políticas opresoras . . . (D, 92)

Goytisolo's primary concern in *Disidencias* is with the socially subversive force of the body and the relation between the body and literary expression. He quotes Castro, saying 'la castidad de la expresión escrita fue primero un aspecto de la tarea defensiva de Castilla contra los moros y para proteger su ya inmutable carácter más tarde' (D, 91–92). Goytisolo's admiration for the way authors like Góngora or Rojas react against their society's repressive attitude to the body finds a contemporary parallel in what Goytisolo terms 'la rebelión actual del cuerpo contra la filosofía moral del progreso y sus construcciones racionales omnímodas' (D, 182). The awareness of the Christian repression of the body that took place from the fifteenth century onwards is reinforced by the reading of Octavio Paz's *Conjunciones y Disyunciones*, published in 1969 and discussed by Goytisolo in the essay 'El lenguaje del cuerpo'.

In *Conjunciones y Disyunciones*, Paz analyses the history of society in terms of its attitude to the twin terms body and non-body (or mind, spirit), concluding that the present day is witnessing a 'rebelión del cuerpo' after centuries of repression. Goytisolo highlights Paz's discovery in the pre-Reconquista period of Spanish history, when the Islamic influence was strong, of a different mode of thought:

> un pensamiento que no niega el cuerpo, no lo abstrae, no lo reprime que antes bien le da la palabra y auspicia la reconciliación del hombre consigo mismo. (D, 176)

Paz confirms Goytisolo's own findings of an attitude in Spanish culture, from the fifteenth century on, which is anti-intelligence and also anti-body because of their, respectively, Judaic and Islamic connotations (D, 178). Paz's theories also confirm Goytisolo's allegiance to a libertarian philosophy which sees the re-affirmation of the corporal as the only means of combating reification in modern society both of the capitalist and the socialist type:

> Hoy cuando España parece adaptarse por fin, al esquema de un mundo racional y útil, sometido a las leyes económicas y la necesidad de un trabajo

alienador y alienado, el cuerpo recobrará quizá la virulencia subversiva del grito. (D, 182)

Goytisolo's concern throughout *Disidencias* is with how this reaction to repression is manifested in literary terms, the way a prevailing rationalist ideology is resisted by the literary manifestation of this 'rebelión del cuerpo', and such a consideration dictates Goytisolo's literary preferences. Hence his admiration for the work of Rojas, whose sense of alienation from his social environment and its values results in a more comprehensively unconventional text.[31] For Goytisolo, Rojas is the perfect example of the 'excéntrico, periférico' (D, 17) and the result is a text which is a radical critique of 'la opinión común', 'la obra más virulenta y subversiva de la literatura de lengua española' (D, 17). Using concepts derived from Roland Barthes and the Russian Formalist, Yuri Lotman, Goytisolo gives as the reason for this enduringly subversive quality of the text the fact that it transgresses on both the formal and the thematic level.[32]

> Si nos atenemos a la moderna doctrina de lo verosímil, en su doble acepción de conformidad a las leyes del género y a la ideología de la época, *La Celestina* es obra totalmente inverosímil por excelencia [...] se sitúa en las antípodas de la 'estética de identidad'. (D, 17–18)

The link between the body and writing manifests itself in different ways. In the case of Quevedo, it expresses itself in a coprophilia, an excremental vision. While a staunch supporter of the status quo, Quevedo's work in its predominantly excremental style reveals the neurosis of someone who has, like the society around him, attempted to deny the body. The repression of bodily pleasure expresses itself in a twisted form by an obsession with the scatological.[33] In a more positive way, this repression of the body in society finds a literary compensation in someone like Góngora who 'sensualizes' language.[34] Where Quevedo's reaction against the repression of the body took place at the (unconscious) level of content, with Góngora it is on the level of language. While Quevedo is obviously an influence on Goytisolo, particularly in a novel like *Juan sin tierra*, the example of Góngora is more decisive as it represents a subversion carried out at the level of language.

This emphasis on the formal aspect of the literary work, as well as tying in, via the connection between sexuality and writing, with Goytisolo's interest in the Arab tradition[35] and the politics of libertarianism, finds reinforcement from Goytisolo's interest in literary theory. Goytisolo's interest in structuralist linguistic theory, especially that of Jakobson and Benveniste, had led him towards the cultivation of a more formal approach to writing. Jakobson influenced his preference in literary analysis for the approach of narrative poetics,[36] which in turn influences Goytisolo's evaluation of his own and others' literary activity:

> todo un sector—el más consciente—de la novelística actual tiende a abandonar la vieja función del género, de representar el mundo exterior, para fijar su atención en el lenguaje; esto es, a pasar de la copia, del lenguaje transparente, a la escritura, a la autonomía del discurso. (D, 164)

This critique of reality through its language entailed a foregrounding of the sign itself, or more accurately, of the signifier over the signified. It was a rejection of Realism which, in its focus on content and tendency to disguise the process of enunciation, fostered the illusion of language as a transparent vehicle. In this light, the significance of the example of Góngora becomes clear:

> El arte elusivo de Góngora, ese empeño típicamente suyo en evitar la mención de los objetos a fin de hacer salir al idioma de su transparencia ilusoria es, en verdad, el resultado de una lucha grandiosa, titánica para que el lenguaje cobre cuerpo—de una demencial porfía en imponernos, a brazo partido, la presencia opaca, densa, casi física de las escurridizas palabras. (D, 181–82)

Góngora's 'sensualization' of language finds a perfect explanation in Jakobson's definition of the poetic function of language which, 'by promoting the palpability of signs, deepens the fundamental dichotomy of signs and objects'.[37] Jakobson saw the poetic function as the 'dominant' function in all literary works, thus distinguishing them from everyday uses of language in which the referential or communicative function of language dominates.

In all of Goytisolo's analyses it is clear that his attraction to Structuralism is founded primarily on the challenge that such a theory posed to the standard thinking on the language and literature of Western bourgeois society. The artist can adopt a critical approach to the prevailing ideology and its corresponding literary orthodoxy and create works that conform to Lotman's 'aesthetics of opposition', works in which 'el autor lucha contra las leyes rutinarias y prejuicios del público imponiéndole su propio modelo o perspectiva del mundo' (D, 71). Goytisolo demonstrates a clear preference for those which set out to infringe the rules of the genre to which they belong, and in so doing challenge and subvert the prevailing modes of perception, themselves dependent on prevailing ideologies:

> La escritura es entonces un acto sutil de traición y la obra del escritor marginal un 'cuento de horror' cuyos gérmenes—como nos muestra la vigencia actual de La Celestina—prosiguen su clandestina labor de zapa en el espíritu del lector y—aún al cabo de cinco siglos—lo conmueven, inquietan, trastornan y dulcemente, lo contaminan. (D, 34)

The Art of Transgression

Disidencias also shows Goytisolo to have reached a much clearer idea of the kind of role as an intellectual and artist which he finds suitable. His concept of this role has changed from the classic humanist one of someone who lays claim to the intellectual and moral high ground within a society, to that of the *marginado*. Goytisolo defines this role in the interview with Julio Ortega:

> A la verdad, toda mi actual experimentación literaria va acompañada de un deseo o propósito de descalificación moral: de decir lo 'indecible', de desautorizarme a ojos del intelectual humanista clásico. (D, 301)[38]

Goytisolo adopted the position of the marginal intellectual on society's periphery, an 'autor de la periferia' (CC, 96), committed not to the balanced and impartial analysis of social issues, but to the provocative gesture.[39]

In 'La novela española contemporánea', Goytisolo develops the idea, taken from Vargas Llosa, of the novelist as a 'provocador', outlining two levels of provocation: that in repressed societies which can take place at a thematic level, and that in a liberal society where in the absence of taboo themes, the provocation must be internalized into the language (D, 166–67).[40] While *Cien años de soledad* is praised for reviving the lost Cervantine tradition and presenting 'la posibilidad de crear ficciones liberadoras, desmesuradas, magníficas', its traditional approach to narrative and language makes it less subversive than the works of Sarduy, Fuentes and Cabrera Infante, where 'la subversión que descubrimos no es la del orden real sino la del lenguaje narrativo' (D, 320).

In 'De la literatura considerada como una delincuencia', Goytisolo reaffirms his belief in the duty of the writer to be a 'criminal' and his writing a 'crime', challenging the monopoly of Official discourse.[41] While recognizing the ability of modern liberal society to tolerate and assimilate such a 'conducta ética y artísticamente "delictiva"', he firmly believes that such an attitude of dissidence is not futile but rather 'podrá desenvolver una labor centrífuga y energética, capaz de contrapesar, gracias a su radical virulencia, la tendencia centrípeta, integradora, de la cultura oficial o paraoficial' (CC, 185).

The Politics of Self-Reflexiveness

It is through Formalist and Structuralist principles emphasizing the way language constructs the world that Goytisolo manages to blur the distinction between literary language and social discourse:

> Todavía hoy, en España, gran número de escritores 'comprometidos' que atacan la casta social que ocupa el poder emplean, sin darse cuenta, el mismo lenguaje que ésta—una misma retórica, aunque de signo opuesto. (D, 165)

The fundamental principle that Goytisolo accepts from the Formalist canon is that 'la vinculación de todo texto con el corpus literario de su tiempo es siempre más intensa que la que le une al contexto' (LLL, 90). This implies a rejection of Realism, especially of that of the nineteenth century in which the novel 'seguía aferrada a la reproducción ilusoria del mundo exterior, a su encarnizada "concurrencia al estado civil"' (D, 323). However, there is a more political motivation to Goytisolo's opposition to Realism which is especially evident in a novel such as *Juan sin tierra*, but in a less virulent way suffuses all of his writing in the post-*Señas* period. In common with certain structuralist or post-structuralist thinkers such as Barthes, Goytisolo perceives a connection between a prevailing bourgeois ideology, intent on presenting itself as 'non-ideological', characterized by common-sense, eternal values, and bourgeois literature, exemplified by the primacy of realism. The characteristic of bourgeois society, according to this trend of thought, is to mask its signs, to project itself as natural.[42] This Barthesian analysis can be glimpsed in his comments on *La lozana andaluza*, where he praises the author's constant appearances in his own fiction:

> recordándonos así su función de cronista y a la realidad material del hecho literario (colmo de desvergüenza para el burgués, preocupado siempre—en literatura como en política—por la disimulación de sus signos). (D, 59)[43]

In conventional realism, more emphasis is placed on the meaning of words than on their form, which it presents as natural. The focus is on the signified as opposed to the signifier. Not only does this suggest that language is innocent, neutral, transparent, it also presents events and ideas as given, pre-existing their textual expression as opposed to textually produced.

Combating such a tendency to conceal the sign explains Goytisolo's adoption of a self-conscious technique. Influential in this change in his and others' writing was the distinction between a style characterized by *discours* in the Benvenistian sense of 'toute énonciation supposant un locuteur et un auditeur, et chez le premier l'intention d'influencer l'autre en quelque manière' and one characterized by *histoire*, defined by Benveniste as narrative where 'les événements sont posés comme ils se sont produits à mesure qu'ils apparaissent à l'horizon de l'histoire. Personne ne parle ici; les événements semblent se raconter eux-mêmes.'[44]

However, the Benvenistian distinction is much more complicated than Goytisolo makes out in the essay concerned.[45] As critics such as Genette have pointed out, *discours* and *histoire* cannot be totally separated.[46] What is not absolutely clear from Goytisolo's citing of Benveniste in *Disidencias* is that the move to *discours* is not simply towards a subjective narrative in which the presence of the narrator is clearly revealed, as opposed to the traditional third-person form. Many straightforward realist texts, including works of Goytisolo like *La isla* and the travelogues, are written in the first-person discursive style. Yet the thrust of Goytisolo's argument in the essay 'La novela española contemporánea' is not simply for a return to subjective narration, but to a narrative that draws attention to its textuality, its status as language and writing. This is the implication throughout and reinforced by the reference to those novels which, in line with Jakobson's theories about the poetic function, 'centran la atención ... en el signo y no en la cosa representada' (D, 164). Goytisolo's interest in *discours* is based on a concern with writing that draws attention to its status as writing, the process of enunciation of the text. In *Disidencias* Goytisolo praises Cervantes' novel for precisely this feature: 'en ningún momento disimula el proceso de enunciación; antes bien, claramente lo manifiesta' (D, 205).

In a later essay, reproduced in *Contracorrientes*, Goytisolo produced a more subtle analysis of the concept of *discours*, and employs the terms 'enunciation/enounced' which, without achieving total clarification of this narratological issue, at least makes clear that his concern is with producing a text which draws attention to its production as text. Following Jenny Simonin-Grumbach,[47] he proposes to call *discours* 'aquellos textos donde hay una señalización con respecto a la situación de enunciación' (CC, 57). Simonin-Grumbach's refining of the Benvenistian principle has the effect of clarifying the significant distinction as being that between narrative illusion (*énoncé*) and the self-conscious narrative process (*énonciation*).

Goytisolo's admiration, therefore, is reserved for those works which draw attention to their status as fiction, deliberately destroying the referential illusion and, as the Russian Formalists would say, 'laying bare the device'.[48] Such self-consciousness has a clear social aim. What Goytisolo says about codified literary discourse ('Todo lo que sea poner en guardia al lector ante cualquier discurso literario codificado tiene un efecto muy saludable')[49] applies equally to non-literary discourses. For Goytisolo's novels incorporate all manner of linguistic codes: the codes of politics, advertising, the media, science, literary criticism. Parody of these codes draws attention to them as codes, ideologically and culturally determined sets of discourses which require to be treated with scepticism.[50]

Goytisolo's self-consciousness has a 'ludic' dimension which has similar social repercussions. The 'ludic' approach is one which indulges in textual play for its own sake and constitutes a contravention of the traditional view of literature as a serious vehicle of ideas and moral values. The ludic approach of someone like Sarduy 'suele tener, como es lógico, muy mala prensa entre los críticos tradicionalistas y conservadores de todo pelaje, preocupados tan solo por captar el Mensaje, el "fondo", la ideología' (D, 58). Ludism is the textual equivalent of eroticism and hedonism, seen as a subversion of traditional bourgeois ideology:

> la del muy burgués time is money: nada de perder el tiempo y malbaratar palabras, nada de gasto inútil: erotismo no, acto procreador, derroche no, economía; juego de escritura, barroquismo, figuras retóricas, vade retro!: pura información, lenguaje denotativo: expropiación de la plusvalía productiva, fisiológica, verbal. (D, 58–59)

Such a quotation illustrates the paradox that even Goytisolo's ludism has a political motivation.[51] Goytisolo's approach after *Señas* is to perceive the intimate relationship between the text and the world and, by enacting his rebellion on a textual level, to imply extra-textual repercussions. On the one hand, ludism has a liberational aspect; the text that foregrounds the content and relegates language and form to mere vehicles of a message is a restriction on the reader's freedom. In *Disidencias* he praises *Don Quijote*, in which 'la lectura única cede el paso a una disyuntiva o variedad de interpretaciones que preserva nuestra libertad de elección y juicio' (D, 251). This, he says, confers on an essentially aesthetic activity 'una profunda justificación moral que rebasa, como es obvio, los límites de la literatura' (D, 251). In his essay on Carlos Fuentes' novel *Terra nostra*, Goytisolo advocates a text which not only encourages an active reading, 'una lectura alerta' (D, 253) but one where the reader is able to detect multiple readings, some contradictory, 'múltiples y antagónicas lecturas' (D, 249) and finally unable to elucidate all the enigmas. Thus the text is opened to future readings (D, 256).

On the other hand, the freedom of the reader, as well as a potential source of pleasure, is also a profoundly disquieting experience because access to an active reading is at the price of a removal of conventional narrative reference points on which the reader bases his normal interpretive strategies. In Fuentes' novel, and in a novel like *Don Julián* or *Makbara*, themes, motifs are juggled, characters metamorphose and disappear, the narrative viewpoint changes continually, fact mingles with fiction, reality with myth. The reader's normal narrative footholds are withdrawn. The process of reconstructing the text is a permanent one since there is no ultimate reality, no stable story. Hence the circularity of many of the novels or their open-ended structure.

In this sense Goytisolo's views reveal clear affinities with aspects of post-structuralist thinking. Jacques Derrida's seminal essay, 'Structure, Sign and Play in the Discourse of the Human Sciences', delivered in the United States in 1966, created a furore with its critique of structuralism and introduction of the concepts of a decentred structure and the free play of the signifier. This essay introduced the idea of a liberating attitude to the world and the text based on the renunciation of a nostalgia for a fixed origin of meaning, a 'transcendental signified' and abandonment to the play of meaning. On the level of individual experience this involved 'a decentring of the "subject" in relation to language [...] a recognition that subjectivity is constituted in and through language, rather than providing its ultimate source and ground'.[52] On the level of literary studies it drew attention to the way the subjectivity of the writer was recreated in the text in the sense of a fixed perspective from which to view the events narrated, and in so doing create a stable perspective for the reader in the reading. Post-structuralist criticism attempts to resist that 'interpellation' of the reader by the text, to read against the grain and in so doing open the text up to new meanings, revealing the ideology that underpins it. This involved the rejection of the notion of the author and his intentions as the 'authority' for an interpretation of the text.[53]

Goytisolo's ludic approach shares with Derrida the aim, in the words of one commentator, to be 'subversive of all authoritarianisms' and to constitute a 'politics of demystification through relativization'.[54] *Don Julián* explicitly plays with the notion of a narrative whose meaning escapes its own author and perplexes the reader. On a formal level, as we shall see, its play with narratorial perspective creates a permanent narrative ambiguity which is developed by subsequent novels. If we accept that subjectivity is produced in the text, the reader is created as a subject by the text, the novels of Goytisolo attempt to undermine that stable sense of subjectivity by creating a decentred structure, with a narrative perspective that is continually changing, the discursive equivalent of nomadism.[55] Hence the importance in Goytisolo's novels of multiple points of view, unsynthesized into a single viewpoint. This approach comes most fully to fruition in *Makbara* and is extended in subsequent novels, but the process of unfixing the subject is noticeable even from *Señas*. The reading experience, the nexus between the world of the text and the world beyond, becomes the scene of the novel's process of subversion.

Myth and Countermyth

Echoes of post-structuralist thinking can be discerned too in relation to the treatment of myths in Goytisolo's writing. The early encounter with Barthes' *Mythologies*[56] led to an awareness of the inevitable gap that separates the real from its representation in language. The two coexist as related but separate dimensions. Goytisolo's structuralist leanings lead him to attach more importance to the semiotic representation of the real as being the only aspect that can be dealt with. The real is not dismissed. It is simply that there can be no possibility of unmediated access to this real. The individual is inextricably caught up in a realm of signs from which there is no escape. The most important sign system of all is, of course, language. Hence the author's role is to engage with the text of reality, the text of history, and effect a constant process of demythification. This attitude was first made clear in the interview with Emir Rodríguez Monegal where Goytisolo's discussion of the approach to myth in *Señas de identidad* reveals the affinity with the Formalist concept of 'defamiliarization': 'Uno de los objetivos del arte ha sido siempre destruir todo automatismo, todo lo que es mito' (57). While some of Goytisolo's comments in this interview indicate a concern to strip away myth and reveal the reality, as when speaking of the Cuban chapter, excised from the first edition of *Señas*, he says, 'he intentado subrayar esta ruptura dolorosa entre mito y realidad, entre la realidad cruda y la realidad embellecida por el mito' (57), the approach that prevails in *Señas* and predominates in the subsequent novels is better described as 'actualizar la imagen antigua y al mismo tiempo proponer una imagen nueva que la destruya' (57). In other words, all demythification is a further mythification.[57]

The essays in *Crónicas sarracinas*, published in 1981, constitute a critique of the discourse of the West about the Arab world, and part of that is a critique of Goytisolo's own role. Goytisolo recognizes a debt to the writer Edward Said and his book *Orientalism*, itself heavily borrowing from Foucault's theory of discourse, in which Western writings on the Orient are shown to be less a truthful reflection of the reality than a 'discourse' through which the West invents its own image of the East in an urge to control it (CS, 27–30). In 'De *Don Julián* a *Makbara*: una posible lectura orientalista', Goytisolo makes plain that the picture of the Arab world in these novels is not a 'realistic' one. Unlike his non-fictional writings, in which he defends the cause of the real-life Arab, the novels are directed at a European audience and are meant as an attack on European values. Part of those values is the mythology surrounding the Arab as an image of 'the Other'—both a threat and a seduction. To combat that mythology Goytisolo uses the myths themselves, inverting them, taking advantage of their power to disturb, shock and fascinate a Western, especially Spanish, audience. Hence Goytisolo reaffirms his constant claim to demythification, but not in the name of 'reason'; rather he seeks to combat myth with myth.

In 'Miradas al arabismo español', Goytisolo returns to this point, revealing an awareness of its dangers and a modest concern that he himself may not entirely have avoided them. He recognizes that the combating of myths involves the creation of new ones:

> Al decir esto, y combatir los mitos y fantasmas negativos que envuelven nuestra percepción 'occidental' de la cultura y sociedad árabes, no excluyo, no obstante, en el plano artístico y literario, la elaboración de nuevos mitos,

una mitogénesis en la que una serie de elementos irracionales actúen de forma libertadora y compensatoria, cuando menos para el lector europeo. (CS, 195)

The essays in *Crónicas* illustrate Goytisolo's acute awareness of the risks involved in the demythificatory process, and, indeed, one of the commonest criticisms levelled at Goytisolo is that, instead of combating myths, he merely inverts them through parody and thus merely serves to perpetuate them.[58] However, Goytisolo is quick to point out that this myth-creating process, if it is to be truly 'desalienador', must not simply invert opposing terms and in so doing serve to perpetuate a mythic polarity rather than create something new. His proposed solution is to undermine the standard opposition between the terms East and West:

> Negar la oposición irreductible de los conceptos 'Oriente' y 'Occidente', desprendernos de nuestras telarañas, adoptar una perspectiva desinteresada pero comprometida y abierta, observar esta sociedad musulmana en tantos aspectos afín a la nuestra con la ventaja que procuran la distancia y el conocimiento, sería a mi entender la alternativa más válida. (CS, 196)

He goes on to propose that the project to be carried out is a decentralizing one, showing that no one culture, neither the technologically advanced, progressive and 'rational' European one, nor the non-European ones, have the monopoly on solutions. Above all, rather than an opposition between East and West, the attempt should be made to unite cultures in opposition to a common enemy, modernity, which threatens them: 'la modernidad incontrolada que las niega' (CS, 196).

It is important to note, therefore, how Goytisolo does not envisage an escape from myth to the stability of history. In 'Vigencia actual del mudejarismo'[59] he reiterates that his attitude to the oriental world is essentially 'mitopoiético' in that, rather than seek an accurate portrayal of the orient—the role of the true 'arabista'—the author attempts to use those myths, work with them for his own artistic purposes. Again, Goytisolo is arguing for art's duty to explore the mysterious, non-rational side of experience on its own terms:

> pues todo texto literario rico, profundo y complejo no se compone sólo de ingredientes racionales sino que cala en las honduras y entresijos del subconsciente individual y colectivo en donde se esconde el mito. (CC, 11)[60]

The choices on offer to the novelist are between a static mythology and a dynamic one:

> Pero este componente mitopoético, si quiere desempeñar un papel desalienador debe evitar una polarización irreductible de los términos de la contradicción. En caso contrario, corre el riesgo de consolidarla aun en forma invertida, pasando así de la categoría de mito estimulante y dinámico a la de estático y muerto. (CS, 195–96)[61]

Return to the Radical Roots

Goytisolo's express interest in linguistic theory spanned the period between 1965 and 1975, though as *Contracorrientes* shows, he was still taking an interest in the early 1980s.[62] After this date, the signs are that his interest waned somewhat and his comments in more recent interviews indicate that his attention has turned more towards Islamic culture and the re-reading of certain classical Spanish texts. Yet the encounter with Russian Formalism and Structuralism was a formative one, and the tenets of these related schools continue to inform his thinking on literature, as can be seen from the frequent references to Russian Formalism in the most recent books, *El bosque de las letras* and *Cogitus interruptus*. What does seem to be the case is that Goytisolo's interest in literary theory stopped short at Structuralism's successors in the Deconstructionist school. His comments in the 1980s reveal if anything a slight disdain for the followers of Derrida, Lacan and the *Tel Quel* school.[63] Nonetheless, critics have noted certain affiliations between Goytisolo's most recent novels and post-structuralist thinking.[64] His appreciation of texts like the *Libro de Buen Amor* is predicated on a radically 'modern' valuing of the activity of linguistic subversion, in which the influence of the Russian Formalist thinker, Mikhail Bakhtin, is explicitly acknowledged.[65] Hence he is quick to point out the link between the Arcipreste's practice and the post-Joycean tradition.[66] In a 1984 essay, 'Medievalismo y Modernidad: El arcipreste y nosotros', Goytisolo expands on a theme which dominates his thinking in this period, that is that the modern avant-garde has much in common with the great works of popular culture in the Middle Ages. Both are characterized by an anarchic, heterogeneous, open structure that mixes a variety of styles and registers in stark contrast to the monolithic structures of official culture:

> Si definimos la modernidad en términos de apertura, insumisión a las reglas establecidas, mescolanza de escritos al servicio de una unidad estética superior o reflexión del autor sobre la propia escritura y configuración del texto, un acercamiento incluso limitado y superficial a una serie de obras representativas de otras épocas nos descubrirá muy pronto que deberían ser incluidos también en dicho apartado o rúbrica. (CC, 14)

Goytisolo sees the *Libro de Buen Amor*, the *Corbacho* and *La lozana andaluza* as characterized by formal features vaunted as radical and subversive by the modern avant-garde. Hence while Cervantes laid the foundations for the modern European novel, a book like the *Libro de Buen Amor* actually stands as a precursor of the post-Joycean tradition with 'su diferente concepción del personaje, argumento, lenguaje novelescos' (19). It is in this period that Goytisolo starts to shun the term 'vanguardia' which had hitherto characterized his attitude and, out of solidarity with the subversive texts of the past, designate his position, somewhat mischievously, as in the 'retaguardia'.[67]

What Bakhtinian theory and pre-Renaissance Spanish literary practice offer Goytisolo is a model for discursive transgression against the accepted norm which is, on a social level, conventional official discourse (for example, the media, advertising and academic-scientific discourse parodied in *Makbara*) and, at a literary level, the prevailing tradition of the realist, 'monologic' novel. This forms the basis of the novels *Makbara* and *Paisajes después de la batalla*.

By the mid-1980s Goytisolo's thinking and practice of writing evolve in a slightly different direction, towards mystical writing, and poetry in particular. This leads one critic to see a theoretical sea-change in his writing:

> En las cinco novelas pre-autobiográficas, Juan Goytisolo se deja guiar por las teorías sobre la cultura carnavalesca de M. Bachtin [sic] para conseguir su objetivo desmitificador [...]
> Y si Bachtin es su mentor en la etapa desmitificadora, San Juan de la Cruz lo será en la etapa mística o escatológica.[68]

However, rather than a sea-change, it is an evolution towards a new form of combating society's ills and new methods of transgression. The most recent non-fictional writing collected in the volumes of essays *El bosque de las letras* and *Cogitus interruptus*, from 1995 and 1999 respectively, show, on the one hand, a reiteration of the allegiance to Russian Formalism dating from the 1960s, but a new focus to the critique of modernity according to which the reification of the individual by capitalist materialism is combated, not by a rebellion of the body, but by a preservation of man's spiritual dimension, viewed as a necessary complement to the physical. It is undoubtedly the case that Goytisolo shares implicitly the critique of modernity made by critical theorists like Marcuse and members of the Frankfurt School and postmodernist thinkers such as Foucault, Baudrillard and Lyotard, for whom modernity is characterized by a repressive scientific rationality. Goytisolo's interest in the classics, and even his recent move towards mysticism and contemplative thinkers such as Ibn Arabi, Miguel de Molinos and San Juan de la Cruz, is strongly conditioned by a contemporary critical awareness.[69] In this new perspective, literature remains vital since literature in its purest form (in particular poetry, through its preservation of 'las palabras sustanciales'), as opposed to the rhetoric of contemporary capitalist society, is essential to man's survival, man as 'el hombre integral'. He cites the Bosnian poet, Dzevad Karahasán, for whom 'la poesía es producto del hombre integral y se dirige al universo integral'.[70] Aside from the apparent novelty of Goytisolo's increasing spiritual preoccupation in these essays and the novels from *Paisajes* onwards, the emphasis on poetry and the power of language is merely a variation on a familiar theme. Faced with a society governed by instrumental rationality, in which the majority literary expression is a familiar, non-transgressive form of literary entertainment which Goytisolo dubs 'la producción editorial', intended for 'consumo instantáneo', Goytisolo advocates a form of literature which is difficult, at times hermetic, on the surface elitist, and which demands from the reader a commitment to 'rereading'. The aim of this is the familiar one of resistance to society's norms and the liberation of the individual:

> Reivindicar la radicalidad sagrada de la palabra es reivindicar la particularidad irreductible del ser humano: su integridad y gloriosa diversidad.[71]

It is not difficult to see in Goytisolo's defence of the hermetic and irreducibly literary nature of writing, its resistance to instant consumption and the explicitly political motivation behind this approach, clear connections with the earlier Barthesian commitment to writing for a transformation of society. His literary ideal in this latest period, not very different from the motivation underlying *Señas de identidad*'s approach to language, is to achieve 'el lenguaje integral del hombre integral, la universalidad de una palabra no limitada ni pervertida por su instrumentalización partidista e interesada'.[72]

The characteristic of this later period is that the emphasis of Goytisolo's attack has widened to be global capitalism, what he terms 'la llamada Tienda Global, el Gran Mercado del Mundo' (CI, 234), and its ally technoscience. The threat is still the reification of man by the social system, and while the earlier response of a playful, erotic rebellion of the body, conveyed through an explicit textuality, has not been renounced, prominence is now given to a rebellion of the spirit, of which literature is one of the most important reserves. From the 'lenguaje del cuerpo' of Góngora to the 'palabras sustanciales' of Valente, San Juan and Ibn Arabi constitutes an evolution, but not a change. The similarities between the two are considerable. In both instances, too, Goytisolo's utopian aim is harmonious integration.

Conclusion

Goytisolo's radical theory and practice of the later, post-*Señas* period has evolved towards a notion of the performative function of literature which comes to supersede the earlier more naive sense criticized in *El furgón de cola* and *Disidencias*. This again is a clear legacy of Structuralism which Terry Eagleton has defined in a way that is appropriate to my interpretation of Goytisolo's approach:

Literature may appear to be describing the world, and sometimes actually does so, but its real function is performative: it uses language within certain conventions in order to bring about certain effects in a reader. It achieves something in the saying: it is language as a kind of material practice in itself, discourse as social action.[73]

From *Señas de identidad* onwards, Goytisolo's novels aim to achieve what, in the words of Roland Barthes, is the characteristic of contemporary fiction, that is, 'to transpose narrative from the purely constative plane, which it has occupied until now, to the performative plane, whereby the meaning of an utterance is the very act by which it is uttered';[74] what Goytisolo, citing Barthes, repeatedly refers to as 'convertir en posibilidades de discurso las imposibilidades del referente' (BL, 79). The text's performativeness is limited, in other words, to the reading process. However, this is an 'active' approach which constitutes a compromise solution to the question of literature's effectiveness.

NOTES

1 A. Carlos Isasi Angulo, 'La novelística de Juan Goytisolo (Entrevista con el autor)', *Papeles de Son Armadans* LXXVI(226) (1975), 78.

2 Luis Sanz, 'Entrevista con Juan Goytisolo', *Camp de l'Arp* 43–44 (1977), 19.

3 See 'Nota del autor', in *El sitio de los sitios* (Madrid: Alfaguara, 1995), 183.

4 Goytisolo has to date produced some 15 books of essays, some exclusively political or concerned with Spanish and Islamic culture. The most interesting ones from the point of view of his literary principles are *Problemas de la novela*, *El furgón de cola*, *Disidencias*, the 'Presentación crítica de José María Blanco White', *Crónicas sarracinas*, *Contracorrientes*, *Libertad, Libertad, Libertad*, *El bosque de las letras*, and *Cogitus interruptus*.

5 Goytisolo himself disapproves of this approach. *Contracorrientes* (Barcelona: Montesinos, 1985), 52–53.

6 'Goytisolo as a writer is not a leader, not even a mere cog in a historical continuum, but expressly a follower, swayed by the fickle currents of his time.' John W. Kronik in a review of Génaro Pérez's *Formalist Elements in the Novels of Juan Goytisolo*, *Modern Language Notes* XCVI (1981), 468.

7 Compare 'Las palabras no son los nombres transparentes de las cosas, forman una entidad autónoma, regida por sus propias leyes: la relación entre literatura y "realidad" existe, pero no tiene, por consiguiente, el carácter simplista, de mera transposición mecánica, que lectores y críticos se empeñan, ingenuamente, en imaginar, y la función del escritor radica, quizás, en hacer salir al lenguaje de su transparencia ilusoria' ('Juego de espejos', *Quimera* LXVIII (1987), 40) and the introductory remarks to the essay 'Estebanillo González, hombre de buen humor', in *El furgón de cola* (Barcelona: Seix Barral, 1976), 97. See also *Disidencias* (Barcelona: Seix Barral, 1977), 63. See too the numerous references to Russian Formalism in his most recent essays in *El bosque de las letras* (Madrid: Anagrama, 1995), 28, 79, 197 and *Cogitus interruptus* (Barcelona: Seix Barral, 1999), 244, 255, 266.

8 In *Disidencias* he states: 'La convergencia de Benveniste y el formalismo y estructuralismo eslavos que se manifiesta en autores como Barthes, Genette, Todorov y, en general, en el grupo *Tel Quel* ha influido igualmente en el camino de ruptura que

inicié con *Señas*, aunque creo que mi proceso personal a la literatura no encaja en ninguna de las escuelas que actualmente se disputan la escena parisiense' (322).

9 *Insula* CXLVI (1959), 6, 11.

10 In the article 'Para una literatura nacional popular', as well as reiterating his attack on Ortega's elitist and aestheticist theory of the novel, Goytisolo also attacks the other dominant post-Civil War literary trend of Nationalist literature of such authors as Eugenio Montes and Giménez Caballero, which he saw as presenting an equally distorted and untrue picture of Spanish reality. The articles collected in *Problemas* were published mainly in the journal *Destino* between 1956 and 1957, and include in an appendix articles and extracts from writers such as Lukács, Malraux, Brecht and Vittorini.

11 So called because they use quotes from Machado's poem 'El mañana efímero' as introductory and concluding epigraphs. Goytisolo's pre-*Señas* production is usually divided into three periods: an initial subjective period that includes *Juegos de manos* (1954) and *Duelo en el Paraíso* (1955); the more politically committed, social realist period of the trilogy comprising *Fiestas* (1958), *El circo* (1957), *La resaca* (1958); and, finally, the attempt at a more objective realism in the work comprising *Para vivir aquí* (1960), *Campos de Níjar* (1959), *La isla* (1961), *Fin de fiesta* (1962) and *La Chanca* (1962). See Ramón Buckley, *Problemas formales en la novela española contemporánea* (Barcelona: Península, 1973), 149–50; José Francisco Cirre, 'Novela e ideología en Juan Goytisolo', *Insula* CCXXX (1996), 1,12; and J. M. Martínez Cachero, 'El novelista Juan Goytisolo', *Papeles de Son Armadans* XXXII (1964), 124–60.

12 'El arte según Ortega, es un juego gratuito propio de aristócratas. Para el escritor, los hechos y sucedidos mediocres de la vida corriente carecen de interés. Lo que cuenta es el refinamiento estético, la búsqueda de "los filones secretos del alma". El artista ha de dirigirse a las minorías. En una palabra, debe deshumanizarse el arte. Desterrados los problemas de orden concreto, las preocupaciones de índole social y humana, la novela, propone Ortega, debe tender a una pureza difícil, alejada de la vida real y sus vulgaridades' (PN, 83).

13 'Para volver a ser universal, nuestra novela debe españolizarse. Para reanudar su contacto con el público debe esforzarse en reflejar la vida del hombre español contemporáneo, tal como hicieron en su día Baroja, Galdós y los grandes maestros de la Picaresca' (PN, 86).

14 Goytisolo himself in the later book of essays *El furgón de cola* refers to them as 'mis poco meditados articulillos recogidos en el volumen Problemas de la novela (felizmente agotado hoy)' (FC, 141). In *En los reinos de taifa* he refers to the *Insula* article as 'producto de una bulímica lectura de Gramsci' (21) and notes the disparity between the ideas it expressed and the actual practice of his novels up to that point with the exception of the failed exercise in social realism *La resaca*.

15 Goytisolo states in the prefatory note: 'Su único denominador común radica en el propósito de abordar los diferentes aspectos y problemas de la creación literaria desde el punto de vista—tan importante como olvidado—de su motivación social' (PN, 7).

16 'La civilización neocapitalista de empresarios, técnicos y especuladores, de gente que vive por el rendimiento y para el rendimiento condena de modo inapelable las "virtudes" humanas de nuestra sociedad primitiva. La nobleza, la lealtad, el desinterés que caracterizaban hasta hace unos años a los españoles son barridos hoy despiadadamente por el credo de la nueva religión industrial y con ellos desaparecen, asimismo, las razones sentimentales y morales de nuestra adhesión a la causa del pueblo que las encarnaba' (FC, 13).

17 'Los pinitos teóricos de mi acercamiento a Lukács y Sartre cuajarían en cambio en unas reflexiones que en vez de ser fruto de mi experiencia de lector y escritor,

reflejarían más bien, como en la mayoría de mis colegas novadores de la época, una penosa indigestión de lecturas.' *Coto vedado* (Barcelona: Seix Barral, 1985), 196.

18 Jean-Paul Sartre, *Qu'est-ce que la littérature?* (Paris: Gallimard, 1948), 341.

19 'Luego en París, empecé a leer al propio Marx, Engels y, sobre todo, Lukács que fue desdichadamente, por espacio de cuatro o cinco años, mi inseparable mentor.' *Contracorrientes*, 220.

20 Writing of Barthes, Frank Lentricchia notes: 'His kind of structuralism represents a commitment to both traditions [Sartrian commitment and Kantian aesthetic self-sufficiency] ... [t]he formalism of structuralist thought ... is integrated with "responsibility".' Frank Lentricchia, *After the New Criticism* (London: Methuen, 1983), 137.

21 'Supeditando el arte a la política rendíamos un flaco servicio a ambos: políticamente ineficaces, nuestras obras eran, para colmo, literariamente mediocres; creyendo hacer literatura política, no hacíamos ni una cosa ni otra' (FC, 87).

22 'Since Cernuda experienced a profound sense of alienation in the society in which he lived, the longing to end the separation between himself and the world frequently became a desire to seek refuge from the world in a private haven.' Derek Harris, *Luis Cernuda: A Study of the Poetry* (London: Tamesis Books, 1973), 2, 16. Harris later in the study qualifies that view of Cernuda in a way that, as we shall see, shows striking parallels with Goytisolo's approach to his art.

23 'A mi manera me parece que [...] toda obra literaria es a la vez huída y una forma indirecta de acción. Yo creo que en *Don Julián* como en mis novelas anteriores, el ansia de evasión y el deseo de cambiar el mundo actúan simultáneamente.' José Hernández, 'Juan Goytisolo—1975', *Modern Language Notes* XCI (1976), 351.

24 This was a position that characterized Cernuda. As Harris states, Cernuda reached the view that 'a poem should have a basis of personal experience to give it authenticity'. *Luis Cernuda*, 16.

25 'Juan Ruiz [...] gracias a él me reconcilio también—a lo menos en el lapso de su lectura—con la gente de habla española'. *Disidencias*, 179. For an excellent discussion of Goytisolo's relationship with his literary precursors, see Alison Margaret Kennedy, 'Dissidence and the Spanish Literary Tradition in the Later Novels of Juan Goytisolo' (unpublished DPhil thesis, University of Oxford, 1996).

26 In the interview with Isasi Angulo carried out in 1975, Goytisolo admitted: 'En general soy partidario de un socialismo libertario.' 'La novelística de Juan Goytisolo', 84.

27 R. N. Berki points out that it is 'not an accident that the dominant and ideological base of libertarianism should be the United States, the inner fortress of Western advanced Capitalism.' R. N. Berki, *Socialism* (London: Dent, 1975), 140.

28 'La defensa de todas las formas eróticas no procreadoras, tiene por otra parte un valor capital: me parece que fue Marcuse quien dijo que la aceptación de las normas sexuales de la sociedad termina por una aceptación de todos los criterios morales, sociales y políticos de la misma.' Hernández, 'Juan Goytisolo—1975', 346.

29 Henry Kamen has noted: 'For long periods, close contact between communities had led to a mutual tolerance among the three faiths of the peninsula: Christians, Muslims and Jews.' Henry Kamen, *The Spanish Inquisition: An Historical Revision* (London: Phoenix, 1997), 1.

30 'La influencia islámica en la obra de Juan Ruiz, que como tan agudamente captó Américo Castro, hizo posible "la pacífica convivencia del erotismo y la religión"' (D, 90).

31 'Frente a una pirámide social absurda, asfixiante y tiránica que tritura a los hombres en sus inexorables mecanismos Rojas, como tres siglos más tarde Sade, reivindica la primacía de la impulsión erótica y su también ciega, inexorable furia' (D, 28).

32 Lotman defines the 'aesthetic of opposition' as constituted by 'systems whose code is unknown to the audience before the act of artistic perception begins'. Yuri M. Lotman, *The Structure of the Artistic Text* (Ann Arbor, MI: University of Michigan, 1977), 292. The 'aesthetic of identity' is the opposite, a work which presents reality in a way that is easily recognizable, complete with clichés. For structuralists, like Barthes, *vraisemblance* referred to a text's conformity to the expectations of the public about life or art. A text is *invraisemblable*, and therefore potentially subversive, if it departs from such expectations. See Jonathan Culler, *Structuralist Poetics: Structuralism, Linguistics and the Study of Literature* (London: Routledge, 1975), 138–60.

33 'En contra de lo que suele decirse, la coprofilia de Quevedo, en vez de ser reflejo de una mente enferma, es, paradójicamente, un síntoma de buena salud: el autor del Buscón expresa a su modo la neurosis general de la humanidad, dando libre cauce a las obsesiones y fantasmas ligados al reconocimiento de nuestra realidad corporal ...' (D, 120).

34 Here Goytisolo finds support in Paz who says: 'Si el siglo XVII había olvidado que el cuerpo es un lenguaje sus poetas supieron crear un lenguaje que, tal vez a causa de su misma complicación nos da la sensación de un cuerpo vivo' (D, 181).

35 Referring to the baroque style of Lezama Lima, Goytisolo says: 'las palabras muertas del diccionario cobran vida, se agrupan sensualmente delante de nosotros, dibujan figuras exquisitas en el blanco de la página, se transmutan en "cuerpo" como en la poesía árabe'. *Disidencias*, 263

36 'Dicho esto, entre los diferentes métodos de análisis crítico, mis preferencias personales van al de la poética, tal como nos ha sido definida por Jakobson. Creo, como decía Northrop Frye, que la crítica literaria tiene necesidad de un principio coordinador o hipótesis de base que permita considerar las obras aisladas como partes constituyentes de un conjunto global.' *Libertad, Libertad, Libertad* (Barcelona: Anagrama, 1978), 89–90. In an interview in 1976, Goytisolo commented that he had taught classes in structuralism. Mauro González Ruano, 'Una literatura total', *Ozono* XI (1976), 58.

37 Roman Jakobson, 'Linguistics and Poetics', in *The Structuralists: From Marx to Lévi-Strauss*, ed. R. and F. DeGeorge (New York: Anchor, 1972), 93.

38 In this we can see echoes of ideas expressed at the time by Michel Foucault. In the early 1970s Foucault was redefining the role of the intellectual away from 'the "universal" intellectual [...] the man of justice, the man of law, who counterposes to power, despotism, and the abuses and arrogance of wealth the universality of justice and the equity of an ideal law'. Michel Foucault, *Power/Knowledge: Selected Interviews and Other Writings, 1972–77*, quoted in *The Foucault Reader: An Introduction to Foucault's Thought*, ed P. Rabinow (London: Penguin, 1991), 70.

39 Goytisolo, as well as the confessed influence of Marcuse, shows signs of an affinity with Foucault's similar, but distinct, theory of the need to resist oppression by a dual strategy of discourse politics and bio-politics; in the former, 'marginal groups attempt to contest the hegemonic discourses that position individuals within the straitjacket of normal identities to liberate the free play of differences'. Bio-politics was a variant on the Marcusian liberation through sexuality, discussed above, and in Foucault involved exploring 'the transgressive potential of the body'. Steven Best and Douglas Kellner, *Postmodern Theory: Critical Interrogations* (London: Macmillan, 1991), 57–58. Brad Epps also notes: 'Sounding out the failure of (revolutionary) faith, we find that despite Goytisolo's explicit reliance on Marcuse, his text presents a world that has just as much to do with Foucault, a world of contradiction and confusion, a world that manifests itself in and as an intricate, uncontrollable web of power'. Brad Epps, *Significant Violence: Oppression and Resistance in the Narratives of Juan Goytisolo, 1970–1990* (Oxford: Clarendon Press, 1996), 248.

40 This idea had its echoes in Marcuse's thinking, also. Speaking of Marcuse's analysis of the avant-garde writers of the French Resistance, Barry Katz sums up his theory thus: 'As the revolutionary *content* of theory or art came increasingly to be adjusted to the prevailing order, the alienation from this order, which transmits the critical force of the *oeuvre*, was transferred to the aesthetic form itself'. Barry Katz, *Herbert Marcuse and the Art of Liberation: An Intellectual Biography* (London, Verso, 1982), 121.

41 '... un delito más o menos tipificado en los distintos códigos de "defensa social y moral" establecidos por los poderes que imponen el monopolio de su propio discurso identificándolo abusivamente con la voz del pueblo' (CC, 179).

42 'In Barthes' view the chief energizing force behind myth is bourgeois culture which succeeds in making itself nearly anonymous by cloaking its purposes in the twin images of Nature and the Eternal Man.' Lentricchia, *After the New Criticism*, 134.

43 In *Disidencias*, Goytisolo makes the analogy once again between bourgeois society and the bourgeois novel when speaking of *Paradiso* by Lezama Lima (258).

44 Emile Benveniste, *Problèmes de linguistique générale*, (Paris: Gallimard, 1966), 241–42. See also *Disidencias*, 164.

45 See Culler, *Structuralist Poetics*, 197–200 for an account of this issue

46 Gérard Genette, *Figures of Narrative Discourse* (Oxford: Blackwell, 1982), 141.

47 Goytisolo was doubtless referring to the article 'Pour une typologie des discours', in *Langue, discours, société: pour Emile Benveniste* (Paris: Seuil, 1975), 85–121. Simonin-Grumbach's exposition of the distinction is on p. 87: 'Il faudrait donc, sans doute, reformuler l'hypothèse de Benveniste en des termes un peu différents, et je proposerai d'appeler "discours" les textes où il y a repérage par rapport à la situation d'énonciation (= Sit E), et "histoire" les textes où le repérage n'est pas effectué par rapport à Sit E mais par rapport au texte lui-même. Dans ce dernier cas, je parlerai de "situation d'énoncé" (= Sit E). Il ne s'agit donc plus de la présence ou de l'absence de *shifters* en surface, mais du fait que les déterminations renvoient à la situation d'énonciation (extra-linguistique) dans un cas, alors que, dans l'autre, elles renvoient au texte lui-même.'

48 '... junto a una mayoría de ficciones literarias que [...] disimulan sus signos y el proceso de enunciación del autor—el hecho de que, como maese Pedro, está siempre detrás de sus personajes de papel, moviendo los hilos—bajo un barniz de "realismo", verosimilitud y "naturalidad" existen otras—mucho menos numerosas, es verdad, pero cualitativamente esenciales—que destruyen aposta la ilusión realista del lector mediante la intervención directa, y a veces perfectamente arbitraria, de un novelista que pone al desnudo su técnica, sus trucos, su procedimiento' (D, 57).

49 C. A. Molina and Luis Suñen, 'Juan Goytisolo o la heterodoxia consciente', *Insula* CCCLXVII (1977), 4.

50 As Terry Eagleton has noted: 'Many modernist literary works [...] make the "act of enunciating", the process of their own production, part of their actual "content". They do not try to pass themselves off as unquestionable, like Barthes's "natural" sign, but as the Formalists would say "lay bare the device" of their own composition. They do this so that they will not be mistaken for absolute truth—so that the reader will be encouraged to reflect critically on the partial, particular ways they construct reality, and so to recognize how it might all have happened differently.' Terry Eagleton, *Literary Theory: An Introduction* (London: Blackwell, 1983), 170.

51 Hence later, in an interview in *Contracorrientes*, he displays an impatience with the fashion of ludism (CC, 234). The same can be noted in *Paisajes*, 193.

52 Christopher Norris, *Derrida* (London: Fontana, 1987), 221.

53 See Catherine Belsey, *Critical Practice* (London: Methuen, 1987), Chapter 3, for a good account of this theory.

54 Andrew Milner, *Contemporary Cultural Theory: An Introduction* (London: UCL Press, 1994), 89.

55 In his interview with Julián Ríos, Goytisolo, speaking of *Juan sin tierra*, says 'este nomadismo se traslada a la estructura misma de la obra'. J. Ríos (ed.), *Juan sin tierra* (Madrid: Fundamentos, 1977), 14.

56 See Goytisolo, *En los reinos de taifa* (Barcelona: Seix Barral, 1986), 6.

57 Stacey Dolgin, *La novela desmitificadora española (1961–1982)* (Barcelona: Anthropos Editorial del Hombre, Ambito Literarios/Ensayos, 1991), 30.

58 Michael Ugarte, *Trilogy of Treason: An Intertextual Study of Juan Goytisolo* (Columbia, MO, and London: University of Missouri Press, 1982), 78; Carlos Blanco Aguinaga, 'Sobre la *Reivindicación del conde Don Julián*: la ficción y la historia', in *De mitólogos y novelistas* (Madrid: Porrúa Turanzas, 1984), 51–71; Claudia Schaefer-Rodríguez, *Juan Goytisolo: del 'realismo crítico' a la utopía* (Madrid: Turner, 1975), 94–95. Jo Labanyi, in her book *Myth and History in the Contemporary Spanish Novel* (Cambridge: Cambridge University Press, 1989), also follows this line of criticism in her analysis of *Don Julián*, stating at one point: 'What starts as an attack on the irrationalist mythifications of Nationalist ideology ends as an equally irrationalist rejection of the Western intellectual tradition' (213).

59 In *Contracorrientes* (1985). This volume gathers together many incidental journalistic pieces and several essays and book reviews along with one interview—all dating from the late 1970s and early 1980s. In this volume the familiar ideas recur with added emphasis and the interview gives a useful insight into the development of Goytisolo's political views in the direction of the anarchist tradition.

60 This does not mean recourse to pure irrationalism. In his interview with José Hernández, Goytisolo advocates an 'alianza integral de la razón crítica y la imaginación que adopta a veces la forma engañosa de la alucinación, la locura: pero en estos delirios, en estos sueños, en estas evasiones oníricas de Goya encontramos una crítica mucho más eficaz, mucho más real del mito español que si nos mantenemos a un nivel puramente racional como hicieron los ilustrados' (Hernández, 'Juan Goytisolo—1975', 350).

61 This recalls Derrida's comment that 'the discourse on the acentric structure that myth itself is, cannot have an absolute subject or absolute centre ... In opposition to epistemic discourse, structural discourse on myths ... must be mythomorphic. It must have the form of that of which it speaks.' Jacques Derrida, 'Structure, Sign and Play in the Discourse of the Human Sciences', in *Modern Criticism and Theory*, ed. David Lodge (London: Longman, 1988), 116.

62 'Leí mucha lingüística de mil novecientos sesenta y cinco al setenta y cinco, pero en los últimos años ha dejado de interesarme'. Milagros Sánchez Arnosi, 'Juan Goytisolo: la creación literaria como liberación', *Insula* CDXXVI (1982), 4. The essay 'El novelista: ¿crítico practicante o teorizador de fortuna?', dates from 1981.

63 See *Contracorrientes*, 16. In a private interview, Goytisolo admitted that he could not read a word of Lacan, finding it unintelligible (a sign at least that he had tried). *Paisajes* contains a satiric swipe at this kind of theoretical terrorism, especially as applied to his own work, when he describes a pair of intruders into his protagonist's study as a 'mili-tante histérica, lacaniana' and her 'secuaz, una discípula con todo el aspecto de una prima fea y tonta venida de provincias, que repetía las palabras de la otra como un periquito, enriqueciéndolas con un fuerte acento catalán' (176).

64 Gustavo Pellón, 'Juan Goytisolo y Severo Sarduy: discurso e ideología', *Hispanic Review* LVI (1988), 483–92; Gonzalo Navajas, 'Retórica de la novela posmoderna española', in *Teoría y práctica de la novela española posmoderna* (Barcelona: Ediciones del Mall, 1987), 13–40.

65 'De *Don Julián* a *Makbara*', in *Crónicas sarracinas* (Paris: Ruedo Ibérico, 1981), 45 and 53.

66 Luce López-Baralt, in *Huellas del islam en la literatura española: de Juan Ruiz a Juan Goytisolo* (Madrid: Hiperíon, 1985), notes that 'Podríamos decir que, en buena medida, las lecturas modernas de Goytisolo coadyuvan a afinar el prisma a través del cual el escritor ha releído y reentendido a Juan Ruiz y a los árabes' (182).

67 'El objeto de mi interés, en los últimos veinte años, es precisamente esa relación con lo que he llamado el árbol de la literatura española. Por eso he negado siempre ser un autor de vanguardia, puesto que mis obras conectan con textos medievales o clásicos. En rigor se me podría tachar de escritor de retaguardia.' Miguel Riera, 'Regreso al origen (entrevista)', *Quimera* LXXIII (1988), 37.

68 José M. Martín Morán, 'La escritura mística de Juan Goytisolo', *La Torre* VIII(29) (1994), 26.

69 '¿puede el mundo de hoy, sometido a la tiranía planetaria de la tecnociencia, sobrevivir sin el *mundus imaginalis*, despojado de su anterior espiritualidad y metafísica de la naturaleza?' *El bosque de las letras*, 151–52.

70 *El bosque de las letras*, 12.

71 *El bosque de las letras*, 13.

72 *Cogitus interruptus*, 234.

73 Eagleton, *Literary Theory*, 118.

74 Roland Barthes, *Image–Music–Text* (London: Fontana, 1984), 114.

CHAPTER TWO

Señas de identidad

Señas de identidad is the inauguration of what Goytisolo himself refers to as his 'mature period'.[1] It is the first instalment of the Mendiola trilogy and the first fruit of the major existential crisis, the 'desgarra-dora labor de autocrítica—política, literaria, personal' (D, 343), which the author underwent in 1963.

Critics have been quick to stress that *Señas* is a transitional work,[2] and Goytisolo himself frequently points out that it contains the flaws and imperfections of its author's search for a new mode of writing. He compares it to *Tiempo de silencio*, 'una obra aún vacilante, desnivelada y con bastantes aristas [...] el comienzo de una nueva etapa' (D, 165). For this reason one must guard against the tendency to treat *Señas* as an aesthetically accomplished work. Indeed a large part of its interest and subversive effect, as we will see, is due to its imperfection, for it reveals the situation of an author in crisis. Its uneven texture, narrative dislocations and ambiguities are the signs of the author's attempt to break free of a restrictive tradition.

Señas, and even subsequent novels, tends to be interpreted in terms of realism. Most critics point to the importance of language and form. José Ortega notes how in *Señas* 'predomina todavía el referente o realidad social, pero el motivo o significado va cediendo al significante o lenguaje, y el personaje [...] va transformando la aventura moral [...] en aventura lingüística'.[3] Ortega sees Alvaro as alienated and setting about substituting history with a new mythology in which the relation-ship of language to reality is put in question. Carlos Fuentes also stresses that the focal point of *Señas* and subsequent novels is on language, seen as the root of experience and the site of ideological control.[4]

Critics, then, often treat *Señas* in one of two ways: either the innovatory form serves the interests of greater realism,[5] or form and content parallel each other, Alvaro's dilemma and critique of Spain constituting an implicit attack on the ideological appropriation of language.[6]

There is, however, a much more radical project at work in *Señas*. Even at this early stage the principles of Structuralism and Russian Formalism were starting to make their mark on the author's work. Goytisolo's undermining of the traditional realist novel, questioning of language and self-conscious treatment of the artist's role—all issues that will form the basis of the subsequent volumes of the trilogy—are encountered in embryonic form in this novel.

Narrative Levels

On the surface, *Señas* is the account of a process of self-examination. Alvaro, the rebel son of a bourgeois family in Barcelona, returns home after a period of voluntary exile in Paris. Departure from Spain had been motivated by a desire to escape the suffocating, repressive environment of both the family home and the country, with whose values the protagonist had long ceased to identify. Throughout his stay in Paris, interspersed with frequent travels abroad—Cuba, Italy, Holland, Switzerland—the protagonist had experimented with traditional forms of dissidence in an effort to combat the conservative, authoritarian system prevailing in Spain, with which he sees himself as inevitably linked by birth.

Alvaro the protagonist, in spite of his many biographical links with Goytisolo himself, can clearly stand as a national archetype. His family is a version in miniature of Spain itself, split into two opposing sides, represented by the maternal and the paternal wings. The latter is the prevailing branch of the family, represented by a right-wing father, supporter of Franco and descended from a grandfather who made his fortune in the sugar industry in Cuba in the nineteenth century, and peopled by other characters such as the snobbish and religious Aunt Mercedes and the pro-Hitler uncles Cesar and Eulogio.

The maternal side of the family represents the other Spain, liberal, progressive, enlightened. Significantly, this Spain has been eradicated from the picture:

> La familia materna no figuraba en el álbum. En virtud de un estricto criterio selectivo alguien había eliminado de sus páginas aquella otra estirpe burguesa más cultivada y sensible que la de los Mendiola. (49)

The maternal side includes the maternal grandmother, Aunt Gertrudis and Uncle Néstor. All of these relations on the maternal side are associated with art and progressive, radical ideas. Their fate has linked them to death, madness and ultimate oblivion. Alvaro, it is clear, identifies with this side of the family:

> Alvaro era el último brote del árbol condenado y enfermo, suspendido al latido de un corazón frágil, a merced del mal que podía fulminarlo, precipitándolo de un soplo en el olvido. (49)

Hence, the family stands as a representation of Spain, the traditional 'dos Españas', one predominant, the other persecuted. In this way Goytisolo combines an exploration of a personal crisis with an examination of a national dilemma.

The essentially critical stance of the novel is a result of the narrator Alvaro's natural allegiance to the maternal side of the family, characterized by 'una inteligencia aguda y crítica, dudosa de su verdad y de sus razones, incrédula de su misión y sus quehaceres' (49). However, this will not be simply a liberal critique of Spain written by a representative of the other side. The narrator makes it clear that this side is also a spent force, 'igualmente injustificable que ésta por la caducidad e insignificancia de sus frutos' (49). What *Señas* shows is the search for a 'third way', an attack on bourgeois society in general and identification with the outlawed minorities, the *marginados*, the representatives of the Third World.

The novel depicts Alvaro, during the three or four days spent at the family residence in Barcelona, looking back over his life and taking stock. The novel's structure seems to follow the temporal chronology of the days spent at the Mas and charts Alvaro's mental processes, memories, association of ideas, snatches of conversation with friends who turn up at the Mas and readings of various documents. This fragmentary structure, however, arranges itself into chapters which focus on particular stages in Alvaro's biography, and these stages tend to follow Alvaro's life in chronological fashion from his childhood (Chapter I), through his university days (Chapter II), his visits to the south of Spain in the late 1950s (Chapter III), his experiences in Paris in the late 1950s (Chapter IV), his association with the Republican exiles in Paris (Chapter V), his relationship with Dolores (Chapter VI), his attempt to make a documentary film on the plight of the Spanish emigrants (Chapter VII), and the present (Chapter VIII). Although within the chapters there is a constant movement from one temporal level to another, the chapters themselves follow the biography of Alvaro.

On the surface, the reader can identify two basic levels in the novel: the level of the past life of Alvaro, commencing before his birth (the story of his great-grandfather in Cuba) up to a few days before the narration begins ('captada por ti diez días antes' [367]) and the level of Alvaro's meditation over the space of three or four days (it is not clear exactly how many days are involved) at the family home. The former level had taken Alvaro to Paris and through various failed forms of escape and dissidence, culminating even in a failed attempt at suicide on the Boulevard Richard Lenoir. The second level takes us through these stages and ends with a trip to Montjuich, where the protagonist rails against Spain and his past and affirms his irrevocable dissociation from the country and determination to abandon it definitively. At the last moment he resolves first to leave some kind of record of his existence and his protest for the sake of posterity.

Critics are virtually unanimous in locating the narrative on the level of Alvaro's experience in the Mas. For Levine, *Señas* is a novel 'que busca captar las recordaciones y proceso mental de un personaje cuya vida abarca un periodo de treinta y dos años', and in so doing 'rehúsa seguir los esquemas "simétricos y rígidos" de la novela tradicional e intenta comunicar la naturaleza "multiforme, ondulante y contra-dictoria" de la vida misma' (89). Robert Spires in *La novela española de postguerra* claims that the aim of the novel is to transform reality into aesthetic terms. In his view, the novel is 'basada en técnicas dispares con el fin de dar realidad estética a la desintegración de una sociedad y del individuo que pretende sobrevivir en ella' (224).

In this sense the 'action' of the novel is the psychological experience of Alvaro during the three days as he both seeks to recuperate his lost identity and at the same time dispense with it. Events from the earlier level, that of his past life and beyond to the time of his ancestors, are incorporated in the form of memories, documents and photos, and punctuate that inner experience. However, the novel implicitly contains a further third level which is the level of textual organization, an aspect of *Señas* which is made deliberately conspicuous.[7] The question *Señas* raises is the relation between these levels. For most critics the relation is essentially mimetic.[8] The text is seen to be organized in such a way as to 'represent' or reflect the fragmented reality of Spain or the inner turmoil of Alvaro. There are, however, signs that the textual level in the novel has an independent role.

An interpretation of the novel in terms of the experience of Alvaro at the Mas is unsatisfactory in that it fails to account for the activity of the novel on the formal level and, more importantly, it is thematically illogical. On the plane of action, nothing actually takes place during those three or four days. Alvaro ranges mentally over the past and the reasons remain unclear. At the beginning we are told:

> habías vuelto no porque las cosas hubieran cambiado y tu expatriación hubiese tenido un sentido, sino porque habías agotado poco a poco tus reservas de espera y, sencillamente, tenías miedo a morir. (15)

At another point in the first chapter, referring to a moment in his late teens, he speaks of having:

> logrado cortar a tiempo las amarras sin conseguir por eso liberarte del todo. Familia, clase social, comunidad, tierra: tu vida no podía ser otra cosa (lo supiste luego) que un lento y difícil camino de ruptura y desposesión. (55)

Alvaro has from an early age, certainly late adolescence (see p. 55), been rebelling against his identity and trying to escape from it in a variety of ways (exile, political dissidence, the love relationship, the documentary) without ever quite succeeding. During the stay in Barcelona he spends most of the period at the Mas trying to resurrect the past and piece it together. Why does he try to reconstruct an identity that has oppressed him and from which he has assiduously endeavoured to escape? In Chapter II we learn that Alvaro's fear of death is that of dying before he has managed to make the definitive break with his identity (65–66). At the end of the novel Alvaro's conclusion is that the only thing that links him to Spain is language and that the solution is exile among non-Spanish-speakers (420). At first this is going to be an act of stoic, silent resignation, reminiscent of Pedro in *Tiempo de silencio*, but at the last moment he determines to leave some kind of record: 'deja constancia al menos de este tiempo no olvides cuanto ocurrió en él no te calles' (422). This introduces an element of circularity into the novel and converts the novel itself into an integral part of the theme.[9] However, one critic's comment that the end signifies Alvaro's opting for 'bearing objective witness to his time'[10] sits awkwardly with the critique that the novel makes of the 'novela testimonial' and the whole notion of bearing objective witness to anything. It is more natural to see the end as pointing in circular fashion to the novel we have just been reading. *Señas de identidad* would emerge thus as a variation on the self-begetting novel,[11] and Alvaro the protagonist would be the author of the text we are reading. What has appeared to be an account of a spiritual crisis, product of an anonymous author, would, in fact, be more than that: it would be the literary outcome of that crisis, the consequence of a realization that the only way to effectively carry out the break with the country and one's identity was through art, through writing, through a subversion of that fundamental link between the individual and the world which he inhabits. In this way, the writing process, the artistic dimension, becomes incorporated into the theme of the novel. This is to be one of the characteristic features of the later period. Goytisolo thematizes the writing process, integrating the levels of language and literature into the existential and social concerns at the centre of the novels.

This identification of a circular, self-begetting structure has enormous implications for our reading of the novel. First, it obliges us to look back over the novel, rather than beyond it into the fictional future of the character Alvaro. The text becomes the consequence as opposed to the mere account of the crisis at its centre. The aesthetic nature of the text ceases to be mimetic in function and becomes autonomous, a recognizable practice of writing. We can thus distinguish three narrative levels in the text:

1. the level of Alvaro's past life;
2. the level of Alvaro's thoughts during the three to four days in Barcelona;
3. the level of Alvaro the writer-narrator subsequently composing the novel that we are reading.

The positing of this third level as an important level in itself is suggested by many details in the text, but more importantly it will lead to a more coherent reading of the novel, showing the exact nature and extent of the *ruptura* involved and indicating how *Señas* forms part of the more explicitly radical project of the following novels. To view *Señas* solely in terms of levels 1 and 2 as most criticism has tended to do is to treat it as a modernist text, more self-consciously literary, representing reality in a more complex way through the inner perspective of the character, and, above all, still essentially mimetic in its premises. To postulate the third level is to recognize *Señas* as more properly post-modernist, tending to a greater self-referentiality in that the writing process becomes the central activity, and rather than accepting mimesis, the primary aim of the writing process is to call into question the relation between language and the world.

To analyse the way the text operates it is necessary to look at the following aspects:

1. the chronology of the novel;
2. the narrative process;
3. self-conscious features;
4. the theme of language.

Chronology

Strangely the chronological aspect of *Señas* has received scant attention in spite of the fact that it is one of the most striking features of the architecture of the novel.[12] It is extraordinarily complex, and is clearly meant to serve more than to merely force the reader into a more active role as Levine suggests.[13] The repeated and detailed references to the chronology throughout show that it is important in its own right. The matter is not made any simpler by the fact that there have been two editions of the novel, as well as an English translation which came out in 1969, immediately prior to the second and definitive Spanish edition, and in which Goytisolo was apparently involved. Mary Ellen Bieder has analysed the differences between these two editions and taken the rather unusual view that in spite of Goytisolo's own statement that the novel covers a period of three days, the chronology of the narrative actually takes place in the space of 24 hours:

> While five separate days are distinguishable, the events from the announcement of Professor Ayuso's death (62–63A) to two days after the funeral occur prior to the narrative present. Thus the novel commences within the framework of the narrated present and rejoins this framework at the end of Chapter VII as the progression of events following the funeral merge with the hour at which the novel opens. The temporal framework of the chapter on Cuba moves the narrative present through the night to the following morning.[14]

Bieder does not specify what the five days are nor how they correspond to the chapters exactly, but she seems to imply that the events at the Mas occur before the narrative present, which begins on the evening in which the novel opens, continues through the night (of the chapter on Cuba [Chapter VIII] in the first edition) and ends in the episode on Montjuich (the final chapter in both editions). This leads, for her, to a chronological error in the novel:

> In the final chapter of both editions the day is specified as: ... esta sofocante jornada de agosto del año de gracia del 63 ... un mes justo después de tu regreso a España cuarenta y ocho horas más tarde del entierro de Ayuso (478A). Since the funeral occurred in the late afternoon (85A) and since in Chapter VII two days have already passed since the funeral (382A), obviously some sixty or more hours have elapsed, for the morning heat is now bearing down on Montjuich. (302 n.11) [In both passages the letter A stands for the first edition.]

Another elaborate study of the chronology of Señas is made by André Gallego and Henri Guerreiro. They study in considerable detail the relationship between the levels of *discours*, which they see as the level of Alvaro at the Mas, and *histoire*, his past life. Their conclusion, however, is the relatively standard one that Alvaro's meditation on the past results in a decision to break with his identity and side with the pariahs. The to-ing and fro-ing between past and present is a reflection of a 'conscience dechirée entre deux temps et de multiples espaces', and the writing process assumes importance as the only way the narrator can try to mend this split in himself: 'Tel est le va-et-vient agonique [...] que le narrateur ne peut momentanément dominer que par l'écriture'.[15] Gallego and Guerreiro, like Bieder, see the novel as covering a space of five days, with the final chapter on the fifth and the funeral of Ayuso on the second. Thus, although they do not draw attention to it, their account also conflicts with the text's mention of a 48-hour gap on page 414.

It is generally supposed by most other critics that the chronology follows that of Alvaro's stay in the Mas. However, the critic Robert Spires sees convincing evidence for a considerable degree of chronological dislocation between the sequence of events as they occur in the Mas and their presentation in the novel. Spires is also one of the few to use the extremely useful terms, derived from Russian Formalism, of *fabula* and *sujet* to distinguish the levels of the disposition of material in the text (*sujet*) from the order in which the events are supposed to happen in 'real' life (*fabula*).[16] According to Spires, the relation *sujet/fabula* is as follows:

	Sujet		Fabula
I	Day one, after ch. VI	VI	Day one
II	Day two, funeral	I	Day one, after VI
III	Day two, after funeral	II	Day two, funeral
IV	Day two, evening	III	Day two, after funeral
V	Day two or three	IV	Day two, evening

VI	Day one	V	Day two or three
VII	Day four, evening	VIII	Day four, morning
VIII	Day four, morning	VII	Day four, evening

According to Spires, the reason for this chronological dislocation is to produce a sensation in the reader akin to that of the protagonist.[17] The rearrangement of the chronology of the *fabula* in the *sujet* creates a sense of atemporality that reflects the experience of Alvaro and transmits the same sensation to the reader.

Spires' explanation from a mimetic point of view has a certain validity. It is undoubtedly true that *Señas* in its constant references to time and its general setting of these references within a temporally vague, 'timeless' realm—the unspecified number of days spent at the Mas, a world set apart from the real world of action—certainly conveys the mood of a man whose acute awareness of the passing of time and the imminence of death are set against his sense of being in a 'presente incierto' (15). However, this mood can be said to be sufficiently conveyed by the details mentioned, the contrast of precise temporal reference with temporal vagueness, without resorting to such structural rearranging.

First it must be pointed out that there are several problems with Spires' analysis of the chronology. Chapter III, for example, ends with nightfall and everyone going to bed. So Chapter IV is the following day (day three?) and not later on the same day. Note how on page 160 everyone is 'reunidos los tres como la víspera'. Chapter IV starts as a summer's day: 'En la clara y luminosa jornada de verano [...] el sol matizaba con distributiva justicia ...', and ends at dusk: 'El sol acababa de desaparecer tras la montaña y un último rayo bermejo agonizaba entre las ramas de los alcornoques'. The temporal location of Chapter V in the *fabula* is difficult to establish, except that it again ends towards nightfall: 'en el fresco nocturno de la terraza' (312). However, it could be assumed to refer to the evening of day three.

The situating of Chapter VI before Chapter I in the *fabula* is also difficult to prove. According to Spires, 'para reconstruir ésta [i.e. the *fabula*] hay que empezar con el capítulo VI. Alvaro está a solas con Dolores en este capítulo antes de la llegada de los amigos y observa el cielo: "Nubes grandilocuentes, pomposas, como anunciando una obertura de ópera, discurrían en dirección al mar, tras el verdor desnudo de los árboles." La acción de la *fabula* sigue en el capítulo I cuando Alvaro se despierta de una siesta: "Las nubes habían escampado durante tu sueño y el sol se obstinaba en el cielo enardecido del crepúsculo".'[18]

Other details, not mentioned by Spires, which help to confirm this are the references to the bottle of wine which Dolores puts on ice (343) and opens (355). In Chapter I Alvaro is seen to be drinking from a bottle chilling on ice. It may be a subsequent night that is referred to in Chapter VI, however; given the suggested concern that Dolores is seen to show over Alvaro's drinking in Chapter I, it is unlikely that she would be encouraging further drinking. On page 13 we read: 'Dolores se presentaría [. . .] dirigiría una mirada lacónica a la botella inmersa en el cubo . . .' and in Chapters II and III, presumably on day two, Alvaro is seen to gradually drink a whole bottle of Fefiñanes and get drunk, leading Dolores to urge him: 'No bebas más' (135).

A close examination of the temporal references seems to allow us to establish the following chronology:

> Chapter I 6.50 p.m. in the evening of the first day. The chapter ends with the arrival of Ricardo and Artigas along with two Danish girls, followed by the arrival of Antonio who announces the death of Ayuso.
>
> Chapter II the following day (see page 80 'la víspera, después de la llegada de Antonio') around 5.00 p.m. at the funeral.
>
> Chapter III the same day, day two, after the funeral (page 110 'De vuelta al Mas—tras la amargura del entierro de Ayuso'). Antonio is obviously staying with Dolores and Alvaro. The chapter ends with first Dolores (148) and then Antonio (149) going to bed, followed shortly after by Alvaro himself (158).
>
> Chapter IV, presumably day three, ends at dusk with the arrival of Paco, Artigas and Ricardo to spend the weekend with them (236).
>
> Chapter V cannot be precisely located in time but takes place in the 'fresco nocturno' of the garden and is the result of conversations with Paco, Artigas, Ricardo and Antonio. If, as we see, Chapters VII and VIII take place two days after the funeral, i.e. on day four, it would seem that Chapter V is the night of day three.
>
> Chapter VI cannot be located for certain, but it is a few minutes before the Angelus, i.e. probably just before 6.00 p.m. The fact that Dolores and Alvaro are alone suggests that it is before the arrival of the friends on day one to spend a few days.
>
> Chapter VII is the evening of the fourth day ('en el lento y cálido atardecer, dos días después del entierro del profesor Ayuso' [380]).
>
> Chapter VIII is the morning of the fourth day (414).

While the temporal location of Chapter VI cannot be determined with any certainty, it seems clear that it cannot follow in straightforward linear fashion from Chapter V. Unless we accept an error by Goytisolo, the non-linear arrangement of Chapters VII and VIII is equally clear.

It is difficult to judge the degree of importance to attach to these chronological details. *Señas de identidad*, as Bieder's article showed, is a novel which has undergone several changes, each of which has involved radical omissions and rearrangement of sections. Furthermore, the idea of simple textual errors is not impossible. *Señas* contains several textual inaccuracies, especially concerning the age of the protagonist. For example, we know that the protagonist is 32 in the narrative present,

August 1963 (367). Yet on page 20 he says that Srta Lourdes gave him the religious book for his seventh birthday and that it had been his bedside book during the early months of the Civil War, meaning that the latest date of his birth was 1929. In the same section on page 20 the narrator refers to the clothes of Srta Lourdes in a photo dated 1936 still seeming to give off their scent after 25 years, making the present 1961 instead of 1963. Slight irregularities such as these are difficult to account for in a novel as carefully constructed as *Señas*. However, it seems unlikely that they are anything other than oversights. The rearrangement of the chapters is harder to explain in terms of error, especially when, as Gimferrer has shown, such attention is paid by the author to minor details, such as the repetition in significant contexts of the phrase 'mira quin parell' (30 and 403).[19]

Certainly, if we accept the rearrangement of the chapters, the motive for such play with the text would appear to reinforce the point made earlier about the implied autonomy of the textual level from a mimetic dependence on the level of the narrated events. As we have seen, Spires himself uses the terms *fabula* and *sujet*. These terms are intended to illustrate the artifice of narrative, the way fiction necessarily shaped the apparent reality it represented (*fabula*) in a way that was totally artistic and artificial (*sujet*). The terms are close in their significance to the terms later taken up by the structuralists, and Goytisolo: *histoire* and *discours*. Unlike *fabula* and *sujet*, these terms do not refer to distinct levels of the same narrative, but rather to two modes of narration. Their similarity lies in the way they each emphasize the distinction between story and presentation, between the referential object and the rhetoric of a narrator.[20] As I explained in Chapter One, Goytisolo's interest in *discours* as a mode of narration implied the text's foregrounding of its linguistic, textual status. Any distinction between *sujet* and *fabula* draws attention to the former, the level of artistic composition. This can be naturalized mimetically, as Spires does, in terms of character portrayal. Another way of viewing it is to see it as self-consciously drawing attention to the process of composition itself, destroying thus the referential illusion. This interpretation is more consonant with *Señas* if we view it in conjunction with other characteristics of the text.

In other words, *Señas* reveals the beginning of a self-conscious approach to the narrative process, a form of writing which Goytisolo later referred to as 'escritura y no copia'.[21]

The Narrative Process

The narration of *Señas* is one of its most complicated aspects and has attracted a variety of interpretations. The most prominent feature is the use of the *tú* form. In the text this is combined with the standard third-person form as well as other forms such as the first person (the *biografía* of the emigrant) and the first person plural. On one level this is, of course, evidence of Goytisolo's attempt to break free of the restrictions of the first and third person and the imperfect tense as advocated in *El furgón de cola*. However, there is clearly more to this than the exploration of 'las inmensas posibilidades de la sintaxis' (FC, 93).

Again, following the tendency to interpret the novel in terms of greater realism, many critics have seen the alternation of the two main modes – *tú* and *él*—as Goytisolo's way of presenting reality both objectively and subjectively. The narrator of the novel seems to suggest as much when he speaks of 'conjugando de modo armonioso la búsqueda interior y el testimonio objetivo' (159).

For Spires, '*Señas de identidad* trata de una doble búsqueda de identidad—la de una nación y la de un ser humano individualizado. Para descubrir esta doble identidad, el narrador-personaje hace uso de dos modos narrativos—uno objetivo y otro subjetivo.'[22] Levine actually posits two separate narrators, a traditional third-person narrator who eventually disappears from the text and the personal narration of Alvaro in the second person. She even goes so far as to suggest that the objective, i.e. reliable, narration of the former serves to point up the inaccuracies of the narration of Alvaro. In her view the removal of the third-person narrator towards the end of the novel reduces the ambiguity of the novel.[23]

It is in the nature of the forms that the third person should seem to objectify the experience narrated and the second person make it seem more intimate. Reed Anderson sees the two forms as representing different ways in which Alvaro sees himself, the third person as bearing objective testimony to the events of his life and the second person as 'elaborating his past experience at a subjective and more intimate level'.[24] However, in practice the uses do not always correspond to such a distinction. There are many examples of the same category of experience being narrated in both forms. For example, the events of the few days in the Mas are narrated sometimes in the second (13–16) and sometimes in the third person (31–40, 60–63). Similarly, certain traumatic and intimately relevant episodes in Alvaro's life, such as his visit to his grandmother, when she does not recognize him, are narrated in the third person. Alvaro is even capable within the *tú* sections of seeing himself in the third person: '(Y cuántas veces tú, el propio Alvaro ...)' (230). His sense of alienation is inherent in both forms, the third person and the second.[25]

If we reject the explanation for the alternation between the third and second person in terms of the qualitative difference between the experiences referred to, we are left with the other, that is, the need to give different perspectives, one objective, the other subjective, on the life of Alvaro. However, the interesting thing about *Señas* is that this alternation of the two forms, particularly glaring and disconcerting in the sections dealing with Alvaro himself, is done in such a way as to attract the reader's attention. Rather than heightened mimesis, the effect is to foreground the constructed nature of the text and the contrasting narrative modes.

The two modes alternate in a noticeably systematic, mechanical fashion, which only serves to highlight the contrast between them. The reader is led not only to ponder the different aspects of the same experience, but also the way similar experience can be treated in different ways in narrative. To this extent the narrative 'defamiliarizes' narrative convention itself, showing how reality can be mediated in various ways. Given that the third-person narrative form can be taken to correspond to the traditional style of realism and the pre-*Señas* novels of Goytisolo, what *Señas* does is to juxtapose it with other forms and then eventually abandon it in favour of the second person.

The fundamental difference between the *tú* and the *él* forms corresponds to the theoretical distinction that Goytisolo made between *histoire* and *discours*. The terms, as we have seen in the introduction, correspond with the linguistic theories of Benveniste. *Histoire* is a form which disguises the position of the speaker and directs attention towards that which is spoken about. In the sections where the narrator refers to himself, it hides the narrating self and focuses on the self represented in narration. The *discours* sections in the *tú* form draw attention to the narrating voice as subjective source of the narrative. Hence the self-conscious contrast of these two narrative modes, rather than presenting a more balanced, all-embracing picture of reality, in fact tends to undermine any referential illusion by foregrounding the narrative process. The reader's attention to the narrated events is disturbed by the revelation of the process of narration and the textual format of the novel. This 'split' between the two levels, narrated events and narrative act, Alvaro the protagonist and Alvaro the narrator, is further emphasized by the deictic features of the novel.

Deixis is characteristic of *discours* and consists of those figures of speech which refer to the situation of utterance, and so draw attention to the act of enunciation or speech-act.[26] To naturalize a text we must be able to construct a discursive situation that is stable. *Señas* indulges throughout in a play between the level of discourse and the level of story. One aspect of this is the presentation of the protagonist's thoughts. At times these are framed by the use of verbs such as *decir*, *pensar*, *reflexionar*, and the use of the past tense, thereby establishing a distance between the thoughts of the protagonist relayed by the narrator. For example:

> pruebas documentales, fehacientes, del niño pintoresco y falaz que habías
> sido y en el que no se reconocía el adulto de hoy, suspendido como estabas en
> un presente incierto, exento de pasado como de porvenir, con la desolada e
> íntima certeza de saber que habías vuelto no porque las cosas hubieran
> cambiado y tu expatriación hubiese tenido un sentido, sino porque habías
> agotado poco a poco tus reservas de espera y, sencillamente, tenías miedo a
> morir. *Así reflexionabas a tus solas* mientras la tarde dilapidaba su esplendor
> ... (15) (emphasis added)

Sections like these emphasize a temporal gap between the thoughts of Alvaro the protagonist and the narrator's subsequent relaying of them. In other cases this discourse is presented directly, unframed. The use of the present tense seems to belong at the level of discourse, relaying the thoughts of the narrator:

> Adiós para siempre, adiós. Tu desvío te lleva por nuevos caminos. Lo sabes
> ya. Jamás hollarás su suelo. (199)

A similar reflection on Spain is framed:

> Los vamos a pagar caro (te decías) la perdida guerra civil, los veinte años de
> miedo hirsuto, la ominosa facilidad que nos invade. (230)

Again at other times this device is used to locate the reflection at the present of the narrator:

> En las interminables horas grises todos los caminos conducen allá (al tobogán y
> al síncope) como si nada (*te dices ahora*) absolutamente nada pudiera aplacar
> (oh place de la Bastille) tu densa apetencia de muerte. (366) (emphasis added)

Throughout *Señas* there is a continual shifting between the levels of narration and narrated events, discourse and story. By moving to and fro between the two levels, the reader cannot naturalize the text unproblematically on one level or the other.[27] This is compounded by the ambiguous use of deictics. The *tú* form itself is a deictic in that it draws attention to the speech-act, the moment of utterance. One of the effects of the *tú* form is the way it dramatizes a split in the speech-act that is only implicit in the first person.[28] This is a feature of discourse that figures prominently in Lacanian psychoanalytic and literary theory and can have useful applications to Goytisolo's works. We will return to these later in our discussion.

Other deictics of interest in *Señas* are the demonstratives, adverbs of place and tenses. At different times, referring to the events at the Mas, the narrator opts for 'este' or 'aquel', 'aquí' or 'allí'. For example:

> y al cabo de largos años de destierro estabas de nuevo *allí*, en el doliente y
> entrañable país de tu juventud. (12)

> la temida irrupción de personas extrañas en *aquel* analgésico y tierno remanso
> de paz ... (13)

> Imaginaste al caballero Don Quijote con su lanza, su yelmo y armadura
> cociéndose al sol de *esta* bochornosa mañana de agosto de 1963 ... (402)
> (emphasis added)

In the last example, the tense ('imaginaste') creates a distance between narrator and protagonist while the demonstrative ('esta') abolishes that distance.[29]

Sometimes in parenthetical asides there are differences in tense, for example:

> Fue también—¿lo recuerdas?—casualidad pura ... (46)

> Esto fue todo—o a lo menos así lo recordabas—ninguna pregunta tuya ... (47)

These changes from one to the other have the effect of varying the distance between the story and the discourse, the speech-act and the narrated events. Some commentators explain these shifts as a desire to make certain scenes more vivid for the reader.[30] However, as the last chapter of the novel shows, the shifts occur within the same section and seem arbitrary. The effect is to emphasize a split between the narrator on the level of enunciation, and the protagonist's thoughts as he wanders around Montjuich. A further feature of the last chapter which militates slightly against the mimetic reading is the inclusion of the sections in italics referring to Alvaro's Cuban connections. These do not seem to form part of Alvaro's thoughts but rather to be texts taken from another source (as indeed they are, extracted from the first edition) and juxtaposed with the rest of the chapter.

The effect of this to-ing and fro-ing between levels is that the reader cannot opt unproblematically for one or the other but is led instead to entertain the two and move from one to the other. Furthermore, the coherence of the reading in terms of the level of narrated events having been disturbed, the only way to resolve the doubt is to naturalize the novel at the level of the writing process, the discourse of the narrator composing the text.[31] In this case the confusion of levels can be read as a sign of a writer divided between two narrative postures, on the one hand the mimetic representation of experience (the situation of Alvaro at the Mas) and on the other the thoughts and feelings that occur to him as he composes the novel.

In *Señas* the confusion revealed by the deictics is a sign of the text's transitional status, abandoning the formal features of realism and advancing towards the new discursive mode of the final chapter. It is possible to interpret the deictic uncertainty, not as a deliberate ploy on the part of the writer, but as a genuine symptom of a narrative crisis undergone and charted in the writing of *Señas*, the same crisis which prevented Goytisolo from continuing with the narrative in the first person,[32] and brought about the use of the *tú* form. This is an example of a crisis that some theorists, drawing on the theory of Lacan, relate to the inability of the individual to accept the discursive practices of society, resulting in a split subjectivity, between the subject of the enunciation and the subject of the enounced. Catherine Belsey in *Critical Practice* links this split subjectivity with a challenge to society's stability and with the possibility of social transformation:

> It is this contradiction in the subject—between the conscious self, which is conscious in so far as it is able to feature in discourse, and the self which is only partially represented there—which constitutes the source of possible change. (85)

Such confluence between a writer's sense of crisis within a particular culture, especially as manifested in discourse, and the urge to subvert and achieve change, is particularly appropriate to the situation of Goytisolo from *Señas* onwards. That this is a crisis which is gradually worked out (though never entirely resolved) in the course of the novel can be seen if we examine the process that the character Alvaro undergoes in the attempt to deal with his past, since this emerges as a metaphorical comment on the nature of writing itself.

Failed Integration

The situation of Alvaro as portrayed in the few days at the Mas is one of existential insecurity. He has returned home to convalesce after a near fatal heart tremor deliberately induced by a trip on a fairground big dipper in the Place de la Bastille. We learn that the episode was a final step in a long attempt to destroy his hated identity. Recovery in a Paris hospital found him strangely liberated of his past identity, 'sin señas de identidad'. At the Mas he is in a kind of limbo, both alienated and, in a way, free from his past self after a long series of evasions, rebellions and assaults on his continued existence (the abortion of his and Dolores' baby, the near suicide) and, at the same time, aware that the true break with his identity has not been made. The protagonist faced with a death which he now knows to be certain is obsessed with the idea of oblivion, dying without leaving a trace and in particular dying before succeeding in effecting the break with his inherited identity (31, 65–67).

In spite of his awareness of his life as a 'lento y difícil camino de ruptura y desposesión' (55), the narrator is caught between the contradictory urges to reject the past and all it stands for, and to attempt to reconstruct that past in a search for a lost unity. Indeed, for most of the novel, the latter activity predominates. Alvaro's activity at the Mas is one of reminiscence, patient reconstruction of the past, 'recuperar el tiempo perdido y hacer balance de tus existencias' (54). To do so Alvaro makes use of all possible aids to complete the picture: photos, documents, writings, newspaper clippings, atlas, conversation with others. At the end of Chapter IV, the arrival of more friends leads him to comment: 'gracias a su ayuda, confiabas en avanzar un paso más en el conocimiento y comprehensión de los hechos' (236). He goes on to say:

> Tu vida se reducía ahora a un solitario combate con los fantasmas del pasado y del resultado de la lucha dependía—lo sabías—la liquidación de la hipoteca que pesaba sobre tu angosto y casual porvenir. (236–37)

It is as though Alvaro must fully understand the past before he can successfully break free from it. Yet this is never stated. His sole urge seems to be to resurrect the past. To do so he must supplement his limited subjective vision with external aids. Remembering the episode with Srta Lourdes, he speaks of the Barcelona of the time, saying: 'podías recomponerlo fácilmente gracias a los documentales y retro-spectivas de la cinémathèque de la rue d'Ulm' (28).

He goes on to speak of imagining, with the aid of memory of these films, the streets of the time 'colmando así los huecos existentes en un relato exclusivamente hilvanado con elementos dispersos y truncos' (28). The verbs 'reconstruir' and 'reconstituir' recur throughout (56, 59, 77, 81, etc.). At the beginning of Chapter IV the narrator remarks: 'Tus esfuerzos de reconstitución y de síntesis tropezaban con un grave obstáculo' (159). This obstacle is Alvaro's absence from many of the important events of Spain's history. This impedes the achievement of the total picture aspired to: 'Vacía tu memoria por diez años de destierro, ¿cómo rehacer sin daño la perdida unidad?' (159). He attempts to surmount this obstacle by including the testimony of others who were present, and also by the use of the imagination to recreate scenes, again with the purpose of 'atando cabos y rellenando huecos' (160).

However, the more the novel progresses, the more these attempts at reconstitution prove futile:

> con la conciencia clara de que la realidad se descomponía entre tus dedos ... (181)

> Algo importante tal vez, se escurría con agilidad entre tus dedos y tus esfuerzos por apresarlo se perdían en el vacío. (236)

> Horas y horas empleadas en reconstituir la existencia de aquellos años ... el tiempo parecía escaparse a medida que pretendían calar en él, ofreciéndoles tan sólo un revoltillo de imágenes aisladas escenas truncas, recuerdos descoloridos y borrosos ... (312)

The narrator never does manage to achieve a unified picture of himself or his past ('sin llegar jamás a fundirlos del todo' [160]). As such, the novel is in fact a demonstration of the impossibility of capturing with any authority or claim to objectivity the reality of experience.

Furthermore, throughout the narrator's experience there has been a contrast between two opposing faculties, memory and imagination. Alvaro's attempt at reconstitution of the past has been based on memory. But memory only provides an incomplete and unreliable vision: 'Discontinua, huidiza la memoria se limitaba a proponerle una serie inconexa de gestos y ademanes' (80). The limitations of memory are supplemented whenever possible by documentary evidence and others' witness, but what interests the narrator most is the ability to resort, where possible, to imagination:

> La familia materna (casi extinguida ahora) permitía no obstante a tu fervor minucioso, gracias a la ausencia casi total de elementos reales, el juego excitante de las hipótesis y conjeturas ... (55)

> Sin documentos, sin pruebas, sin testigos, podías decorar a tus anchas los fastos de la detención en la demolida casa materna ... (152)

> Sometida a los cánones imperiosos de lo real tu imaginación se resarcía componiendo con morosidad las situaciones, limando las aristas del diálogo, atando cabos y rellenando huecos, manejando con soltura su influjo catalizador. (160)

Sometimes there is even confusion about which of these faculties is responsible for an image:

> Uno de tus primeros recuerdos infantiles—¿o era una creación posterior de tu imaginación sobre la base de una anécdota repetida a menudo en familia? (124–25)

In this way there is a tension in the narrator between the urge to reconstitute reality and the pleasure he acquires from invention. This tension between memory and imagination is the tension between history and fiction, between fiction parading as history (realism) and fiction that recognizes its fictionality (metafiction).

This contrast is related to the alternation between the third person and the second person, between a realist mode of narration which attempts to conceal its status as discourse and focus attention on the narrated events presented as real, and a subjective mode that draws attention to its status as discourse, with no pretence to objectivity. The fact that these are juxtaposed, unintegrated, and that eventually the third person is abandoned in favour of the *tú*, is a sign of the impossibility of an integrated representation of reality and the preference for the freedom of subjective discourse, not because it was any more accurate in its grasp of reality, but simply because it is more honest. However, there is more to it than simply a rejection of objectivism in favour of subjectivism. Already in *Problemas de la novela* Goytisolo had criticized authors who sheltered behind 'la impersonalidad de la tercera persona gramatical', and insisted that 'en la moderna novela ya no hay juicios inapelables ni verdades absolutas, sino parcialidad, ambigüedad, relativismo' (PN, 40). The adoption of a more self-consciously subjective style, *discours* over *histoire*, is only part of a broader shift in *Señas de identidad* towards a more textual approach. In addition to the features we have noted thus far, the reader's attention is drawn to certain self-conscious features which emphasize the importance of this third level in the narrative.

Narrative Self-Reference

The identification of the three levels within the narrative has one immediate significance: the level of reality is placed at several removes. As opposed to the 1950s novel which attempted to capture reality in all its immediacy—hence the 'camera-eye' technique of Sánchez Ferlosio in *El Jarama*—in *Señas* the level of narrated events, the *fabula*, is placed in the background. Alvaro's active experience, in other words, his life prior to the stay in the Mas, is mediated through the process of meditation and reminiscence at the Mas. This in turn is further mediated by an implied third level, a second reworking of that experience in the writing-narrating process of the text itself. The presence of the levels and their recognition by the reader has the effect of impressing upon him or her the necessarily mediated nature of our perception of reality. The level of Alvaro at the Mas engaged in his act of reminiscence represents the level of subjectivity; the further level, that which for the first time assumes primary importance in *Señas*, the all-important mediating level of language.

Unlike, for example, *Juan sin tierra*, or even to a lesser degree, *Don Julián*, *Señas* does not draw attention to the construction of the text in an explicit way. However, in a variety of ways the text does point to its own construction.

First, there are the occasional explicit references to the act of writing:

> Desde entonces (anota bien la fecha : octubre de 1952) (159)

> Evoca (transcribe) esta escena por que no muera contigo. (389)

There is another reference to a suggested level of composition of the text, subsequent to the events of the Mas:

> asociaciones de ideas y recuerdos no filtrados aún por el severo tamiz de la memoria (pertenecientes a épocas distintas, sin ningún denominador común) interpolaban de modo caótico el relato de Antonio sobre su detención y confinamiento (*rehecho luego por ti con ayuda de Dolores*). (160) (emphasis added)

Antonio's account of his house arrest is taking place at the supposed narrative present—that is, the time at the Mas (cf. 'la emoción que te embargara entonces ante el interés apasionado de tu interlocutor por tu discurso la *revives ahora (aprovechando una breve pausa en el relato minucioso de Antonio)*' [211], emphasis added). Hence the account of the episode that appears in the text is composed by Alvaro and supplemented with information from Dolores.

Second, there are details that point to the present text being the artistic fulfilment of the crisis alluded to. In the novel we know that Alvaro considers himself an artist, albeit as yet an unsuccessful one: 'Desertaste de la acción para ser un artista y, a fin de cuentas, ¿qué eres?' (377). There is mention of an early recognition of the need to express his dissidence via a work of art:

> Te fuiste de España (abandonando a tus amigos en medio de una lucha política difícil e incierta) para realizar la obra que llevabas (o creías llevar) dentro de ti ... (377)

Alvaro, of course, is by profession a photographer, and the only attempt at a 'work of art' that we know of was the failed documentary. However, as he contemplates the fate of Uncle Néstor, he realizes that he must channel his rebellion into 'some' form or other:

> su rebeldía contra la sociedad española de su tiempo murió con él como morirá sin duda la tuya si no le das forma concreta y precisa si no logras encauzarla antes ... (346)

This connects with Alvaro's final injunction to himself, 'deja constancia', at the end of the novel.

The failed documentary in Alvaro's case is the equivalent of the *novela social* in the context of the Spanish post-Civil War novel and in particular Goytisolo's own production, that is, a politically motivated art-form using documentary realism as a means of criticizing the Régime. The *novela social* is also represented within the novel by the account of Antonio's house arrest. This, both stylistically and in terms of content, bears a marked similarity to the 1950s novel, especially those written by Goytisolo himself. Critics have noted the parallels between Antonio and Alvaro, especially in the use of parallel phrases.[33] However, the purpose of this is less to establish a parallel between the two than to show important differences. In many ways Antonio is a vestige of the heroes of Goytisolo's pre-*Señas* production, a rebel in search of a fixed identity in opposition to the values of the society around him. He dreads ambiguity and longs for solid values on which to cling. Hence he speaks of the house arrest in his native village removing him from 'el cómodo maniqueísmo de la prisión' and projecting him into 'un universo maleable y ambiguo' (176). In order to resolve this state of intolerable ambiguity, Antonio actively 'commits' himself by publicly insulting the local potentate, Don Gonzalo, thus gaining the opprobrium of the entire village. As a result, 'la ambigüedad desapareció' (231). Such open political commitment, with its corollary of 'la condena muda de los otros', helps Antonio define himself, 'la señal indeleble que le marcaba' (231) and thus escape the threat of the 'mundo ambiguo ... universo aparentemente venturoso y tranquilo' (235).

Alvaro goes through a similar process on another level. After the insularity of his childhood, in a world of manichean values, the freedom of university and later the travels with Dolores disrupt those firm values and sense of identity. In Chapter VI he speaks of 'la imaginación infantil y el mito adolescente' being substituted by 'la realidad ambigua, contradictoria y compleja del recuerdo vivido' (317). Thanks to his travels with Dolores, 'las fronteras y límites que antes os aprisionaran habían sido abolidos de golpe' (317). The difference between Alvaro and Antonio is that, where the latter dreads ambiguity and to avoid it makes a political gesture that restores the 'cómodo maniqueísmo', Alvaro in the course of Señas appears to accept the ambiguous, contradictory nature of the reality and resolves to struggle against it in his own personal fashion.

Interestingly, the contrast is most marked in a reference to language. Antonio's stay in the village is a period of quasi-freedom in which 'podía abandonarse otra vez a sus fantasmas' (221). He describes his world as 'un universo ambiguo en el que las palabras perdían su primitiva significación y asumían intenciones huidizas y cambiantes, como nubes ligeras impulsadas por el viento. Libertad y prisión se mezclaban en una realidad imprecisa y, a momentos, creía imposible escapar de aquel engranaje' (222). The ambiguity of Antonio's situation reflects itself in a linguistic uncertainty, both of which he finds unacceptable and must escape from through the act of political commitment. Alvaro, on the other hand, throughout the novel is acutely aware of the ambiguous nature of reality's representation in language, but instead of wishing to escape from such linguistic uncertainty back into the real world of political action, he is seen in the last chapter to recognize the supreme importance of language and the need to carry out his protest on that level. It is interesting to note also the difference in profession of the two. Whereas Alvaro considers himself an artist, Antonio is a translator for whom linguistic certainty and the exact meaning of words are important.

Antonio's story, therefore, both in its style and content recalls the novela social of the 1950s. Its inclusion within the novel Señas serves to contrast its limitations with the complexity and ambiguity of the framing novel. Antonio is deliberately likened to Alvaro in order that the reader, having detected the clear parallelisms, is led to ponder the equally clear differences. The result is that Antonio's story acts as a parodic critique of the novela social. This internal parody of the hitherto prevailing literary norm adds to Señas' self-conscious style.

A third self-referential aspect of the novel is that, while not explicitly referring to its own writing process, it frequently thematizes this through the meditative activity of Alvaro at the Mas. This leads to a curiously contradictory stance on the part of the narrator: on the one hand, the narrative seems to follow his random thoughts and memories, and on the other, he seems to be engaged on a conscious project of construction of the past (of the text). This brings us back to the memory/imagination distinction noted earlier. This was a distinction between a passive and an active approach to the narrative. Although even within the theme of memory there is a similar distinction between someone who is a passive receiver of memories, 'el escenario ... se había impuesto de modo paulatino a tu memoria' (110), or '¿Dónde estás? ¿Qué estrato de la memoria te importuna?' (147), and another who actively sets out to 'desempolvar de tu memoria algún recuerdo tardío, meditar aún mientras estabas a tiempo' (155).

This dual and contradictory urge within the narrator, to passively relive the past and to actively recreate it, is played out in the novel and draws our attention to the literary process, for while the reliving of the past, the urge to resurrect the past in memory emphasizes the importance of a preordained reality which the narrator endows with meaning ('perdida clave', 'perdida unidad') and tries to recapture (re-present), the creative act of recreating reality through the imagination emphasizes the primacy of the process of composition itself.

This dichotomy can be observed in the composition of *Señas*, for while the structure of the novel seems superficially to be determined mimetically by the representation of the protagonist's confused mental state during the few days at the Mas, a closer look at the novel shows it to be highly wrought, extremely systematic in its structural use of symmetry and juxtapositions. Rather than representing a character on the point of disintegration, it reveals the purposeful technique of the artist.

This contradiction is highlighted in one of the sections already mentioned. It is where the narrator most self-consciously alludes to the activity of composition of the narrative, and although the implication is that the narration takes place on the level of the protagonist's mental processes, the very explicit reference to the activity of narrating, of composing, draws attention also to the textual level:

> El diario de vigilancias de la Brigada Regional de Investigación Social (confiado a Antonio por su abogado defensor después del proceso), expedientes y actas del Juzgado de Instrucción que viera la causa, asociaciones de ideas y recuerdos no filtrados aún por el severo tamiz de la memoria (pertenecientes a épocas distintas, sin ningún denominador común) interpolaban de modo caótico el relato de Antonio sobre su detención y confinamiento (rehecho luego por ti con ayuda de Dolores). (160)

I have already discussed the significance of the last phrase, but it can be seen that what is said here does not correspond with the actual composition of the narrative, where the juxtapositions and sequence of sections are anything but chaotic.

As seen in the earlier section on the figure of Alvaro, the ambiguity of his position in the novel dramatizes the split we have noted throughout. He is at once a protagonist undergoing a crisis of conscience and also a narrator figure who mirrors, on the level of narrated events, the narrator of the text *Señas de identidad*. This last role is most noticeable when at the beginning of Chapter IV we read:

> Merced a los documentos y pruebas atesorados en las carpetas podías desempolvar de tu memoria sucesos e incidentes que tiempo atrás hubieras dado por perdidos y que rescatados del olvido por medio de aquellos permitían iluminar no sólo tu biografía sino también facetas oscuras y reveladoras de la vida en España. (159)

It is sections such as this that mark *Señas de identidad* as a limit text between the realist, representational phase of Goytisolo, here lingering on in the figure of a protagonist, and the incipient self-referential, metafictional phase.

The features which I have identified as self-conscious are, it has to be admitted, slight. However, they are there and, in disturbing a straightforward reading, require to be recognized and naturalized by the reader. Their significance is reinforced when viewed in relation to the other features I point out. Their tentative nature is a sign of *Señas de identidad*'s transitional status. Goytisolo is working his way towards a more explicitly textual approach to the act of writing. *Señas* marks the beginning of this recognition of the importance of language, not only in the literary process, but also as a fundamental mediating element of experience in general. In *Señas* language acquires an ontological dimension, as a crucial factor in the construction of the individual's own reality and that of the world around him.

Thematization of Language

Throughout *Señas* there are references to reality as represented in language. Most noticeable among these are:

- the association of people with literary texts
- the religious books
- the gravestones and prints
- the tourist discourse

The Association of People with Literary Texts

In *Señas*, one of the ways of describing characters is in terms of art, and in particular literature. Hence the pro-Nazi tío Eulogio lends Alvaro books by Spengler, and the equally pro-German tío Cesar is an avid reader of *Mein Kampf*. Enrique in his right-wing period, on hearing of the defeat of the Germans, cries in his room to the strains of Wagner. When Alvaro visits his maternal grandmother, he finds her playing Ravel's *Pavane pour une infante défunte*. One of the few vestiges of her is the painting hanging in the dining room (50). More dissident members of the maternal line are tía Gertrudis, a devotee of the music of Satie and the theatre, and tío Néstor, reader of Baudelaire and Verlaine, Clarín and Larra, translator of Yeats into Catalan and lover of a wild Irish poetess who was a supporter of Sinn Fein. Similarly Alvaro's anarchistic student friend, Sergio, is a reader of even more audaciously progressive literature: 'Sobre el diván, en ejemplar desorden, los libros de cabecera de tu amigo: Blake, Quincey, Lautréamont, Gerard de Nerval' (86). This identification of characters with works of art and, in particular, texts is part of a general significance attached to the written word, to literature and art in general. In *Señas*, art is generally associated with dissidence, rebellion against the status quo. Alvaro identifies with the maternal side of his family, all associated in some way with art and all characterized by an 'inteligencia aguda y crítica' (49).

Religious Books

When Alvaro goes in search of the religious book that marked his childhood so deeply, he cannot locate it and recalls an earlier failed attempt to find it. This had led to him searching for it in a Barcelona bookshop. The shop assistant could not find the same book but found one similar:

> La empleada te tendía un tomo de formato mediano en cuya sobrecubierta un Niño Jesús (rubio) abrazaba a un santito (rubio) bajo la mirada complaciente de dos angelotes (rubios), estrictamente reducidos por el artista a una cabeza rosa y mofletuda adornada con dos alas. (21)

The parenthetical remarks are ironic readings of the ideological bias of the images used in the works involved. It is noticeable, however, that the protagonist remarks that the book and the original were written 'aproximadamente en el mismo lenguaje' (21). In other words, the language is a principal feature.

Gravestones and Prints

Language, the written word, is thus associated with the ideological foundations of the individual and society. Other details endow language with an ontological dimension. As he wanders around the graveyard on Montjuich, Alvaro reads the epitaphs and notices others that have been vandalized: 'Invocaciones, plegarias, consejos, sentencias, vanos señuelos de inmortalidad' (79).

Chapter II is full of references to the theme of death and the idea of remembrance of the dead. This is only achieved by the record of a photograph or the printed word:

> Agreste y huraño hasta el fin, muerto cortado de la comunidad hispana por una escritura hermética e incomprensible, ¿qué compatriota extraviado, te decías, recogería su último y desolado mensaje? (98)

Here language is both a source of non-communication (if the code is not shared) and of possible retrieval from oblivion.

The Tourist Discourse

This theme of retrieval from oblivion through language is prominent in the first chapter. Alvaro tours the house and finds prints, some identified and others not. He toys with the idea of his power over the preservation of the identity of the people portrayed:

> Un sentimiento oscuro, de íntima y gozosa profanación, acompañaba el lento desfilar de aquellas páginas evocadoras de un pasado desaparecido y muerto, fantasmagórica ronda de personajes identificables sólo gracias a la inscripción piadosa de un nombre y una fecha que los salvaba así—¿por cuánto tiempo?—del irrevocable y definitivo olvido [...] Por una ironía feroz del destino dependía de él—¿quién le impedía borrar los pies con una goma, rasgar caprichosamente las páginas?—que el recuerdo mismo de su existencia se perdiese igualmente [...] se disolviese en la nada ... (19)

In subsequent chapters, the fear of oblivion is omnipresent and the only apparent remedy is the written word. Hence the reference made earlier to tío Néstor. Throughout, the ontological is closely linked with the theme of writing. Above all, language is associated with identity. It is not just that non-expression in language commits one to oblivion, non-existence; it is that unless one manages to define oneself clearly in language, one runs the risk of being submerged in the prevailing identity of the society in which one finds oneself. Hence the graves of the Protestants, with inscriptions written in English, German and Cyrillic, in the Barcelona cemetery lie engulfed in an alien environment, anonymous, unless a compatriot, one who understands the language, comes along to decipher it and rescue them from oblivion. Similarly, in the last chapter, the past history of Montjuich, the history of the Republican prisoners during the Civil War, has been eradicated from present-day official discourse—represented by the tourist guide. It is as though the past has not existed and produces in the protagonist a sense of unreality, of hallucination:

> sin saber con certeza si el pasado reciente de tu patria era real o se trataba sencillamente [...] de una alucinación un mal sueño una resaca característica de borracho un prosaico y vulgar fenómeno de espejismo ... (414)

Señas, then, reveals reality to be constituted by language, and language is seen to be the product of the prevailing forces in society.

This awareness of the importance of language in the configuration of society and the individual explains the exact nature of the conclusion reached by the protagonist at the end of the novel. The final link between him and his identity is language. Hence the proposed solution cannot be the mere abandonment of the country in a fit of pique,[34] nor the mere testimony of the experience undergone. To effect the break, something more radical is needed. The protagonist determines to affirm his identity in negative fashion, against the prevailing standards of the country. The circumstances lead us to expect that the transgression will take place on a linguistic plane, destroying that last vital link and also attacking what has been shown to be the vital substance of reality, its linguistic and ideological foundation. In his own way Alvaro aims to produce an 'escritura hermética e incomprensible' in the hope that 'alguno comprenderá quizá mucho más tarde' (422).

A Textual Approach

In the preceding pages I have suggested how *Señas*, while remaining to a large extent characterized by the features of realism, introduces and superimposes self-conscious features on to that realist base. As a result, the novel signals the beginning of Goytisolo's new aesthetic approach of engaging with social reality through an engagement with and subversion of its discursive practices.

One critic, Michael Ugarte, does point out that in *Señas* the author creates a clash of differing texts or discourses, but sees them essentially as 'Goytisolo's tools in the re-creation of Alvaro's past', thus interpreting them according to a criterion which is essentially realist.[35] Ugarte ends, for example, by claiming that Alvaro's search for identity is 'Goytisolo's search for a meaningful voice through writing' (70), and goes on to say, 'The quest for texts, however, falls short in *Señas*. Neither Alvaro nor Goytisolo likes what he finds; their own identities are repugnant to them both' (71).

However, everything in *Señas* points to Alvaro as not only the protagonist but the writer-narrator of the novel itself. The novel is the aesthetic response and solution to the existential dilemma that is depicted on the thematic level. The text itself, as the consolidation of Alvaro's revolt into some tangible form that will outlive him, is the solution to his existential and artistic quest. This is a constant in Goytisolo's later work (cf. the Sadeian epigraph of *Don Julián* and the final pages of *Juan sin tierra*), and it is not merely a case of the novel as record, as 'testimonio', but as an enduring agent of linguistic and literary subversion.

The novel has stressed the ontological nature of language and art. Hence, the association of characters with texts was not merely a form of artistic shorthand, as Ugarte would have it, but a sign of the importance of language as a defining characteristic of an individual's identity. It served as a parallel on an internal level of the relationship between Alvaro's existential crisis and the text of *Señas*. In conjunction with the broader motif of the ontological status of language itself, it served to suggest the relevance of the literary process to the non-literary realm. As such, the novel posits a new form of literary commitment to counter the discredited version of 1950s realism. Even without considering the textual level of the novel, it is interesting to note how the novel viewed on a superficial level contrasts the levels of action (Alvaro's biography from childhood protest to suicide attempt) with that of contemplation (the three days at the Mas), contrasting the total futility of the former with the changes wrought by the latter. The suggestion is that any solution to Spain's crisis is to come less from attempts at direct action than from a process of careful, and painful, analysis.

Where *Señas* goes further is in the recognition of the radical importance of language not only as a tool for analysing reality but as the essential stuff of individual and social reality. In this way *Señas* constitutes the first manifestation of the language-oriented aesthetic which will characterize the subsequent novels. Fundamental to this new aesthetic is the notion of the individual as a subject constructed in language. In *Señas* this is brought to the fore by the gradual emergence of the level of the self-conscious narrator. I have stressed how much Goytisolo's new aesthetic owes to the influence of Structuralism, and it is interesting to observe the light shed on the narrative situation of *Señas* and its potentially subversive effect by a brief look at the theory of Jacques Lacan.

Christian Meerts has given a detailed Lacanian interpretation of Alvaro's character in terms of the symbols and motifs that run through the novel. His study is useful, if difficult at times to follow, which is unsurprising for anyone with a familiarity with Lacan's thought. Our intention is not to apply Lacan's theory to the novel in such depth, but merely to point to an aspect of that theory which has a curious appropriateness to the narrative situation of the novel.

According to Meerts, Alvaro's search for his past, his 'señas de identidad', is a classic illustration of the individual's sense of loss of 'the Imaginary'—the perfect pre-Oedipal relation with the mother. Alvaro's dilemma in the novel is the frustrated attempt to unify the self, to recover his 'señas'. The work itself becomes the only way he can do so, a means of achieving a surrogate unity. As Meerts puts it, Alvaro fails to unify 'les deux aspects, l'intérieur et l'extérieur, "l'Innenwelt" et "l'Umwelt", sinon dans le moule imparfait, le trouble miroir de l'oeuvre'.[36] Meerts ends by saying: 'Si Alvaro est incapable de se définir, d'agir et de sortir d'un "moi" néantisé, du moins a-t-il parlé et porté témoignage sur lui-même et son pays' (24). This, however, is to fail to recognize the tension present in *Señas* between the level of Alvaro the protagonist at prey to his crisis and the more active level of the narrator attempting to transcend the crisis on a linguistic and literary level.

Lacanian theory is extremely interesting in the context of *Señas* for the striking parallels between its own motifs and those prominent in the novel, in particular, as Meerts effectively illustrates, the motif of the mirror. The theory is also interesting in the context of all of Goytisolo's later production for the importance it accords to language.

Lacan's theory is complex, but for our purposes we can identify three basic concepts that characterize his thought. These are the 'Imaginary', the 'mirror-phase' and the 'Symbolic order'. A useful definition is provided by Catherine Belsey in her book, *Critical Practice*:

> The child has no sense of identity, no way of conceiving of itself as a unity, distinct from what is 'other', exterior to it. During the 'mirror-phase' of its development, however, it 'recognizes' itself in the mirror as a unit distinct from the outside world. This 'recognition' is an identification with an 'imaginary' (because imaged) unitary and autonomous self. But it is only with its entry into language that the child becomes a full subject. If it is to participate in the society into which it is born, to be able to act deliberately within the social formation, the child must enter into the symbolic order, the set of signifying systems of culture of which the supreme example is language.[37]

For Lacan, a fact of the individual's nature is a split between the perceiving self and the self that is perceived (as in the mirror). In order to function successfully, the individual suppresses that split by identifying fully with the perceived self. In linguistic terms this is reflected in the signified/signifier split. In literary terms it would be the distinction between that which is narrated, represented, and the act of narration, representation. Suppressing the signifier, the process of utterance, is to suppress the self that perceives and so create stability and conformity to the Symbolic order. To draw attention to these aspects of language and the self is to subvert that order. As Belsey says, 'the child who refuses to learn the language is "sick", unable to become a full member of the family and of society' (60).

Alvaro in *Señas* is clearly suffering from this 'sickness'. In Chapter I, for example, we see him recalling his experience with Srta Lourdes. The ideology of his family is summed up in this chapter in the Christian ethos represented by the 'lecturas piadosas y edificantes de los tíos' (19). The aspect of these books that is emphasized is the language. Hence when Alvaro cannot find the particular book that he sought, *Historias de niños mártires*, he acquires another 'redactado aproximadamente en el mismo lenguaje' (21). These books present a certain ideal image: 'un Niño Jesús (rubio) abrazaba a un santito (rubio) bajo la mirada complaciente de dos angelotes (rubios) ...' (21). Interestingly, in view of the Lacanian theory mentioned, Alvaro recalls standing in front of a mirror:

> Ingenuamente habías intentado imitar las actitudes de los mártires dibujados en el libro con una corona de santidad milagrosamente sostenida sobre su rubia y angelical cabeza, observándote horas y horas en el espejo del cuarto de baño y preguntándote si los niños morenos y saludables como tú podían aspirar al favor y protección de las potencias celestes ... (23)

Alvaro, in other words, looks into the mirror, hoping to see it return the ideal image, but is faced only with confirmation of his difference. The search for the 'perdida unidad', as Meerts suggests, is doomed. However, contrary to Meerts' view, the novel, rather than providing a surrogate unity, actually emphasizes the split. This is seen in the use of the *tú* form. The third person, *histoire*, suppresses the act of utterance and presents the illusion of a stable and unified self, Alvaro. Even the first person, which according to Lacan carries implicitly the split between the 'I' who speaks and the 'I' who is spoken, can disguise the split.[38] The use of the *tú* form dramatizes, by making explicit, the Lacanian split.

The other features I have pointed to that draw attention to the textual surface of the novel further dramatize for the reader the split between speaker and spoken, narration and narrated, language and the real. The abandoning of the third-person form and definitive assumption of the *tú* in *Señas* is a sign of Alvaro's acceptance of this 'sick' posture. His new-found identity and aesthetic (the two become synonymous) is revealed, not in the notion of 'bearing objective witness', but in the cultivation of an oppositional voice:

> aléjate de tu grey tu desvío te honra
> cuanto te separa de ellos cultívalo
> lo que les molesta en ti glorifícalo
> negación estricta absoluta de su orden esto eres tú ... (419)

Such a split communicates itself to the reader also. For the reader identifies with the subject of the enunciation, the speaker, and in so far as the *tú* form seems to oscillate between the protagonist Alvaro in the Mas addressing himself mentally, and the author Alvaro referring to himself in the narrating process, the reader is forced to oscillate in his interpretation between the two levels. He is unable to secure a stable point from which to naturalize.

Señas, then, in spite of the possibility that its author may have begun by attempting to achieve a unified and comprehensive picture of his own and Spain's situation (by the combination of multiple perspectives and subjective [*tú*] and objective [*él*] versions), never really achieves such a picture. As the novel progresses this is gradually accepted. The third-person form is discarded and the narrator accepts definitively the *tú* form. In so doing he is abandoning the claim to recover or even represent reality objectively in language in favour of language as explicit self-expression. The protagonist in the end finds his identity in the adoption of a subjective discourse, reflected most fully by the free verse of the final chapter.

The protagonist in Montjuich reaches an awareness that language is the last link between him and Spain, between him and his inherited identity. At first the choice is escape, to another country, to another language, to silence. This is rejected in favour of bearing witness, 'deja constancia'. Yet elsewhere he exhorts himself to cultivate his sense of difference, and this, on a textual level, is what he is clearly doing, adopting a language which in form and tone stands as a virulent and defiant challenge.

Throughout the novel, another of the important textual features is the stylistic contrasts in the different types of discourse. There is, however, a basic contrast between a monotonous prosaic register, as in the Voces and the Diario de Vigilancias and also the long sections of conventional prose, and a more lyrical, poetic (and for that reason self-consciously textual) register seen in certain key sections such as Chapter VI, but especially in Chapter VII with the diary of José Bernabeu.

The latter chapter opens directly with the discourse of the 'portavoces oficiales'. Alvaro feels despair at the triumphalist tone and the way that it distorts and masks reality. He takes some consolation, however, from the equally unerasable—because transcribed—testimony of the emigrant, José Bernabeu, which he goes on to include. At first these two opposing discourses vie with each other, until Alvaro eventually exerts his one privilege; he actually terminates the spokesman's discourse ('con un dedo, extirpaste bruscamente la Voz' [382]) and gives free rein to that of the emigrant. The episode reflects in a very graphic way what Goytisolo's texts will aim to do: that is, set discourses in contrast and opposition to one another, but also create a discourse that in some way represents the voice of the marginalized groups in society. Part of this is seen in *Señas* in the adoption of a poetic style, one that rhythmically, syntactically and typographically contrasts with the prose of the conventional novel, but also with the monotonous prose that characterizes the Voces, the 'portavoces oficiales' and the 'Diario de Vigilancias'. A stylistic measure of the success of this subversive discourse is the one we have already noted in the last chapter where the discourse of the Voces, which had haunted and oppressed the protagonist in the opening pages, makes a reappearance and this time is present only in fragments, within the narrator's own poeticized discourse.

A central theme of the novel is that the essence of identity is linguistic. Alvaro's discovery during his meditation at the Mas is that reality both external and internal is precarious, subject to change. Above all, it is discursively produced, and the control of discourse about reality, and therefore of reality, is a condition of power. The power which Alvaro realized he had over the continued 'existence' of the people remembered in the prints in Chapter I is a variation on the power society and its rulers have over the reality of Spanish history. An example is the last chapter in which the reality of the existence of the Republican prisoners in the Civil War is effectively obliterated from the discourse of the tourist guide.

The critique which the novel provides of this situation is, however, not one-sided. It is not simply a question of reminding us of aspects of the past which have been forgotten, using the novel as a way of supplementing a deficient or partial reporting of reality by the powers-that-be, as was the motivation behind the *novela social*. In *Señas* reality is shown as constantly renewing itself. Hence Chapter III and Chapter VIII are designed to show the folly of applying an idea of a past reality to the present. To continue to consider the Spanish people as the same as they were during the war is as mistaken as attempting to deny the existence of aspects of the past altogether. The Spaniard of 1963 is different from that of 1936 because the whole social circumstances are different. This is what Goytisolo meant when he referred to his purpose in *Señas* as to show the gap between myth and reality, 'la realidad cruda y la realidad embellecida por el mito'.[39] But the last chapter of *Señas* shows the narrator unsure about the 'reality' of what he sees in the present; it seems equally unreal, a hallucination, a new 'myth'. In the end, given the uncertainty surrounding the real and its objective verification, there is only one solution, and that is the cultivation of a personal rhetoric to set in opposition to that of society.

In this way the novel as a whole and the last chapter in particular direct our attention to the novel itself as an arena in which language, and by extension reality, can be challenged. As Goytisolo is later to put it in *En los reinos de taifa*:

> La literatura extiende el campo de nuestra visión y experiencia, se opone a cuanto reduce o anestesia nuestras virtualidades perceptivas, nos condiciona cultural, ideológica y sexualmente [...] frente al discurso, el contradiscurso. (113)

It will not, however, be sufficient to indulge in a personal rhetoric. As *Don Julián* is to make clear, 'la invectiva no te desahoga' (DJ, 16). It is necessary for that rhetoric, in this case the rhetoric of the novel, to have a truly subversive effect. In *Señas* this is achieved by the introduction of a degree of self-consciousness which challenges the reader's naturalization of the text in a more radical way than at first appears.

Conclusion

The difficulty with *Señas* is that it manifests an ambiguous status, both rejecting traditional mimesis while preserving many mimetic features, and tending towards narrative self-consciousness without assuming its consequences fully. This once again is due to its transitional nature. Goytisolo has stated that *Señas* was the last novel he wrote according to a plan,[40] which suggests that the overall architecture of the novel was disposed prior to writing. However, it is also clear that the novelist himself underwent a development during the writing process. Goytisolo has stated:

> paralelamente al argumento, al desarrollo de la fábula, hay un proceso constructivo que conduce a un resultado, a esa maldición gitana de Alvaro contra su ciudad en el último capítulo. Si la acción progresa por un lado, la construcción también. El verso libre narrativo que empleo en las páginas finales es el resultado de mi experiencia de escritor durante la construcción del libro [. . .] es el resultado de un proceso que se desarrolla a la vista del lector.[41]

This quotation comes to support the distinction I have made between the formal level and the level of narrated events, and the lack of strictly mimetic coordination between the two. The free verse style used at the end of the novel is less a technical device to render a particular narrative content, than the artistic climax of the writing process.

In so far as the ambiguities, contradictions and dislocations are, as far as the reader can ascertain, not fruit of a deliberate literary project but rather of the writer's uncertainty searching for a practice of writing while still clinging on to a vestigial mimetic technique, *Señas* can be construed as a failed novel. This certainly is how Goytisolo sees it.[42] However, the novel only appears a failed text if we apply to it criteria such as coherence of authorial intention or formal unity. *Señas* reveals a variety of factors at work in the composition of the novel, and the tension between them, the sensation of crisis they suggest about the author and produce in the reader, constitutes an essential feature of the novel's subversive effect.

In this way, it can be seen that at the deepest and most important level, the situation of the implied author whom we have identified as Alvaro Mendiola himself, and the real author, Goytisolo, coincide. This is not a case of interpretation in terms of the biography of the author, but rather an illustration of the new approach to literature outlined in Chapter One of this study. This was summed up in the notion of 'compromiso total' which Goytisolo took from Leiris (FC, 87; cf. also 58), according to which the biographical realities of the author are used to give greater authenticity to the writing process.

NOTES

1 Miguel Riera, 'Regreso al origen' (entrevista), *Quimera* LXXIII (1988), 36.

2 Linda Gould Levine, in her seminal study, *Juan Goytisolo: la destrucción creadora* (Mexico City: Joaquín Mortiz, 1976), has stated that *Señas* is an 'obra bifronte y texto de Jano, que sirve como puente íntimo entre las primeras novelas y *Don Julián*' (11). Carlos Fuentes, in *La nueva novela hispanoamericana* (Mexico City: Joaquín Mortiz, 1969), describes it as 'la novela de tránsito de Juan Goytisolo', and goes on to add that it is 'no solamente la preparación de su obra maestra, Reivindicación del Conde *Don Julián*, sino, en cierto modo, una crítica de lo que él y su generación han escrito' (78).

3 José Ortega, 'Estilo y nueva narrativa española', in *Actas del Sexto Congreso Internacional de Hispanistas* (Toronto: University of Toronto, 1980), 548.

4 Fuentes, *La nueva novela*, 80.

5 Héctor Romero, for example, sees *Señas* as an attempt to fuse subjectivism and objectivism in the interests of a superior realism: 'Lo que el autor busca en *Señas de identidad* es presentar una imagen completa de todos los aspectos de la realidad, desde un punto de vista objetivo y subjetivo, uniéndose así a las nuevas corrientes de la novela actual'. *'Señas de identidad*: una nueva etapa en la novelística de Juan Goytisolo', *Hispanófila* I(53) (1975), 73.

6 Aline Shulman, '*Marks of Identity*: Identity and Discourse', *The Review of Contemporary Fiction* IV(2) (1984), 147.

7 In his interview with Emir Rodríguez Monegal, Goytisolo commented: 'He introducido en la novela una serie de materiales sin integrarlos del todo en su estructura, los he dejado un poco con el culo en el aire para que se vea la carpintería'. Emir Rodríguez Monegal, 'Destrucción de la España sagrada: diálogo con Juan Goytisolo', *Mundo Nuevo* XII (1967), 53

8 Santos Sanz, in *Lectura de Juan Goytisolo* (Barcelona: Pozanco, 1977), notes: 'También los elementos formales ayudan a esa primera impresión de desorganización. Su función, sin embargo, es la de dotar al relato de una mayor verosimilitud en la transcripción de una compleja realidad' (92).

9 Levine sees this as pointing towards the next novel in the trilogy, *Reivindicación del conde don Julián* (*Juan Goytisolo*, 119).

10 J. E. Lyon, 'The Structure of Juan Goytisolo's *Señas de identidad*', *Quinquereme* I(2) (1978), 256.

11 Stephen G. Kellman has defined the self-begetting novel as 'an account usually in the first person, of the development of a character to the point at which he is able to take up his pen and compose the novel we have just finished reading'. Stephen G. Kellman, *The Self-Begetting Novel* (New York: Columbia University Press, 1980), 3.

12 Jaime Martínez Tolentino has produced a painstaking study of the chronology of the novel which, while useful in elucidating the complexity, offers little by way of interpretative conclusions. *La cronología de 'Señas de identidad' de Juan Goytisolo*, Problemata Literaria 13 (Kassel: Reichenberger, 1992).

13 Levine sees *Señas*' fragmented and disordered chronology as serving on the one

hand to avoid 'los esquemas "simétricos y rígidos" de la novela tradicional', and on the other to oblige the reader to restore the original order, thus avoiding a 'concepción unívoca de los problemas de la sociedad y la cultura' (*Juan Goytisolo*, 89–90).

14 Mary Ellen Bieder, 'A Case of Altered Identity: Two Editions of Juan Goytisolo's *Señas de identidad*', *Modern Language Notes* LXXXIX (1974), 302 n. 11.

15 André Gallego and Henri Guerreiro, 'Pour une chronogénèse de *Señas de identidad*: temps escamoté, temps anéanti, temps dominé', in Jacques Beyrie et al. (eds), *Deux romans de la rupture?*, Table ronde organisée par l'UER d'Etudes Hispaniques et Hispano-Américaines, Toulouse 28–29 February 1980, Travaux de l'Université de Toulouse–Le Mireil, Tome XIII (Toulouse: Université de Toulouse–Le Mireil, 1980), 123–41 (137).

16 The terms 'fabula' and 'sujet' are the versions Spires chooses. The original terms used by the Russian Formalists are 'fabula' and 'suzhet' or 'sjuzet'. This is sometimes rendered as 'fable' and 'sujet'. See Robert Scholes, *Structuralism in Literature: An Introduction* (London: Yale University Press, 1974), 80. While dealing with Spires' ideas, I have opted to use the terms as he has used them.

17 'Esta construcción retrospectiva de la *fabula* revela una paradoja temporal que caracteriza la experiencia del lector; éste tiene la sensación de atemporalidad pero no puede ignorar la existencia de señales de un orden temporal. Tal sensación paradójica refleja la experiencia psíquica de Alvaro; siente la atemporalidad de su existencia al tratar de reconstruir el pasado pero no puede escapar de la realidad de su cercana muerte.' Robert Spires, 'Modos narrativos y búsqueda de identidad en *Señas de identidad*', *Anales de la novela de posguerra* II (1977), 57. See also his *La novela española de posguerra: creación artística y experiencia personal* (Madrid: Cupsa, 1978), 205–06.

18 Spires, 'Modos narrativos', 56.

19 Pere Gimferrer, 'Riesgo y ventura de Juan Goytisolo', prologue to volume I of *Obras completas* of Juan Goytisolo (Madrid: Aguilar, 1977), 34.

20 See Jonathan Culler, *Structuralist Poetics: Structuralism, Linguistics and the Study of Literature* (London: Routledge, 1975), 197, and Patricia Waugh, *Metafiction: The Theory and Practice of Self-Conscious Fiction* (London: Methuen, 1984), 152 n. 5.

21 Julián Ríos (ed.), *Juan Goytisolo* (Madrid: Fundamentos, 1975), 143.

22 Spires, *La novela española de posguerra*, 202.

23 Levine, *Juan Goytisolo*, 101. Lyon in his article also posits a third-person narrator, distinct from Alvaro, which he calls 'straight third-person'. Lyon, 'The Structure of Juan Goytisolo's *Señas de identidad*', 245.

24 Reed Anderson, '*Señas de identidad*: Chronicle of Rebellion', *Journal of Spanish Studies* II (1974), 10. For Jesús Lázaro too, the third person, apart from its use by the narrator in sections describing the activities of others (Antonio, for example), is used by Alvaro to refer to himself. Lázaro accounts for this thus: 'De este modo podemos deducir que el empleo de la tercera persona se debe a un proceso paralelo de distanciamiento y objetivación. Alvaro la utiliza para poder ver más claro lo que sucede y, simultánea-mente, los acontecimientos le repelen de tal forma que se aleja de ellos desencantado.' Jesús Lázaro, *La novelística de Juan Goytisolo* (Madrid: Alhambra, 1984), 158. For Lázaro the third person serves as a way of recounting events in the distant past of the protagonist from which he feels alienated. The second person deals with more intimate self-analysis, 'la exploración personal y la organización de los contenidos de conciencia' (159), but also conveys the sense of self-alienation that would have been absent from the first person. It is interesting that both Lázaro and Anderson see Alvaro as the narrator of both the *tú* and the *él* passages. Anderson actually sees Alvaro as the 'author and protagonist' of the novel (3). However, his study does not attach any importance to Alvaro's status as writer. Lázaro sees Alvaro as narrator in the sense of the point of view

from which the novel is seen. This is that of Alvaro's mental experience at the Mas. *Señas de identidad* is for Lázaro 'una novela de pensamiento' (160).

25 Goytisolo himself has said of the use of the second person: 'hay en Alvaro una especie de desdoblamiento que hace que cuando monologa se habla a sí mismo como si fuera otro. Es decir, el tú corresponde más a este desdoblamiento que el yo.' Rodríguez Monegal, 'Destrucción de la España sagrada', 54.

26 'Deictics (or shifters) are "orientational" features of language which relate to the situation of utterance ... the most interesting are first and second person pronouns (whose meaning in ordinary discourse is the "speaker" and the "person addressed"), anaphoric articles (articles used to avoid repetition of a word) and demonstratives which refer to an external context rather than to other elements in the discourse, adverbials of place and time whose reference depends on the situation of utterance (here, there, now, yesterday) and verb tenses, especially the non-timeless present'. Culler, *Structuralist Poetics*, 165.

27 Culler, *Structuralist Poetics*, 170.

28 Patricia Waugh explains this split as follows: 'To write of "I" is to discover that the attempt to fix subjectivity in writing erases that subjectivity, constructs a new subject. The insight is not entirely post-modernist, however. *Tristram Shandy* desperately attempts to dissolve past, present and future "selves" into the moment of discourse, the "now" of his act of narration. He discovers, in the words of the twentieth-century phenomenologist Merleau-Ponty, "I am never at one with myself"... And "I" never will be. To write about oneself is implicitly to posit oneself as an "other", to narrate or historicize oneself as a character in one's own discourse.' Waugh, *Metafiction*, 134–35.

29 Other examples of deictics in the novel are: 'esta sofocante jornada' (414), 'aquel verano' (417), 'aquel agobiador verano español de 1963' (73), 'el hondo amor que desde niño presentías ¿era éste?' (78).

30 'Cuando los hechos pasados se expresan en presente—de uso no específico entonces—el narrador acorta arbitrariamente la distancia entre ellos y sí mismo, da la ilusión de que vuelven a ser vigentes en el momento de la enunciación por el inmenso deseo que tiene Alvaro de vivirlos, pese a la cronología lo que se pierde en el terreno de la objetividad se gana en "tensión".' D. Cardaillac, 'Algunos problemas de enunciación en *Señas de identidad*', *Les Langues Neo-Latines* LXXIV(234) (1980), 51.

31 Jonathan Culler sees this as a characteristic of Structuralist criticism in general in which, 'instead of attempting to resolve difficulties so as to produce themes or statements by a persona about a particular problem one may seek to preserve those difficulties by organizing the text as an illustration of certain problems. At the highest level they are problems of language itself.' Culler, *Structuralist Poetics*, 160. It is part of the effect of *Señas*, attributable in large measure to the Structuralist influence, to disturb the reading in such a way as to actively encourage this kind of reading in terms of language and literary form.

32 'Por ejemplo, en un principio al personaje de Alvaro lo quería tratar en un doble plano: en tercera persona, visto desde fuera, y metiéndome en su interior, hablando en primera persona. Pero en determinado momento me di cuenta que tenía que emplear la segunda persona en vez de la primera porque hay en Alvaro una especie de desdoblamiento, que hace que cuando monologa se habla a sí como si fuera otro.' Rodríguez Monegal, 'Destrucción de la España sagrada', 54.

33 Christian Meerts comments that 'Antonio est très exactement un "double" purement "fonctionnel" d'Alvaro en Espagne pendant le séjour de celui-ci en France'. Christian Meerts, *Technique et vision dans 'Señas de identidad' de Juan Goytisolo* (Frankfurt: Vittorio Klostermann, 1972), 59.

34 Anderson, '*Señas de identidad*: Chronicle of Rebellion', 18.

35 Michael Ugarte, *Trilogy of Treason: An Intertextual Study of Juan Goytisolo* (Columbia, MO, and London: University of Missouri Press, 1982), 65.

36 Meerts, *Technique et vision dans 'Señas de identidad'*, 15.

37 Catherine Belsey, *Critical Practice* (London: Methuen, 1980), 60.

38 Belsey, *Critical Practice*, 64–65.

39 Rodríguez Monegal, 'Destrucción de la España sagrada', 57.

40 Jesús Lázaro (ed.), *Juan Goytisolo*, Serie España, Escribir hoy 11 (Madrid: Ministerio de Cultura, 1982), 153.

41 Ríos (ed.), *Juan Goytisolo*, 114.

42 'Mi brega diaria con las sucesivas versiones de *Señas de identidad* se distinguía cualitativamente de mis forcejeos anteriores con la literatura; debía ser un texto de ruptura y salto al vacío: iniciativo, genésico, fundacional. Como advertí más tarde, al releer la novela impresa, no alcancé el objetivo sino a medias. Compendio y superación de la narrativa pasada, *Señas* sería finalmente el híbrido de la nueva subjetividad conquistada y un esquema formal, del que no conseguí escapar del todo'. *En los reinos de taifa* (Barcelona: Seix Barral, 1986), 230.

CHAPTER THREE

Reivindicación del conde don Julián

Reivindicación del conde don Julián, published in 1970, is the second instalment of the Mendiola Trilogy and is certainly a much more fully rounded and accomplished novel than *Señas de identidad*. The transitional phase of the earlier novel has largely been overcome and the author now pursues his new aesthetic with greater confidence and sense of purpose. It is a multifaceted work which can be read in a variety of ways. Goytisolo himself has commented:

> Este libro como otras obras de la novelística actual admite y se propone una pluralidad de lecturas; oscila, a la vez, de la poesía a la crítica, del sicoanálisis a la interpretación histórica.[1]

As with *Señas*, critics have tended to see the novel in a dual light as portraying the personal crisis of the central protagonist, his sense of alienation, inner crisis, his status as an exile from Spain and his rebellious nature, and at the same time, emphasizing its own break with the traditional novel and its upsetting of conventional linguistic and narrative usages. In the majority of cases, these two aspects are drawn together in an 'expressive' function: the narrative experimentation is seen to 'reflect', to 'express' in novelistic, aesthetic terms the human crisis portrayed by the novel.[2] In many cases, the novel is read even more literally as an expression of the problems of the real author Goytisolo.[3]

The formal elements in *Don Julián* are interpreted, as with *Señas*, in terms of reflecting the protagonist's, and Spain's, reality.[4] The novel's satiric and parodic attack on the literary tradition of Spain can be accounted for by the protagonist's exiled status as someone who is outside the country and, as Goytisolo himself said, 'ha renunciado a la realidad física de su país, pero no a su cultura; a la tierra, pero no a la palabra'.[5] It is a continuation of the end of *Señas* where Alvaro recognized that the only thing linking him to Spain was language. It is against language that the attack must be carried out.

In spite of the interrelationship between the levels of form and content, there is an important extent to which they conflict with one another and produce narrative dislocations which the reader must, in turn, naturalize. Such features emerge from a consideration of the way *Don Julián* develops the metafictional mode that we had noticed emerging in the previous novel. For this reason it becomes interesting to take the lead from the novel itself, bearing in mind the comment by

Goytisolo that 'toda obra literaria importante lleva su propia teoría incorporada, contiene sus propias claves'.[6]

The metafictional nature of *Don Julián*, while frequently recognized, nonetheless receives scant attention.[7] Yet there is justification for considering it as central to the meaning of the text, for once a novel includes self-conscious elements, it alters radically the reader's approach to the narrative illusion. The reader's primary reaction on encountering a text is to naturalize it as coherently as possible, and the most common way is by locating a stable narrator or speaking subject who can be posited as the source of the narrative communication. In so far as such identification of a stable narrator is disrupted the reader is forced to naturalize such disruption.[8]

The self-conscious elements of *Don Julián* disrupt the traditional narrative scheme, based on mimesis, and draw the reader's attention to the process of writing itself. Goytisolo himself has emphasized this aspect of the novel when he said 'este libro pone el acento sobre la novela en tanto que construcción puramente verbal'.[9]

However, the novel, as is common in metafictional writing, does not permit this reading in terms of writing to take place unproblematically. The 'traditional' reading in terms of representation, mimesis, is not abolished entirely, but rather maintained in order to be subverted, disrupted, and in this way to focus the reader's attention to the interrelation of the differing levels.

Recognition of this problem at the centre of the novel brings us closer to the true functioning of *Don Julián*'s subversive process. The novel's theme revolves around the idea of transgression and subversion, in particular the speaker's desire to enact a 'crime' that will have an enduring effect. The epigraph to this effect is from Sade and the motivation behind the novel, and it helps to read the Sadeian epigraph in the light of Roland Barthes' interpretation of Sade in *Sade, Fourier, Loyola*. Barthes' approach to Sade is to see him as first and foremost a writer in the self-conscious rather than the realist mould. He says:

> Etant écrivain, et non auteur réaliste, Sade choisit toujours le discours contre le référent; il se place toujours du côté de la sémiosis, non de la mimesis : ce qu'il 'représente' est sans cesse déformé par le sens, et c'est au niveau du sens, non du référent, que nous devons le lire.[10]

The implication of this is that Sade's criminality was a purely discursive one. The subversive effect of the novels is one which belongs firmly to the world of discourse. As Goytisolo, quoting from Barthes' analysis of Sadeian discourse, puts it:

> Podemos decir que *Don Julián* escoge siempre el discurso contra el referente. O, por emplear una brillante fórmula de Roland Barthes, pretende 'transformar las imposibilidades del referente en posibilidades de discurso'.[11]

The key to the novel then is the search for the enduring subversion, the 'crime dont l'effet perpétuel agît, même quand je n'agirais plus'. The answer to that quest is clearly to be found in writing, and this is the philosophy behind the whole change in Goytisolo's writing from *Señas* onwards.

However, this leads us to the more serious question which is what exactly constitutes this subversive effect in *Don Julián*, how is it achieved and how successful is it? There is a tendency for the novel's subversion to be reduced to its portrayal of a subversive and aggressive protagonist who pours hatred and scorn on his homeland from the first page to the last. Added to this is the constant parody and satire of the Official Spanish literary tradition, as cherished by the apologists of the Franco regime. Finally, due recognition is given to the novel's formal experimentation, its complex style and its departure from traditional realism.

However, a more important and fundamental subversion is taking place within the novel itself, on the level of the reading process. *Don Julián* sets itself up as a practice of writing which aims through the writing and reading process to enact the permanent rebellion to which the epigraph refers. A close study of the novel, of the complex relationship between the referential and the self-referential levels, will reveal an irreconcilable tension which is the source of a permanent troubling of the reading process.

Naturalization

On one level, *Don Julián* is an account of a typical day in the life of a Spanish ex-patriot in Tangiers: 'la vida de un emigrado de tu especie se compone de interrumpidas secuencias de renuente y laboriosa unidad' (20). The novel begins when he wakes up and it follows him through the day until he returns to his apartment in order to go to bed. The novel appears to follow the mental processes of the central protagonist as he enacts his daily routine, which consists primarily of an elaborate fantasy in which Spain is invaded once again by the Moorish hordes in a recreation of the 711 invasion. According to legend, this had been provoked by the desire on the part of Count Julián for revenge on the Visigothic king, Rodrigo, for the latter's rape of the Count's daughter, Florinda. The implication is that this daily fantasy of invasion is the only way for the tortured protagonist to establish his identity. Having abandoned Spain and rejected his inherited identity, he can only preserve that rejection by a continual reiteration of it. His new identity comes to be constituted by that very act of imaginary aggression against Spain. His new identity is in other words an anti-identity, in which he defines himself negatively by rejecting everything Spanish.

For this reason too, the daily fantasy culminates in the torture and incitement to suicide of the image of the protagonist's former self, Alvarito. Hence the daily act of destruction against Spain is also an act of self-destruction, in which the protagonist provokes his own suicide and rebirth in the new, non-Spanish, Muslim persona he longs to be:

> y he aquí que el muñeco resucita y recobra súbitamente la vista y uso e integridad de sus miembros : vestido con blanca chilaba, ceñido de níveo turbante invoca en árabe puro el nombre de Alá, manifiesta su vivo deseo de ser musulmán. (238)

As the novel progresses it becomes clear that the protagonist's battle is not so much against Spain as against 'Official Spain', the image of Spain projected and fostered by the dominant forces in Spanish society since the Reconquest, in particular the Franco Regime.[12] To this end, the protagonist sides with those aspects of Spanish history and culture excluded from this official image. On a historical and cultural level, this leads to an identification with the Arabs. On a literary plane the predominant figure is Góngora.

The context of fantasy in which this occurs and the subsequent return to reality as the protagonist comes home to his apartment and goes to bed admitting to himself, 'lo sabes, lo sabes : mañana será otro día, la invasión recomenzará' (240), makes clear the awareness of the futility of the protagonist's posture, the impossibility of altering in any real way one's cultural identity. Having said that, the novel implies that, in this situation, the best course of action is a determined resistance to the 'facts' of reality through the imagination. Fantasy becomes the last bastion of resistance to the real.

This, then, is the thematic level of the novel. However, the novel does not consist solely of this level. The level of 'story' is complicated throughout by the level of 'discourse'. It is impossible for the reader to read the novel simply on the level of the story, for this is interrupted continually by elements that refer the reader back to the level of discourse.

In Chapter One of our study, we saw how in his essays Goytisolo has stressed the importance of the role of fantasy or imagination in the process of resistance to repression in society. But, as I also pointed out, he makes a qualitative distinction between those writers who display an imaginative freedom encased in a conventional narrative form—García Márquez for example—and those others, like Fuentes, Sarduy and Cabrera Infante, who encapsulate that imaginative freedom within an exploration of the possibilities of language. The principle underlying this is the constant with Goytisolo that one cannot challenge the 'real' or the status quo through imagination alone. The challenge that is represented by fantasy must also be accompanied by a challenge to the forms in which that real is usually channelled. Hence it is significant that the principal fantasy writers whose influence pervades *Don Julián* are Sade and Lautréamont, writers who challenged the social norms with a fantastic vision which was embodied in a subversion of literary norms. Rosemary Jackson has noted of Sade's writings that they are 'as important on a syntactic level as on a semantic one. It is not only the themes of transgression which make his work subversive, but the means of their representation', adding that 'Sade's fantasies do not actually break syntactic structures: they push syntax to its limits, eroding, yet sustaining it'.[13]

It is clear that in Goytisolo's scale of priorities, fantasy, important as it is, takes second place to the exploration of language. It is the text's self-referentiality which is the predominant concern in so far as it draws attention to the materiality of language and literature and the discursive practices of society. Hence the truly subversive effect of *Don Julián* is not merely the way that it attacks the Spanish tradition or mocks sacred values, but the way that it continually challenges the reader's attempt to fix a stable meaning on the text itself.

In coming to terms with a text, two of the major devices of orientation for the reader are the recognition of the identity of a narrator and of a coherent fictional world.[14] *Don Julián* can be seen to disturb the reading process in both these aspects.

The Problem of the Narrator

Don Julián is most commonly interpreted as the anguished monologue of its central protagonist, the exiled Spaniard living in Tangiers.[15] Mary Ellen Bieder concludes that he is an example of those 'narradores que crean sus historias en su mente como historias que se cuentan a sí mismos'.[16] In this way *Don Julián* is viewed as a form of interior monologue. The text represents, expresses, the inner mental babbling of the alienated, neurotic, exiled protagonist.[17]

The narration is complicated by the predominance of the *tú* form which has led critics often to speak of the possibility of a dialogue between the author (as the concealed *yo*) and the protagonist, the interlocutory *tú*.[18] Even Goytisolo, while not suggesting an author-protagonist dialogue, does imply addresser and addressee as separate entities:

> En *Don Julián* el texto tiene [...] la verosimilitud inherente al acto de comunicación puesto que todo es un pseudo-diálogo entre un narrador que habla a un personaje y el texto entero de la novela queda incluido en este pseudo-diálogo del que el lector es testigo indirecto y oblicuo.[19]

However, while undoubtedly there are two separate narrative components, narrator and protagonist, one who enunciates the narrative and one who is represented in that narration, it seems the case that, as Bieder suggests, these two aspects correspond to the same person. This impression is reinforced when in brief instances of first-person narrative the speaker is the same as the *tú* figure, that is, Alvaro-Julián, addressing Spain: 'tierra ingrata, entre todas espuria y mezquina, jamás volveré a ti : con los ojos todavía cerrados [...] dibujados ante ti, lo admites ...' (11). As we have seen in our study of *Señas*, the narration in the *tú* form strikes the reader most forcibly as a single protagonist-narrator addressing himself, as suggested in Goytisolo's reference to 'una especie de desdoblamiento que hace que cuando monologa se habla a sí como si fuera otro'.[20] Sobejano has neatly referred to this as a 'monodiálogo interior'.[21]

Martín Morán has also shown how *Don Julián* does not correspond to the definition of interior monologue but rather to a discourse derived from the 'desdoblamiento' of the narrator, since as he says 'existe un interlocutor a quien va dirigido el discurso y no un simple fluir de una conciencia'.[22] Given this definition, he perceives too much organization and motivation in the discourse of the novel to enable it to qualify as interior monologue and, in passing, notes how the discourse of *Don Julián* displays certain signs of the 'narrative act':

> En *Reivindicación del conde Don Julián* nos encontramos con las ya citadas frases cambiarás el final, pasarás, pues a las clases prácticas, que constituyen una clara inclusión de la instancia narrativa en el discurso. (320)

Earlier he had noted how these comments correspond to 'la función de organización, propia del narrador' (318). In other words, Martín Morán dismisses the idea of interior monologue and substitutes for it the idea of the 'desdoblamiento' of the central protagonist into a narrator-protagonist. It is interesting too, although Martín Morán does not pursue the idea, that the narrator at moments reveals himself to be *consciously* narrating.

According to these views, then, the narrator is the protagonist, Alvaro-Julián, engaged in a one-sided mental conversation with himself. The narrator thus becomes the central character in the novel and the narration an indirect characterization of its narrator. The referential realm of the narrative, the world in which the narrator-protagonist moves, is strongly preserved. We see him awaken in a room, get up, get dressed, go out into the streets of Tangiers, spend a day visiting the library, the café, smoking kif, dreaming, returning home, entering his apartment, undressing, going to bed and admitting that the process will take place again the following day.

However, the narrative situation of *Don Julián* is much more complex than this. For while on the one hand the novel focuses on the protagonist's situation in which he carries out an imagined invasion and destruction of Spain, there is clearly also the level of the narration itself, in this case a self-conscious narration of a text which is a literary assault on the official culture of the Regime. A close look at the opening pages reveals the interweaving of these two levels.

*   *   *   *   *

The novel opens by locating us as readers in the consciousness of a protagonist waking up in Tangiers. According to Levine: 'existe una armonía perfecta entre el tiempo verbal y el proceso psíquico del personaje que no sigue una continuidad cronológica'.[23] The narrator seems identified with this protagonist as he directs a diatribe against Spain, 'tierra ingrata, entre todas espuria y mezquina, jamás volveré a ti'. He then directs the discourse against himself: '... dibujados ante ti, lo admites, con escrupulosidad casi maníaca' (11).

The opening pages, then, create a character, a centre of consciousness, a subjectivity that belongs to a fictional world. This fictional world is expressly depicted: 'mirando a tu alrededor en un apurado y febril inventario de tus pertenencias y bienes' (14).

The reader's naturalization of the narrative as the representation of the psychic flow of a protagonist, registering his circumstances, is modified when he reads the following:

> abres un ojo : techo escamado por la humedad, paredes vacuas, el día que aguarda tras la cortina, caja de Pandora : maniatado bajo la guillotina : un minuto más, señor verdugo : un petit instant : inventar, componer, mentir, fabular : repetir la proeza de Scherezada, durante sus mil y una noches escuetas, inexorables : érase una vez ... (13)

The narration here takes on a more self-conscious aspect, presenting itself as a narration in the Scheherezadian mould. Like Scheherezade, the protagonist is a narrator, one whose life depends on his storytelling, his life is his storytelling. The ensuing narrative no longer presents itself as the unconscious rendering of the central protagonist's thoughts and movements but his conscious narration of his life.[24]

In other words, a form of psychological realism is substituted by the theme of fiction, of storytelling, of artifice. The effect is to introduce an element of confusion between life and art, reality and fiction. This effect is reinforced with the theatrical references—a recurrent feature of the novel—equating the beginning of the novel with the raising of the curtain:

> tres metros, incorporarse, calzar las babuchas, tirar de la correa de la persiana : y : silencio, caballeros, se alza el telón : la representación empieza : el decorado es sobrio ... (13) [25]

This duality in the protagonist reveals the conflict between the realms of reality and fantasy. The protagonist in his wanderings through the city will waver from one to the other, registering his experiences and his imaginary transformation of them. But this dramatization of a fictional protagonist's state of mind is also continually interrupted by sections revealing a more self-conscious narrator occupied in the task of textual production. The implications of this for the overall interpretation of the novel are several and will be discussed in a later section. One of the effects is the undermining of a standard feature of conventional narrative, that of character.

The Concept of Character

Since the tendency in *Don Julián* is to naturalize the narration in terms of a narrating character, the novel's treatment of the narrator is related to the treatment of character. It is by now a commonplace that the twentieth-century novel has done much to subvert and alter our basic notion of character. More recent theory and practice has the effect of doing away with character in the novel completely, and replacing it with what is called the 'pronominal hero' or, as Barthes called it, 'the linguistic person', which he says is 'never defined by states of mind, intentions or traits of character but only by its (coded) place in discourse'.[26] In *Don Julián* Tariq, Peranzules, Séneca, are not characters in any real (or conventionally fictional) sense, but mere names that appear and disappear according to the needs of the narrative.

However, the central protagonist himself, in spite of the somewhat unreal, anonymous nature of his description, is clearly not on the same level as the other 'characters' or 'linguistic persons' mentioned. He is the focus and, as we have seen, the apparent source of the narration throughout. The narrative follows the workings of his consciousness from the moment of waking up until he retires to bed. The other figures in the narrative may have their unreality explained as being figments of the narrator-protagonist's imagination, memory or kif-induced hallucinations. This narrator-protagonist does evidence some signs of 'espesor psicológico'. As Goytisolo says, he is a 'ser anónimo que desde Tánger contempla la costa española'. Later we find he has a profession as a reporter (58). There are enough intertextual links also to establish the narrator as the same character, Alvaro Mendiola, as in *Señas de identidad* (see pp. 57–58). In so far, then, as this picture of the central protagonist in Tangiers is built up and presented as the narrator, *Don Julián* does not eliminate entirely the notion of a central 'human' character who in this case also appears to act as the narrator of his own story.

And yet, as Martín Morán points out, the traditional narrative expectations about this narrator-protagonist are not satisfied, he remains a shadow, a mere function of the discourse.[27] What is important, therefore, is the way the novel deliberately fosters the image of a psychological persona only to undermine it, cast doubt on it. The text does encourage a reading in terms of psychological realism, according to which the text relays the mental processes of a 'real' character. This indeed is how most critics view the novel.[28] The character, for example, has a past: 'años atrás, en los limbos de tu vasto destierro habías considerado el alejamiento como el peor de los castigos' (13). The move out of the present tense into the past has the narrative effect of reinforcing the fictional world. The allusion to the past is a feature of conventional realism; Genette refers to it as 'external analepsis' or retrospection to a point beyond the beginning of the discourse.[29] However, in *Don Julián* such 'realist' details are counterbalanced by the impression that this character is a mere textual entity, what Goytisolo refers to as 'agent', existing solely on the page. Hence the text begins with the protagonist waking and ends with him going to bed, events marked by references to the curtain rising (13) and falling (230).

The strong impression the reader has of the character at the centre of the narration is simultaneously weakened by certain features that undermine the classical notion of character. Martín Morán speaks of his 'presencia [...] casi fantasmal' and tentatively suggests that the 'entidad protagonista queda así reducida a un pronombre personal, a una forma vacía que no tiene ningún referente externo'.[30]

A principal feature is his anonymity. The novel genre in general, and the classic realist text in particular, were of course characterized by the opposite, eponymy.[31] Anonymity is not merely an inversion of a narrative convention but more importantly participates in the broader attack waged by the novel on the yearning for epistemological certainty, a central issue in all the novels of Goytisolo's later period. Throughout *Don Julián* there is a combat against the desire to fix meanings, construct stable world-views. For this reason, the central protagonist not only remains nameless but identifies with a character with both a dubious historical identity and a variety of names, as García de Valdeavellano's epigraph to the novel attests:

> un misterioso personaje al que los historiadores musulmanes llaman casi siempre Ulyan y que probablemente se llamara Julián o quizás Urbano, Ulban o Bulián.

The historical ambiguity surrounding the identity of the legendary *Don Julián* contributes to the novel's blurring of the distinction between fiction and fact, history and myth, language and reality. Julián is a figure at once historical and mythical, in the same way that Alvaro-Julián is a 'realistic' character and a 'linguistic person', a product of the textual process. The contrast between, on the one hand, Count Julián's doubtful historical existence and, on the other, the 'real' force of his mythical presence serves also as a comment on the ultimate victory of the latter over the former, an indirect justification of the author's rejection of realism in favour of an engagement with myths. Furthermore, the doubt over Julián's actual identity acts as a metaphor for the indeterminacy of character promoted by the novel's treatment of its protagonist. Finally, the figure of Julián stands as a comment on the precarious status of history itself, and its claims to truth.[32]

By frustrating the reader's attempt to establish meaning by locating a clear, well-defined and stable narrating persona, the novel is transgressing one of the essential features of conventional narrative. Similarly, the treatment of character offers the contradiction of a 'real' central character represented in the discourse of the novel and a 'pronominal hero' whose only function is as part of the literary project of subversion in so far as it subverts a standard convention of traditional realism.[33]

Narrative Levels

The ambiguity surrounding the notion of narrator and character applies also to the notion of a fictional world in the narrative. The identification of such a world constitutes one of the primary ways of making sense of a text. Goytisolo himself distinguished two separate levels in the novel:

> pese a la ausencia de personajes 'psicológicos', acciones realistas, etc., el elemento narrativo predominaba aún sobre los otros, había una línea argumental, una unidad de acción y de lugar, un tiempo 'referencial' exterior al tiempo de la escritura.[34]

According to this view, the referential dimension still exists and predominates over the textual features of the novel. This fits awkwardly with Goytisolo's major pronouncements about the development of his and other contemporary novels. As we noted, in 'La novela española contemporánea' Goytisolo's concern in his mature novels was for *discours*, drawing attention to the sign and away from the fictional world of *histoire*. In so far as he sees the 'línea argumental' or 'tiempo referencial' as still predominating in *Don Julián*, one might adjudge it a failure in his terms. However, the relation between *discours* and *histoire* in *Don Julián* is more complex than this, as Goytisolo himself was subsequently to recognize.

The terms *discours* and *histoire* have been largely replaced in modern criticism by the terms *énonciation* and *énoncé*. The former refers to the actual narrating act and the latter to that which is narrated. Much *discours*, for example, the voice of a narrating protagonist or the stream of consciousness of a character, still belongs firmly to the realm of the *énoncé*, in other words, the fictional world, and need not draw attention to the actual materiality of the text.[35]

Hence, within *discours* it is possible to have a narrative voice belonging to a character in the referential realm, and this discourse is firmly contained within the level of the narrated events (*histoire*), and does not necessarily draw the reader's attention to the text itself. For the latter to occur, the *discours* must belong to the persona responsible for enunciating the text.

Goytisolo appears, in a later essay, to realize the complexities of the distinction between *discours* and *histoire*. He defines 'true' *discours* as 'aquellos textos donde hay una señalización con respecto a la situación de enunciación', and *histoire* as 'aquellos donde la señalización no se efectúa en correspondencia con la situación de enunciación sino en relación con el texto literario mismo, esto es, la situación del enunciado' (CC, 57).

This means that in *Don Julián*, in so far as we interpret the 'discurso narrativo' as the narrative voice of the Alvaro-Julián protagonist, located in Tangiers, the 'discurso' belongs to the realm of *histoire*. As I have argued, this would make *Don Julián* not very different from the stream-of-consciousness novel and would draw the reader's attention not to the 'sign', but to the psyche represented by those signs; in other words, another form of psychological realism. *Don Julián*, on the other hand, works in numerous ways to impede such straightforward naturalization and draw our attention to the surface of the text and the process of writing.[36]

In the same essay in *Contracorrientes*, Goytisolo shows an awareness of the ambiguity of levels and narrative voice in *Don Julián* that this new perspective on *discours* gives rise to:

> vista desde esta nueva y enriquecedora perspectiva una novela como *Don Julián* no sería un texto de discurso, a pesar del empleo continuo de los tiempos verbales del presente y futuro y el uso de la segunda persona gramatical. El 'tú' que abre el surco de la escritura no es el destinatario de la narración desde el momento en que nada permite identificar el sujeto del enunciado con el de la enunciación y no hay por tanto identificación posible entre la situación de enunciación y la de enunciado, antes bien, una situación imprecisa y ambigua que se extiende como un *no man's land* entre ambas. (CC, 57)

It would seem clear that Goytisolo, from the final pages of *Señas de identidad* onwards, was working towards a form of pure discourse, pure enunciation, what Todorov referred to as 'a certain tendency of modern writing [which] does not propose to make us see anything whatever: it is discourse without being fiction'.[37] It is a situation which Goytisolo obviously feels he has attained more successfully in *Juan sin tierra*, about which he comments that 'cada vez que el relato empieza a cobrar impulso y se desdibuja la trama argumental—esto es, la ilusión del referente—el narrador interviene para imponernos su presencia: todo es escritura, nos hallamos ante un objeto específicamente literario'.[38]

As the quotation implies, there is a similar metafictional tension in both novels between the pull of the narrative illusion and the self-conscious features. The difference is in the degree of overtness of the metafiction. However, while *Juan sin tierra* may be more explicitly metafictional, there is a case for seeing *Don Julián*'s much more ambiguous mixture of textuality and referentiality as both equally metafictional and more subversive. *Juan sin tierra*, for all its dissolution of the novel form, has an essentially stabilizing factor in the writer in the 'cocina-escritorio' self-revealed as the producer of the text we are in the process of reading. *Don Julián*, on the other hand, lacks any such centring device and consequently the reader himself is decentred, torn between identifying with a 'subject of the enounced', the protagonist, located in Tangiers, and a 'subject of the enunciation', an author-narrator figure composing the text of *Don Julián*.

The interrelationship between the referential and the textual in the novel has not been fully explored. Levine stresses the relation between external reality, that is, the setting in Tangiers, and the inner world of the protagonist. The former she sees as gradually giving way to the latter in a process she terms 'desrealización'.[39] The textual features of the narrative represent that descent into fantasy. Yet she, like many other critics, has recognized the self-conscious aspects of *Don Julián*, asserting:

> El hecho de que Goytisolo articule su traición lingüística a lo largo de la novela reafirma la identidad de *Don Julián* como obra que nos habla de su propio proceso de creación y que pone al centro del texto una tensión implícita entre teoría y praxis literaria.[40]

She draws attention to the analogy between the referential realm and the text when she claims that Tangiers is both the 'sitio donde ocurre la acción externa y lugar cuya estructura física es simbólica de la construcción de la novela misma' (53). Nonetheless she does not pursue the consequences of this assertion and her interpretation remains essentially mimetic. The novel, however, does deliberately play on the relation between the city and the text, a favourite analogy in all of Goytisolo's work, but in a way that inverts the usual mimeticism in that the city becomes a metaphor for the text. The effect of this is to place the textual plane in the foreground but at the same time to grant a greater significance to the writing process by implying the interrelationship of the textual and the real. This also has relevance to the literary model for the novel, Góngora. Speaking of the *Soledades*, Goytisolo has commented:

Si la realidad se vislumbra como una metáfora de la escritura y el universo como un entramado de signos, la escritura será, lógicamente, 'acto de naturaleza'. (CC, 123)

Such a comment reveals a clear sense of the fundamental relevance of self-conscious literature to the world outside the text, to 'reality'. Goytisolo's novels in their increasingly metafictional form will always emphasize this interrelationship between the world of literature and the real world beyond.

One critic who does examine Goytisolo's fiction in terms of metafiction and the play with narrative levels is Robert Spires. He has argued that *Don Julián* merely foregrounds its literary codes and those it borrows, and therefore belongs to the same category as parody. For Spires, true metafiction is where the novel violates the levels of *énonciation* and *énoncé*, and this *Don Julián* does not do, whereas *Juan sin tierra* does. Yet, as I shall point out, *Juan sin tierra*, for all its overtness, does not actually violate narrative levels whereas this is precisely what does occur in *Don Julián*.

Like Levine, Spires interprets *Don Julián* in mimetic fashion. The disorienting features of the text are interpreted in terms of the central protagonist's mental state. In this way, Spires synthesizes *Don Julián*'s textual fragmentation by locating a non-problematic narrative persona, a fixed point that 'centres' the text. For Spires, the novel deals with an imaginary destruction of Spain, and the aesthetic techniques are to make the reader share the experience of the protagonist, feel it as 'real'. Of course, the destruction fails, reality reasserts itself at the end, but 'el lector implícito ha experimentado que una libertad estética lograda por medio de la imaginación creativa es también una realidad palpable'.[41]

In other words, the protagonist imagines the destruction of Spain and the text recreates that on an aesthetic level. The inevitable failure of the imaginary destruction is compensated by the reality of the (surrogate) aesthetic experience. This interpretation resembles Meerts' approach to *Señas de identidad*, as we saw in the last chapter. The relationship between the text and extra-textual reality is extremely important in Goytisolo's novels, but the novel attempts to go beyond the view of art as a surrogate for real action towards a more critical and productive reading of the relationship between the text and reality. And it does so precisely by the violation of the fictional codes. Let us examine the relationship of the narrative levels as it develops throughout the novel.

*   *   *   *   *

I have discussed the ambiguity in the novel between the protagonist as character situated in Tangiers and the author-narrator of the text we are reading. This is reflected in the interplay between the levels of the referential and the textual. While the first part opens in a style in which, although convoluted and baroque, and therefore to an extent self-consciously literary, the referential dimension seems to be intact, section six of Part One suggests much more a narrator concerned with the writing process:

> enredados en tu memoria, tal implicantes vides, los versos de quien, en habitadas soledades, con sombrío, impenitente ardor creara densa belleza ingrávida : indemne realidad que fúlgidamente perdura y, a través de los siglos, te dispensa sus señas redentoras en medio del caos ... (39)

He associates himself with the Poet, Góngora, whose verses are now described in terms of a 'reality' which is more durable than ordinary, physical reality. This reference alone raises questions about the relation between art and reality. It also makes the reader wonder as to the precise nature of the Gongorine influence.[42] We know that a book of Góngora's poems constitutes the protagonist's bedside reading (see pp. 15, 240). The poet's influence is also clearly behind the baroque style of the text and lines from the *Soledades* and from the 'Fábula de Polifemo y Galatea' (for example on p. 26: 'no es sordo el mar, la erudición engaña') are interwoven into the narrative. The lines might, then, suggest that the alienated protagonist finds consolation and inspiration in the beauty of the verses of Góngora. Alternatively the lines point to the writer of the text, reflecting on his own project, dialoguing with his literary inspiration and model. The chaos, the labyrinth of spongy material, can either be viewed as external reality, from which he redeems himself through writing, or it can refer to language itself, the material from which he has to work and produce the crafted object, the text. A similar idea is introduced in Part Three where the protagonist imagines himself 'adentrándote audazmente en la híspida e inculta maleza : parásito feliz del erizado bosque' (152) in what is both the whiskers of Tariq, 'ásperas selvas son sus dos bigotes' (152), and a prose style:

> prosa anárquica y bárbara, lejos de vuestro estilo peinado, de vuestra anémica, relamida escritura! : y, abriéndote paso entre la manigua, inaugurarás caminos y atajos, inventarás senderos y trochas, en abrupta ruptura con la oficial sintaxis y su secuela de dogmas y entredichos ... (152)

There is a constant semantic ambivalence in lines which, while seeming to refer to the situation of the protagonist in Tangiers, also point to the textual activity of the novel which consists of a satire and parody of the Spanish cultural canon. Even in terms of the situation of the protagonist, there is an occasional confusion of the two levels. For while the protagonist's experience is not self-consciously literary—he dreams of a 'real' second invasion of the Moors with 'llamas, dolores, guerras, muertes, asolamientos, fieros males' (16)—his acts at times have a 'literary' nature as, for example, in the scene in the library. His squashing of the insects is a metaphoric parallel of the narrator's activity on the textual level, satirizing and parodying the 'sacred' texts of the Spanish canon. Nevertheless, except for these occasional moments when one level merges into the next, the two remain separate and the narrative moves to and fro between them.

The phrase 'la impresión sensorial o la memoria del verso' suggests the same contrast between life and art. It can refer to the mental state of the protagonist in his wanderings, caught between his memories of Góngora's poetry and his sense impressions of the Moroccan reality. It can also suggest the writer constructing his text and wondering which actually forms the basis of his inspiration, reality or the literary corpus. The phrase 'oscilando de una a otra mientras caminas dibujando jeroglíficos' (39) intertwines the referential and the textual in a manner appropriately reminiscent of Góngora.[43] Like Góngora in the *Soledades*, the author is uninterested in the representation of reality. Instead he is moving within a world of codes and conventions. In Góngora it was the Renaissance poetic tradition, in Goytisolo it is on one level the canonical Spanish literary tradition and, on another, the traditional realist novel genre. In *Don Julián* the depiction of a character inhabiting a fictional world is interwoven with a self-conscious narrator caught up in the systems of social and literary discourse.

The same process of 'oscillation' from the referential to the self-referential is detectable in the following excerpt:

> inmerso en la multitud, pero sin integrarte a ella : a diferente diapasón : captando sutilmente la presencia (irrupción) de signos que interfieren (violan) el orden aparente de las cosas : movimientos bruscos, ruidos desabridos, gestos ásperos ... (40)

This refers ostensibly to the protagonist in his wanderings through Tangiers, reading that reality in a semiotic fashion. But it also uses the alien reality of the city as a metaphor for the subversive text itself, composed of signs which violate the order of the discursive and linguistic system, a text resistant to interpretation: 'ecuación cuyos términos desconoces, escritura que inútilmente quisieras descifrar' (40). This Gongorine play between the referential realm and the writing process is continued a few pages on when the narrator is led to posit the creation of a text whose meaning escapes even its creator (52). Such a notion contains certain post-structuralist, Barthesian echoes of the liberation of the text to a plurality of meanings free of the authority of the author.[44]

The end of the first part intertwines in quite startling fashion the textual and the referential. Trying to escape from one of his daily tormentors, Don Alvaro Peranzules, the protagonist takes refuge in what seems like a Turkish bath. The reality of the bath on the one hand and the literary, linguistic project on the other mingle in the narrative:

> mientras el sudor escurre por el cuerpo como si te hubieran baldeado y, poco a poco, naufragas en la languidez bienhechora: con los versos miríficos del Poeta incitándote sutilmente a la traición: ciñendo la palabra, quebrando la raíz, forzando la sintaxis, violentándolo todo ... (85)

The passage perfectly illustrates the way the text entertains simultaneously two related but entirely distinct projects, the protagonist's fantasy and the literary process. As the protagonist descends into dream, the literary project is born: 'sólita epifanía del verbo!' (85). The lines take the reader from a position within the protagonist's psyche, vividly sharing his physical sensations ('mientras el sudor escurre por el cuerpo') out of the referential dimension on to the textual process ('forzando la sintaxis') without any attempt to naturalize the link between the two within the narrative itself.

*   *   *   *   *

Part Two similarly opens with ambiguous hints of psychic introversion and textual self-consciousness. The protagonist is entering the café with his friend Tariq. The use of the name is deliberately intended to initiate the confusion of levels of reality and dream. We know from early in Part One that the protagonist has a friend called Tariq (14), but the name recalls the other Tariq involved in the original invasion of Spain. The reader is unsure if this is part of the dream following on from the previous section or a real part of the protagonist's daily itinerary.

> hacia dentro, hacia dentro: en la atmósfera algodonosa y quieta, por los recovecos del urbano laberinto: como en la galería de espejos de una feria, sin encontrar la salida y con los papamoscas, en la acera riendo de cada uno de tus tropiezos ... (89)

Following on from the protagonist's apparent slide into sleep at the end of Part One, this suggests a descent into dream, an 'atmósfera algodonosa'. The enigmatic images of the protagonist's self-consciousness, 'con los papamoscas, en la acera, riendo de cada uno de tus tropiezos : pagando para devenir objeto de mancomunada irrisión' (89), give a psychological solidity to the narrator-protagonist and his world. He appears as someone afflicted with acute self-consciousness, bordering on a schizoid personality. This is understandable in terms of his position as an exile, alienated from his native land and his inherited identity and thus prey to a chronic case of ontological insecurity:[45]

> las calles están desiertas ahora y la luz de los faroles agiganta desmesuradamente vuestras sombras e invalida, de rechazo vuestra precaria, insegura realidad ... (89)

The regular use of the *tú* form had emphasized this image of a split personality. All of this then serves to reinforce the sense of the 'real' human identity of the protagonist and to see the narrative as charting his mental processes, the formal features, such as the *tú* form, reflecting his condition. Yet at the same time this 'human' reality is complicated by further references to fictional artifice:

> las viviendas se superponen como maquetas de cartón y el nocturno cielo nublado imita un decorado ingenuo de bambalinas ... (89)

The image of an ontologically insecure individual is present in this passage and in the novel as a whole, but can be seen as part of a wider and more self-reflexive project which is the subversion of the notion of an ontologically convincing fictional character: 'falso, falso : personajes de una obra no escrita, inexistentes los dos' (89). It is tempting to read the 'obra no escrita' as the work of mimesis that *Don Julián* refuses to be.

At this stage the reader is led to question whether the confusing, disorienting appearance of the narrative has a mimetic or an anti-mimetic purpose, whether it is intended to convey more vividly the tortured psyche of the protagonist or to undermine the illusion of a protagonist altogether. The self-reflexive allusions have the effect of alerting the reader to his own role. The phrase 'la duda es tu única certeza' (89) acquires a sense of appropriateness for him as well. Already the protagonist's trip 'por los recovecos del urbano laberinto' (89) of Tangiers or of his own mind can suggest the voyage through the labyrinthine meanderings of the text, as planned by the writer-narrator himself (see p. 52). The mention of the 'galería de espejos' is a not inappropriate metaphor of the text itself.[46]

Part Two has a dual focus, both aspects motivated by images on the television screen in the café. The first part (91–109) develops the fantasy of Alvarito and the snake-charmer, motivated, it would appear, by certain childhood experiences such as the trauma of a Natural Sciences class and the dread inspired by the sermons of Tithamer Toth. This part develops the theme of the protagonist's psyche, delving into aspects of his past related to his sexual awakening. It will expose all the protagonist's sexual hang-ups which later sections of the novel will develop.

In the second part (109–124) the psyche of the protagonist gives way to a more national theme, constituting as it does a satire of all the sacred myths of the Regime: Seneca, stoicism, the liberation of the Alcázar of Toledo, the 98 Generation's mythologization of the Castilian landscape. The dual focus of this chapter corresponds with Goytisolo's assertion that the novel is 'a un tiempo psicoanálisis de un individuo y de un país'.[47] However, whereas in the first section the set is towards the level of *histoire*, the personality of the protagonist, in the second the level of *discours*, the process of enunciation of the text as literary parody, comes to the fore.

The first section builds up a strong sense of the personality of the central protagonist and the psychological quirks of his character: his sense of trauma left over from childhood experiences and the influence of a tyrannical school-teacher, the early awakening of sexual feeling and accompanying guilt. Reminiscence ('rostros y rostros ...' [91]) and imagination (e.g. the child's visit to the snake charmer's hut and witnessing of copulation between the latter and Putifar [98]) merge in a hallucinatory fashion.

This psychological background is defined in terms of certain texts. Lengthy sections of Little Red Riding Hood and the sermons of Tithamer Toth appear regularly and are juxtaposed in an overt way with repetitions from earlier parts of the novel. Little Red Riding Hood is accompanied by references to overheard conversations about neighbours' perverse sexual habits and the episode of voyeurism referred to earlier. This prefigures the end of the novel where the story will provide the frame for a sadistic sexual fantasy.

Similarly, Toth's sermon is regularly interrupted by references to the protagonist's situation in Tangiers, as though to point out how the protagonist's life has become a perfect illustration of the dangers he was warned against as a child. Indeed, towards the end of the novel, the dire consequences that the religious strictures warned of will be gleefully enacted by the protagonist's new self.

Even in this section, the omnipresence and evidence of texts can serve to divert the reader's attention away from the tortured psyche toward the level of discourse itself. The emphasis on the textual is reinforced when in the second section of Part Two, the personal gives way altogether to a parodic attack on national culture and literary myths. Here the intertextual clearly predominates over the mimetic, and any reading in terms of *histoire* gives way to attention to the play of the *discours*. The culmination of this is the final section in Part Two.

This passage (124–27) constitutes the most explicit reference to the textual proceeding in the novel. It stands in many ways as the aesthetic manifesto of the novel. It is worth noting how the passage still plays with the two levels, the protagonist and his fantasized invasion ('pero detente : no galopes : la traición se realizará : tu sierpe tenaz aguarda el secular desquite' [126]), and the narrator and his project for linguistic subversion ('tu vuelo acariciante ciñe el lenguaje opaco de un esplendor sombrío' [126]), without explicitly linking the two. The most natural interpretation of the two levels is in terms of complementarity. The formal subversion parallels and complements the thematic transgression.[48]

In practice, however, the effect is much more complex and confusing. The reader is aware of the clash between reading the text as representing the hallucinatory mental meanderings of the protagonist or as the process of enunciation of a writer bent on an act of linguistic revolt. In spite of the fact that Goytisolo may have intended to create a complementarity of form and content, the actual effect is one of narrative dislocation which nonetheless achieves magnificently the aim of disturbing a conventional reading.

*   *   *   *   *

Part Three develops out of the latter section of Part Two. After the apparent preliminary dreaming, induced by kif and the television images in the café, the protagonist seems to have resumed his wandering around the city, directing himself towards a blood-donation centre:

> DONNEZ VOTRE SANG SAUVEZ UNE VIE
> el llamamiento te persigue obsesivamente y esta misma tarde, al oscurecer (la tiniebla favorece de ordinario tus negros designios) te presentarás en el lugar indicado ... (131)

That this too is a fantasy is indicated by the aside: '(no estás en Tánger, sino en España ...)'. What follows is the imaginary invasion and desecration of Spain, starting with the protagonist's infection of the peninsula with rabies and the subsequent invitation to the Moorish harka to lay waste his homeland. The 'invasion' soon reveals itself as a textual assault through parody, pastiche and satire of the Spanish tradition and the linguistic subversion of traditional prose (see especially p. 152). Just as the process is initiated by the sight of a slogan which sums up the humane values of the hated society which the protagonist aims to subvert by doing the opposite (causing death through infection), the passage outlining the fantasy is a description of the symptoms of rabies taken directly from a medical encyclopedia: '(en los manuales de medicina al uso se acostumbra a distinguir tres periodos ...)' (133).

The rest of the chapter deals systematically with all aspects of the post-Civil War literary canon, especially the devotion to the 98 Generation's mystical glorification of the Castilian landscape, and other patriotic works. Don Alvaro symbolizes this whole tradition, and his deflation and disintegration under the steady attack of parody is merely a comic representation of the textual process:

> moscas, abejas, hormigas, tábanos, arañas que entran y salen de los libros, devoran el papel, corrompen el estilo, infectan las ideas : la máscara de don Alvaro se deshincha y arruga, y sus miembros se abandonan a un irresistible baile de San Vito ... (180)

In Part Three, on the story level, the situation of the protagonist is eclipsed by his fantasy which occupies the whole chapter. However, the

fantasy is almost entirely overshadowed by the activity of the enunciation, linguistic and literary self-consciousness. An example is the second
section. This commences with a statement that is a corruption of the
well-known adage 'La ignorancia es la madre de todos los males'. In the
text this becomes 'La patria es la madre de todos los vicios' (a version
Goytisolo has admitted to hearing from Buñuel: see CC, 187). The
importance of the phrase in the context lies especially in its status as a
play on words. The passage goes on to develop the theme of treason
with further plays of language:

> y lo más expeditivo y eficaz para curarse de ella consiste en venderla, en
> traicionarla : venderla? : por un plato de lentejas o por un Perú, por mucho o
> por nada ... (134)

The passage is characterized by a joyfully arbitrary choice of words
with little regard to their meaning:

> a quién? : al mejor postor : o entregarla, regalo envenenado a quien nada sabe
> ni quiere saber de ella : a un rico o a un pobre, a un indiferente, a un
> enamorado : por el simple, y suficiente, placer de la traición ... (134)

The passage continues a ludic approach to language as an example
of a hedonistic indulgence in gratuitous pleasure: 'abandonarse al juego
excitante de las combinaciones'. Treason against one's country is
enacted in a play with the word 'treason': 'traición grave, traición
alegre : traición meditada, traición súbita : traición oculta, traición
abierta ...' (135).

In the penultimate section, the invasion is given an explicitly
linguistic purpose. Julián and his invaders intend to rescue the Arab
words from the Spanish lexicon. As well as an intertextual homage to
Cervantes, this is an imaginative rendition of the perspective on Spanish
history promoted by Américo Castro regarding the debt owed to Islam
in the forging of what is today recognized as Spain. Goytisolo satirizes
the notion of 'pureza' by urging the Arabs to 'adueñarse de aquello que
en puridad os pertenece' (196) in the understanding that it will
'paralizar la circulación del lenguaje' (196). The grammarian's concern
for 'la pureza del idioma' will be a certain cause of the Spaniard's death.
The passages in Cuban, Mexican and Argentinian slang are both a
statement of the enriching, life-giving consequences of linguistic plurality and also a comment on the link between language and colonialism.
The reader is made aware of the political implications of linguistic
diversity, the way language can channel opposition to a system of
cultural and political hegemony.

*   *   *   *   *

If Part Three was an extension and development of the latter section of
Part Two, Part Four takes up and develop the earlier section dealing

with themes and motifs of Alvaro's childhood. Part Four seems at first to refer most forcefully to the realm of the referential, the protagonist and his inner conflict, his childhood trauma and his desire to destroy his former self. Here the textual features seem to push the reader in the direction of the *énoncé*.[49] Yet it is also true that the literary, self-conscious references are equally strong in this part, reinforcing the split already mentioned.

The chapter begins with references to the theory of information and oblique references to Spanish censorship. Levine says of the opening that it 'satiriza la pretensión de verosimilitud del Ministerio de Información y el dogma religioso'.[50] Clearly, there is a pun, given the historical circumstances, with the inappropriate name of the Spanish Ministry. However, the subsequent quotation from Umberto Eco takes up the reference and projects us towards a linguistic theory of the text. In the 'Presentación crítica de Blanco White', Goytisolo referred to the theory of information and Genette's concept of *vraisemblance* to describe both the kind of conventional narrative he was trying to get away from, 'la obra cerrada, reiterativa, insignificante, que no quita ni añade nada al corpus de las obras anteriores a ella', and the ideal form of writing he was trying to cultivate.[51]

Umberto Eco, in *The Open Work*, outlines the difference between 'meaning' and 'information':

> The meaning of a message [...] is a function of the order, the conventions, and the redundancy of its structure. The more one respects the laws of probability (the pre-established principles that guide the organization of a message and are reiterated via the repetition of foreseeable elements), the clearer and less ambiguous its meaning will be. Conversely, the more improbable, ambiguous, unpredictable, and disordered the structure, the greater the information—information here understood as potential, as the inception of possible orders.[52]

In information theory an increase in 'information' leads to a decrease in 'communication'. Poetry is traditionally a form of language which lacks the usual redundancy that allows everyday communication to take place. Poems are thus semantically dense, producing a richer set of messages than any other form of language. Clearly, *Don Julián* can be viewed as a novel that aspires towards 'information' in the sense meant by Eco of a range of possible 'meanings' as opposed to one fixed, unambiguous meaning. Eco goes on in *The Open Work* to distinguish between the kinds of art that result from these different concepts. Traditional art uses common conventions and, while still producing unusual and original meanings because of its departure from straightforward communication, nonetheless does little to alter our perceptions:

> 'classical' art avails itself of sudden deviations and temporary ruptures only so as to eventually reconfirm the structures accepted by the common

> sensibility it addresses, thereby opposing certain laws of redundancy only to
> re-endorse them later, albeit in a different fashion ... (94)

Contemporary art, on the other hand, aims at breaking with the laws of probability and placing the common discourse in crisis. The contemporary artist aims to

> break with the conventions of accepted language and the usual ways of
> linking thoughts together, so as to offer his reader a range of possible
> interpretations and a web of suggestions that are quite different from the kind
> of meaning conveyed by the communication of a univocal message. (95)

Don Julián aspires towards a 'contemporary' as opposed to a 'classical' approach. Doing so involves a move away from the classical mimetic tradition which, by its adherence to the principles of verisimilitude and its founding of the meaning of the text on the central point of view of the narrator, encourages the 'mensaje unívoco'. By disrupting the mimetic reading in terms of the psyche of the narrator-protagonist and by its self-referential process drawing attention to the surface features of the text, *Don Julián* posits the text not as the product of a single source but as 'una posibilidad de interpretaciones, una serie de sugerencias'.

Part Four, therefore, reveals an enhanced tension between the apparent psychological interiorization of the narrative—the total separation from external reality and entry into the psychic fantasy of the protagonist, and the equally apparent self-referential elements that constantly flaunt the reality of the text, of writing and discourse, of the fictive process. Part of this again involves the fantasy of Alvaro-Julián, lived out as if it were a story or a theatrical performance. The whole of Part Four, as indeed the three previous parts, enacts Eco's theory alluded to in the first page. The parodied version of the Little Red Riding Hood story serves as a framework for an accumulation of disparate discourses, from ecclesiastical and journalistic to commercial.

Once again the reader is drawn empathetically to the climax of the narrator-protagonist's neurotic struggle with his past self, his childhood traumas and his attempt to destroy once and for all an identity to which he feels no longer any attachment, but at the same time propelled outwards to an awareness of the puns and plays of meaning, the combinations of discourses, the intertextual literary references. The text refuses to synthesize these two tendencies and the reader is unable to do so.

The reader might try to synthesize the duality by claiming that this is how the protagonist exorcizes the demons of his past, by deliberately and outrageously distorting certain classical discourses: the children's fairy-tale and the religious sermon. A mimetic motive for the choice of the Caperucito story can be posited if we interpret the first occurrence of the story in Part Two (95–100) as suggesting the coincidence of the story, read by the 'abnegada sirvienta', with some childhood sexual trauma, the sexual awakening of the protagonist. However, this still does not explain the self-referential features. The protagonist is not recognized as the writer of the text. He and the text-author remain separate entities. Hence, looking at the narrative in terms of the protagonist, the importance of texts suggests, if anything, the notion of a character who, rather than an individuated subject, the archetype of the conventional, realist novel, is in fact structured by social discourses, a common characteristic of the post-modernist hero. Charles Russell has described this phenomenon as follows:

> The environment that post-modern characters confront is described as a fictive construct, as systems of social discourse. These characters, positioned self-consciously within the social framework, encounter no natural world, but rather a cultural reality, a reality structured by the patterns of social desire, discourse and ideology which manifest themselves throughout the environment and the character's lives.[53]

This corresponds closely to the situation in *Don Julián*. It must be remembered that Goytisolo commented of his narrator that 'ha renunciado a la realidad física de su país, pero no a su cultura; a la tierra, pero no a la palabra'.[54]

Throughout the rest of the chapter, textual features intrude which break up the narrative, seem arbitrary displays of the story-teller's authority. As the fantasized destruction of Alvarito begins, the narrator cannot avoid entering the picture:

> (siguen, aquí, diversas apreciaciones anatómico-morales del interesado : piel blanca, manos finas, pestañas rizadas, carácter tierno, virtud acendrada mutatis mutandis según el código significante de los diferentes órganos informativos y su finalidad gnoseológica) ... (206)

More than a mere display of narratorial omnipotence, the aside draws attention to narrative conventions and stereotypes. The reader senses that rather than, or as well as, the narrator-protagonist indulging in a fantasized torture and execution of a side of his personality, he is witnessing a writer taking pleasure in violating a cultural stereotype. Part of this is the 'corruption' and 'perversion' of the traditional fairy story by having it recast in homosexual terms.

The unfolding of the fantasy is characterized by further self-conscious references distracting attention from the 'content' of the fantasy towards the method of telling. There is a sense of the novel generating itself by association of ideas. An example is the section in which 'tortas' is substituted by 'torrijas' (206) and then gives way to the recipe which has no apparent motivation and seems merely to follow on automatically from the reference to 'torrijas'. This is followed by similar interruptions relating to the 'superurbanización GUADARRAMA' and the Rolex watch (208–09). Such associations are difficult to naturalize. Viewed in mimetic terms, they can possibly be read as reflecting the state of mental crisis and perturbation at this stage of the protagonist's daily fantasy, his imagining interfered with by random recollections of earlier experience or images on the TV. However, this is unsatisfactory. These intrusions are not random or chaotic. They appear as the result of a deliberate, playful rewriting of a classic tale:

> soy Caperucito Rojo y traigo unas torrijas y un bote de manteca de parte de
> mamá anda, entra, hijito: levanta el pestillo y empuja la puerta interior
> funcional adecuado a las categorías axiológicas del paisaje: decorado sobrio,
> luz indirecta, chimenea de hogar ... (208)

Throughout the rest of the chapter there are numerous details alluding to the narrative process. If we read this section as the protagonist's fantasy, it is a fantasy which assumes the explicit form of a narrative. There are images of the theatre: '(alarmado)' (206); 'la cortante caída del telón' (230); 'teatralmente' (231); the cinema: 'fondo sonoro' (210); 'los espectadores sensibles' (212); 'la luz, el ambiente' (213); and to narratorial choice: 'no no es así' (210); 'eliges definitivamente la segunda versión' (220), as too the earlier reference in Part Three to 'trujamán de la escena' (185).

Such deliberately visible textual features have the effect of undercutting the psychological base of the narrative at this point and leading the reader to interpret the fantasy as a subversive rewriting of certain conventional discourses. One of these, the most obvious one, is the traditional story of Red Riding Hood. At another level is the discourse of the traditional novel itself which *Don Julián* throughout, but especially in this last chapter, has set about formally undermining. At yet another level is an entire set of social codes and values relating to sexuality, attitudes to children, relations with parents, honesty, duty, which the novel similarly seeks to transgress. Such social codes are usually enshrined in morality tales such as Red Riding Hood and the sermons of Tithamer Toth as well as, on a grander scale, in a society's literary canon.[55]

In this connection, another important feature of this section of the novel which contributes to a textual reading is the intertextual link with Lautréamont's *Les Chants de Maldoror*. Levine, in her book, recognizes the influence of Lautréamont. She points to the similarities and parallels between Part Four of *Don Julián* and the sixth book of the *Chants*, in particular 'el afán de liberación en los dos protagonistas y el modo en que se autodefinen en oposición a los valores que les rodean' (231). Levine stresses the similarity of values expressed by the two authors, and her account presents an interesting analysis of the thematic parallels and contrasts between them.[56]

There is, however, another important dimension to the intertextual link between Goytisolo's novel and the *Chants* on the aesthetic level, the two works' approaches to language and literature, and the implicit socio-moral implications of these. Goytisolo's empathy with Lautréamont is not only on an ethical level, but also on the aesthetic level. Lautréamont's masterpiece is not only an attack on the bourgeois tastes and values of his time, but it is above all an ethical attack carried out through a radical subversion of literary conventions. According to Paul Knight, Lautréamont's works

> call in question and undermine 'innocent' assumptions about the essential problems of fiction: the relation between the written text and the world (or 'reality'), between the writer and the reader; the arbitrariness of the fictional text, the dangers and absurdity of expecting an easily digestible meaning; the relation of literary forms and devices consciously and ironically played against one another; the question of originality. It is the problem of writing fiction which is continually posed in these texts.[57]

Another point which Knight makes is that 'Maldoror presupposes the traditional novel with all its assumptions, deliberately breaks all its rules. It has to be read with these texts in mind, parallel with them, as a form of counterfiction which is continually pointing back to them'. He goes on to add that 'the traditional novel cannot be abolished. But it can be subtly undermined, its forms can be experimented with, its philosophical structure and its pretensions exposed' (21). According to Knight, the killing of Mervyn in Book VI is really the killing of the traditional novel, the 'little novel' (21). Similarly, in *Don Julián*, just as Alvaro Peranzules is the representative of the staid Spanish literary tradition, and is 'killed' in a prolonged act of literary parody and satire, it is clear that Alvarito, the former self of the narrator, is, at the same time, his former literary self for whom the writing of the text *Don Julián* constitutes an act of literary suicide and artistic rebirth.

The intertextual dialogue with Lautréamont underlines the literary nature of the final chapter and reminds the reader that the text's activity is to be understood on an aesthetic plane. The ethical message of *Don Julián*, as with the *Chants*, requires that it be read in literary rather than realistic terms, and for this it is essential to disrupt the mimetic interpretation of the text.[58]

In this way, the final part of *Don Julián*, while seeming to be the most 'interior' section, delving into the psyche of the central character, and lending itself most strongly to an interpretation in terms of psychological realism, reveals itself at the same time to be the most flagrantly intertextual and literary. Alvarito's relationship with Julián is another version of the Mervyn–Maldoror relation and the chapter, as with the *Chants*, becomes a play with the possibilities of fiction and a parody of traditional narrative. The reader is left hesitating between identification with a character who, via fantasy, enacts a tortured act of self-immolation, and a narrator who deliberately carries out a literary transgression.

Language in *Don Julián*

The same contrast observed throughout between the narrator-author and narrator-protagonist, *énonciation* and *énoncé*, is discerned also in the treatment of language between the word and its meaning, or more accurately, between the signifier and the signified. The novel sets out to undermine the standard link between the signifier and the signified which places the priority on the signified. In this, naturally, Goytisolo reveals a broader target of attack than merely the Spanish literary tradition. The ideas in *Don Julián* are very much in accord with contemporary post-Saussurean linguistic theory and its critique of the sign.

The central passage of the novel in this connection is the one which ends Part II. After an invocation to Góngora, the 'altivo, gerifalte Poeta', the speaker makes an impassioned plea to attain a level of linguistic autonomy in which the signifier is free from the attachment to the signified:

> móvil, móvil : sin otro alimento y sustancia que tu rica palabra : palabra sin historia, orden verbal autónomo, engañoso delirio : poema : alfanje o rayo : imaginación y razón en ti se aúnan a tu propio servicio : palabra liberada de secular servidumbre : ilusión realista del pájaro que entra en el cuadro y picotea las uvas : palabra-transparente, palabra-reflejo, testimonio ruinoso yerto e inexpresivo ... (125)

This section prefigures the theoretical principles that will underlie *Juan sin tierra*. It echoes the critique by contemporary semiotics of the realist approach to the process of signification. Goytisolo, as we have already pointed out, described *Don Julián* as 'escritura y no copia'. In *Don Julián* the approach to language echoes the structuralists' critique of positivism's confident use of language as a transparent tool to describe reality and in particular the literary manifestation of this in classical realism.[59]

The literary presence which hovers over this project in *Don Julián* is that of Góngora. Goytisolo has summed up Góngora's style as 'hacer salir al idioma de su transparencia ilusoria [...] imponernos, a brazo partido, la presencia opaca, densa, casi física de las escurridizas palabras' (D, 181–82). The debt to Góngora in *Don Julián* has been remarked by several critics, in particular Sobejano and Lázaro.[60] The latter provides a list of Gongorine forms used by the novelist: *cultismos, alusiones mitológicas, adagios, fórmulas, hipérbaton, metáforas, perí-*

frasis alusivas, aliteración, paranomasia, plurimembración, unión de opuestos, hipérboles.[61] All of these baroque techniques have the effect of foregrounding language, endowing language with a degree of opacity, semantic density, which substitutes the passive consumption of the meaning with a more active perception of the play of meaning:

> tu vuelo acariciante ciñe el lenguaje opaco de un esplendor sombrío, el verbo encadenado se libera, su arquitectura deviene fluida, la mezquina palabra despierta y ejecuta la implacable traición ... (126)

The liberation of language from the referential illusion and creation of an 'orden verbal autónomo' is not a flight into an escapist realm of art but rather a restoration to art, to literature of properties inherent to it. The passage, and especially the term 'palabra sin historia', have provoked criticism of Goytisolo for wanting to escape from reality into art. Jo Labanyi criticizes Goytisolo for wishing to produce 'a text whose artificiality makes it autonomous and therefore unaccountable to history'.[62] If this means a discourse whose ultimate 'truth' cannot be verified by appeal to some stable reality or 'history' outside the text, then this is undoubtedly true. One of the purposes of the novel, as we have seen, has been to reject the notion of a 'true' 'historical' discourse. As Labanyi rightly says, Goytisolo's novel, by emphasizing the literary discourse of Francoism, 'also emphasizes that it was a man-made product and not "given" or "natural"' (210).[63] However, by emphasizing its own textuality and its inevitable dependence on the discourse of the culture and society in which it is produced, the novel implies that escape from discourse into some objective realm of history is impossible.

On one level the term can be read as reaffirmation of what is a fundamental feature of literary language but often ignored. As Linda Hutcheon reminds us, 'the autonomy of the referents of literary signs in relation to real referents is [...] not a modern radical realization of recent criticism' but 'a reality of the novel genre'.[64] The speaker invokes the freedom of the artist to create and use language without the constraints of verisimilitude, the 'ilusión realista'.

The significance of 'palabra sin historia' would seem also, in the context, to suggest a text that transcends its historical context. In *El furgón de cola*, Goytisolo had reflected on the enduring nature of Góngora's verse beyond the historical period in which it was produced, whereas the work of those poets of the eighteenth century concerned with social issues was forgotten (FC, 280–81). The continued relevance of Góngora's poetry derives from its artistic and literary qualities, not from any reference it makes to the socio-historical circumstances of the time. Goytisolo's aim in *Don Julián*, as the epigraph from Sade tells us, is to produce a similarly enduring text that will transcend its historical context. 'Palabra sin historia' comes to mean, therefore, language which is atemporal, not in the sense of lacking reference to a particular reality or to reality in general, but language which is timeless, capable of being appreciated by and affecting the reader in any period. The way the text does this is, as we have stressed throughout, by using language and form to challenge the reader, much as Góngora did in his verse. This, the text hopes, it will continue to do long after the satire of the culture of the Franco regime has ceased to interest a future reader.

One of the text's principal techniques is a form of linguistic opacity which has the effect of alerting the reader to the signifying potential of language. One of the best examples is the passage in question. The syntax, reducing the passage to a succession of phrases, reduces syntagmatic coherence. As Antony Easthope remarks, referring to Saussurean theory, 'the relationship of signifier and signified becomes stabilized as signifiers are strung together sequentially along a temporal line'.[65] By disrupting normal syntax, Goytisolo's narrative releases the potential for language's associations. This leads to an increase in its capacity for 'information' as opposed to 'communication' in the terms of information theory. This passage typifies the novel as a whole in its use of baroque language to avoid the usual term, draw attention to language and expand the range of connotations. It uses neologisms ('zapateril'), intertextual references (to Fray Luis' poem 'Profecía del Tajo' in the phrase 'el fluvial profeta') and draws on the Arabic roots of words to add to their connotation ('guadalajara verbal').[66] The reference to the television as an 'artefacto' whose 'ciclópica pupila aspira a inmovilizarte' includes a reference to Góngora's 'Fábula de Polifemo y Galatea', as well as the suggestion of the medium's ability to ensnare the individual into accepting and identifying with its ideology. The academicians are described as 'hinchas' of the 'estoico filósofo', and later 'babeando siempre ante el inaccesible antro o la ampulosa excrecencia inútil'.

The language combines sexual and literary allusion in a way that characterizes the novel as a whole. The 'inaccesible antro' relates to the regular metaphor in the text for the vagina and projects back to the 'españolita' mentioned in Part One and her 'gruta sagrada' (27). 'Ampulosa excrecencia inútil' could refer to the girl's figure ('la brusca y candorosa insurgencia de los pechos' [27]) or the Academician's useless sexual member or the empty style they seek to preserve ('cuánta proliferación cancerosa e inútil, cuánta excrecencia parasitaria y rastrera!' [156]). The phrase 'mesiánico adorador de sus cadenas' links a historical criticism of Spaniards as being willing victims of repression and the idea of signifiers chained to signifieds ('el verbo encadenado se libera' [126]). Spain is described as a 'lugar común del lechuguino concepto' which again merges connotations of linguistic banality, ordinariness, meanness and sexual inadequacy ('la robusta culebra suplantará su concepto mísero y lechuguino' [127]). This combination of the connotations of repressed sexuality, intellectual pusillanimity and linguistic and literary rigidity contributes to the text's striving after polysemy.

Don Julián not only parodies the discourses of Official Spain but explicitly points to the social control of language. A normative, prescriptive attitude to language is associated with the ideology of Official Spain:

> imagen de nuestra alma
> reflejo de nuestro espíritu
> nuestro, nuestro, nuestro
> apostólico
> trascendental
> ecuménico (193)

Official Spain is seen to show a bourgeois possessive attitude to language:

> los carpetos reivindican con orgullo sus derechos de propiedad
> sobre el lenguaje (192)

Against this bourgeois ideology, the narrative ranges an anarchistic one:

> LA PROPRIETE C'EST LE VOL
> ET
> TOT OU TARD
> LA CLASSE POSSEDANTE SERA DETRUITE (195)

The repetition of the stock notions about the export of the language to South America as part of a moral crusade, a beneficial transfer of values, 'nosotros lo llevamos a la otra orilla del Atlántico con la moral y las leyes, la espiga y el arado, la religión, la justicia' (193) emphasizes the element of colonial dominance, language as a form of colonial control. Against this the text opposes the mocking sections in South American dialect. The quasi-unintelligibility of the dialectal sections, their witty, irrepressible critique of the attitude of the mother-country, illustrate the linguistic revenge of these ex-colonies. These passages serve to suggest the connection between linguistic independence and political and ideological independence, but they also point to an essential theme of the novel, the resistance to interpretation as a means of subversion and asserting one's independence.

Section Three of Part III accumulates a series of images of Spanish culture, 'nuestros símbolos vetustos' (136), making it clear that they are the target of the invasion. The Moorish invasion takes the form of a contrasting juxtaposition of images from the enemy culture, 'imágenes líricas, suntuosas' (136). The technique of this passage prefigures the rest of the chapter; traditional images, quotes, symbols, names are gathered in such a way that their context is removed and they are presented as mere names, labels, signifiers. Goytisolo's novel explicitly contrasts images which are dynamic, 'acuden en tropel', with ones which are static, 'yacen arrinconados' (136).

The passage obviously implies a value judgement on the part of the speaker, but the important point is simply the reality of those images as components of a rhetoric, an ideological discourse which is self-sustaining rather than as manifestations of some eternal essence. The passage also suggests, in its reference to the 'mask', the ideology that controls the individual, locates him as a subject acting out a preordained role: 'la máscara nos pesa : el papel que representamos es falso' (137). The hold of ideology as represented in discourse must be broken. The irreverent subversive prose of Don Julián aims to answer 'una imperiosa necesidad de aire' (137). The arbitrary collection of names and images implies that, far from being a true reflection of transcendent values, they represent merely a discourse, a collection of clichés.

The Role of the Reader

One of the features of the self-reflexive nature of Goytisolo's later novels is the increasing recognition of the reader's role. In Don Julián the self-reflexive elements can be seen to refer not just to the writing process but also to the concomitant process of reading. As we have already seen, the protagonist in Tangiers is often shown to register reality in a semiotic fashion. In his walk around the city he is seen to be 'captando sutilmente la presencia (irrupción) de signos que interfieren (violan) el orden aparente de las cosas' (39–40). Goytisolo is fond of the analogy between the urban landcape and the text. He calls Juan sin tierra a 'texto-Medina'. The same could be said of Paisajes después de la batalla, where to gaze at the map of the Paris metro is described as 'ceder al recuerdo, evasión, desvarío; abrirse a la utopía, la ficción y la fábula' (110). In Makbara one can point to the last chapter, 'Lectura del espacio en Xemaá-el-Fná'. By the end of Part One of Don Julián the protagonist's daily periplus through the labyrinthine streets of Tangiers reads like a metaphor for the reader's intricate passage through the complexities of the text where everything is

> extraño todo : el designio, la fábrica y el modo : avanzando a tientas por una realidad porosa y caliza, ajena a las leyes de la lógica y del europeo sentido común ... (70)

and where the reader, like the protagonist, his conventional procedures of intelligibility frustrated, advances 'absorto en la esotérica motivación del itinerario' (83).

The novel takes as its aim the disturbance of the reader's interpretive strategies. Early on we see the narrator-protagonist concerned with finding 'the truth':

> indemne realidad que fúlgidamente perdura y, a través de los siglos, te dispensa sus señas redentoras en medio del caos: rescatándote del engañoso laberinto: de tu cotidiano periplo por dédalos de materia incierta, esponjosa: sin saber dónde está la verdad: en la impresión sensorial o la memoria del verso: oscilando de una a otra mientras caminas dibujando jeroglíficos ... (39)

This search for truth and certainty mirrors exactly the reader's hermeneutic urge on encountering a novel of the complexity and obscurity, at first, of Don Julián:

> y el despertar ambiguo en ciudad anónima sin saber dónde estás: dentro, fuera?: buscando ansiosamente una certidumbre ... (14)

The analogy between the protagonist's predicament and the one that the text creates for the reader is reinforced in the continuation of the quotation cited earlier:

> captando sutilmente la presencia (irrupción) de signos que interfieren (violan) el orden aparente de las cosas : movimientos bruscos, ruidos desabridos, gestos ásperos : pequeñas (sordas) explosiones de violencia : ecuación cuyos términos desconoces, escritura que inútilmente quisieras descifrar ... (39–40)

By dissolving the illusion of a rounded character or 'human' narrator, and by dethroning the figure of the author, the text discourages the reader from a fixing of its meaning in some transcendent, pre-linguistic realm and instead encourages an active reading of the textual surface as a play of signs. The text dramatizes this and shows the narrator-protagonist (and, by extension, the reader) caught early on in this complex sign system which is the world, still entertaining a nostalgic hankering after a stable truth, a reality:

> al acecho de la realidad oculta tras el engañoso barniz : mensaje cifrado cuyas señas llegan con intermitencia hasta ti, requiriendo bruscamente tu atención y extinguiéndose al punto ... (42)

The protagonist experiences the world as text and his experience mirrors the reader's in reading Don Julián. Meaning is seen to be a fluid and unstable affair, less a truth to be discovered than an effect to be constantly produced. It recalls Barthes' account of contemporary écriture as 'writing [that] ceaselessly posits meaning ceaselessly to evaporate it, carrying out a systematic exemption of meaning'.[67]

The protagonist's attempts to decipher the reality that surrounds him lead to a curious episode:

> un muchacho que avanza transistor en mano ... han escuchado ustedes, señoras y señores, una selección del balé, la sífilis de Federico Xopén : sífilis o sílfides? : igual da : el mensaje está ahí ... (42)

The message that he receives is the idea for the contamination of Spain via syphilis/rabies that will constitute the basis of Part III. However, what is interesting is the communication of the message. The Chopin reference is arbitrary but the title 'Les Sylphides' ('sílfides' in Spanish) provides the opportunity of the acoustic equivalent of a slip of the tongue. The protagonist hears 'sílfides' but thinks 'sífilis'. This can be explained in Freudian fashion by the presence of unconscious forces or mental conflicts. The protagonist, in a throwback to his rigidly moralistic upbringing, is clearly preoccupied by the possibility of contracting syphilis—hence the daily injections at the local chemist's, and the elation on leaving (31). It leads him to plan his revenge in the form of contamination.[68] However, the episode and the verbal pun, suggestive as it is of a precarious relation between the signifier and the signified, points to the linguistic nature of the novel's real process of subversion which will involve a freeing of language from its fixed meanings.

The protagonist has momentarily lost contact with the 'meaning', the signified, of the voice on the radio. Left with the signifier, the ambiguous acoustic image, 'sífilis o sílfides', he rapidly abandons any concern with establishing the true meaning, 'igual da', and instead accepts the inspiration provided by the linguistic ambiguity. The implication of the phrase 'el mensaje está ahí' is that the linguistic subversion consequent on liberating the signifier is the key to the attack on his homeland. Since in the context of the novel the thematic level (contamination through syphilis) is never really developed, whereas the linguistic and literary process assumes ever greater prominence, it is clear that *Don Julián* institutes a formalistic inversion of the traditional narrative process. The text's lateral commenting on its formal and linguistic processes, while at first seeming subordinate to the thematic or mimetic level (the representation of the personal situation of the central protagonist), in fact emerges as its primary level of functioning.

The protagonist's wanderings serve as a sign of the narrator's aspiration to a text which will resist interpretation and whose meaning will escape even his authority:

> perdiéndote en dédalo de callejas de la Medina : trazando con tus pasos (sin previsores guijarros ni migajas caducas) un enrevesado dibujo que nadie (ni siquiera tú mismo) podrá interpretar ... (52)

The text manages to do this since the narrator-protagonist is a decentred subject for the reader. He can locate a stable source of the narrative neither in the character, Alvaro, nor in the author-narrator. This absence of a centring subjectivity contributes for the reader to the undecidability of the text.[69]

Towards the end of Part One the protagonist (and by extension the reader) seems finally to recognize the unattainability of a stable truth and accept reluctantly an active reading of the urban signs:

> a tientas y a ciegas : abandonado a tu reacia, alicorta inspiración : a derecha, a izquierda? : persiguiendo activamente los signos ... (83–84)

This may be read as an implicit thematization of a change in the reading role from a quest for the meaning lurking behind the semiotic surface of reality to an acceptance of this surface as 'reality', the only reality to which one can have access. The abandonment of the quest for truth in favour of an active pursuit of signs echoes certain principles of post-structuralist theory. Derrida, in a famous passage of the essay 'La structure, le signe et le jeu dans le discours des sciences humaines', subsequently included in *L'écriture et la différence*, speaks of two forms of interpretation: 'L'une cherche à déchiffrer, rêve de déchiffrer une vérité ou une origine échappant au jeu et à l'ordre du signe'. The other is characterized by 'l'affirmation nietzschéene, l'affirmation joyeuse d'un monde de signes sans faute, sans vérité, sans origine, offert à une interprétation active'.[70] It is not necessary to posit a Derridean influence on Goytisolo's thinking, although the appearance of Derrida's essay in 1966 corresponds almost exactly with the initiation of *Don Julián*. However, there is a clear coincidence between certain deconstructionist principles such as decentring, the critique of Western logocentrism and the overturning of hierarchical oppositions and the principles that begin to underlie Goytisolo's essays and fiction at this time.

Goytisolo in his own criticism expresses a similar version of the ideal 'active' reading process in his discussion of Carlos Fuentes' *Terra Nostra*:

> Dichas dudas y posibilidades, abiertas en abanico se desplegarán ante el lector incitándole a intervenir, a abandonar el papel pasivo de quien se ve forzado a aceptar la versión única de los hechos, de lo cual nada puede [...] participará en fin en el proceso de construcción de la novela mediante múltiples y antagónicas lecturas. (D, 248–49)

The reading process implied here is an active process, not in the conventional sense of working to establish the 'true' order of events on the level of 'story', recovering some single truth, but producing a variety of readings, some contradictory. The text, in other words, is not a repository of a single signified, but a catalyst to a process of signification.

Having abandoned the search for a 'certidumbre' and embarked on an active 'pursuit of signs', the narrator of *Don Julián* at the start of Part Two declares (and the reader with him): 'la duda es tu única certeza' (89). By Part Three the exhortation will be to 'abandonarse al excitante juego de las combinaciones' (135).

Conclusion

I have emphasized the constant split in *Don Julián* between the referential and the textual levels and maintained that their relationship is one of tension and difference rather than complementarity. The existence of an independent level in the novel in which a text-author is composing a radical narrative which will constitute the Sadeian crime 'dont l'effet perpétuel agît, même quand je n'agirais plus' not only prevents the conventional reading of literary form as a 'representation' of that which is taking place on the level of story or content and focuses attention on the two levels of form and content; it also, most importantly, encourages, indeed demands, some kind of reflection on the differences between the two.

In *Don Julián*, not only does the textual level reveal itself to be independent of, rather than merely a vehicle for, the story level, but the level of story on numerous occasions appears as a kind of 'representation' of what is taking place on the textual level. The conventional hierarchy is inverted. An example of this is the death of Alvaro Peranzules which comes about after the narrator's relentless satire of the Spanish literary tradition. Another example is the insect-squashing incident which is merely a narrative metaphor for the assault on literary tradition carried on at the textual level.

The effect of this dislocation between the levels of discourse and story is to draw attention to the difference between them while foregrounding the former. This takes a stage further the process observed in *Señas de identidad*. There, too, there was a tentative attempt to move away from the depiction of events and even from the depiction of subjective experience to a foregrounding of the writing experience as a possible solution and means of transformation. In *Don Julián*, having established the distinction between the level of story and discourse, between that of the protagonist in the narrative and that of the text-author, the reader is led to posit separate interpretations of the ending. The protagonist's story ends on a decidedly downbeat note. His fantasy ended, he returns to his apartment resigned to the knowledge that nothing in the 'real' world, as witnessed by the repeated description of his room, has changed and that he is fated to repeat the same fantasy the following day. On the textual level, too, the closing of the book heralds the return to the 'real world' for the reader, a world in which likewise nothing will have changed. However, the assault on the literary tradition in the form of the writing of the book will have constituted a liberation for the writer; he will not have to write the book again the next day and so his experience is superior to that of the protagonist.[71] Moreover, of course, there is always the possibility that the book will have changed something through its interaction with the reader, through a form of literary contagion. The permanence of the text and its potential for infinite future readings allow it to constitute the Sadeian 'crime'.

The text's foregrounding of itself as linguistic play endows its formal aspects with a performative quality which the interpretation in terms of mimesis lacks. The mimetic element of *Don Julián*, the existence of a referential dimension and a recognizable central protagonist, are still present, but only in order to be subverted, deconstructed in order to draw attention to the linguistic level. By maintaining this conventional level only to disturb it, the novel keeps the reader in a state of perpetual doubt and he is thus led to attempt to naturalize the narrative at a higher level, that of literary convention and the problems of language. As we will see in the next chapter, *Juan sin tierra* attempts to take that process a stage further by eliminating mimesis entirely. However, eliminating one side of the opposition effectively removes the tension and, with it, the novel's subversive force

NOTES

1 J. Ríos (ed.), *Juan Goytisolo* (Madrid: Fundamentos, 1975), 142.

2 See Jesús Lázaro, *La novelística de Juan Goytisolo* (Madrid: Alhambra, 1984), 133. Linda Gould Levine, in *Juan Goytisolo: la destrucción creadora* (Mexico City: Joaquín Mortiz, 1976), comments that 'la desintegración de la prosa viene a ser la representación estilística de la desintegración de su ser' (98).

3 Michael Ugarte, *Trilogy of Treason: An Intertextual Study of Juan Goytisolo* (Columbia, MO, and London: University of Missouri Press, 1982): 'One witnesses a struggle between opposing forces: the real world versus the world of artistic creation, reality versus artifice. The struggle between these two forces is Goytisolo's quest for self' (110). See also Kessel Schwartz, 'Juan Goytisolo: las coacciones culturales y la *Reivindicación del conde Don Julián*', in Ríos (ed.), *Juan Goytisolo*, 156; and Levine, *Juan Goytisolo*, 136.

4 Manuel Durán, 'El lenguaje de Juan Goytisolo', in Ríos (ed.), *Juan Goytisolo*, 65. Levine, *Juan Goytisolo*, 116.

5 Ríos (ed.), *Juan Goytisolo*, 141.

6 Miguel Riera, 'Regreso al origen (entrevista)', *Quimera* LXXIII (1988), 39.

7 Levine comments that '*Señas de identidad*, igual que *Don Julián* en años futuros, pertenece a la categoría de obras que nos hablan de su propia creación' (*Juan Goytisolo*, 96). At another point she says, 'el verdadero tema o argumento de *Don Julián* viene a ser su estructura misma' (148). Spires, in 'The Metafictional Codes of *Don Julián* versus the Metafictional Mode of *El cuarto de atrás*', *Revista Canadiense de Estudios Hispanicos* VII(2) (1983), 306–09, admits that *Don Julián* 'assimilates at least some of the perspectives of criticism into the fictional process, and to some degree it is a gloss on its own fiction—both discursively and allegorically—and it is blatantly self-conscious' (308), but rules out its belonging to the 'metafictional mode that violates the very conventions on which fiction is based' (308). This as we shall see is far from the case.

8 Jonathan Culler, *Structuralist Poetics: Structuralism, Linguistics and the Study of Literature* (London: Routledge, 1975), 149–50.

9 Ríos (ed.), *Juan Goytisolo*, 143.

10 Roland Barthes, *Sade, Fourier, Loyola* (Paris: Seuil, 1971), 41.

11 Ríos (ed.), *Juan Goytisolo*, 143.

12 David Herzberger in his recent study of post-Civil War Spanish fiction has spoken of how 'rather than draw its referent from history (the so-called facts of the matter), fiction reaches into time through the discourse of history (historiography) in order to subvert the narrative principles upon which the telling of that history is premised'. David Herzberger, *Narrating the Past: Fiction and Historiography in Postwar Spain* (Durham, NC, and London: Duke University Press, 1995), 3.

13 Rosemary Jackson, *Fantasy: The Literature of Subversion* (London: Methuen, 1981), 75–76.

14 Culler, *Structuralist Poetics*, 189, 200.

15 Ricardo Senabre says: 'el anónimo personaje de *Reivindicación del conde don Julián* contempla el país desde fuera, instalado en Tánger, y procede a una sistemática destrucción mental de unos determinados aspectos españoles'. Ricardo Senabre, 'Evolución de la novela de Juan Goytisolo', *Reseña* (January 1971), 9. Santos Sanz describes him as follows: 'Alguien misterioso residente en Tánger, desde su habitación o a lo largo de sus paseos por la ciudad, clama en un monólogo angustioso y desesperado contra su país, su gente, su tradición.' Santos Sanz, *Lectura de Juan Goytisolo* (Barcelona: Pozanco, 1977), 98.

16 Mary Ellen Bieder, 'De *Señas de identidad* a *Makbara*: estrategia narrativa en las novelas de Juan Goytisolo', *Revista Ibero-americana* CXVI–CXVII (1981), 90.

17 Goytisolo himself has contributed to this grounding of the narration in the mind of the central protagonist: 'El narrador es un ser anónimo que desde Tánger contempla la costa española ... Este narrador sueña en una nueva invasión de España, cuyos efectos duren también ocho siglos.' Ríos (ed.), *Juan Goytisolo*, 138.

18 Levine, *Juan Goytisolo*, 136.

19 José Hernández, 'Juan Goytisolo—1975', *Modern Language Notes* XCI (1976), 342.

20 Ríos (ed.), *Juan Goytisolo*, 115.

21 Gonzalo Sobejano, in Ríos (ed.), *Juan Goytisolo*, 46.

22 José Manuel Martín Morán, 'La palabra creadora. Estructura comunicativa de *Reivindicación del conde don Julián*', in *Reivindación del conde don Julián*, ed. Linda Gould Levine (Madrid: Cátedra, 1985), 319.

23 Levine, *Reivindicación del conde don Julián*, 54.

24 Robbe-Grillet defined the modern narrator thus: 'he is no longer just a man describing the things which he sees, but he is also the person who invents the things around him and who sees the things he invents'. Cited in Ann Jefferson, *The Nouveau Roman and the Poetics of Fiction* (London: Cambridge University Press, 1980), 113.

25 Levine interprets these lines as follows: 'El narrador recién despierto y deseoso de evitar el nuevo día y la caja de Pandora que constituyen su pan diario, intenta componer al estilo de Scherezada, fábulas y cuentos que le salven momentáneamente de la realidad que acecha al otro lado de la costa.' However, in *Don Julián* the 'fábulas y cuentos' are not seen as a way of escaping from reality. They are the means of engaging directly with the hated reality, of attacking it. These 'fábulas y cuentos' are his 'pan diario', they constitute his very mode of existence. Levine, *Reivindicación del conde don Julián*, 85 n. 9.

26 Roland Barthes, *Image–Music–Text* (London: Fontana, 1984), 114. Goytisolo echoes this approach: 'La narrativa ha vivido durante siglos sin esta noción de personaje individualizado, de "espesor" psicológico; bastaría citar los ejemplos de las *Mil y una noches*, de Boccaccio, de toda la literatura medieval. En estas obras, como dice Todorov, no podemos hablar de personajes, sólo de participantes, de agentes. Es decir, el personaje es un mero nombre, la acción un verbo [...] en mi opinión este tipo

de personaje [i.e. 'de espesor psicológico'] está hoy día abandonando el campo de la novela [...] asistimos a la muerte de este tipo de personaje y su sustitución por un nuevo tipo de personaje "lingüístico", de personaje sometido a las necesidades retóricas del texto. En *Don Julián* y en *Juan sin tierra* no hay personajes de "carne y hueso" sino que estos surgen, desaparecen, se transforman siguiendo el "murmullo discursivo del narrador".' Hernández, 'Juan Goytisolo—1975', 349. See also Goytisolo, *Disidencias* (Barcelona: Seix Barral, 1977), 245–46.

27 Martín Morán, in 'La palabra creadora', comments: 'no tenemos ni una sola referencia a su aspecto físico; nuestros escasos conocimientos de su pasado no llegan casi ni a intuiciones; en muy contadas ocasiones oímos su voz. Podemos decir, como lógico colofón, que nos encontramos ante un protagonista que carece de materialidad, de corporeidad, de entidad en una palabra ... Ahora bien, si es verdad que no hay una persona física que ocupe el lugar primordial, entonces ¿quién es el protagonista? No parece que descabellado afirmar que *Reivindicación del conde don Julián* tiene por protagonista al discurso frente a la historia, a la palabra frente al hecho' (311).

28 Lázaro, *La novelística de Juan Goytisolo*, 174–75.

29 Gérard Genette defines analepsis as 'any evocation after the fact of an event that took place earlier than the point in the story where we are at any given moment'. Gérard Genette, *Narrative Discourse* (Ithaca, NY: Cornell University Press, 1980), 40.

30 Martín Morán, 'La palabra creadora', 311.

31 Jefferson, *The Nouveau Roman*, 74, 76.

32 In an interesting article, Linda Ledford-Miller explores the way the traditional 'objectivity' of history is being placed in doubt by contemporary historians themselves and replaced with the Nietzschean notion of history as a form of art or mythology. In her view, this blurring of the two, history and myth, corresponds exactly to the technique of *Don Julián*. Linda Ledford-Miller, 'History as Myth, Myth as History: Juan Goytisolo's *Count Julián*', *Revista Canadiense de Estudios Hispánicos* VIII (1983), 21–30.

33 'What one might call the "pronominal heroes" of Sarraute's *Les Fruits d'or* or Sollers' *Nombres* function not as portraits but as labels which in their refusal to become full characters imply a critique of conceptions of personality.' Culler, *Structuralist Poetics*, 231.

34 Cesar Alonso de los Ríos, 'Juan Goytisolo sin Tierra', *Triunfo* XXX(673) (1975), 26.

35 Catherine Belsey, *Critical Practice* (London: Methuen, 1980), 30–31.

36 Stephen Heath speaks of the 'practice of writing' of the French New Novel as 'profound experience of language and form and the demonstration of that experience in the writing of the novel which, transgressed, is no longer repetition and self-effacement but work and self-presentation as text'. Stephen Heath, *The Nouveau Roman: A Study in the Practice of Writing* (London: Elek, 1972), 22.

37 Tzvetan Todorov, *Introduction to Poetics* (Brighton: Harvester Wheatsheaf, 1981), 37.

38 Alonso de los Ríos, 'Juan Goytisolo sin Tierra', 26.

39 Levine, *Juan Goytisolo*, 141–44.

40 Levine, *Reivindicación del conde don Julián*, 40.

41 Robert Spires, *La novela española de posguerra: creación artística y experiencia personal* (Madrid: Cupsa, 1978), 302

42 Goytisolo in *Disidencias* has remarked that Góngora was the inspiration for the novel on the linguistic level (D, 314).

43 The 'Dedicatoria' of the *Soledades* opens with the verses: 'Pasos de un peregrino son errante / cuantos me dictó versos dulce Musa / en soledad confusa, / perdidos unos, otros inspirados'. Luis de Góngora, *Soledades*, ed. John Beverley

(Madrid: Cátedra, 1980), 71. Beverley points out how the 'peregrino' not only refers to the protagonist, but can also be read as referring to the poet himself and the reader (21). Maurice Molho, in a way that resembles our reading of Goytisolo's text, notes how the above lines from Góngora can mean both that the verses of the poet recount the 'pasos' of the protagonist and that they constitute the 'pasos' of the poet himself in constructing the poem. Maurice Molho, *Sémantique et poétique. A propos des 'Solitudes' de Góngora* (Bordeaux: Editions Ducros, 1969), 49–53.

44 Roland Barthes, 'The Death of the Author', in *Image–Music–Text*, 142–48.

45 The protagonist of *Don Julián* bears many similarities to the definition of the schizoid individual given by the psychologist R. D. Laing in *The Divided Self* (London: Pelican, 1965), in particular, the split between self and his 'personality', the recourse to fantasy and the characteristic of self-consciousness (73, 84–85, 106). Levine refers to the parallels with Laing's theory in *Juan Goytisolo*, 228–29.

46 Goytisolo says of Fuentes' novel *Terra Nostra*: 'mientras recorre la fascinadora galería de espejos que reflejan el mundo y se autorreflejan, no pierde nunca de vista la historia real'. *Disidencias*, 234.

47 Alonso de los Ríos, 'Juan Goytisolo sin Tierra', 28.

48 This is clearly what Goytisolo meant when he stated: 'Tenía que ir acompañada la "traición tema" con la "traición lenguaje" y cesar, por tanto, la distinción entre fondo y forma'. César Antonio Molina and Luis Suñen, 'Juan Goytisolo o la heterodoxia consciente', *Insula* CCCLXVII (1977), 4.

49 According to Gonzalo Sobejano: 'Para mi objeto, baste decir que la parte última, la más interiorizada, apenas contiene referencias a la literatura de España como aspecto de ese pasado presente que el sujeto se afana por demoler. Al contrario las otras tres partes están cuajadas de tales referencias ...' Gonzalo Sobejano, 'Don Julián, iconoclasta de la literatura patria', *Camp de l'Arpa* XLIII–XLIV (1977), 9.

50 Levine, *Reivindicación del conde don Julián*, 271 n.254.

51 'Originalidad, individualidad, creación se sitúan por tanto en los antípodas de lo verosímil y la obra más innovadora y rica será la que, rechazando sus servidumbres implícitas, asumirá sin explicaciones el desafío de su enigmática opacidad.' Juan Goytisolo, 'Presentación crítica de José María Blanco White', in *Obra inglesa de D. José María Blanco White* (Buenos Aires: Formentor, 1972), 104.

52 Umberto Eco, *The Open Work* (London: Hutchinson Radius, 1989), 93.

53 Charles Russell, 'Individual Voice in the Collective Discourse: Literary Innovation in Postmodern American Fiction', *Substance* XXVII (1980), 33. Goytisolo makes a similar comment in relation to Sarduy's *De donde son los cantantes*: 'En *De donde son los cantantes* [...] el novelista se mueve con desparpajo, dialoga con los personajes, emite juicios erróneos y a continuación se desdice de ellos, cambia simultáneamente de estilo y decorado, parodia frases de autores clásicos etc., recordándonos así que el paisaje realista—o por ser más exactos, referencial—de las novelas ordinarias es acá otro discurso. En vez de un mundo "natural" nos movemos en un universo estrictamente cultural. Las transgresiones, como en Góngora, cobran un matiz superretórico: pastiche de la cultura, cultura al cuadrado' (D, 188). R. O. Jones has noted: 'Góngora ... his mind richly stocked with the literature of Classical Antiquity and the Renaissance, viewed life "through the spectacle of books" (as Johnson said of Milton)—or at least he wrote as if he did.' R. O. Jones, *Poems of Góngora* (Cambridge: Cambridge University Press, 1966), 6.

54 Ríos (ed.), *Juan Goytisolo*, 141.

55 Abigail E. Lee has given a very good account of Goytisolo's reworking of the original fairy-tale 'Little Red Riding Hood' in her article 'La paradigmática historia de Caperucita y el lobo feroz: Juan Goytisolo's use of "Little Red Riding Hood" in *Reivindicación del conde don Julián*', *Bulletin of Hispanic Studies* LXV (1988), 141–51.

56 She concludes by distinguishing between the motivations underlying Goytisolo's treatment of his character and the equivalent in Lautréamont and Sade: 'No es un acto obrado como exaltación del mal universal como en Sade, ni una protesta contra la situación del hombre empeñado en destruir la ilusión de la superioridad humana, como en Lautréamont, sino una manifestación del dolor íntimo del autor mismo, unión compleja del odio y del amor.' Levine, *Juan Goytisolo*, 237.

57 Paul Knight, 'Introduction', in Comte de Lautréamont, *Maldoror* (Harmondsworth: Penguin, 1978), 12.

58 Goytisolo makes clear his view that Lautréamont's text must not be taken literally when he says: 'Sólo a un imbécil se le ocurriría la idea de buscar en Maldoror una propuesta cualquiera de aplicación concreta y práctica'. Goytisolo, 'Sobre literatura y vida literaria', *Quimera* XXIII (1982), 21.

59 According to Terence Hawkes, contemporary semiotics 'frees the sign from its subservience to that "reality" or (presence) which it was supposed to serve'. Hawkes goes on to note that for semiotics, writing 'does not "reproduce" a reality beyond itself, nor does it "reduce" that reality. In its new freedom, it can be seen to cause a new reality to come into being.' Terence Hawkes, *Structuralism and Semiotics* (London: Methuen, 1977), 148.

60 Sobejano, '*Don Julián*, iconoclasta de la literatura patria', 13–14. Lázaro, *La novelística de Juan Goytisolo*, 200.

61 Lázaro, *La novelística de Juan Goytisolo*, 201–02.

62 Jo Labanyi, *Myth and History in the Contemporary Spanish Novel* (Cambridge: Cambridge University Press, 1989), 211.

63 Stephanie Sieburth makes a similar point in 'Reading and Alienation in Goytisolo's *Reivindicación del conde don Julián*', *Anales de la Literatura Española Contemporánea* VIII (1983), 85.

64 Linda Hutcheon, *Narcissistic Narrative: The Metafictional Paradox* (London: Methuen, 1984), 96–97.

65 Antony Easthope, *Poetry as Discourse* (London: Methuen, 1983), 36.

66 See Bernard Loupias, 'Importance et signification du lexique d'origine arabe dans le *Don Julian* de Juan Goytisolo', *Bulletin Hispanique* LXXX (1978), 241.

67 Barthes, 'The Death of the Author', in *Image–Music–Text*, 147.

68 This is an interesting example of Goytisolo's use of myth to combat myth in *Don Julián*. As the memories of the Tithamer Toth sermons of his childhood show, Alvarito was sexually oppressed by the myth that indulgence in sex would lead to contamination. Hence when it is a question of Alvarito attacking and undermining the motherland, he turns the same myth, the fantasy of contamination, against it. See *Coto vedado* (Barcelona: Seix Barral, 1985): 'La idea del pecado—del pecado mortal, con sus espeluznantes consecuencias—me torturó por espacio de algunos años' (122).

69 'The self has long been one of the major principles of intelligibility and unity. One could suppose that an act or text was a sign whose full meaning lay in the consciousness of the subject. But if the self is a construct and result it can no longer serve as source'. Culler, *Structuralist Poetics*, 29–30.

70 Jacques Derrida, *L'écriture et la différence* (Paris: Editions du Seuil, 1967), 427.

71 It is interesting to note that Goytisolo has commented that '*Don Julián* ha sido una liberación. Por eso ese estado de paz conmigo mismo'. A. Carlos Isasi Angulo, 'La novelística de Juan Goytisolo (entrevista con el autor)', *Papeles de Son Armadans* LXXVI(226) (1975), 85.

CHAPTER FOUR

Juan sin tierra

Juan sin tierra, published in 1975, is the last instalment of the Mendiola trilogy. In it Goytisolo carries to the extreme the process of rupture with the past, subversion of Spanish and Western values, the assault on literary tradition and search for a freer form of writing. *Juan sin tierra* shares the same concerns that characterize the trilogy as a whole and sets out to take them to a more profound level, with a view to effecting the definitive stage of the process of destruction. As Goytisolo himself said, 'concibo *Juan sin tierra* como una obra última, el finis terrae de mi propia escritura en términos de comunicación' (D, 317).

This development operates at all levels. Hence, in terms of the narrative persona, whereas in *Don Julián* he had been an exile, located in Tangiers, on the very edge of Spanish territory and still very much fixated with the mother country, in *Juan sin tierra* the central figure is an even more shadowy character, situated in a small 'escritorio-cocina' in Paris, still an exile but one who has assumed his status of 'Juan sin tierra' and who revels in this lack of territoriality. The exile from Spain that was still a source of latent bitterness and neurosis to the protagonist of *Don Julián* is no longer a problem. However, the protagonist is still not free. He has achieved one form of freedom from the constraints of national identity, but he is still oppressed by a wider identity, that of Western society. Hence, the location in Paris is appropriate since the focus of the protagonist's ire is Western values in general. This wider focus was present in *Don Julián* but now comes to the fore. The horizon of the novel has broadened and the perennial presence of the Arab as a symbol of subversion is extended to include the more general figure of the 'pariah'.

Juan sin tierra is the final stage of the project of 'defining oneself negatively' first referred to in the closing pages of *Señas de identidad*. In *Juan sin tierra*, at one point the narrator exhorts: 'defínanse negativamcntc' (240). All the values espoused in *Juan sin tierra* are, in traditional European terms, 'negative', and this for the narrator is the source of their 'positive' significance for him. Their focal point is the notion of treachery or betrayal.[1]

It is therefore misleading at the outset to judge *Juan sin tierra* in terms of the alternative values it proposes. The negative, revolutionary values forwarded in the text lose all their meaning when divorced from the positive conventional opposites. Any meaning generated by the text is based on the tension between these opposing values. This is sometimes seen as a flaw in the novel.[2] However, Goytisolo has always insisted that the destructive process has implicit within it a creative function.[3] In Goytisolo's novels, creativity is not seen in terms of substituting new, 'positive' values. The creativity inheres rather in a form of creative deconstruction of repressive structures in such a way as to open a new way forward. Goytisolo's thinking is self-avowedly influenced by the anarchist tradition, and he has claimed that *Juan sin tierra* required a reading in terms of a 'revolución de tipo bakuniano'.[4] This is part of the utopian impulse that characterizes Goytisolo's vision and which starts to emerge clearly as a theme in *Juan sin tierra*. It makes explicit a characteristic of all his novels which is that they are utopian texts. Tom Moylan defines the utopian text in the following way:

> To write utopia is to indicate what cannot yet be said within present conceptual language or achieved in current political action. To write utopia is to perform the most utopian of actions possible within literary discourse. The form is itself more significant than any of its contents.[5]

This coincides with Goytisolo's comment in *Disidencias*, 'toda mi actual experimentación literaria va acompañada de un deseo o propósito de descalificación moral: de decir lo "indecible"' (301).

Goytisolo's emphasis throughout the later period is on the formal features of the text—only language can be subversive in the context of a modern democratic society. In such a context, taboo themes are rare. Speaking of *Juan sin tierra*, Goytisolo referred to the coprophilic impulse as being perhaps one of the few lingering taboo themes. In the essay on Quevedo, written at approximately the same time, and included in *Disidencias*, Goytisolo had linked 'escritura, impulso sexual y excremento', arguing that the denial of the body in Spanish and Western culture had resulted in a literary tradition devoid of reference to the body, a 'represión sistemática del cuerpo mediante su radical desposesión del verbo' (D, 124). The exceptions to this, according to Goytisolo, would be Góngora, who reacted by creating a poetry that was sensuous in its material celebration of language, and Quevedo, an upholder of the prevailing ideology who nonetheless reveals the repressive tensions that it created in a morbid fascination with excreta.[6]

The celebration of the body in *Juan sin tierra* and the explicit celebration of the excretive processes in their most natural, undisguised fashion of the 'zanja común' is an attempt to reverse the process:

> Devolver la voz al cuerpo nos parece todavía una empresa quijotesca, casi descabellada—incursión temeraria en terreno minado, en el corazón del campo enemigo. (D, 124)

This essay on Quevedo explains the political motivation for the aesthetic practice of *Juan sin tierra*:

> La civilización, como sabemos, ha sido el resultado de una lucha feroz por la existencia que ha supeditado la satisfacción de los impulsos primarios del individuo a imperiosos objetivos sociales. (D, 124)

Goytisolo's use of the excretive process as the central motif of *Juan sin tierra* locates him half-way between Rabelais and Swift. As Norman Brown pointed out, while for Rabelais and Aristophanes 'the anal function is a part of the total human being which they make us love because it is part of life, for Swift it becomes the decisive weapon in his assault on the pretensions, the pride, even the self-respect of mankind'.[7] Goytisolo is both trying to reconcile us to an alienated side of our nature and also, using the same motif, repel us and undermine our conventional attitudes.

In the conflict between 'libido y productividad' (D, 124), *Juan sin tierra* acts to glorify and indulge the former. The self-referential nature of the text is a textual analogue of the open, unconcealed practice of the 'zanja común', the overturning of an excessively neurotic culture that seeks continually to disguise its signs. The primacy of the formal in *Juan sin tierra* means that the themes of homosexuality, sodomy, bestiality, onanism that recur throughout the novel act as the thematic 'shadow' of the primary activity conducted at the level of the textual process. At one point in *Juan sin tierra* the narrator says: 'atentados, pillajes, razzias, descarrilamientos servirán en adelante de pretexto a los juegos sutiles de la escritura' (126).

The novel does not set out to tackle socio-political issues on their own terms, but first relates those issues to an aesthetic theory and proceeds to carry out the battle on an aesthetic level. In an interview in 1978, Goytisolo himself referred to this process. Speaking of the novel's call for 'una revolución de tipo bakuniano', he says:

> Cuando lo escribí, Franco vivía aún, no había espacios de discusión y, una propuesta como la mía, traducida al lenguaje estrictamente racional del ensayo, no cabía en el estrecho marco político de aquellos años, no ya en el campo de lo tolerado por el régimen, sino de lo admitido por la oposición. Para decir lo que quería decir debía recurrir a un lenguaje nuevo. La novela fue el producto de esta estrategia de la invención. (CC, 233)

This quotation illustrates the essentially political nature of Goytisolo's aesthetic. As he says earlier in the interview, 'estimo que se trata de la novela más política que he escrito o, si quieres metapolítica'.[8] However, he also emphasizes, in a prelude to the previous quotation: '*Juan sin tierra* es un texto literario, y hay que aceptarlo como tal' (CC, 233).

It is true that *Juan sin tierra* is the novel where Goytisolo pins his political colours most firmly to the mast, and it is equally true that it is the novel in which he declares his aesthetic principles most explicitly. Moreover, due to its overtly metafictional nature, it is the novel where the intimate relation between the two is most obvious. The novel not only refers to its own process of composition but explicitly theorizes about its aesthetic principles and the link between these principles and the two dominant themes of the novel, which are sexuality and (political) power.

It might be useful at this point to consider *Juan sin tierra*'s relation to *Don Julián* in order to identify the areas in which the later novel has carried the aesthetic project forward. It will also be helpful to do so in the light of Goytisolo's own comments on the novels.

From *Don Julián* to *Juan sin tierra*

Goytisolo himself has remarked on the broader scope of *Juan sin tierra*'s intertextual references in comparison to *Don Julián*:

> Esto es, las referencias son mucho más amplias: el mundo de los clásicos es sustituido por el del cine, la literatura de masas y algunas obras marginales de escritores-aventureros fascinados como yo por el mundo musulmán. (D, 314)

Thematically, too, the scope has widened beyond the domain of Spain and its culture to embrace the wider culture of the West. There is a similarity in the theme of the opposition between repression and sexuality. For where *Don Julián* was founded on the repression of the body by Christian Spain since the Reconquest as a reaction to the myth of Spain's fall to the Moors due to a sexual misdemeanour, *Juan sin tierra* presents Western culture since the Middle Ages as characterized by a similar denial of the body.[9]

Still the Spanish focus remains dominant and Chapter Four in particular of the novel is a parody of the way a repressive morality has dominated Spanish literary history since the *Corbacho*. It is in this section that the author develops the theory, also expressed in the essay on Quevedo in *Disidencias*, that the poverty of Spanish literature, 'esas obras indigestas, compactas, recias, amazacotadas' (D, 237), is the result of a form of constipation, an anal retentiveness which is just Goytisolo's typically corporal, physiological metaphor for repression.

Given the theory that coprophilia is the ultimate Western taboo, it is not surprising that Goytisolo, ever eager for 'temas provocadores', should structure the novel around it.[10] However, as we have also observed, it was Goytisolo's opinion that in a free society there were no truly provocative themes; true provocation must operate at the formal level. Hence, the formal features of *Juan sin tierra* are even more to the fore than in *Don Julián*.

On a formal level, Goytisolo distinguishes *Juan sin tierra* very clearly from *Don Julián*. Whereas the latter was a closed, tightly knit, hermetically structured work, *Juan sin tierra* is on the contrary 'una obra abierta, desplegada en múltiples direcciones como las varillas de un abanico' (D, 306). This can easily be seen. *Don Julián* revolved very strictly around the protagonist and his day in Tangiers. The novel, like a symphony—an analogy that critics have used and Goytisolo concurred with—worked like a series of variations on a single theme. Goytisolo described it in this sense as 'centripetal'. *Juan sin tierra*, on the other hand, has a centrifugal structure. Its components seem at first sight to be unrelated and therefore the novel gives the impression of being open, disconnected. The structure of *Juan sin tierra* aspires to a mobility, lacking a centre:

> No hay unidad de tiempo ni de lugar ni de personaje (aunque al principio pueda parecer lo contrario). No hay un centro fijo, bien que oculto como en *Don Julián*; el centro es nómada, varía en cada secuencia. (D, 315–16)

Yet Goytisolo does admit to one 'centripetal' element in *Juan sin tierra*. Unlike *Don Julián*, which to an extent preserved the classical unities of time, space and action, the only unifying factor in *Juan sin tierra* is the process of writing itself:

> se compone de un conjunto de secuencias discursivas, ligadas entre sí por el proceso organizador de la escritura, por la fuente misma de producción textual.[11]

Juan sin tierra, according to Goytisolo, finally does away with the traditional linear structure of plot, actions and characters. Instead, the novel is composed of textual segments where the relationship is one of 'afinidades electivas secretas, como en la arquitectura y las artes plásticas' (D, 307).

For Goytisolo, the structure of *Juan sin tierra* can best be defined in terms of spatial form. The emphasis is on how the elements are arranged on the page and the reader is obliged to read the novel 'en virtud de una combinación de repeticiones y juegos simétricos que se llevan a cabo sobre el blanco de la página' (D, 316). *Juan sin tierra*, according to Goytisolo, 'no se funda en relaciones de orden lógico-temporal, sino que se desarrolla en el plano espacial, lo mismo que un poema'.[12]

Nonetheless, he does not regard it as a 'texto poemático', insisting that a narrative element persists and that it is important that it does so, since one of the major effects of the novel will be to disrupt the narrative flow at regular intervals and destroy the fictive illusion, reminding the reader that it is a text he is reading:

> los elementos narrativos existen cuanto menos a nivel de la secuencia. Lo que ocurre es que cada vez que el relato empieza a cobrar impulso y se desdibuja la trama argumental—esto es, la ilusión del referente—el narrador interviene

para imponernos su presencia: todo es escritura, nos hallamos ante un objeto específicamente literario.[13]

One of the important features of *Juan sin tierra* is a more explicit incorporation of literary theory into the novel. Goytisolo sees this as a characteristic of contemporary fiction: 'Una nueva concepción del hecho literario aúna los elementos narrativos, poéticos y críticos en el interior del espacio textual'.[14] Where *Don Julián* still retained, according to Goytisolo, the notion of character, in *Juan sin tierra* the protagonist has disappeared from the novel and instead 'el productor del discurso [...] es un mero "personaje lingüístico"' (D, 306):

> Los pronombres personales del discurso narrativo no expresan una voz individual sino todas las voces o ninguna [...] los yo, tú, nosotros no se refieren a una realidad del discurso, sino a un mero proceso de enunciación. (D, 316)

This has the effect, according to Goytisolo, of confusing the reader:

> Ni el tú interpelado, ni el yo interpelador poseen una identidad precisa y concreta y el lector no sabe a ciencia cierta quién es el sujeto emisor y quién el receptor. (D, 316)

Goytisolo clearly sees *Juan sin tierra* as carrying the subversion of the traditional novel form to its culmination. *Don Julián*, for all its radical form, had preserved certain vestiges of this tradition, such as linear structure, the concept of character and the referential realm. In the last chapter I argued that, if *Don Julián* did retain these features, it was in a highly extenuated form and solely for the purposes of placing them in doubt. *Juan sin tierra* sets itself the task of a much more explicit dynamiting of these forms. Goytisolo himself commented:

> yo sabía que [...] después de un libro como *Don Julián*, podía llevar aún más lejos mi proceso personal a la literatura, la disolución del lenguaje y de las formas narrativas tradicionales. (D, 317)

In *Juan sin tierra* this consists almost wholly of a self-reflexive revolt against the conventions of the traditional novel with the dual intent of foregrounding for the reader the textuality of the novel and exploiting the unlimited narrative possibilities of a text freed from the constraints of the narrative illusion. Goytisolo's comments also highlight the importance, fundamental to metafiction, of the relationship with the reader. This is primarily one of unsettling, disorienting, confusing.

The Metafictional Mode

The principal characteristic of *Juan sin tierra*, then, is its overtly metafictional mode. While undoubtedly the metafictional mode was fashionable in Spanish fiction of the 1970s,[15] a form of narrative self-consciousness was intrinsic to Goytisolo's aesthetic approach from *Señas* onwards and corresponded less to literary fashion than to a deep-seated affiliation with certain important currents in contemporary fiction and critical theory. All of Goytisolo's novels from *Señas* onwards are self-conscious in varying degrees, and this responded to a concern for artistic authenticity and intellectual honesty which constitutes the ethical basis of Goytisolo's approach to his craft. Having said that, it is necessary to recognize the extent to which certain aspects of *Juan sin tierra*'s metafiction display a certain modishness which we shall discuss later.

Many critics who have focused specifically on the self-referential dimension have difficulty harmonizing it with what they perceive to be the overall impression yielded by the novel. In most cases, the problem can be summed up by saying that *Juan sin tierra* aims to be autotelic but cannot avoid reference to the world.[16]

For Robert Spires '*Juan sin tierra* could well be considered the manifesto for the whole Spanish self-referential novel movement', and he sees its importance precisely in the fact that it violates 'the laws of fiction by challenging the very distinction between the world from which one narrates and the world of which one narrates'.[17] The novel foregrounds both the activity of the novel coming into being as a new form of writing and the novelist creating himself as a new kind of novelist. The world from which one writes eventually supplants the world of which one writes, the act of narration supplants the novel as product. For Spires, the novel achieves autonomy by 'freeing language from externally imposed meaning', which it does by transforming cultural codes into narrative codes, as when he transforms the culturally coded white colonizers–black slaves dichotomy into the narrative code of 'dos bloques opuestos de palabras'.[18]

Spires's point would seem to be the rather conventional one that it is only within the confines of the literary text that the writer can use language freely, and in so doing forge for himself an identity different from that accorded to him by his place in a particular cultural milieu. The weakness of *Juan sin tierra* is, in his view, that that liberating process is limited to the space of the text: 'with the end of the linguistic process' exterior reality imposes itself, and the text and the text author are reduced to 'static black markers on a white page' (87). At the end Spires sees some hope in the figure of the reader, since 'as long as there are readers of *Juan sin tierra* the static black markers will be transformed into the text author's eternal quest for a new novel and a new artistic being' (87).

Spires's view of the novel as offering mere artistic salvation, freedom on the page, for the author, and the potential for surrogate freedom and pleasure in the reader's recreation of it,[19] underplays the political dimension of the novel, its paradoxical play between the concept of textual autonomy and socio-political significance. The metafictional nature of *Juan sin tierra*, its attention to itself as a text being created on the basis of other texts, is less concerned with freeing itself from externally imposed meaning (whatever that means exactly) than with drawing attention to the way reality is culturally coded, one of the major manifestations being precisely written texts. The novel, more than a satire, aims at a more active subversion of a common ideology coded in different discourses ranging from the Christian doctrine of denial of the body to conventional realism's antagonism to literary experiment.

Spires updates his argument in a more recent study, incorporating more elements of postmodernist theory, especially Bakhtin, to show how Goytisolo's creation of a narrative heteroglossia 'challenges and subverts authoritative discourse',[20] but his argument remains unconvincing and rather contradictory. On the one hand, he sees Goytisolo as striving to 'authorize novelistic creation as a new divinity', but at the same time in 'his attempt to go beyond poetics, he has had to resort to and reaffirm the very discursive practice that he has up to this point discredited' (61). However, there is something, as we will see, in his assertion that the author of *Juan sin tierra* 'has now defined himself as the new centripetal force' (61).

Michael Ugarte reads the self-conscious technique in terms of an authorial quest for identity.[21] His focus is principally on the intertextual nature of Goytisolo's novels, the way they attack Spanish and Western culture via a system of linguistic corruption and contagion of the texts of sacred Spain with textual allies such as Sade, T. E. Lawrence, and Anselm Turmeda. While seeming to engage with the novels in terms of their application of structuralist theory, Ugarte's study remains rather traditional and even biographical in its approach to Goytisolo's fiction, the linguistic enterprise being seen as 'the Spanish author's search for his own identity in writing'. Strangely, for Ugarte, rather than finding his true identity in *Juan sin tierra*, Goytisolo only manages to split 'his self into a variety of entities'. Viewing the novels as a form of 'psychoanalytic therapy, as a tool to re-form the self into an integrated unit', Ugarte concludes that the novel is a failure since Goytisolo's neurotic self resurfaces in *Makbara* (145). I would disagree both with the idea of narrative splitting in *Juan sin tierra* and with that of a neurotic author in *Makbara*.

Closer attention to the function of metafiction in Goytisolo's literary practice will reveal the way self-reference is reconciled with social concern expressed in the novel. In addition, it will be necessary to examine the relation between the literary theory incorporated into *Juan sin tierra* and its own practice, and relate both to the social concern of the novel.

Metafictional Levels

The metafictional context of the novel is established early on in the first chapter. The narrator recounts his experiences as he sits in his room surrounded by books, records and documents. Focusing on the record sleeve of the Cuban singer, the narrator enters the world depicted in the background to the photograph 'dando la vuelta, a fin de sortearla'. This is both an allusion to the return in imagination to his family's past in Cuba and a clear reference to the metafictional process, the move from one level (the situation of the writer-narrator, i.e. within the fictional world of the novel, the level of 'reality') into another (the level of artistic representation, in this case a photograph). This opening narrative 'incident' initiates the entry into the world of fictional creation, the text we are reading, and sets the tone for the novel as a whole for it shows the two-way focus of the text, both towards a world (the narrator's past, the real world of the Cuban slaves) but also, self-consciously towards the text, recognized at every moment as text. It also makes clear that the text's engagement with that world referred to is going to be via the reworking within this textual space of the discourses and texts that relate to that world. There is explicit reference to the sources on which the narrative will base itself:

> desperdigados sobre la mesa, en la tabla que cubre el fregadero de latón, por
> los estantes de un mueble clasificador desgalichado y ridículo los Seeco
> Record de la gorda explosiva ponen una fogosa nota de color relegando a un
> segundo plano los restantes comparsas de tu memoria : el libro en rústica, de
> cubierta verdosa [...] la fotocopia de una sobrecogedora 'Explicación de la
> doctrina cristiana acomodada a la capacidad de los negros bozales' ... (14)

The natural concomitant of the text's foregrounding of the process of its production is an undermining of the premises of the realist novel. The initial incident mentioned above was an example. Instead of gesturing solely outwards towards a fictional referential world, the novel deliberately moves inwards, focusing the reader's attention on the process of narrative composition, the creation of a textual reality, 'recreando tu mundo en la página en blanco' (126). *Juan sin tierra* describes scenes in a way that reveals their textual nature but also makes an allusion to the structuralist critique of realism. The description of the sugar plantation is done in such a way as to self-consciously parody a feature of realism that Barthes had termed 'l'effet de réel':[22]

> te interrumpirás unos segundos a fin de completar el decorado : sofás,
> mecedoras, hamacas, un piano de cola ... (15–16)

This effect is added to by the reference to the 'use' of components from costumbrista novels such as *Cecilia Valdés* by the Cuban novelist Cirilo Villaverde (16).[23] This invokes the structuralist principle of 'intertextuality' according to which all texts, rather than reflecting the real, are, in fact, reworkings, transformations and citations of previous texts. This had also been implied in the opening of the novel where the narrator makes clear that he is surrounded by books which will aid him in the composition of the text we are reading. For example, there is the implication that the 'voice' or discourse of Vosk the chaplain is a parodic reworking of the 'Explicación de la doctrina cristiana acomodada a la capacidad de los negros bozales' mentioned on page 14.

At one point the narrator pauses to make an explicit reference to the method of composition: 'dividirás la imaginaria escena en dos partes : dicho mejor : en dos bloques opuestos de palabras' (30). Such a reference, as well as undermining any referential illusion and showing the novel as the result of an operation with words and not the reflection of an external reality, draws attention to the way the representation of reality in words can be coded ideologically, so that white equates to good, and black to bad. The binary division of terms is yet another symptom of the structuralist mentality that characterizes *Juan sin tierra* and that the author uses deliberately as part of his strategy of subversion of the traditional realist attitude. The reference points up a fundamental principle of *Juan sin tierra* which is that meaning inheres primarily in the internal system of language rather than in the extralinguistic realm:

> a un lado sustantivos, adjetivos, verbos que denotan blancor claridad, virtud : al otro, un léxico de tinieblas, negrura, pecado ... (30)

According to this example, once one establishes a code or enters into an already existing one (such as this deliberately simplistic example of a cultural code in the system of representation, familiar to any viewer of Westerns), meaning will inhere in that code irrespective of any 'referential' dimension. This reveals a strategy *Juan sin tierra* will take in two ways. One refers to the way the text will play with established codes, in the form of binary oppositions, in order to provoke. So, for example, in the oppositions master/slave, white/black, WC/zanja, heterosexual/homosexual the text will glorify one over the other, deliberately choosing the non-privileged element in the binary hierarchy.

The other is the way *Juan sin tierra* will establish its own network of relations and analogies so that it can refer to different things at the same time. The most important of these is the analogy between sexuality and writing. Once this is established, references to onanism, homosexuality, eroticism come to 'signify' self-reflexive, ludic, subjective, baroque writing and sexual orthodoxy equates to realism.

The establishing of these narrative codes does not, as Spires would suggest, 'free language from externally imposed meaning' but rather reminds us of a feature of all language, i.e. that it is not dependent on extra-linguistic reality, the referential realm alone, for the generation of meaning, but obeys its own internal rules and conventions, and that in most circumstances these conventions can be artificial ones, ideological ones. In Western culture we do occasionally invest the colour code with ideological significance. Clearly Goytisolo's metafiction, by turning away from 'reality' towards language, is telling us something about the way we structure reality in language.[24]

However, the result of the explicitness of the metafictional form of *Juan sin tierra* is that there is no violation of levels, and therefore the reader's perception of the 'ontological boundaries'[25] within the novel is not disturbed. *Juan sin tierra* presents itself as a book about a writer writing the book we are reading. Its intent to explode the traditional novelistic, 'realist', conventions is similarly overt, as is its alliance with Formalist and Structuralist theory in this project. Once the reader recognizes that situation, which he does in the initial chapter, the narrative context is clear. The metafictional form of *Juan sin tierra* is such that, rather than undermining the traditional novel, the text constitutes an overt reflection on a critical debate in which it takes very clear sides.

Literary Theory

As is common in metafiction, *Juan sin tierra* includes within it not only reflections on its own narrative activity but also on narrative theory in general. As was suggested in the previous section, literary theory in *Juan sin tierra* consists mainly of a concerted attack on the doctrine of literary realism, employing to that effect some implicit or explicit allusions to structuralist thinking.

Chapter II of the novel makes clear the narrator's identification at all levels with unorthodoxy. The chapter develops the central analogy of the novel between sexuality and writing. Sexual orthodoxy is represented by the 'Parejita Reproductora'. The narrator's inability to describe the copulation leads to the couple's sexual impotence, which in turn becomes a linguistic impotence. The real theme is the narrator coming to terms with his inability to write conventional descriptive prose which would win him critical acclaim:

> los adjetivos más luminosos del idioma acudirán en tropel a tu pluma y te convertirán en un novel, nobelable bardo de la patermaternidad! : [...] el flujo tumulario no se producirá [...] la voz pasiva y los modos compuestos no caben en el nupcial paradigma ... (70–73)[26]

The apparent 'content' here, the incident of the Parejita, is really the pretext for the true content of the passage which is the writing of the narrative itself. However, the 'content', far from being irrelevant, is intimately bound up with the theme of writing in a network of binary oppositions which equates conventional writing with heterosexuality, Europeanness, 'normality'.

In a later passage the narrator announces his intention to carry on his subversion via a deliberate project of expressing the unsayable, 'cantarás a partir de ahora lo indecible, aberrante y enorme' (77–78). As this chapter progresses, the narrator charts his gradual process of discarding the values of his society ('lentamente te has despojado de los hábitos y principios de tu niñez' [83]), but insisting that the true dispossession must take place on a linguistic level:

> no basta con echar por la borda rostro, nombre, familia, costumbres, tierra : la ascesis debe continuar : cada palabra de tu idioma te tiende igualmente una trampa : en adelante aprenderás a pensar contra tu propia lengua ... (83)

At this point it is not clear what form this linguistic process will take, the narrator merely making an allusion to the omnipotence inherent in the writing process (85). The narrator then ends, however, with an emphatic statement of his subversive intent, one which takes the form of a rebellion of the body:

> a su espíritu de autoridad y jerarquía, fundado en prohibiciones y leyes, opondréis la subversión igualitaria y genérica del cuerpo parado, desnudo el sexo, sí, el sexo ... (88)

In Chapter III the narrator is drawn in imagination to the Arab workers in the Paris streets and is reminded of his guilt complex at belonging to a privileged caste:

> justo en el punto en que el odio irreductible a tus propias señas (raza profesión clase familia tierra) crecía en la misma proporción que el impulso magnético hacia los parias y toda la violencia impuesta en nombre de la grey civilizadora (a la que exteriormente aún pertenecías) ... (94)

Once again he seeks 'redemption' in the writing process along with the 'gozo de profanar su blancura' (96). The writing process is seen to have two related consequences: the principal one is the possibility of writing as salvation; the secondary one is that of pleasure, a pleasure intimately linked to the act of profanation. In this case the desire to identify with the Arabs in writing leads to a rejection of the technique of mimetic realism based on 'una escueta descripción linear' and 'la ilusoria operación de nombrarlos' (97). Instead, the method chosen will be to convey their physical presence by the use of an explicitly baroque linguistic style:

> imponiendo su existencia física en el papel gracias a una suntuosa proliferación de signos, al cúmulo exuberante de figuras de lenguaje ... (97)

Chapters III and IV centre on the twin dimensions of space and time respectively, seen as the 'binomio opresor espacio-tiempo' (141). The limitations of the spatio-temporal realm govern not only the real but, by implication, any literary mode that aims at verisimilitude. Hence the novel vaunts its freedom to disregard these restrictions, the narrator claiming 'has recorrido de un extremo al otro el ámbito del Islam' (174) by means of the power of writing 'sin abandonar por eso un instante el surco genitivo de la escritura' (99). The novel continually displays its ability to do whatever it chooses, the space of writing is a realm of absolute freedom: 'todo es posible en la página' (114). The speaker, as happens frequently in metafiction, refers to his divine status in the text (119).

One of the ways the novelist-protagonist reveals his attitude to writing is through his identification with alter egos. There are three main alter egos in the novel, T. E. Lawrence, Père Charles de Foucauld, the French missionary in Africa, and the apostate Anselm Turmeda (1352–1432) who became Ibn Turmeda when he converted from Christianity to Islam in 1386.[27] The principal alter ego is T. E. Lawrence, someone whose relation with the Arab world resembled Goytisolo's own, characterized by a mixture of sexual attraction and moral guilt at being a member of the colonizing class, and also someone whose ambiguous relation with the victim in real life was superseded and 'redeemed' in a work of art. In the section 'El octavo pilar de la sabiduría' there is an intertextual reference to the theories of Jakobson in the recognition of the difference between the sign and the referent, 'descubriendo con candoroso asombro el margen que separa el objeto del signo y la futilidad de los recursos empleados para colmarlo' (126),[28] and Barthes, who, in the face of the limitations of a pseudo-realism's attachment to the referent, proclaimed the liberating possibilities of discourse: 'la habilidad del relato suplanta la dudosa realidad de los hechos' (126).[29] This had been mentioned earlier in the novel when the narrator, in his panegyric of King Kong, had proclaimed his project of sexual-linguistic subversion, 'sacrificando el referente a la verdad del discurso' (77; cf. also p. 304).

The section reveals the narrator's rejection of any mode of writing which makes a pretence to objective representation. The contrast is made between history and art. Lawrence had stated in *Seven Pillars of Wisdom* that 'the history is not of the Arab movement, but of me in it' and was keen to reject any claim to history, viewing it rather as a personal account.[30] Lawrence's book is indeed an extremely literary, artistic work more concerned with reassessing his own personal and political motivation than with giving an objective account of events. The narrator sides with Lawrence in renouncing any claims to represent reality in favour of engagement with the reader through a personal writing style:

> decidirás abandonar para siempre tus hueras presunciones de historiador :
> renunciando a las reglas del juego inane para imponer al lector tu propio y
> aleatorio modelo en lucha con el clisé común ... (126)

Later in Chapter V the narrator, echoing the terminology of Benveniste and Barthes, will reject the realist mode in favour of a more subjective and imaginative alternative (231). The use of the term 'aleatory', a favoured term in Goytisolo's vocabulary as well as a favourite concept of the twentieth-century avant-garde in general, in relation to the novel, as with the narrator's stress on the 'arbitrariness' of his narrative (115, 311) and its subjective mode, is a constant disclaimer of any kind of truth in the sense of objective knowledge of reality.

The novel, in other words, like *Don Julián* is aiming at producing an epistemological shift in the reader. Foregrounding language and literary conventions traditionally taken for granted is part of this 'defamiliariz-ing' procedure. But as with *Don Julián*, this novel is not merely seeking to renew perception but to subvert at a more profound level certain cherished epistemological traditions. This is a trend of the postmodern novel in general.[31] We can see this in the section 'Variaciones sobre un tema fesí', which invokes the non-representational, non-teleological principles suggested by Arabic architecture as a model for textual construction. Here, too, the reader is mentioned. The narrator sees his purpose as to use his imagination to confuse the reader: 'extraviarás al futuro lector' (145). There is also the implication of an extra-textual motivation for the process of reader disorientation: 'soltarle otra vez al mundo, enseñarle a dudar' (146). Part of this disorientation is achieved, the text implies, through the exploitation of the natural ambiguity of the personal pronouns 'I/You' (158)[32] to suggest the fundamentally autonomous nature of literary language:

> mudan las sombras errantes en vuestra imprescindible horma huera, y
> hábilmente podrás jugar con los signos sin que el lector ingenuo lo advierta:
> sumergiéndole en un mundo fluyente, sometido a un proceso continuo de
> destrucción ... (159)

Barthes refers to these grammatical categories of the person as ones that 'can only be defined in relation to the instance of discourse, not to that of reality'.[33] The novel claims for itself a narrative ambiguity through the reader's inability to establish with any certainty who speaks. Yet the extent to which this is actually accomplished is dubious. It was Benveniste who defined discourse as the form of speech which enables a speaker to posit himself as subject:

> C'est en s'identifiant comme personne unique prononçant 'je' que chacun des
> locuteurs se pose tour à tour comme 'sujet'.[34]

For Benveniste, 'you' and 'I' were empty signifiers whose signifieds were only provided in the context of the speech act. Goytisolo's text echoes this when it says 'pronombres apersonales, moldes substantivos vacíos!' (158). The problem, we shall see, is that the reader's tendency is always to naturalize the narrative as a communicative situation. In a way, Goytisolo himself reveals the weakness of the assertion with the term 'lector ingenuo'. For any experienced reader will assume this ambiguity and naturalize it at a higher level. In *Juan sin tierra* this level is the level of the text writer-narrator. With the alter egos the reader rapidly becomes accustomed to recognizing that the narrator 'assumes' the voice of the character (Lawrence, Foucauld or Turmeda) incorporating quotes from the original, as when the narrator mentions 'to imitate their mental foundation y cameleónicamente take on Arab skin' (98), echoing Lawrence's words in *Seven Pillars of Wisdom*.[35] The narrator slips in and out of the alter ego, establishing an affinity with him and using his identity as a way of expanding on his own dilemma. A reader familiar with structuralist theory would recognize immediately the explicit intertextuality. In the novel it is made explicit when the writer-narrator remarks on how 'de un mero trazo de pluma os hago asumir el dictado de mis voces proteicas, cambiantes' (158). One of the difficulties, therefore, with *Juan sin tierra* is that the explicit theorizing on the actual narrative practice, as in the above quotation, has as its corollary the effect of defusing the intended subversive impact. There is, in other words, a clash between narratorial orientation and the aim of textual disorientation.

Chapter V of the novel introduces the theme of utopia. This is immediately given a literary connotation in the link between utopianism and the renunciation of realism:

> saltarás al futuro verbal...sin aval de la tercera persona del aoristo propia de la enunciación histórica y su lustroso barniz de verdad ... (231)[36]

Utopian thinking has traditionally attempted to liberate us from the conventionally restricting notions of space and time. As Vincent Geoghegan has said:

> By playing fast and loose with time and space, logic and morality, and by thinking the unthinkable, a utopia asks the most awkward, the most embarrassing questions.[37]

Juan sin tierra's critique of realism involves a critique of that convention's adherence to the restrictions that affect reality, the 'binomio opresor espacio-tiempo' (141). Chapter III flouts the traditional spatial conventions of the novel by having the narrator range at will over the entire geography of the Arab world. Chapter IV demonstrates a similar freedom in the temporal realm by satirizing the anti-sensual bias of the Spanish cultural tradition beginning with the *Corbacho*. Chapter V deliberately chooses the unconventional future tense in opposition to the 'tercera persona del aoristo propia de la enunciación histórica y su lustroso barniz de verdad' (231). The effect is to mark the novel's break with traditional realism but also to emphasize the point that the apparent 'realism' of the conventional novel is as much an illusion as Goytisolo's metafictional fantasy. This chapter also underlines Goytisolo's view of the essentially utopian nature of literature. Previous utopian visions are satirized for being too rationalistic, failing to come to terms with man's physical side. Goytisolo's thinking is more in tune with the utopian thinkers such as Fourier and Lafargue, the 'postergado yerno' (245). Geoghegan has pointed out how Fourier's achievement

> was to go beyond the Enlightenment clichés on the natural goodness of humanity by radically redefining the good and its origins. He rejected the impoverishment involved in the spiritualization or dematerialization of humanity by giving due importance, for example, to the sensual passions of sight, hearing, touch, smell and taste.[38]

Chapter V is therefore a deliberately hyperbolic celebration of the body as a provocative counter to the emphasis of the traditional utopian vision on reason. In its eccentric and unworkable ideas it captures the flavour of Fourier's 'mad notions',[39] but it is intended less as a utopian vision in its own right than as a subversive parody of the traditional utopia which is seen as suffering from the same dependence on reason and denial of the body as the bourgeois society it criticized.

As we have already seen, at several points the link between utopia and the textual process is made explicit:

> paraíso, el tuyo, con culo y con falo, donde un lenguaje-metáfora subyugue el objeto al verbo y, liberadas de sus mazmorras y grillos, las palabras al fin, las traidoras, esquivas palabras, vibren, dancen, copulen, se encueren y cobren cuerpo ... (234)

The textual analogue of the utopia posited by the narrator is a 'lenguaje-metáfora', released from the instrumental, communicative function. Later, speaking of the ideal pattern of sexual relationships in this utopia, the narrator speaks of the alternative to the Parejita Reproductora:

> nuestro remedio? : muy simple : una ars combinatoria de elementos dispares (individuos de todos los sexos, razas, edades) de acuerdo con los principios que rigen la peculiar construcción artística (incluyendo imponderables de improvisación y de juego) : tríos, cuartetos, septetos, décimas de estructura mudable, ligera ... (243)

The idea of the 'construcción artística' of the couplings draws attention to the link, as does the subsequent reference to the Calder mobile:

> postulando mejor la elasticidad de esos móbiles airosos de Calder, cuya esbelta trabazón obedece a una corriente multilateral y secreta, hecha de atracciones y repelencia, fuerzas centrípetas y disgregadoras : arquitecturas en equilibrio fugaz y precario, de acróbata, bailarín o funámbulo, propicias al

> virtuosismo lúdico, artesanal : campo magnético en el que opera la búsqueda
> zahorí del poeta ... (243–44)

The reference to the 'ars combinatoria' both recalls structuralist
theory and points ahead, as does the whole account, to the passage in
Chapter VII in which the narrator outlines his aesthetic manifesto:

> improvisando la arquitectura del objeto literario no en un tejido de relaciones
> de orden lógico-temporal sino en un ars combinatoria de elementos
> (oposiciones, alternancias, juegos simétricos) sobre el blanco rectangular de
> la página ... (311)

That this was how Goytisolo himself saw the novel is clear from the
comment in *Disidencias*:

> En *Juan sin tierra* el orden lógico y el temporal son sistemáticamente
> destruidos y la estructura de la obra, como la de un poema, se desarrolla en el
> plano espacial. El lector deberá 'leerla' como un móvil de Calder. (D, 316)

The themes of utopia and textuality are intermingled, with the
emphasis falling naturally on the latter. The text of the novel is a
literary equivalent to the utopia of sexual liberation. The text's
liberation from conventional literary meaning, which in Goytisolo's
view 'seguía aferrada a la reproducción del mundo exterior' (D, 323),
and its creation of a dynamic space of plural meanings, is a textual
surrogate for the unattainable utopia on the level of reality.

Chapter VI carries out a humorous critique of the realist novel not
only by parodying its conventions and revealing them as such, but by
giving a potted history of the novel from the Pastoral novel, by way of
Cervantes, to the modernist novel and its destruction of the traditional
concept of the novelistic character. In doing so it shows Realism to be
merely a historical category. The narrator takes issue in particular with
the Lukacsian principle, dominant in the Spanish social realist novel of
the 1950s, of the 'encargo social', that is, the belief that the author had a
moral obligation to society and his novels must engage with reality and
social problems. Instead the narrator argues for a more personal,
subjective approach to literature, its right to be ludic and experimental,
with no social or moral purpose at all.

The epigraph to Chapter VII, taken from *La Celestina*, as well as
being a clear act of solidarity with that other *marginado*, Fernando de
Rojas, implies that the narrator in the previous chapters has succeeded
in exorcizing the social responsibility of the artist and freed himself. It
would seem that the conventions of realism and referentiality having
been undermined, the narrator is free to proclaim and construct his
ideal text:

> Pues agora sin temor, como quien no tiene que perder, como aquel a quien tu
> compañía es ya enojosa, como caminante pobre que sin temor de los crueles
> salteadores va cantando en alta voz ... (309)

The first passage of Chapter VII is a virtual manifesto that advocates removal of representationality ('teatralidad'), plot ('peripecia'), rounded characters ('personaje de carne y hueso') and in their place the production of meaning via the internal relations between the narrative elements within a self-consciously textual space.

What the speaker is arguing for here is the essentially limitless possibilities of the writing process which are unnecessarily restricted by the demands of realism:

> con la pluma en la boca, asaetando a balazos (palabras) las múltiples orientaciones posibles : causalidad restrictiva, determinismo avaro del triste pájaro en mano antepuesto a la embriaguez de la centena aerícola : acciones lógicas, sintaxis coherente, motivaciones claras! (312)

Again the text makes an allusion to structuralist theory, in this case, Jakobson's model of linguistic communication:

> completando las funciones de representación, expresión y llamada inherentes a una comunicación oral cuyos elementos (emisor, receptor, contexto, contacto) operan también (aunque de modo diverso) en el instante de la lectura con una cuarta función (erógena?) que centrará exclusivamente su atención en el signo lingüístico ... (312–13)

Jakobson is invoked to argue the case for literature's natural set towards the message (which in Jakobson's analysis means the act of verbal communication, not its content). This Jakobson defines as its 'poetic' function as opposed, among other things, to its referential function:

> Poetic function is not the sole function of verbal art but only its dominant, determining function, whereas in all other verbal activities it acts as a subsidiary, accessory constituent.[40]

Cast in Jakobsonian terms, *Juan sin tierra* implies that conventional, realist literature ignores the true dominant and instead treats as its dominant the referential function. The 'autonomía del objeto literario' claimed in the text must also be understood in this context not to mean that the text is hermetically sealed and unconnected to the world, but merely that the 'dominant' laws for the production of meaning are those of literature ('un ars combinatoria de elementos [oposiciones, alternancias, juegos simétricos]' [311]) not those of verisimilitude. This, of course, is a principle which applies to all literature and therefore, like most metafiction, *Juan sin tierra* foregrounds facets of the novel in general that are disguised by the referential illusion.[41]

The novel advocates self-consciousness in the sense of a continual foregrounding of the process of enunciation, of the author in the act of writing the novel (126). It also advocates maximum foregrounding of the signifier, and in so doing plays on its naturally ambiguous nature.

This prioritizing of the signifier on the level of language has its correlative on the level of literary form in the rejection of mimesis and referentiality in favour of self-conscious and self-justifying form. *Juan sin tierra*, carrying on from *Don Julián*, aims to undermine what it sees as a teleological urge in Western man, compelled by a desire to establish fixed meanings and ascribe a moral purpose to literature. The implication is that this constitutes the pursuit of a chimera that results in the denial of enjoyment in the here and now. This is seen as an unfortunate outcome of the combined effect of the prevailing ideology of progress and the Christian religion that permanently defers pleasure. Hence the Cuban revolution, an example of one of the rational utopias, is criticized for 'suprimir la libertad viva de hoy en nombre de la imaginaria libertad de mañana' (14). Alvarito is likewise counselled by the Angel to put off present pleasure (in defecation) in the interests of his soul. Hence too the Cuban dancer on the record sleeve is described as

> cuerpo real sin duda que no acata otra ley que el soberano disfrute [...]
> partidario resuelto de un hic et nunc muy precisos [...] dando a entender que
> ella, la gorda, sólo aspira a dar placer y a recibirlo pues la vida es sabrosa y
> debe apurarse sin remilgos ni teorías, con la conciencia tosca pero clara de
> que no hay otra realidad fuera de la que uno ve, gusta y toca ... (13)

In the same way that the novel on the thematic level glorifies the body in opposition to the prevailing denial of the body, on the textual level it advocates a textual hedonism as a counter to the logocentrism that characterizes Western culture. In the essay on Paz and Sarduy in *Disidencias*, Goytisolo reveals his affinity with the post-structuralist mood of the day:

> El logocentrismo de nuestra cultura (o el copiado, fuera de ella, de nuestra
> ideología exportada) conduce a la situación aberrante de un mundo en el que
> el goce debe ocultarse tras la máscara de la razón (política, social, religiosa)
> ... (D, 185)

Essential to this hedonism, clearly redolent of Barthes and his *Le Plaisir du texte*, is the aspiration towards a text devoid of social intent, of moral purpose, and part of this is the hedonistic enjoyment of the materiality of the signifier. All of this is summed up in the frequent analogy between masturbation and writing: 'manipulación improductiva (onanista) de la palabra escrita, ejercicio autosuficiente (poético) del goce ilegal' (313). However, implicit in this, as in Barthes' theory, is the clear ideological and social motivation of this subversive hedonism. This had been summed up in Barthes' comment on Sarduy's novel, *De donde son los cantantes*, which he termed a 'texto hedonista y por ende, revolucionario'[42]—a paradox with which Goytisolo revealed himself familiar in his essay on Sarduy (D, 187).

The literary theory of *Juan sin tierra* must be understood in the context of the post-structuralist mood of the day, in particular the *Tel Quel*ian variety that reigned in the early 1970s. The *Tel Quel* group carried to an extreme a feature common to that 'politicized' branch of the structuralist and post-structuralist movement most clearly represented by Barthes, and that was the intimate link, a kind of homology, between the social, political, economic and linguistic spheres, as a result of which the realist text could be seen as synonymous with bourgeois values and the self-reflexive, modernist text as, therefore, ipso facto revolutionary.[43] Goytisolo's sympathy with this view is clear from the reference, quoted above, to logocentrism. The entire structure of *Juan sin tierra* can be seen to be established on the basis of these homological relationships between realism and Western bourgeois values, especially in terms of religion and sexuality. Similarly, *Juan sin tierra*'s acute self-reflexiveness, its emphasis on hedonism, as well as its assault on referentiality and exaltation of a 'poetic' use of language as inherently revolutionary, situates it close to the *Tel Quel*ian system of values.

Viewed in this context, the conflict between the novel's self-referentiality and what Bernstein calls 'real-life concerns'[44] and Nelson 'transcendent meanings'[45] is only an apparent contradiction. For Goytisolo, as for Barthes and the *Tel Quel*ians, the literary process has a very precise social significance. What I have tried to show throughout this study is that there is really no contradiction between Goytisolo's literary and linguistic self-reflexiveness and his social concerns, but rather that the former constitutes a more sophisticated response to the latter. As he himself put it, he simply transferred his commitment to another level.[46] Nonetheless, there are aspects of Goytisolo's theory and practice in *Juan sin tierra*, related to his affinity with the particular brand of post-structuralist criticism of the day, which present more serious problems and can be seen ultimately to weaken the novel.

The Practice of Theory

Part of the overall metafictional nature of the text is that it combines the practice of fiction with overt theorization on that practice. In *Juan sin tierra* this takes two forms. On the one hand there is the constant self-reflexiveness where the narrator, during the process of the text's construction, reflects on that process itself:

> interrumpirás la lectura de documentos : frases extraídas de los libros y fotocopias se superponen en tu memoria a la carta de la esclava al bisabuelo resucitando indemne tu odio hacia la estirpe que te dio el ser ... (51)

On the other hand, there are sections in which the narrator posits a radically new kind of writing:

> alzarás bloques de piedras sonoras, las sustraerás a la tiranía del razonable uso y les permitirás crecer y agruparse, atraerse, excluirse, dóciles a los campos magnéticos y afinidades secretas que imantan la búsqueda aleatoria del zahorí ... (145–46)

In terms of the former, *Juan sin tierra* can be seen to take narrative self-consciousness to the extreme. The novel becomes a skilful and entertaining 'deconstruction' of the conventional novel. The conventions of realism are exploded as the novel draws attention to the writing process itself. The subject of the novel is its own process of production. However, Goytisolo manages, by a complex network of analogies, to convert this narrative solipsism into political comment. For Goytisolo, self-conciousness is the highest form of honesty on the part of a writer.[47] It has an ideological function in so far as it is the mark of a novel which refuses to disguise its textuality, its 'body', in the interest of a transcendent 'truth'. The novel's network of metaphors and analogies allows the reader to establish the links between self-conciousness on the textual level and the thematic motifs of the slaves and the 'zanja común', openly displaying and revelling in their instinctive urges in opposition to the bourgeois family intent on disguising their nature and aspiring to spirituality. This spirituality of the capitalist family, abetted by Christian doctrine, is shown to be simply a manner of denying the body in the interests of productivity, an example on a reduced scale of the Freudian theory of civilization. The novel sets itself up in opposition to this repressive metaphysics and encourages a celebration of the present moment. This is how *Juan sin tierra* contextualizes the metafictional nature of the novel as an integral part of the ideological critique. In this way the problem most critics see with the novel's self-referentiality and, at the same time, its referentiality (in the sense of its meaningful engagement with the outside world) is not a contradiction, but a deliberately contrived effect. If Goytisolo in *Juan sin tierra* manages, according to Herzberger, to straddle the Word/World conflict, that is because it is his intention to do so.[48]

Part of the problem with *Juan sin tierra*'s self-reflexiveness is that it is accompanied by a large amount of literary theorizing, as I pointed out in the previous section. Rather than merely commenting on its own procedures, 'laying bare the device', *Juan sin tierra* actually advocates a radically new type of text, one which destroys referentiality with the intention, not, as critics like Herzberger would have it, of writing a book about nothing, but rather of creating a polysemically plural text. In this way, *Juan sin tierra* takes part in a textual revolt characteristic of the period in which it was produced. Susan Rubin Suleiman sums up this literary debate as follows:

> The realist novel, founded on the aesthetic of verisimilitude and representation, is one of the most fully realized manifestations of the dialectic between 'poetry' and communication, between spectacle and message. It is precisely against this kind of novel that the modern 'textual' revolt has been directed—a revolt that has taken the form of an attempt to systematically suppress the referential element in writing, and corollarily to emphasize its self-referential element. It has been a revolt against a (single) meaning. To render impossible the emergence of an unambiguous meaning by the production of 'plural' texts, to create works that will communicate 'nothing but the dramatization of their own functioning' (Ricardou)—such has been the programme of modernist writing.[49]

The question of reference is, of course, one of the major bugbears of contemporary theory. Formalism asserted that, as opposed to everyday speech, based on the communicative function, poetic language is governed by its own immanent laws. *Juan sin tierra*, by stressing its textual nature, foregrounding language and revealing its method of composition to come not from reference to the 'real' but to other texts, discourses, which it cannibalizes and weaves into a new text, aligns itself with the Formalist approach. As mentioned earlier, the allusion to Jakobson's theory of communication, rather than denying reference completely, merely urged that the 'poetic' function be the 'dominant'. Such disruption of the normal semantic process is seen as a means of generating, not non-meaning, but a plurality of meanings, polysemy:

> conmutando la anomalía semántica en núcleo generador de poesía y aunando de golpe, en polisémico acorde, sexualidad y escritura ... (313)

Elsewhere, the narrator had proclaimed this possibility of freeing language from referentiality and creating a metaphoric language:

> imponiendo su existencia física en el papel gracias a una suntuosa proliferación de signos, al cúmulo exuberante de figuras de lenguaje : echando mano de todos los ardides de la retórica : tropos, sinécdoques, metonimias, metáforas : tendiendo hasta el límite los músculos de la frase ... (97)

Gustavo Pellón, in a useful article which, unfortunately, fails to develop many of the points made, remarks on this tendency towards semantic disruption in the work of both Goytisolo and the Cuban writer, Severo Sarduy. According to Pellón, both writers 'se dedican al cultivo de las rupturas del eje sintagmático y al deleite del desenfreno paradigmático'.[50] In the case of Sarduy, this is done by 'un discurso saturado de símiles, metáforas y analogías' (486), whereas in Goytisolo 'la ruptura de la sintaxis ... se lleva a cabo por medio de la enumeración, las listas, los catálogos' (486). We can see a reference to this in the text itself when in Chapter VII the narrative advocates

eschewing a 'sintaxis coherente' in favour of 'una enigmática, libera-
dora proliferación de signos' (312). An example is the passage describing the Arab workers in the street:

> cuerpos envueltos en el rigor y la dureza de sus creencias, aferrados a su
> instinto de vida como a un axioma neto e incontestable, dejarás que su
> presencia se imponga con la claridad cegadora de un aforismo : embebiéndote
> poco a poco de su espíritu nómada, de su cálida, bienhechora esencia solar :
> independiente y libre también como un jeque beduino : dueño del aire, los
> vientos, la luz, los vastos espacios, el inmenso vacío ... (97–98)

Liberation is obviously only for the writer in the writing process and
possibly for the reader in the reading process. The 'unliberated'
condition of the Arabs is not altered by the description.

Juan sin tierra effects the subversion of the fixed signifier–signified
link in similar ways to those seen in *Don Julián*. Traditional syntactic
patterns (sentences logically linked to form a narrative), whose function
is to ensure that meaning inheres along the syntagmatic chain, are
abandoned and instead the text juxtaposes short phrases or simply
images. Within the individual sections, narrative elements are out-
numbered by the proliferation of metaphors and associations of ideas.
This can be seen in the reduced number of verbs which would carry
forward the narrative. Those verbs that do occur tend to be in the
temporally ambiguous form of the infinitive or the gerund. *Juan sin
tierra* does not reject reference outright but rejects transparency of
reference. Language's denotative function is subordinated to its connotative function. Hence, for example, in the opening pages the
narrative 'refers' to the photograph on the record sleeve. The text
enacts a minute description of the singer in which language rapidly
takes on a life of its own. The thing referred to is subordinate to the
apparent delectation the narrator takes in the manipulation of language.
Yet it is not impossible to recognize the persistence of a correspondence
between the language and its referent. The photograph is of a sensual
singer representative of the joys of the flesh, 'cuerpo real sin duda'. As
with the reference to the Arabs mentioned above, the text seeks to
provide a textual equivalent to the object in question.

In *Disidencias*, Goytisolo praises Lezama's style which avoids 'el
malthusianismo verbal inherente a la comunicación ordinaria en
nombre de la deliberada opacidad del lenguaje poético'. Still speaking
of Lezama, he goes on to say that 'el poeta reemplaza así el lenguaje
transparente con el lenguaje figurado para imponer la presencia de las
palabras—el lenguaje común con el lenguaje literario para imponer la
presencia de las cosas' (D, 261). In both cases, that of the Cuban singer
and the Arabs in the street, although referents do exist, the text works
to complicate the process of reference, foreground language and make it
the principal protagonist of the narrative. As Goytisolo had said of the

language of Lezama, 'la expansión del lenguaje ... emula con la realidad y la sustituye con un cuerpo verbal' (D, 261).

On other occasions the language is so highly figurative and connotative that the actual signified is almost impossible to determine, and several possible 'meanings' suggest themselves. An example is section 10 of Chapter II. The exact nature of the scene conjured up is difficult to ascertain, but seems to be one of (homosexual?) prostitution in the basement toilets of a cinema. To understand the location in toilets one has to recognize 'los auríferos, no revolucionarios edículos' (83) as an echo of the references in Don Julián to 'desdeñados, oportunos templetes que el generoso Lenin soñara en erigir en oro' (DJ, 54), and again 'la negrísima gruta destinada a aliviar comunes, elementales necesidades : de oro, no : pre-revolucionaria' (DJ, 58), themselves references to the utopian visions of Lenin and More.[51] The passage appears to be a recrimination for four hundred years of repressiveness (since the Reconquest) which has led to such sordid outlets for frustrated sexuality. This passage is one of the most obscure in the novel and typifies the technique of concealing the signified beneath a welter of signifiers alluding to such a variety of different areas (Spanish history and cinematography, utopian literature).

Juan sin tierra's play with the signifier–signified relationship and attack on instrumentality in language is part of a broader subversion of the tendency on the part of the reader to attach meanings, go through the language and the text to an overall meaning or interpretation. To the hermeneutic and teleological nature of narrative and, concomitantly, of the reading process, *Juan sin tierra* proposes a text that resists meaning. The model of Arabic architecture was the example. The image of the text endlessly turning in on itself and eluding interpretation like the intricate web of streets in an Arab city where the foreigner finally gets lost and abandons himself to the mystery of the system was also a dominant motif in Don Julián. The text aspires to a fluidity and mobility which will communicate nothing and merely frustrate the reader's interpretative urge:

> recovecos, escondrijos, curvas de un camino versátil que culebrea de modo arbitrario sin conducir finalmente a salida alguna [...] seguirás el ejemplo del alarife anónimo y extraviarás al futuro lector en los meandros y trampas de tu escritura ... (145)

However, the degree to which the novel actually succeeds in creating this polysemic, plural, endlessly metaphoric text is questionable. It undoubtedly does undermine completely the normal referential illusion and obliges the reader to see the process of textual construction as the subject of the novel. It also manages to give this textual activity a political and ideological significance by its network of analogies. Its use of a predominance of image and metaphor over other elements that would advance the narrative succeeds in arresting the reader's natural urge towards story and reference in favour of a greater awareness of linguistic play. Nevertheless, it is not possible to say that the novel actually does liberate the signifier, nor achieve the category of plural text that it sets for itself. The words of *Juan sin tierra* do not ever manage to 'vibrate, dance, and copulate' free of their referential chains, and it is not merely because words never can. However, we have established that Goytisolo does not aim at non-reference but at plural reference, the liberation of the signifier from a fixed meaning. In many cases, Goytisolo does achieve through metaphor a form of semantic ambiguity, an example being the one mentioned earlier of section 10, Chapter II. The previous sections too, dealing with the 'adoradores del bicho', appear to be an extended homosexual metaphor. Such metaphors are familiar to the reader of Goytisolo. The motif of the snake as a metaphor for the penis and homosexuality was recurrent in *Don Julián* and is understandable in the context of Chapter II with its numerous phallic metaphors.

Nonetheless, such metaphoric discourse is not the same as polysemy. The novel clearly departs from any straightforward referential purpose in the sense of creating a fictionally coherent world, yet stops short of a truly liberating linguistic plurality as suggested in the image of the words breaking free of their 'mazmorras y grillos', i.e. their meanings. *Juan sin tierra*, as the above quotation suggests, aims to liberate the reader by confusing him and by subjecting him to an experience that challenges his normal interpretive strategies, based on a teleological urge for an ultimate meaning.

The novel, then, appears to aspire to the liberating effect of indeterminable meaning. Yet there are two factors which militate against this. One is the rigid system of binary oppositions which underlies the novel's theme. The other is the nature of the narrator in the novel.

As has been pointed out, *Juan sin tierra* is governed by a set of hierarchies that are all variations on the same essential opposition between mind or spirit and body, 'cara' and 'culo'. The novel's attack on the former and celebration of the latter is itself a variation on the post-structuralist critique of a repressive Western rationality. Goytisolo has often been criticized for this tendency to simply invert the existing order of things. The quotation from Mainer mentioned at the beginning of this chapter is a case in point. Schaefer-Rodríguez has also said of *Juan sin tierra*: 'La paradoja de esta llamada "revolución" es su perpetuación de los polos y el antagonismo sin cambios'.[52] One can justify the rigidity of the oppositions presented in the novel as a sign of the intractable nature of repressive reality. Similarly, the novel's predominantly 'negative' stance derives from the view that, given such an implacable enemy, the novel's prime aim is to contest that reality by negating it, by affirming its opposite. *Juan sin tierra* sees itself as a subversive 'artefacto' which is added to the 'monumento' of the corpus of the Spanish novel in order to distil 'el agente (caústico, corrosivo, mordaz) que la corrompe y desgasta' (319). Like a bomb, its sole purpose is to destroy. However, as I stated in the introduction to this chapter, implicit in this destruction is the hope of something better taking its place. Likewise, implicit in *Juan sin tierra*'s assault on the 'cara' and celebration of the 'culo' is the call for a reconciliation of man's dual nature, 'cara y culo parejos, libres y descubiertos, utopía de un mundo complejo, sin asepsia ni ocultación' (234).

Where this rigid dual structure does create problems is in terms of the textual theory proposed by the novel. This hierarchy imposes a fixed interpretive structure on the novel which works against its aim to be a dynamic, mobile, fluid structure. One is led to recall the structural model of Arabic town-planning:

> itinerarios dudosos, periplos inciertos por una maraña inextricable de callejuelas tenazmente ovilladas sobre sí mismas [...] hundiéndote en la angostura cerril de sus uterinas sinuosidades: recovecos, escondrijos, curvas de un camino versátil que culebrea de modo arbitrario sin conducir finalmente a salida alguna ... (145)

Yet the system of oppositions provides the reader with a comfortable hermeneutic framework within which to establish the 'meaning' of the novel. Such a thematic structure acts to 'centre' the text in such a way as to counter Goytisolo's claims for a 'nomadic' structure for the novel:

> este nomadismo se traslada a la estructura misma de la obra. Si todo el mundo viajara, no habría centro ni jefe, ni poder, ni escritura represiva alguna. Muy al revés: libre disposición de cuerpos y bienes, fraternidad leve y móvil, nomadismo de ideas. Esta aspiración descentralizadora y antijerárquica ha desempeñado un papel muy importante en la elaboración del libro.[53]

The second problem, which I will deal with in detail in the following section, concerns the narrator of the text. As we saw with *Don Julián*, another important centring device is the identification of a narrator. Here, too, *Juan sin tierra* presents problems. I had noted Goytisolo's remarks on the way the novel's attempts to gather narrative momentum (on the level of *histoire*) are constantly interrupted by references to the writing process (the level of *discours*). Goytisolo had also commented that the novel had no fixed centre, the narrative voice was 'un yo, o tú baladeur que circulara libremente de un tema a otro'.[54] In the passage referring to Arabic architecture, the narrator proclaims 'seguirás el ejemplo del alarife anónimo', and yet he lacks the essential anonymity and absence of his model. The narrative voice of *Juan sin tierra* may be anonymous in the sense of unnamed (and, even then, the reader can identify him as Alvaro Mendiola), but he is a very definite human presence, a subjectivity, with whom the reader identifies and whom he uses to naturalize the text.

Text and Narration

Juan sin tierra's self-consciousness draws attention to two separate, though related, aspects of the text: the process of narration, which in this case is an act of writing, and the resulting text. It will be useful in this context to refer to Gérard Genette's re-definition of the traditional distinction made between *histoire* and *discours* in *Figures III*. Genette identifies three aspects to the narrative situation: *histoire*, *récit* and *narration*. *Histoire* is the level of the signified, the basic elements of the story. *Récit* is the discourse or narrative text itself in which the elements of *histoire* have been arranged. What Genette adds is the third dimension, *narration*, which is the 'act of narrative production, and, by extension, the real or fictional situation in which it takes place'.[55]

Using this categorization we can see that *Juan sin tierra* manages to eliminate the *histoire*. There is no recognizable level of fictional events. In *Don Julián* this had been retained in the form of the narrator and his daily wandering about Tangiers. In *Juan sin tierra* the 'story' of the novel is, principally, the writing process itelf, the creation of the *récit*. The text does therefore foreground the level of narration, the narrator's act of creating the novel, ensconced in his 'escritorio-cocina' in Paris. Hence, recasting our analysis in Genettian terms, we can say that where in the previous novel we had detected a conflict between the levels of *histoire* (the account of a protagonist in Tangiers) and *narration* (the process on the part of a narrator of constructing a text), in *Juan sin tierra* there is a tension between the levels of *récit* and *narration*, the level of *histoire* having been comprehensively abolished.

Juan sin tierra presents itself both as the culminatory act of self-liberation of the central writer-narrator (Alvaro Mendiola), and as the creation of a text that will stand as a new kind of novel, a permanent subversion of the literary and linguistic tradition. The end of the novel reveals the consequences of both these levels. The narrator 'tells' us through the Arabic inscription that he is 'on the other side'. This and the Arabic imply that he has finally achieved the break with Spanish culture and his Spanish identity. On the level of text, the author tells us that the novel will endure and act as a subverting agent within the body of Spanish language and literature:

> agregando tu artefacto a su monumento, pero destilando al mismo tiempo el agente (cáustico, corrosivo, mordaz) que la corrompe y desgasta ...

> progenitura infame, su (tu) subversión (ideológica, narrativa, semántica)
> proseguirá independientemente su labor de zapa por los siglos de los siglos . . .
> (319–20)

The ending of *Juan sin tierra* is a symbolic one. The transformation of the narrative into Arabic is for artistic effect and is coherent with the trajectory of the novel. The narrator had wished to break away from Spanish culture and identify himself with the pariah, the Other of a different culture. The principal model was the Arab. Given that the novel, and the Trilogy, had emphasized that language was the ultimate constituent of identity, the dissolution of Spanish ('pensar contra tu propia lengua' [83]) and its transformation into Arabic charts symbolically the accomplishment of that process. The narrator achieves his liberation by finally breaking communication with the reader, renouncing thus the essential characteristic of the conventional novel, the narrative contract. All of this, of course, is part of the metafictional game, the play with the reader's expectations.

If we see the novel as an attempt at a plural text, or one arranged spatially like a painting or architectural structure, such an intention would appear undermined by the presence throughout of this narrative voice, which not only centres the discourse of the text, but gives it a human, psychological and even social motivation. In this way the novel, with its preservation of the persona of Alvaro and the provision of the reader at the end, if he did not have it already, with 'la clave que te permite interpretar su trayecto (el del otro) de modo retrospectivo' (313), appears to hold too many interpretive hostages to fortune up to the 'comisario-gendarme-aduanero disfrazado de crítico'. There is a clear contradiction between the 'biographical' detail of the slave's letter which explains the genesis of the text and the incident in the Zoco Grande (314) which explains the birth of the author's aesthetic project, and the text's own claim to the 'autonomía del objeto literario'. Gustavo Pellón had remarked that:

> A pesar de su adherencia a la poética posestructuralista, en las novelas a partir de *Señas de identidad*, hay un aspecto de la escritura de Goytisolo que milita en contra de su poética. Se trata del interés psicológico del autor que se desplaza de los personajes en una novela como *Duelo en el Paraíso* al narrador goytisoliano de la trilogía.[56]

The narrator of the novel is identifiable as Alvaro Mendiola. However, the referential dimension of this narrator has been radically reduced, from the three days and realistic surroundings of the Mas in *Señas de identidad*, to the more ambiguous but still identifiable twelve hours in Tangiers in *Don Julián*, to the tiny 'escritorio-cocina' and time of the text in *Juan sin tierra*. Gonzalo Sobejano has detected an inverse proportion at work here:

> Una proporción puede establecerse en dependencia de la soledad: a mayor impotencia física dentro de la situación de origen [...] mayor potencia expansiva y traslaticia y más libre movilidad mental.[57]

This corresponds to the pattern we have seen in the gradual elimination of the referential dimension and the parallel increase in the metafictional dimension: the 'real' has given way to the 'textual'.

In *Don Julián* we detected an ambivalent picture of, on the one hand, a character who was a 'real person', living in Tangiers and fixated on Spain and its culture, and, on the other, a writer-narrator composing a text that would be a subversive attack on the Spanish literary tradition. Both were distinct and the narrative did not opt definitively for one or the other. In *Juan sin tierra* there is no ambiguity. The protagonist is clearly the author of the text. The text constitutes his attempt to resolve his existential concerns in the writing process, 'la página virgen te brinda posibilidades de redención exquisitas' (51), and reveals him in a process of transforming his identity by transforming language:

> presto a la súbita imantación del cuerpo que atraerá irresistiblemente el tuyo y os acoplará con fuerza magnética como palabras unidas por el poeta en versátil conjunción fugaz [...] hasta el momento en que las búsquedas paralelas se mezclan, el verbo deviene carne y la amorosa cópula alumbra como una esplendente metáfora ... (298)

This recalls Colin MacCabe's comment on Joyce's work that it was 'concerned not with representing experience through language but with experiencing language through a destruction of representation'.[58] However, where Joyce, according to MacCabe, undermined the stable sense of a subject (or author) and refused the reader a normal position from which to naturalize the text, *Juan sin tierra* does not go that far. The subject is stable throughout and the reader's position in reading is equally stable. The only way that *Juan sin tierra* can solve this problem of the subject and its inevitable relationship with the reader is to brusquely remove him from the picture, closing the door of communication in the face of the reader.[59] This, of course, is no more than a symbolic end. It does not have any really subversive effect on the reading process and contrasts with the superficially less radical but far more unsettling end to *Don Julián*.

Viewed in this way the references to the radical text emerge as mere projections of an ideal text to which the narrative and its narrator aspire. Certain features are accomplished such as the elimination of a referential realm and conventional plot ('discurso sin peripecia alguna...'), although one could object that the text substitutes a traditional narrative with the narrative of its own coming into being and of the dissolution of the traditional novel. *Juan sin tierra* certainly does not lack linearity as it moves from the original motivation of the narrative process (the story of the narrator's family in Cuba) towards the climax in the final chapter.[60] Similarly *Juan sin tierra* manages to 'dinamitar la inveterada noción del personaje de carne y hueso' (although this had been quite successfully done in *Don Julián*) without quite subverting the notion of a narrator.

There is a sense in which the novel seems to admit that this radical text is an ideal. The references to it are couched in the ambiguous verbal forms of the infinitive, with its prescriptive tone, the gerund or the future tense: 'eliminar del corpus ... sustituyendo ... improvisando ...' (311).

The oft-quoted passage in the final chapter about the 'autonomía del objeto literario' commences deprived of verbs, decontextualized, so that it is unclear whether this is an account of *Juan sin tierra*, or a literary ideal or a future text to emerge when the destructive process of *Juan sin tierra* is completed. It goes on, significantly using the future tense, to speak of 'una cuarta función que centrará su atención en el signo lingüístico'. As we saw, in Chapter V, the future tense is the tense of utopia. Earlier the narrator had spoken of 'soñando en el desmesurado placer de lo caprichoso e inverosímil' (312), which again suggests the ideal text as a dream, aspired to but not quite achieved. We noted too that this radical text had been linked in an analogy with the utopian image of liberated lovemaking. In this sense, the radical literary theorizing in the novel can be read as the equivalent of the utopian motif, in other words, half intended as an image of an unrealizable literary goal, half intended as a subversive attack on the conventional view of the text.

Whether it is a deliberate contradiction or not, the text obviously shows a marked inability to shrug off some of the most fundamental 'Western' characteristics that it seeks to reject. In the same way that the Arabic identity will forever remain out of reach to the narrator (except in the surrogate form of a symbolic literary gesture), so too will the aspiration towards a text which eludes the Western tradition of rationality. The elusiveness of this ideal was suggested in the reference to an Arabic scene:

> en un decorado quimérico de alminares mezquitas escuelas coránicas, albornoces velos chilabas recatarán las imágenes inseguras que tu memoria no podrá jamás reconstituir ... (145)

The narrator goes on to propose a text that will elude reason and appear self-justifying, something which *Juan sin tierra*, for all its difficulty, is unable to do.

Conclusion

Juan sin tierra, perhaps more than any other novel by Goytisolo, conforms to what he sees as the characteristics of all avant-garde works which 'abocan a una especie de suicidio ejemplar, a un harakiri de las posibilidades expresivas' (D, 318). The metafictional deconstruction of the traditional novel has been carried out to perfection. Goytisolo exposes the inner workings of the narrative process and allows the latter to constantly usurp the fictional illusion.

The result of such extreme metafiction is a contradictory one. On the one hand it is the supreme act of narrative honesty by which Goytisolo set such store. On the other, of course, the loss of the last trace of referential illusion removes the tension on which the novel's subversion must depend if it is to seduce the reader. As Barthes said in the very book whose influence seems to permeate *Juan sin tierra*, 'subversion must produce its own chiaroscuro'.[61] *Juan sin tierra*'s subversion of conventions of realism is skilful and entertaining but has little impact on the reader because his natural susceptibility to the referential illusion is never engaged. Goytisolo himself said of the novel: 'he procurado darle una forma más ensayística que propiamente narrativa'.[62]

As is often the case in overt metafiction, the figure of the reader is thematized and made an integral part of the textual process. Linda Hutcheon comments on the unsettling effect that modern metafiction can have on the reader:

> The unsettled reader is forced to scrutinize his own concepts of art as well as his life values. Often he must revise his understanding of what he reads so frequently that he comes to question the very possibility of understanding. In doing so he might be freed from enslavement not only to the empirical, but also to his own set patterns of thought and imagination.[63]

One of the standard ways that metafiction does this is by disturbing the ontological boundaries of the text, confusing the reader's sense of the relation between fiction and reality, or more accurately, between textuality and fictional illusion. As we noted earlier, Spires claims that *Juan sin tierra* violates narrative levels whereas, in fact, the novel makes the narrative situation perfectly clear.

The lack of confusion over the narrative situation and, above all, the strong presence of a narratorial persona means that the reader does not have any difficulty in naturalizing the text. Its metafictional context is unproblematic. Goytisolo spoke of the way the metafictional elements intrude in order to disrupt the narrative momentum of the text.[64] The comment suggests that this is an unsettling, subversive feature. In fact, the effect is the opposite, for the illusion of a referential dimension in *Juan sin tierra*, unlike *Don Julián*, does not exist. The novel instead clearly foregrounds itself as a novel whose theme is its own process of creation.

Nor does the novel achieve the effect of those texts which Patricia Waugh has termed 'radical metafiction':

> They function through forms of radical decontextualization. They deny the reader access to a centre of orientation such as a narrator or point of view, or a stable tension between 'fiction', 'dream', 'reality', 'vision', 'hallucination', 'truth', 'lies', etc. Naturalized or totalizing interpretation becomes impossible. The logic of the everyday world is replaced by forms of contradiction and discontinuity, radical shifts of context which suggest that 'reality' as well as 'fiction' is merely one more game with words.[65]

Such effects are again much more common in *Don Julián* and would be again in *Makbara* and *Las virtudes del pájaro solitario*.

The reader can, moreover, situate the novel within the context of a well-known critical debate. One of the weaknesses of the novel is that it takes sides in a critical debate that, as Susan Rubin Suleiman commented, now seems slightly outmoded.[66] While *Juan sin tierra* succeeds in taking metafictional overtness to the extreme, it falls short of achieving the apparent aim of the dynamically plural text. Indeed the overtness of the metafiction tends to explicate the linguistic activity in a way that defuses its subversive potential. The novel's emphasis on textual ambiguity and liberating proliferation of metaphors does not match a text which, while semantically dense and rich in images, remains fundamentally lucid.

Juan sin tierra, then, stresses the interrelationship between the social and the textual levels but does not confuse the two. As with *Don Julián*, the author maintains a distinction within the novel between the referential realm and the writing process. In the preceding novel this was clear. Alvaro returned to his apartment; nothing had changed. This absence of effect on the fictional referential realm of the novel indicates that the novel recognizes art's inability to directly transform reality. The activity on the textual plane, however, held out the possibility of an indirect effect.

In this final novel of the Trilogy, the situation of the referential plane is eclipsed by the textual process itself. However, there are details which point to the relationship between the text and 'reality'. The Changó episode in the first chapter can be read as a *mise-en-abîme* of the novel, emphasizing literature's capacity, like fantasy, to conjure up a subversive, sacrilegious vision, in which the West's most cherished myths will be violated, but which ultimately will have no direct effect on reality. The author may transform himself in the text but remain a 'rostro pálido aún, señorito, blanco de mierda' (59). The episode is a sign of both the importance and the limitation of the writing process. Goytisolo himself clearly felt that in *Juan sin tierra*, although his novel could not claim to have contributed in any direct way to liberation in the extra-textual realm, especially for the Arabs and the pariahs with whom he sides, nonetheless a literary liberation has been achieved through which the reader's fundamental attitudes and expectations have been challenged, if only on the level of the reading process. To this effect he has commented, in *Crónicas sarracinas*, that 'la única liberación de *Juan sin tierra*—fuera del sexo y la realidad histórica—se llevará a cabo en el ámbito de la creación literaria o el reino de la utopía' (CS, 43).

However, try as it might, the novel never really manages that literary liberation it sets itself. The novel's recuperability as a communicative situation is not troubled, as in *Don Julián*, but if anything enhanced, and is only destroyed at the very end when the author-narrator removes himself from the picture, leaving the reader faced with a passage in Arabic and then the blank page. This is one way of achieving the aim, but an unsatisfactory one. It implies that the truly liberated text belongs to the realms of the future or the blank page.

Viewed in this way, *Juan sin tierra* emerges as an intriguing reflection of the artist's dilemma and the paradoxical status of literature, deprived of any direct effect on that reality but an essential area of contestation of the real. Unfortunately, *Juan sin tierra* fails to meet the radical standards it sets for itself.

The following novel, *Makbara*, develops that concept of the utopian space of the text and its paradoxical nature, but manages, by a more subtle exploration of the contradictions involved in the issue, to escape the polarized debate evident in *Juan sin tierra*. Goytisolo also turns his attention away from the ultimately sterile—for narrative purposes at least—avenue of radical linguistic and literary theory towards a more vibrant source of subversive inspiration: the oral tradition.

NOTES

1 Goytisolo has said 'la connotación que yo doy a la traición es una connotación positiva', in Karl Kohut, *Escribir en París* (Barcelona: Hogar del Libro, 1983), 99.

2 'Si la literatura dinamita realmente sus caminos a fuerza de reflexionar sobre sí misma [...] lo cierto es que la explosión abre otros nuevos. Por eso solamente cuando imaginación y reflexión no han hipotecado su infinita potencia, cuando el escritor tiene enemigos reales que combatir y no meros fantasmas de guardarropía bibliográfica. Ese es el riesgo actual de Juan Goytisolo: que, mientras que bien muertos han quedado ciertos demonios familiares [...] no parecen apuntar los temas nuevos.' José Carlos Mainer, 'Letras sin tierra: Juan Goytisolo', *Camp de l'Arpa* XXIII–XXIV (1975), 11.

3 'Lo que he dicho sobre la destrucción del lenguaje se ha interpretado, a veces, de una forma disparatada. Cuando hablaba de destruir la frase entendía una recreación, ya que toda recreación parte de una destrucción previa de los materiales antiguos.' Milagros Sánchez Arnosi, 'Juan Goytisolo: "la creación literaria como liberación"' (entrevista), *Insula* CDXXVI (1982), 4. See also J. Lázaro (ed.), *Juan Goytisolo* (Madrid: Ministerio de Cultura, 1982), 155.

4 *Contracorrientes* (Barcelona: Montesinos, 1985), 233. Bakunin had stated: 'The passion for destruction is also a creative passion'. George Woodcock, *Anarchism* (London: Pelican, 1977), 13.

5 Tom Moylan, *Demand the Impossible: Science Fiction and the Utopian Imagination* (London: Methuen, 1987), 39.

6 'La coprofilia de Quevedo se nos ofrece entonces bajo una luz diferente: como respuesta del cuerpo mortificado al proceso alienador que lo sublima.' *Disidencias* (Barcelona: Seix Barral, 1977), 128.

7 Norman Brown, *Life against Death: The Psychoanalytical Meaning of History* (London: Sphere, 1970), 163.

8 As Brad Epps notes, '*Juan sin tierra* champions a non-referential language, that is, none the less, politically motivated'. Brad Epps, *Significant Violence: Oppression and Resistance in the Narratives of Juan Goytisolo* (Oxford: Clarendon Press, 1996), 14

9 '... el blanco de la sátira no es la historia oficial de España y sus valores retrógrados, como en *Don Julián*, sino el inconsciente colectivo de la sociedad occidental, configurada por la civilización judeo-cristiana: de una sociedad entregada rabiosamente a la tarea de negar el cuerpo y la felicidad corporal ...' Juan Goytisolo in César Alonso de los Ríos, 'Juan Goytisolo sin tierra', *Triunfo* XXX (1975), 27–28.

10 'It is in particular the coprophilic impulses of childhood—that is to say, the desires attaching to the excreta—which are submitted the most rigorously to repression'. Sigmund Freud, 'Five Lectures on Psycho-Analysis', in *Two Short Accounts of Psycho-Analysis* (London: Penguin, 1962), 75.

11 Alonso de los Ríos, 'Juan Goytisolo sin tierra', 26.

12 Alonso de los Ríos, 'Juan Goytisolo sin tierra', 26.

13 Alonso de los Ríos, 'Juan Goytisolo sin tierra', 26.

14 Alonso de los Ríos, 'Juan Goytisolo sin tierra', 27. This echoes a view expressed by Philippe Sollers in an interview in 1962: 'le livre par excellence, inclassable [...] à la fois un roman, un poème et une critique'. Quoted in Stephen Heath, *The Nouveau Roman: A Study in the Practice of Writing* (London: Elek, 1972), 180.

15 See Gonzalo Sobejano, 'Ante la novela de los años setenta', *Insula* CCCXCVI–CCCXCVII (1979), 1, 22. Also J. I. Ferreras, *La novela en el siglo XX (desde 1939)* (Madrid: Taurus, 1988), 95.

16 David Herzberger, 'Toward the Word/World Conflict: The Evolution of Juan Goytisolo's Novelistic Theory', in *Perspectivas de la novela* (Madrid: Ediciones Albatros Hispanófila, 1979), 107. Esther Nelson, 'The Self-Conscious Narrator in Goytisolo's *Juan sin tierra*', *Symposium* XXXV (1981), 260, 261. Jerome Bernstein, 'Body, Language and Divinity in Goytisolo's *Juan sin tierra*', in *The Analysis of Hispanic Texts: Current Trends in Methodology*, ed. L. Davis and I. Tarán (New York: Bilingual Press, 1976), 87. See also Rafael Conte, '*Juan sin tierra* de Juan Goytisolo: la destrucción y sus límites', *Insula* CCCXLIX (1975), 5. Goytisolo himself has commented that he has been criticized for holding progressive views but writing an elitist literature. Mauro González Ruano, 'Una literatura total', *Ozono* XI (1976), 58.

17 Robert Spires, *Beyond the Metafictional Mode: Directions in the Modern Spanish Novel* (Lexington, KY: University of Kentucky Press, 1984), 76. See also Spires, *Post-Totalitarian Spanish Fiction* (Columbia, MO, and London: University of Missouri Press, 1996), 62.

18 'With this violation of the story by the act of narrating, the original cultural codes become narrative; what were originally objects from sociohistorical reality have been transformed into linguistic signs guiding the text author in his search for a new, freer mode of novelistic expression. He has taken the first step towards freeing language from externally imposed meaning.' Spires, *Beyond the Metafictional Mode*, 78.

19 Brad Epps largely coincides with Spires on this point, claiming that the text enacts a liberational effect for the reader, adding the proviso: 'If the reader happens to concur with Goytisolo's representation of freedom, if he or she finds it persuasive, right, or true, close or familiar, then that is indeed fortunate for the reader, the author and the text'. Epps, *Significant Violence*, 187. Epps himself finds Goytisolo's images of liberation in the novel unacceptably phallocentric (177) and, ultimately, sees the liberation of the novel as too 'textually bound [...] Liberation reduced to the lonely act of writing', too reliant on the 'erasure of the reading public' (160).

20 Spires, *Post-Totalitarian Spanish Fiction*, 55.

21 Michael Ugarte, *Trilogy of Treason: An Intertextual Study of Juan Goytisolo* (Columbia, MO, and London: University of Missouri Press, 1982), 116.

22 Jonathan Culler sums this effect up as follows: 'In a description of a room items which are not picked up and integrated by symbolic or thematic codes (items which tell us nothing about the inhabitant of the room, for example) and which do not have a function in the plot produce what Barthes calls a "reality effect" (l'effet de réel): deprived of any other function they become integrated units by signifying "we are the real".' Jonathan Culler, *Structuralist Poetics: Structuralism, Linguistics and the Study of Literature* (London: Routledge, 1975), 193

23 A similar effect is sought by the narrator of *La saga de los Marx* (Barcelona: Mandadori, 1993), with his transcriptions and, at one point, his act of sticking a photograph of Helen Demuth to the page in order to avoid an 'enojoso retrato balzaciano' (216).

24 As he has said in an interview with Pilar Trenas in 1981: 'No se puede descodificar la realidad sin descodificar el lenguaje'. Pilar Trenas, 'Juan Goytisolo, ahora sin amargura ni rencor', *ABC* 7 June 1981, 37.

25 Brian McHale, *Postmodernist Fiction* (London: Methuen, 1987), 14.

26 Again, this theme will be taken up in *La saga de los Marx*.

27 Ugarte, *Trilogy of Treason*, 122–23.

28 Terence Hawkes, *Structuralism and Semiotics* (London: Methuen, 1977), 86.

29 *Disidencias*, 304. Barthes has written that 'modern literature is trying, through various experiments, to establish a new status in writing for the agent of writing. The meaning or the goal of this effort is to substitute the instance of discourse for the instance of reality (or of the referent).' 'To Write: An Intransitive Verb?', in *The Languages of Criticism and the Sciences of Man*, ed. R. Macksey and E. Donato (Baltimore, MD: Johns Hopkins University Press, 1970), 144.

30 T.E. Lawrence, *Seven Pillars of Wisdom* (London: Jonathan Cape, 1942), 22.

31 Gonzalo Navajas, in *Teoría y práctica de la novela española posmoderna* (Barcelona: Ediciones del Mall, 1987), comments: 'la novela postmoderna se propone como una vía epistemológica que cuestiona las formas convencionales de conocimiento en general, incluyendo la literatura' (19). See also Spires, *Post-Totalitarian Spanish Fiction*, 61–63.

32 See Barthes, 'To Write: An Intransitive Verb?', 138–39.

33 Roland Barthes, 'Introduction to the Structural Analysis of Narrative', in *Image–Music–Text* (London: Fontana, 1984), 112.

34 E. Benveniste, *Problèmes de linguistique générale* (Paris: Gallimard, 1966), 254.

35 Lawrence, *Seven Pillars of Wisdom*, 30.

36 George Steiner has referred to future tenses in narrative as 'an example of the more general framework of non- and counter-factuality. They are a part of the capacity of language for the fictional and illustrate absolutely central powers of the human word to go beyond and against "that which is the case".' Quoted in Patricia Waugh, *Metafiction: The Theory and Practice of Self-Conscious Fiction* (London: Methuen, 1984), 121.

37 Vincent Geoghegan, *Utopianism and Marxism* (London: Methuen, 1987), 2.

38 Geoghegan, *Utopianism and Marxism*, 18.

39 Geoghegan, *Utopianism and Marxism*, 20.

40 Roman Jakobson, 'Linguistics and Poetics', in *The Structuralists: From Marx to Lévi-Strauss*, ed. R. and F. de George (New York: Anchor Books, 1972), 93.

41 'The autonomy of the referents of literary signs in relation to real referents is, therefore, not a modern radical realization of recent criticism. Self-informing, self-reflective metafiction merely points self-consciously to what is a reality of the novel genre, a reality that structuralists have also made manifest.' Linda Hutcheon, *Narcissistic Narrative: The Metafictional Paradox* (London: Methuen, 1984), 96–97.

42 Roland Barthes, 'La faz barroca', prologue to Severo Sarduy's *De donde son los cantantes* (Barcelona: Seix Barral, 1980), 5.

43 See Fredric Jameson, *The Prison-House of Language: A Critical Account of Structuralism and Russian Formalism* (Princeton, NJ, and London: Princeton University Press, 1974), 180–82. Also Graham Dunstan Martin, 'Structures in Space—An Account of *Tel Quel*'s Attitude to Meaning', *New Blackfriars* (1971), 546.

44 Bernstein, 'Body, Language and Divinity', 87.

45 Nelson, 'The Self-Conscious Narrator in Goytisolo's *Juan sin tierra*', 261.

46 'No he renunciado a la lucha. La he trasladado a otro nivel. A otra perspectiva.' Goytisolo in Enrique Loubet, 'Goytisolo vs el mito español', *Excelsior*, Mexico, 20 February 1970, 17A.

47 Juan Goytisolo, in J. Ríos (ed.), *Juan sin tierra* (Madrid: Editorial Fundamentos, 1978), 21–22.

48 Herzberger, 'Toward the Word/World Conflict', 113.

49 Susan R. Suleiman, *Authoritarian Fictions: The Ideological Novel as a Literary Genre* (New York: Columbia University Press, 1983), 22.

50 Gustavo Pellón, 'Juan Goytisolo y Severo Sarduy: discurso e ideología', *Hispanic Review* LVI (1988), 485–86.

51 Thomas More, *Utopia* (London: Penguin, 1974), 86.

52 Claudia Schaefer-Rodríguez, *Juan Goytisolo: del 'realismo crítico' a la utopía*, (Madrid: Porrúa Turanzas, 1984), 94–95.

53 Ríos (ed.), *Juan sin tierra*, 14.

54 Ríos (ed.), *Juan sin tierra*, 14.

55 Shlomith Rimmon-Kenan, 'A Comprehensive Theory of Narrative: Genette's *Figures III* and the Structuralist Study of Fiction', *PTL: A Journal for Descriptive Poetics and Theory of Literature* I (1976), 40–41.

56 Pellón, 'Juan Goytisolo y Severo Sarduy', 490.

57 Gonzalo Sobejano, 'Valores figurativos y compositivos de la soledad en la novela de Juan Goytisolo', *Voces* I (1981), 28.

58 Colin MacCabe, *James Joyce and the Revolution of the Word* (London: Macmillan, 1978), 4.

59 Ríos (ed.), *Juan sin tierra*, 10.

60 'Another unifying element is the linearity of the verbal text, of the work in process that builds, albeit in a nontraditional way, towards a climax.' Nelson, 'The Self-Conscious Narrator in Goytisolo's *Juan sin tierra*', 260.

61 Roland Barthes, *The Pleasure of the Text* (London: Jonathan Cape, 1976), 32.

62 Ríos (ed.), *Juan sin tierra*, 14. It is perhaps for this reason, too, that a critic like Sanz should have seen an excess of didacticism in *Juan sin tierra*. 'Goytisolo se ha dejado llevar en exceso por una idea en función de la cual crea las situaciones pero éstasdependen demasiado de aquélla y se resiente la totalidad. Más que nada porque siempre queda un regusto didáctico que hace que algunos de esos asuntos adolezcan de cierta ingenuidad narrativa o muestren con demasiada claridad su carácter ejemplar,

ilustrador.' Santos Sanz, *Lectura de Juan Goytisolo* (Barcelona: Pozanco, 1977), 109. It must be remembered too that Goytisolo himself has referred to the novel's critique of realism as 'una lección de literatura'. Interview with González Ruano, 'Una literatura total', 57.

63 Hutcheon, *Narcissistic Narrative*, 139.

64 César Alonso de los Ríos, 'Juan Goytisolo sin tierra', 26. Sarduy also refers to this when he says: 'Para que el simulacro de la ficción no "cuaje", el relator de *Juan sin tierra* se pone constante y explícitamente en escena, sin pudor: los trucos del oficio se desmontan, se advierte al lector que todo es representación'. Severo Sarduy, 'La desterritorialización', in Ríos (ed.), *Juan Goytisolo*, 177.

65 Waugh, *Metafiction*, 136–37.

66 Suleiman, *Authoritarian Fictions*, 241.

CHAPTER FIVE

Makbara

After the publication of *Juan sin tierra* in 1975, it might have been thought that Goytisolo had reached the limit in his process of radical aesthetic revolt. He had sealed the break with Spain and taken the process of dissolving the novel form to its limit, dispensing with narrative plot, the spatio-temporal framework of the novel, the concept of character and finally, in the last few pages, had severed the narrative contract with the reader, announcing 'our communication has ended', and, as though to hammer home the point, doing so in Arabic. The narrator of that novel had also claimed that if he wrote again it would not be in Spanish. Having established a process of creative destruction as his hallmark, it did not seem as though Goytisolo had left himself with any more bridges to burn in the search for 'otros ámbitos de libertad expresiva' (CC, 73). Once again he had manoeuvred himself into the artistic dead-end which he had always considered to be the natural destination of all serious artists in their striving to extend the limits of their medium.[1]

Yet in *Makbara* the author manages to connect with the dominant concerns of the preceding novels and carry them a stage further. Contrary to what critics such as Gil Casado and Schwartz argue in their different ways, it is not the case that the novel introduces no major innovation.[2] Both thematically and technically, the novel manages to break new ground. On the thematic level, Goytisolo has widened the horizon of his critical vision and engages with his target, contemporary society, on a broader front, including the Soviet-style state bureaucracies in his satire. In addition, *Makbara* extends and develops the theme of utopia which had made its first appearance in *Juan sin tierra*. The Arabic dimension is similarly taken a stage further in that the Arab element in *Makbara* is a more ambiguous composite of myth and reality. Large parts of the novel are actually set in Morocco, as indicated by the novel's title, and one of the principal protagonists is a 'meteco', a Moroccan immigrant. In *Makbara*, more than any previous novel since *Señas de identidad*, the parodies in the novel are non-literary, satirizing the discourses of the media, tourism and advertising. This central attention to the ideological and political nature of discourse forms part of an important aspect of the novel, namely, its treatment of the relationship between literature and society.

In this sense *Makbara* reveals itself as a highly political or 'metapolitical' novel, in the sense referred to by Goytisolo in connection with *Juan sin tierra* (CC, 233). Moreover, *Makbara* is a much more ambiguous and contradictory novel than those of the Trilogy and, as a result, the critique of society it carries out is given greater force by the manner in which it dramatizes contradiction. The trenchant, rancorous, destructive satire of the previous novels has been succeeded by a more ambiguous, lyrical approach which is both more unsettling and more thought-provoking.

Juan sin tierra marked the end of the narration as enunciation of a particular author-narrator, the Alvaro Mendiola figure.[3] In *Makbara* the narrative situation is more multi-layered. We find narrating characters, the Angel and the Pariah, as well as instances of 'official' discourse—the voice of Radio Liberty and the commercialism of 'Le Salon du Mariage', an overall storyteller figure, the 'halaiquí nesraní', and the anonymous narrator of the final chapter. Although it is possible to arrange these narrative voices into a hierarchy, such an arrangement is less clear-cut than in the novels of the Trilogy, in which the voices could be traced to the central narrator-protagonist. In this way, the novel aims to undermine that tendency we have identified on the part of the reader to naturalize the text in terms of a communicative situation. This urge is especially strong in *Makbara*, where the disorientating nature of the text is greater than ever.

On the linguistic level, *Makbara* continues Goytisolo's aim of creating a language which encourages the reader's appreciation on an aesthetic level rather than for its communicative function. This was a declared aim of Goytisolo:

> En una época en que propuestas, reclamos y soluciones-milagro de todo tipo nos asaltan sin cesar de la mañana a la noche—desde la propaganda política a la publicidad comercial—la literatura debe reivindicar orgullosamente su derecho a la belleza, el juego, el goce y la inutilidad.[4]

It is with *Makbara* that Goytisolo starts to emphasize the 'prosodic' dimension of the language, the text's value as an 'oral' text, one best appreciated when read out loud. Although Goytisolo claims to have perceived the importance of this aspect around the year 1974,[5] it only came to the fore with the composition of *Makbara* where the intertextual links of the novel are with the oral tradition of the *Libro de Buen Amor* and the contemporary Arabic oral tradition. It is clear from a reading of *Makbara* that the acoustic dimension, the sensuous enjoyment of the rhythmic sonority of the text, is of primary importance.

Makbara marks a change of direction in this move towards an older, more oral tradition. This is undoubtedly partly to do with a certain disillusionment with the direction taken by radical linguistic theory. Goytisolo had said that his interest in linguistic theory ceased around 1975, and we noted in the previous chapter how the image of the 'plural text' was entertained as a radical ideal but never really attained. The exhaustion of this linguistic and textual contesting of conventional Western attitudes to language and literature leads in *Makbara* to a recourse to the possibilities offered by the primitive oral tradition.

This change of direction is also influenced by the encounter, around the same period, with the work of the Soviet critic, Mikhail Bakhtin, in particular the study on Rabelais, *Rabelais and his World*. Bakhtin's study of Rabelais' work had identified its roots in the medieval oral tradition of popular culture and included a theory of the principle of carnival as a subversion of official ideology. The convergence of these influences permits a renewal of Goytisolo's assault on the familiar targets. Although Goytisolo's novels of the Trilogy undoubtedly had carnivalesque elements, such as the glorification of the 'lower' over the 'higher', the corporal over the rational, and the inversion of conventional hierarchies, as in Chapter V of *Juan sin tierra*, the novels were still very much locked into the system that they were criticizing. The technique of the novels was to oppose myth with counter-myth and in so doing reveal the mythic nature of what was often taken as 'given' or natural. This in itself was a valid precondition for social transformation, but laid the novels open as we have seen to accusations of perpetuating, rather than dispelling, myths.

Curiously, such accusations were repeated with even more vigour by critics of *Makbara*,[6] and yet this novel goes a long way to overcoming the deficiencies in this regard detected in the earlier novels. One of the ways that it does so is to introduce a more carnivalesque structure into the novel in which the key elements are those of ambiguity and contradiction. As Clark and Holquist in their study of Bakhtin note:

> Carnival and the grotesque both have the effect of plunging certainty into ambivalence and uncertainty, as a result of their emphasis on contradictions and the relativity of all classificatory systems.[7]

Uncertainty and ambiguity were important elements of both *Don Julián* and *Juan sin tierra*'s critique of the Western mentality, yet, as we saw, those novels' critique of the West showed an inverted logic and rationalism which undermined to a large extent their subversive intent. *Makbara*, on the other hand, creates to much greater effect a world in flux, in which the narrator seeks to undermine all positions, even his own. Before passing on to an examination of this carnivalesque structure, it will be useful to take a look at the novel's approach to two central concepts, the myth of the Orient and the idea of utopia.

The Orient: Myth and Reality

Where the Trilogy had exploited Western myths concerning the East as a weapon in an attack on Western mores, *Makbara* tries to transcend this opposition. In *Don Julián* and *Juan sin tierra*, the image of the Arab and Arabic culture was that of the Western imagination about the East. In *Makbara* this is still the case, but the situation is more complex and the reality of the Moroccan environment is incorporated to render the picture much more ambiguous. For whereas the target of previous novels was Spanish and Western culture and traditions and could therefore be combated by manipulating its prejudices and phobias about an alien culture, the target perceived in *Makbara* is not simply Western values but their universalization, their imposition as an unquestioned norm, and in this the Arab world is itself to an extent a victim. In other words, rather than calling for a destruction of one particular culture, Goytisolo is advocating a cultural relativization which values difference and opposes the cultural and scientific hegemony of one particular tradition. The work of the post-Trilogy period becomes a more balanced celebration of the concepts of heterogeneity and difference.

In the Trilogy, Goytisolo confronted myth with counter-myth, ideology with counter-ideology, 'frente al discurso, el contradiscurso'.[8] In common with other postmodern fiction, Goytisolo's novels refuse to deny that the 'resistance to the dominant culture and its ideology is also an ideology'.[9] The novels are frequently criticized for their refusal to explode myths by combating them with 'the truth' or 'history'.[10] In the Trilogy, the use of a counter-myth was both an attempt at a greater aesthetic effectiveness, using a weapon with the same power as the target, but also a sign of Goytisolo's relativism and distrust of absolutes. The novels' self-consciousness was part of this, a laying bare of their own signifying processes. This left the novels open, however, to the accusation of confirming rather than undermining the polarities, perpetuating a mythic view of the world and denying the prospect of progress or transformation. As I have tried to argue, the novels' revelation of the mythic nature of our perception of reality and their denial of eternal essences establish the necessary conditions for a critical attitude to society which includes the possibility of change.

Nonetheless, the essay in *Crónicas sarracinas* reveals Goytisolo's own concern to be seen as not simply perpetuating a static mythic opposition but aspiring to what he termed 'la categoría de mito estimulante y dinámico' (CS, 196). *Makbara* does attempt to achieve this, and one of the ways it does so is a much more radical erosion of fixed positions within the text.

Goytisolo's treatment of the East in *Makbara* has attracted a considerable amount of critical comment, even from very favourable critics. For López-Baralt, 'el resultado artístico es—lo pretenda o no el novelista—la comunicación de un profundo desafecto hacia el mundo árabe, no su reivindicación histórica y vital'. And again we find the accusation that Goytisolo merely consolidates the existing myths:

> Interesantemente, parecería que con su tratamiento literario 'maniqueo' del mito anti-árabe (por más que sea premeditado e irónico), Juan Goytisolo no logra sino consolidar el mito.[11]

Such comments reveal a tendency to interpret the novels on a literal level. Hence, the sexual behaviour of the protagonists is thought to represent Goytisolo's ideal of love, and the scenes of Morocco his view of the East. Even critics who recognize the importance of the ironic transformation of reality in the novel have difficulty in not taking it literally. Thus Gil Casado says: 'la liberación de la tiranía impuesta por la sociedad consumerista y burguesa, y el definitivo triunfo de los personajes se reduce a un caso de hipergénesis: el pene del negro mide veintiséis centímetros [...] Como resultado, sólo cabe una interpretación: la felicidad es cuestión de hipersexualidad.'[12] Brad Epps, too, objects to the apparent phallocentricism, saying that 'by show-casing the phallus and investing it with revolutionary power, it appears to secure the success of the dominant order by upholding, as it were, conventional values'.[13]

In *Crónicas sarracinas*, Goytisolo states clearly that, in contrast to his essays, in which he voices ideas and opinions, and can deal directly with the reality of the Arab world, in the novels he is writing specifically for a Western audience and working within the cultural framework of the West and dealing with 'una escenografía mental en la que la realidad empírica y las observaciones directas inciden casi siempre de modo secundario' (CS, 31). Hence Sobejano is mistaken when he interprets *Makbara*'s aim as 'la exaltación de los parias y con ellos del mundo árabe o marroquí'.[14] In these essays Goytisolo takes his cue from Edward Said, whose book *Orientalism* was a deconstruction of the Western discourse on the East. Said shows how this discourse had little to do with the actual reality of the Orient but instead was 'a Western style for dominating, restructuring, and having authority over the Orient'.[15] Said's approach is to analyse the texts of Western writers on the Orient to see how, rather than portraying the truth of the Orient, they in fact revealed more about the West's own values and prejudices, especially those relating to its superiority over the East, and thus functioned as an instrument of cultural hegemony.

Said's study was influenced in turn by the theory of Michel Foucault, and there are interesting parallels between the French philosopher's attitude to the Orient and Goytisolo's general approach. According to

Uta Liebmann Schaub, Foucault's approach involved a critique of Western values and of unliberated, repressed Western man, to which he opposed a deliberately vague positive counter-image based on 'some vision of liberated humanity or perhaps "an ancient and familiar archetype of man"'.[16] Similarly in *Makbara* there is no positive image of liberation that can be identified with anything in the 'real world' (not even the plaza Xemaá-el-Fná), but rather such images are clearly consigned to the realm of utopia. Foucault was taken with the inaccessibility of the Orient to the Western mentality, 'the Orient that is presented to the expansionist rationality of the Occident but that remains eternally inaccessible because it always remains the limit'.[17] Liebmann Schaub goes on to interpret Foucault's attitude in terms that are particularly relevant to *Makbara*:

> Correspondingly, if the West is expansionist in its rationality, the spiritual Orient is something that retreats and recoils from that expansionist force. Unable to be conquered and penetrated, it remains the eternally other, the perpetual challenge and frustration for rationality, which, for Foucault, is the West's only cognitive strategy. (309)

According to this account, Foucault's thinking constitutes a probing of the limits and the possibilities of transgression. He aims to break with the basis of Western thought and discourse which is essentially dualist, a logic of antagonistic contradictions. In its place he advocates a paradoxical style, 'not a dialectics that wishes to prove a proposition but, rather, one that wishes to subvert the single-minded confidence in the possibility of proofs. Instead of taking and defending a position, he tries to avoid or elude fixed positions' (311).

This helps us understand the underlying ethos of Goytisolo's novel, particularly the importance attached by Foucault to style:

> His style is thus central to his enterprise; it is, once more, a praxis (which unsettles immutabilities and certainties) rather than a theory (which by its nature aims at immutability). Foucault therefore has to insist on the inseparability of discursive thought and style. Rhetorical style thus becomes the message; it is intended as a 'tool kit' to work change; it is not descriptive, nor is it representational. (311)

Makbara uses an irresolvable ambiguity in its presentation of the Arab in order to preserve its subversive effect on Western discourse but at the same time avoid the substitution of one 'reality' with another. As we see in the characterization of the Pariah, he is a composite of myth and reality, the typical Arab immigrant and the personification of Western myths of the Orient. Throughout *Makbara* the text works to blur the boundaries between myth and reality. It thus suggests the way myth and reality, ideology and 'truth' are inextricably woven together. For the Angel the Orient, as represented by the 'viejo filme de amor', is the promise of (sexual) fulfilment, and, as such, constitutes just one more example of the European myth of the Orient as 'erotic space' and 'escapist lieu'.[18] The mythical and misguided nature of this aspiration is made clear but it is not, for all that, denied or satirized.[19]

Goytisolo employs the image of the Orient both as source of a counter-discourse in opposition to the discourse of technological progress of the West and, in its essential otherness, as a source of subversion while at the same time foregrounding its equally mythic status. He thereby skirts the temptation to consolidate myths by undercutting them within the text itself. We see this in the contradictory position of the two main characters. The image of the East is at once mythically romantic for the Angel (44, 94) and for the Pariah himself as the fantasized plaza in which he imagines himself an *halaiquí*. Yet this image is undercut by the vision of the tannery, as 'aquel lucrativo infierno en el que te pudres' (67), or the image of the inhospitability of the desert in 'Como el viento en la red':

> no hay modo de cobijarse, el abandono es absoluto: planicie huérfana, vibración de arena, indigencia, hostilidad, desam-paro, remolinos de polvo, saña, encono obsesivos ... (179)

The pariah in his home environment is also engaged in a utopian quest for a different life, a different world: 'imaginar otro universo [...] caminar, caminar, sin volver jamás la cabeza' (179). Hence the two worlds, East and West, are presented ambivalently, as both the promise of fulfilment and space of non-freedom. However, the opposition is not a purely symmetrical one which neutralizes the two terms, but one which rather gives way to a new and different opposition, that between reality and utopia: for the Angel, between the West and the mythic East (presented as utopia) and, for the Pariah, between the repressive structures of Western and Moroccan society and the freedom of the plaza similarly associated with fantasy and imagination:

> cerrar los ojos, escapar, huir, anulado el infierno [...] la libertad de la plaza, sus espacios francos, me parecen vedados e inaccesibles : soñar, soñar en ellos, perder la afonía, recuperar la voz ... (70, 72)

Thus, Goytisolo subtly manages both to deconstruct his own fascination with the Orient and his use of the Orient as a literary subtext in his critique of the West while disarming criticism that he is merely countering myth with myth and so reinforcing the antinomy.

The Critical Utopia

Makbara, while operating within the East/West antinomy, aims to deconstruct that cultural opposition without denying its existence or its power. In this way Goytisolo can simultaneously make a critique of the

Orientalist tradition, including his own part in it, as a source of ideological repression, while maintaining its use as a form of 'counter-discourse that appropriates Oriental lore in opposition to Western strategies of control'.[20] An example of such a critique of the Orientalist tradition can be seen in the 'Dar Debbagh' episode in which the discourse of the narrator-protagonist about the maqsuras contrasts with the tourist discourse: 'voici le quartier des tanneurs, Messieurs-dames, the old, local color tannery' (67). The way that the text avoids either the impression of imposing this counter-discourse as an alternative to the criticized Western ethos, and therefore of being guilty of an equal authoritarianism, or the danger of radically undercutting its own status to such a degree that it precludes itself from being taken seriously, is by integrating the East/West antinomy into the theme of utopia and its own textuality.

The thematic level acts as a *mise-en-abîme* of the textual process. The protagonists' fantasies mirror the *halaiquí*'s stories which in turn mirror the text of *Makbara* itself. This *mise-en-abîme* or Chinese-box structure allows the text to indicate by implication the way in which it should be read, both its potential and its limitations. The image of the role of imagination for the protagonists and the act of storytelling for the *halaiquí* reflect inevitably back on the text, *Makbara* itself and its scope.[21] Both the Angel and the Pariah sustain themselves with the thought not only of future happiness but also the memory (whether idealized, distorted or invented, it is hard to tell) of past happiness: 'imposible olvidar, olvidarte' (105).[22] Their experiences are constructed on an opposition between, on the one hand, existing unhappiness and, on the other, future or recalled happiness.

Makbara's utopianism is a contestation of the ideology of established reality as it represents itself in discourse. Its principal means of doing this is within the textual space to create an alternative discursive universe or heterocosm, one which challenges that dominant discourse. However, it goes beyond that by introducing within the text a series of contradictions that place everything, even the utopian vision, in question.

Paradoxically, this reappraisal of the utopian impulse depends for its effectiveness on the recognition of its limits. The Angel and the Pariah are never shown to encounter happiness because their real condition is undeniable. However, their assumption of their condition, their refusal to conform and their ceaseless desire for utopia operates a dual function of keeping their hope alive and subverting the attempted total normalization and homogenization of society by the dominant ideology. The *halaiquí* at the end of his tale is returned to the misery of his condition, but the storytelling gives him and his listeners strength to continue on and trust that all will be better tomorrow, 'con la idea de que todo será mejor mañana' (200).

Similarly, the writer of the novel at the end claims nothing but the freedom of the blank page. However, thanks to the blurring of the bounds of reality and textuality through the uncovering of the semiotic relations between the two in the last chapter, the novel implies that reality, too, is a 'caligrafía que diariamente se borra y retraza en el decurso de los años', a 'precaria combinación de mensaje incierto' which the individual has the capacity to read in his own way. *Makbara* is structured around the opposition between reality and utopia, but this opposition is not a static one, an irresolvable impasse. Rather it reveals the nature of the utopian impulse as a process of constant resistance to oppression rather than a product of the total overthrow of repression.

An example is the dominant motif of movement. The two central protagonists are involved in a quest for an ideal—the love relationship and escape from a repressive reality. Movement in this sense becomes the only solution left to the protagonists and equates with the activity of fantasy as a provisional escape. Movement forms part of a general eulogy of nomadism, which while connecting with the Arab theme echoes also the Deleuzian concept of *pensée nomade* as a radical, Nietzschian subversion of the 'sedentary' ethos of the West.[23] *Makbara* rejects this philosophy explicitly, and proclaims a 'desquite de lo espontáneo, abigarrado, prolífero contra la universal regulación clasista' (205).

In this last chapter the narrator posits the idea of the nomadic principle as the utopian ideal:

> supervivencia del ideal nómada en términos de utopía : universo sin estado ni jefe, libre circulación de personas y bienes, territorio común, pastoreo, pura impulsión centrífuga ... (205)

This nomadism had formed an important part of the previous novel *Juan sin tierra*. However, *Makbara* assumes the principle more fully by achieving a greater decentring of the novel. One of the most obvious signs of this is the way the narrative roams much more freely among the different verbal persons, *yo, tú, él*. In *Juan sin tierra*, as we saw, in spite of the importance placed on a dynamic and ever-changing narration, the novel was always held in place by the writing process, the 'murmullo discursivo' of the author-figure in the 'escritorio-cocina'. In *Makbara* the situation is vaguer. The narrating voices vary and the overall narrator is in doubt until near the end. The figure of the 'halaiquí nesrani', one who adapts his stories to suit the circumstances and the whims of his audience, may or may not be a creation of the narrator of the final chapter who, in any case, is given a dynamic image, located in the open, circulating space of the plaza. The final chapter's image of the palimpsestic reading of a mobile space, the text and its metaphor, the *plaza*, wherein diverse narrative strands, voices, levels, interweave without any resolution or final closure, achieves much more effectively the ideal *Juan sin tierra* had set for itself.

The ideal nomadic existence portrayed on page 204 is a utopian space to be aimed for, and indeed the whole novel is constructed on the principle of movement or aspiration towards the ideal, within the individual chapters and in the novel as a whole. All the chapters dealing with the two protagonists end with a rejection of existing reality and a movement towards the ideal or a version of it. The whole novel is a progression towards the last chapter which focuses on the utopian space of the plaza. *Makbara* on all levels deals with the rejection of reality and the aspiration towards utopia.

That distinction is preserved throughout, but the novel works to interweave and relativize the terms in such a way that reality, while no less real, becomes less fixed, and utopia is posited as less a state than a process in which the individual can participate in different ways. These manifestations of the utopian, nomadic impulse range from the act of physical movement (the Pariah's wanderings through the streets of Paris, the Angel's 'caminar, caminar, perderse en el desierto'), the act of fantasizing or remembering a past state of happiness, listening to a story in the plaza, telling a story, and for the writer and reader, the parallel processes of writing and reading.

Characters

Makbara differs from the novels that immediately precede it in having two central protagonists who are distinguishable from the narrator. It also differs in that the relationship between these two characters appears to be a version of the traditional romantic love affair. In *Crónicas sarracinas* Goytisolo calls it an 'amor imposible' (CS, 44).

A study of the two protagonists reveals a fixity within flux. They continually metamorphose from one episode to the next and yet remain identifiably the same. Goytisolo relates the technique of characterization to the example of the *Libro de Buen Amor*:

> A lo largo de ese librillo 'de buen amor' que es *Makbara*, Juan Ruiz me instruyó, tanto o más que los maestros del siglo XX, en el manejo de las rupturas temporales, digresiones aparentes, disposición autónoma de las partes en la armazón del conjunto, metamorfosis de los personajes— alternativamente jóvenes y viejos—según las exigencias retóricas del texto. (CC, 19)

The Pariah in the first section is a tramp in Paris, in 'Cementerio marino' a handsome former *halaiquí* who returns to his homeland, in 'Dar Debbagh' a worker in the tannery, in 'Aposentos de invierno' and 'Eloísa y Abelardo' a dweller of the sewers below a Western city, in

'Hipótesis sobre un avernícola' a freak discussed by American academics, in 'Como el viento en la red' an itinerant in Morocco. He appears in the sections devoted to the Angel as a soldier whose precise name and identity fluctuates in the Angel's uncertain memory.

The Angel's identity is similarly uncertain. Her changes are mainly sexual. She begins as an asexual, though implicitly female 'angel' in the bureaucratic paradise run like a religious order in which the body and its functions are rigorously denied. After being raped (41)[24] she develops a craving for the sexual pleasures denied her in her 'paradise', escapes, and eventually undergoes a sex-change operation and joins the 'peroleras y busconas de los áscaris y soldados del Tercio' (44). In 'Sic transit gloria mundi' she emerges as an old prostitute, in 'Le Salon du mariage' 'she' is now a 'he', a transvestite who speaks with a 'cultivado acento meteco' (78) planning his/her marriage to Ahmed, the soldier. The circumstances of their encounter vary continually, from their meeting in the Grand Hotel in Jenifra or a building in Bel Abbes or the street (58–59) to their contacting by letter and the Angel visiting him in prison in Targuist (110–11).

Two principles emerge from the character portrayal in the novel, one a constant and the other a variable. There are clear constant features of the nature of the protagonists and of their relationship to each other and to others. Both are outsiders attempting to escape from the constraints of their milieu, unsuccessful and relegated to the dark fringes of society. The Moor is forced to withdraw to the sewers, work in the mines or the tannery, to hide in the cinema or languish in jail. The Angel falls from paradise and ends up in a brothel in a cellar, performing fellatio on the Moor in the back row or the toilets of a cinema, following him into the sewers or pursuing him off into the desert. Both characters attract the opprobrium and revulsion of respectable members of society, are mocked by their companions, and both are in some way sexual misfits: the Moor has a disproportionately long penis and the Angel's femininity is either false (transvestite or merely dressed up asexual angel) or artificial (result of an operation). This constant element is not merely the coincidence of certain characteristics in the various narrative personae or 'actants' of the text. There is a definite unity of character that allows us to perceive them in the different episodes as the same characters, Angel and Pariah, in different guises. The variable element is the way their identities, names, occupations, ages, and circumstances change from episode to episode.

The nature of this characterization differs considerably from the treatment of character, for example, in *Juan sin tierra*, where no characters really existed and the closest approximation to one was Vosk, who was clearly portrayed as a totally protean narrative agent whose function was to act as the symbol of narrative character, an

element of the traditional novel which the author wanted to deconstruct. The 'characters' of *Makbara* come closer to the more ambivalent
(and more metafictionally subversive) character of *Don Julian*, in that
they are clearly narrative components, as Goytisolo would say, there to
comply with 'las exigencias retóricas del texto' (CC, 19), yet also clearly
they do not come across as mere 'personajes lingüísticos' but rather
possess a degree of recognizable humanity. Goytisolo here is returning
to a deliberate play on the conventional empathy of the reader towards
a fictional character to enlist our sympathies for their plight, while at
the same time continuing with the distancing effects to foster a critical
attitude. The mere fact of their love relationship, the constant defining
characteristics, serves to make them almost 'seres de carne y hueso'.
Unlike Vosk in *Juan sin tierra*, whose entirely linguistic and textual
status was dissected before our eyes, these characters show a greater
ambiguity. At the end of Chapter 14 they are revealed as fictional
characters, but of a traditional realist sort, i.e. possessing the verisimilitude of real people. The *halaiquí*'s stories obviously rely to a great
extent on old-fashioned verisimilitude, a narrative illusion which he
maintains to the end: 'unos cuentan ... otros dicen ... algunos afirman
...' (199–200). The *halaiquí* is here playing with narrative illusion in a
very traditional way, treating his story as though it were real yet also, in
the varieties of ending and the final arbitrary choice of one of them,
revealing the implicit fictiveness of his tale.

The characters possess certain features of the oral tradition. They
are 'flat' as opposed to the nineteenth-century convention of 'round-
ness'. They are characterized in the schematic way common to the oral
tradition of fixed, formulaic expressions and epithets.[25] Yet again, these
techniques apply more to the Pariah and his discourse than to the Angel
(for example, the formulaic descriptions of the sought-after woman [53,
183] cannot with certainty be associated with her and, besides, belong
to the Pariah sections of the text). The constant elements make us
identify the characters as stable, recognizably human, if ultimately
fictional, figures, while the variable features of their portrayal argue
for them as mere narrative devices metamorphosing to respond to the
narrative requirements of the text. This ambiguity is deliberate and
corresponds to a series of other contradictions and conflicts in the text,
not least the opposition between the figure of the oral storyteller and the
author of the text, *Makbara*, and by extension the opposition implicit in
the novel between the oral and the literate traditions, between the text,
Makbara, and the 'cuento oral'. These contradictions take *Makbara*
back to the more successful, disturbing metafictional effects of *Don
Julián*. However, in *Makbara* these contradictory features are more
consciously produced and effectively explored than in the earlier novel.

The choice of these characters, Pariah and Angel, one from the East and one from the West, foregrounds the antinomy that structures the novel. The fact that they are each questing after the other, or, in the Moor's case, the world of the other, implies the quest for a rapprochement between the two worlds. The failure of their efforts suggests the obstacles in the way of such a reconciliation. At the same time, the fact that the opposition in the novel is now between the couple, combination of East and West, and modern technological society is a sign of the attempt to break down the antinomy East/West, and displace the focus elsewhere, as Goytisolo had expressed a wish to do in *Crónicas sarracinas* (196).

Each character is a subtle mix of reality and myth. The Pariah is in many ways a recognizable, everyday figure, the Arab emigrant in Western society.

> El *muhaxir* (emigrado) que, después de una infancia huérfana en el Marruecos colonial y el aprendizaje de la esclavitud en el infierno de los curtidores, siembra el horror a su paso por los bulevares de París, podría ser uno de los innumerables obreros magrebís cuya condición ha resumido bellamente Tahar Ben Jelloun en su ensayo titulado *La plus haute des solitudes*. (CS, 44)

But Goytisolo goes on to add: 'Pero es no obstante algo más'. He is also a compendium of the myths, stereotypes and prejudices of the West about the East.

> El 'meteco' no es, pues, un emigrado norteafricano cualquiera. Abrevia también, de forma condensada y caricaturesca, la fantasmagoría occidental sobre el Islam y los árabes ... (CS, 44)

Whereas the protagonist of *Don Julián* was 'una mera concreción de la fantasía hispanocristiana', the Pariah is a 'personaje simbiótico', someone both other than the Westerner and at the same time produced by the Westerner, 'configurado por la mirada hostil y reprobatoria del prójimo con quien se cruza' (CS, 44). His identity as a creation of the West's own prejudiced mentality is indicated by the detail of his being an 'imagen venida del más acá' (15), in other words, rather than being a 'monster' from an alien culture, he actually emanates from within ('acá') the Western mentality. Hence the character is a curious mixture of reality and myth. The two are conflated, so that while we recognize the predominance of mythic elements—the extra-large penis, the lack of ears—and we understand the novel's engagement with these mythic elements, there is no attempt to radically distinguish reality and myth. The two are inextricably woven together.

The Angel, while not associable with a precise type such as the emigrant, is an outcast from within Western society. She is the rebel against her own system who dreams of escape and fulfilment in the 'other' world of the Arab, and in union with him. Her rebellion is a sexual one because her society is one that either denies or debases sex. She too, however, is a mixture of reality and unreality. She begins as an 'angel' in some unearthly paradise which is a cross between a Communist state bureaucracy and a convent. Goytisolo plays here on the ironic similarities between the Christian and the Communist doctrines in their submission of the individual to an ideology.[26] The satire is played out in terms of sexual repression because Goytisolo, following Marcuse, sees this as the defining characteristic of the West's theory of progress: the denial of the body in the interests of economic progress. In this way the rehabilitation of the body is the most effective way of resisting this ideological repression. This was the lesson of *Juan sin tierra* and is carried on here in *Makbara*. Goytisolo in *Disidencias* had spoken of the 'virulencia subversiva del grito' (182). It is interesting that *Makbara* starts off 'al principio fue el grito' (13). In a mission to Earth, which is a parodic version of the Sodom and Gomorrah episode in the Bible, the Angel is raped and thus introduced to the 'delights' of the body, after which she can no longer tolerate the situation in Paradise and escapes. Thus begins her quest for love and sexual fulfilment. She tries capitalist society, characterized by the sexual promiscuity of New York's 42nd street (42), is disenchanted and turns to radical protest groups within that 'free' society only to find they were suffering from the same faults as the 'presunto paraíso yahvista' (43). This leads her to have a sex-change operation and set off for the deserts of Africa where the promise of sexual gratification seems assured.

The Angel's story is an ironic potted sketch of the evolving stance of the radical Western intellectual movement from the 1960s onwards. The critique of the Soviet-style bureauracies, the equally alienating effects of modern industrial, capitalist society, the failure of radical political groupings and solidarity with the Third World are all stages that have characterized the contemporary radical movement, and Goytisolo's own development.[27] The Angel's final solution is a libertarian quest for self-fulfilment and ties in with the novel's suggestion (at the heart of *Juan sin tierra* also) that the concept of utopia, of perfect happiness, is an individual affair, unable to be legislated for by the state or programmed in an ideology.[28]

However, again the ambiguity of the text, the chapter's finale, with its reference to the 'viejo filme de amor',[29] is a sign that the Angel's projected solution is a false one, based as it is on a myth of the Orient. The image is of a character questing for liberation but hopelessly caught up in the ideological web of her own culture and tradition. Her obsession with the fashion magazines of the West as she prepares for her encounter with her lover is a graphic illustration of her susceptibility to the ideological discourses and values of Western consumerism.

Equally, in 'Le Salon du Mariage', we have an image of her

subversive effect on this society, yet clearly this subversion is unwitting. While there are glimpses of the narrator's delight in the disruptive, embarrassing effect the character has on the others ('saborear la violencia brutal del impacto' [78–79]—due to the circulating narrative voice, the narrator's perspective and the character's become inter-twined), we sense that the character 'himself' is eager to be able to participate in this scheme of marital orthodoxy, 'la gracia, ternura, profundidad del sentimiento poético le arrebatan' (91), and is hurt whenever rejected: 'rehusar la realidad, evadirse del público' (94). He is caught up in the ideological structures that work to exclude him.

The novel spans the lives of the two protagonists, from beginning to sad end, when the Angel is an old prostitute alone with her none-too-clear memories in 'Sic transit' and the Pariah in 'Cementerio' is remembering or fantasizing the time when he was 'joven y airoso como entonces' (48). Their relationship is marked by failure and frustration. For the Pariah, the length of his member is an obstacle to his sexual fulfilment ('ninguna mujer querrá probarlo' [182]); it produces admiration but cannot be physically accommodated (184). Only the Angel is prepared to adapt in order to satisfy her lover: 'decidiste aprender, doctorarte, trabajar tus cuerdas vocales ...' (152). Her adaptation takes the form of a cult to the Moor in which she ironically returns to a state similar to the one she escaped from: 'monja de clausura, consagrada exclusivamente a tu culto' (105). Sexual liberation is at the same time an enslavement. It also takes an evidently degraded form, as seen by the Angel performing fellatio in the toilets of a public cinema or in the back row, 'un periódico encima de mi cabeza' (152). The lover in the Angel's accounts clearly comes across as indifferent to her, solely preoccupied with his own pleasure. He heartlessly abandons her after he is satisfied. The Angel never figures in the Moor's accounts, and in her accounts he has a vague identity: 'tu nombre, M'hamed, Ahmed o Mohamed' (59), 'dijiste que te llamabas Abdelli, Abdellah, tal vez Abdelhadi [...] tu nombre es Omar' (62). This confusion of names and spellings is partly allusion to the standard Western difficulty of transcription of Arabic words, thus tying in with what was said before about the East's essential otherness, and as such it adds to the point of the whole situation, that is, that the Angel is in love with an idea, the image of the East as a place of possible fulfilment, attractive because of this otherness, its resistance to Western understanding. On another level it adds to the subversion of the stable notion of character which we saw in the figure of Julián in *Don Julián*.

In this way the Angel character is suffering from the same illusions as Lawrence in *Juan sin tierra*. The East is a place 'para desenvolver su proyecto creativo, ilustrar sus obsesiones, rastrear la propia identidad ...' (CS, 30). The Angel may be the only one capable of loving the

Moor, as Goytisolo tells us (CS, 44), but she is in love with a myth and is thus a victim of myth, and her love is doomed to failure. In this way, both characters are composites of reality and ideology, both are challenges to myth and victims of it. This is one way of interpreting the image of the Pariah's sexual member. It is a symbol of Orientalist discourse on the East and of the repression of the Arab. The attribute is a burden on the Pariah, denying him fulfilment. The Angel's obsession with the penis as the source of her fulfilment is a sign of her equal enslavement to the mythic Orientalist discourse. The account of her love as a devotion, a cult, accentuates that sense of a distorted vision of liberation. Amidst this assortment of myths is the reality of the pro-tagonists' misery and their real need for love and fulfilment. Her position is not unlike the role that Goytisolo in an essay in *Crónicas sarracinas* sketches for himself as inevitably a European writing about the Orient. Hence he says that the Angel's love for the Moor is

> Amor imposible, no por una decisión arbitraria del narrador o halaiquí nesrani que asume el relato en las últimas páginas de la obra sino, una vez más, a causa de la posición estratégica del autor ante el material narrado. (CS, 44)

More than any previous text, *Makbara* reveals the limitations of its utopian vision. The two protagonists of *Makbara* continually escape into a fantasy world. The Angel, as we have seen, turns her back on the world and goes off to the desert, which is the mythical space for the European. In 'Sic transit' this 'utopia' of her encounter with the Arab lover is in the past, located in the realm of idealized memory or fantasy. The Angel's utopia is not only placed in doubt by being portrayed as unattainable, but its very nature is put in question. We have already seen how the image of the escape to the desert is revealed as myth. As well, there is the clear fact that her lover, on whom she pins such hopes for romantic and sexual fulfilment, is clearly indifferent to her and either abandons her when she has sexually satisfied him (152, 158) or rejects her when he sees a photograph (110). Another example of the ambiguous characterization is that this character both is (from the reference to the extra-large member [109]) and is not (in the comment 'tú no habías entrado todavía en mi vida' [108]) the Pariah.

Similarly the Pariah's fantasies are various. There is the dream of sexual intercourse with the 'rubia americana' which is shown to be, in 'reality', out of the question (71). There is an idealized return home in which he is welcomed, admired, resumes his former role as storyteller, and is awaited by the mysterious beauty in the cemetery, in 'Cementerio marino' (which can be seen to follow on from the end of 'Del más acá venido' and so be construed as the fantasy that he began in the cinema [22], subsequently debunked by the parallel but contrasting chapter

'Como el viento en la red'). And finally there is an encounter with the Angel in the catacombs who appears as an elegant 'desposada' and in fact turns out to be a grotesque, aged figure ('lo que se pierde en juventud se gana en savoir faire' [158]) wearing 'falsos sostenes de goma', a set of false teeth and afflicted with colitis. The two lovers are obliged to live out their idyll in the sewers (i.e., as with the cinema, the brothel in the basement, the imagination: the margins or underground of society and the individual unconscious which constitutes the space of the utopian impulse in society) and are rudely interrupted by the lights of PB News.

In this way *Makbara* posits the idea of utopia but also assumes a critical and realistic perspective on its ambiguous function in society. The complex treatment of the relationship of the two characters is a good example of how *Makbara* extends the ideological critique of the previous novels by examining the contradictory and ambiguous nature of its own premises. Goytisolo in this novel is analysing his own and others' ambiguous relation to the marginal elements with which they identify and which they employ in their critique of the West.

Structure

If we turn to the structure, we note similar contradictions. Speaking at the time of preparing the text of *Makbara*, Goytisolo commented:

> Deliberadamente, me he propuesto escribir sin plan premeditado alguno. Estoy redactando una serie de conjuntos textuales, pero sin preocuparme de que la obra final carezca de esqueleto y sea, en definitiva, una criatura monstruosa ...[30]

This indeed is the initial appearance which the novel presents to the reader. Yet when examined, *Makbara* reveals quite a definite structural pattern. This has been described schematically by Evelyne Garcia as follows:

> Cap. I: P – II: O – III: A
> IV: P – V: Ao
> VI: P – VII: Ao
> VIII: P – IX: Ao
> X: O
> XI: [O–P–A–O]
> XII: O
> XIII: P – XIV: Ao
> XV: Lectura del espacio

In García's schema each letter represents the dominant discourse in each chapter: P = the Pariah, A = the Angel and O = the representatives of the official system. In linguistic terms, the Angel's discourse contains an element of the official one. Linguistically, it is the Pariah sections which, according to García, introduce 'la creación lingüística más original'.[31]

One of the conclusions that we can draw from the structural arrangement of discourses revealed by García is that it is symmetrical and therefore, to a large extent, static. We could add that the separate sections devoted to the Pariah and the Angel suggest the lack of communication and true interrelation between them. Their arrangement around a central official discourse which remains intact reveals them as condemned to exist on the edges, opposed not only to the central official discourse but to each other. The final chapter stands outside the oppositional arrangement of these conflicting discourses. García's schema is useful in that it reveals an underlying shape coordinating what at first appears to be a collection of disparate fragments. It also reveals a fundamental contradiction in the dichotomy between order and looseness. As Goytisolo's comment suggests, *Makbara* is motivated by a desire to abandon the constraints of narrative form, and yet the principle of order is difficult to resist. The tension that this creates on a structural level is an integral part of the contradictions we have been observing at other levels. The presence of a fundamental order underlying the text's aspiration to disorder serves to dramatize the principle we have noted elsewhere, i.e. that the decentring, subversive process ultimately depends on a centre, a logos, against which to rebel, just as the concept of utopia is predicated on the existence of a non-utopian reality.

At the end of the penultimate chapter we discover the stories to be the product of an oral storyteller, a revelation which alters our attitude to the structural arrangement. We can now recognize certain features of the oral tradition: the lack of a tight linear plot, the beginning *in medias res*, the episodic structure, etc. It is significant, however, that this revelation is kept until the end. In other words, the reader is led to read the text with the usual expectations of novel reading.

Furthermore, in spite of its looseness, as we have seen, the novel is not without structure, and likewise, in spite of its appearance of being a collection of episodic tales, there is underlying it a recognizable 'story', the 'love story' of the two protagonists. This story, despite constant ambiguities and fluctuations, tends to move in a linear fashion, going from the present of the protagonists (the Angel in the brothel and the Pariah in the sewers) in which they reminisce on their past life and their original meeting, to the final encounter in 'Eloísa y Abelardo', when they are interrupted by the reporters, on the Pariah's trail since 'Radio Liberty', and each captured, the Angel by her former co-religionists and the Pariah by the scientists and academics. The *halaiquí* puts an end to their story by opting for one of several possible dénouements.

The oral tradition does not constitute a model for the novel. The novel both incorporates elements of the oral tradition and adapts them to the peculiar needs and characteristics of the text. The oral tradition acts on an aesthetic plane as the element of otherness represented on the thematic level by the Arab and his culture. The oral narrative corresponds to a social context (medieval Europe, present-day Third World) with which *Makbara* attempts to connect. However, it is not blind to the fact that it cannot deny its ineluctably contemporary character.

It has already been noted that *Makbara* lacks a traditional linear plot. *Juan sin tierra* had self-consciously eschewed such a notion in favour of a more spatial arrangement. Where *Juan sin tierra* tried to deconstruct the linear plot of literacy, *Makbara* tries to capture the non-linear, episodic structure of orality. As with Goytisolo's interest in the medieval tradition in general, this need not be regarded as a nostalgic desire to regress but as a desire to incorporate what was good and lost in the 'civilizing' process and use it to regenerate a tired modernity.[32]

According to *Crónicas sarracinas*, *Makbara* originated in the rereading of the *Libro de Buen Amor* in the *zoco* in Marrakech. Goytisolo explains the reason for the latter work's continued relevance in the present:

> Si al cabo de más de seis siglos, la obra del Arcipreste conserva intacta su ejemplaridad, ello obedece, pienso yo, a su estructura atípica e informe, híbrido de géneros distintos y opuestos, revoltillo genial de dialectos y léxicos; a su carácter espúreo, mestizo, abigarrado, heteroclito, díscolo a normas y clasificaciones ... (CS, 53)

The attraction to the *Libro* is clearly due to this atypicality which characterizes it at every level, especially at the level of its lack of structural form. The value of the book, as Goytisolo's definition states, is dependent on the existence of a 'typical' against which it can react. It is clearly the carnivalesque nature of the work, its status as a deliberate contestation of official literature, that constitutes its appeal, and Goytisolo goes on to mention the work of Bakhtin in relation to this theme in the work of Rabelais (CS, 53). It is the employment of the carnivalesque mode in the contemporary context that underlies the writing of *Makbara*. As Goytisolo said in *Contracorrientes*:

> el atípico Libro del Arcipreste conecta en virtud de su peculiar textura con la aventura literaria posjoyciana y su diferente concepción del personaje, argumento, lenguaje novelescos. (19)

However, there is an important distinction to be made here. Bakhtin's study of carnival notes that, while prior to the mid-seventeenth century the concept of carnival was still a lived concept, people were directly involved in the carnival performances and the carnival attitude, and *'the source of carnivalization was carnival itself'* (italics in original), this changes, and

> ... from the second half of the 17th century carnival almost completely ceases to be a direct source of carnivalization, relinquishing its place to already-carnivalized literature: thus carnival becomes a purely literary tradition [...] The carnival elements in this literature, which is already cut off from carnival, its direct source, undergo certain changes of form and meaning.[33]

As it loses its roots in popular carnival tradition, the carnivalesque becomes a purely literary activity, a counter-literature to the norms of official literary discourse. This is the nature of the carnivalesque mode of contemporary post-Joycean literature. *Makbara*, however, finds a counterpart of the original carnival tradition in the *zoco* of Xemaá-el-Fná.[34] By thematizing the modern oral tradition of the Moroccan storyteller, the novel draws our attention to an important contradiction. The space of the carnival for the Westerner no longer exists. It is a utopian space and its nearest equivalent, the Arab *zoco*, is clearly ambiguous and presented as so, since its carnival spirit perceived by the Westerner is determined by his status of being Western, and to this extent its utopian character is a myth. The last chapter of *Makbara* makes this 'posición estratégica' of the narrator clear when it says: 'predispone el ánimo del forastero' (215), and doubly so when it makes clear that this carnival space is all taking place on the page, is only carnivalized literature. As the last chapter ends, the narrator describes the gradual closing down of the plaza for the night. Reality (in the shape of the apparent description of the plaza Xemaá-el-Fná) gradually gives way to and merges with the literary reality of the Arabian nights:

> figones de quita y pon, olores de fritura y potaje, comino, té con hierbabuena que avivan el apetito del caminante y lo atraen a los banquillos del tenderete de su elección sucesión de luminosos bodegones proyectados en una linterna mágica : ilustraciones de alguna remota edición de 'Las mil y una noches' con mercaderes, alfaquís, artesanos, mancebos de botica ... (222)

The description of the plaza ceases to be merely compared to the images of literature; there is an ambiguous sense in which the images of this literary tradition colour the perspective on reality: 'aprehensión del universo a través de las imágenes de Scherezada o Aladino'. The reality of the plaza is recognized as a literary reality which supplants reality itself: 'la plaza entera abreviada en un libro, cuya lectura suplanta la realidad' (M, 222). This literary reality suggests the text of *Makbara* itself. The reality of the plaza reveals its significance as a metaphor of the literary text and, as such, a utopian space capable of substituting, albeit temporarily, the real world.

The experience of carnival, backed up by its literary counterparts, was itself utopian, but at least it was a lived experience. The realization that our only type of utopian experience belongs to the realms of fantasy or literature is a comment on both the extreme repressiveness of Western society and the role of literature as one of the important last bastions of the utopian, carnival spirit.

The awareness in the last chapter of the mythic nature of the utopian space of the *zoco* for the Westerner is enhanced by the clear move to a different level of narration. The last chapter has an anonymous narrator who is the writer of the text. The space he refers to is one of orality and otherness. The chapter revolves around the constant theme in Goytisolo's work of the desire for identification with the Other and the awareness of the inescapability of one's own identity. This fits into the overall framework of the distinction between reality and utopia, and in the last chapter (implicitly in the novel as a whole) this distinction is posited in terms of the contrast between orality and literacy.

Narrative Levels

In the same way that the Angel can be interpreted as representing a particular ambiguous attitude of the Western intellectual to the Arab world, and the Pariah as a metaphor of the aesthetic effect that the author would like to produce with the novel—as seen in the phrase 'reto, provocación, tentativa de movilizar contra él' (16–17) and the whole of the 'Hipótesis sobre un avernícola' chapter—so too there is a parallel between the storyteller, the *halaiquí nesrani*, and the narrator of *Makbara* in that they are both in a sense caught astride two cultures – *halaiquí* in so far as he engages with Arabic culture in the form of the oral storytelling tradition of the *zoco*, and yet unavoidably *nesrani*, i.e., Western. Luce López-Baralt refers to him as 'el halaiquí nesrani o narrador "europeo" de la halca'.[35] By identifying the storyteller as such, the novel hints at its *mudéjar* nature, its affinity with the art of Juan Ruiz, 'un clérigo con gustos y aficiones de goliardo, embebido a la vez de la tradición literaria latina—la de los joca monachorum y farsas religioso-profanas—y la cultura arábiga—narraciones eróticas, poesía juglaresca' (CS, 53). However, there is also a sense of the narrator's awareness of his own ambiguous nature, drawn to a culture from which he is, of necessity, excluded, and it points up too the essential dichotomy within the text between a rejection of Western culture and approximation to that of the oral tradition of the *zoco*, and the irredeemably Western nature of the text.

In this sense there is also, as well as a parallel, a contrast between the *halaiquí* and the narrator of the final chapter, between the oral storyteller and the writer. *Makbara* evokes the world of the public storyteller and places that figure at the centre of the narrative. Yet any reader will be immediately struck by the contradiction between its form, which is highly literate, dependent for its major effects (in spite of Goytisolo's view of it as a 'texto oral') on being read in its printed form by a Western reader, and the influence of the oral tradition. An awareness of this paradox can be detected in its dedication: 'A quienes la inspiraron y no la *leerán*' (my emphasis).

A look at the structure of the novel revealed the way the presence of the *halaiquí* was deferred to the end of the penultimate chapter, thereby altering our perception of the novel—showing it to be an oral narrative —and at the same time leaving us unaware of this oral structure on a first reading. The effect of the introduction of the *halaiquí* at this stage must be deliberate and does not respond to the influence of the oral tradition, for if oral narratives tended to start *in medias res*, they did not tend to disguise the presence of the oral narrator who frames the stories. The *Libro de Buen Amor* flaunts the narrator's presence and begins with an invocation to God to help him compose the book:

> Tú, Señor e Dios mío, que al omne formeste,
> enforma e ayuda a un tu arcipreste,
> que pueda facer libro de buen amor aqueste
> que los cuerpos alegre e a las almas preste.[36]

The late introduction of the figure of the oral narrator means that the contemporary reader can be forgiven for approaching the text as a radical break with conventional narrative form and as postmodernist in nature. The discovery of the *halaiquí* at the end of the penultimate chapter does not change that. At most, what it prompts is a reflection on the part of the reader on the relationship between the *halaiquí* and the contemporary Western writer. This is encouraged further when the voice of the *halaiquí* gives way to and is subsumed within a higher narrative voice, that of the writer-narrator of the last chapter and his meditation on the writing process.

Jesús Lázaro, in *La novelística de Juan Goytisolo*, makes a similar point when he says that the introduction of the *halaiquí* forces the reader to

> cambiar los presupuestos de lectura, a reinterpretar lo leído a la luz del nuevo descubrimiento, a dar un nuevo valor a la crítica, a considerar, en definitiva, la necesidad de alterar la idea de un novelador occidental para pensar, ponerse en el lugar de un juglaresco vendedor de sueños, para el que no existe sólo la palabra, sino también el mimo, la imitación, los ruidos. (244)

However, Lázaro's comments show an unwillingness to confront the numerous contradictions that *Makbara* throws up and which are essential to the proper assessment of the radical project of the novel. The introduction of the *halaiquí* does not simply transform the novel into an oral work; the reader is not led straightforwardly to 'releer la novela desde esta nueva posibilidad, verla en su escenificación en la plaza pública' (244). Essential to the impact of *Makbara* is the projection towards a human space and a literary form that is essentially inaccessible except in radically altered form, and this paradox is what gives depth and complexity to the novel.

One incongruous detail, an example of where the disjunction shows through, is the section on page 221 which is a passionate vindication of the giving voice to those individuals in society and those aspects of human nature that are usually silenced by social norms. At one point the text states: 'literatura al alcance de analfabetos, mujeres, simples, chiflados' (221), a sentence that could certainly not apply to this novel (or any of Goytisolo's later novels). No matter how hard he might try, there is no way that Goytisolo, a Western writer, can recreate fully the effects of a primary oral tradition. This sentence brings out the communal, fraternal quality of oral narrative, binding teller and audience in an intimate relationship.

The fact that *Makbara* preserves the distinction between the *halaiquí* figure and the anonymous, Western narrator of the last section, who both closes the text and refers us back to the beginning for a re-reading, shows that Goytisolo assumes the contradiction and makes it work for him in elucidating the complex nature of the utopian theme. The oral tradition in the form he admires of the Arab *halaiquí* and the medieval *juglar* is one he can identify with, show an allegiance to, but never recapture fully for the obvious historical and literary reasons. But there is also underlying this literary question the obvious human one of the nostalgia for certain values that characterize the society of orality, inappropriately named 'primitive'. Walter Ong makes clear how the distinction between orality and literacy relates to human values and social attitudes. Literacy effectively restructures the consciousness:

> many of the contrasts often made between 'western' and other views seem reducible to contrasts between deeply interiorized literacy and more or less residually oral states of consciousness.[37]

Makbara displays an affinity with and a desire to recapture a particular attitude that contrasts with the prevailing rationality characteristic of modern society. It is not an unusual development in Goytisolo, resembling as it does the dilemma he faced in the 1960s in relation to the beautiful but barren landscape of Almería and the 'aesthetic of poverty' (see FC, 'Examen de conciencia') and which recurs in similar form in relation to the context of Morocco.[38] Ong reveals a similar dilemma with regard to the question of the distinction between orality and literacy.

> There is hardly an oral culture or a predominantly oral culture left in the world today that is not somehow aware of the vast complex of powers forever inaccessible without literacy. This awareness is agony for persons

who also know very well that moving into the exciting world of literacy means leaving behind much that is exciting and deeply loved in the earlier oral world. (15)

Makbara both connects with and displays a distance from that oral realm and all the values that attach to it. The embedded narrative levels operate an alternating movement. The novel at first strikes the reader as very contemporary, a series of narrative segments whose connection is uncertain and whose narrative voice adopts various grammatical persons in a deliberately disorienting fashion characteristic, it could be said, of a postmodernist concern to decentre the subject.[39] The introduction of the *halaiquí* for a moment transforms the reading and 'explains' several points: the segments are narrative episodes, stories related in the plaza, organized around a common theme but changing according to the vagaries of the oral storytelling process. The reader's attempt to attach a stable meaning to the confusing narration is rendered less urgent by the arbitrariness with which an ending is produced; the intriguing enigma of the text gives way to the simple pleasure of the storytelling process. The constantly shifting narrative voice becomes 'explained' by the common technique of the oral story-teller to combine performance with recitation. Sobejano notes how 'el empleo simultáneo de yo-tú-él para un solo sujeto [...] es menos polifonía de juglar que ventriloquismo de bululú'.[40]

Ong has also shown how this circulating narrative viewpoint is characteristic of the oral narrator's empathetic relationship with his characters, itself a sign of the participatory and communal nature of the oral tradition (46). However, this oral explanation of the text is then rendered problematical by the final chapter, which has the effect of subsuming the *halaiquí*'s discourse within a further level, that of an explicitly written text and the reflection on the writing process.

While the importance of orality in *Makbara* and the text's oral qualities have been widely recognized, few critics have focused on the contradictory relation between orality and literacy in the novel.[41] As Ong's book shows, there are important distinctions between the oral and the literate mentality. It is impossible not to see the theme of orality in *Makbara* as related to the protest against modernity, which Goytisolo emphasized as the new target of radical resistance and which clearly lies at the heart of the ideological critique of the novel. The theme of oral narrative invites the reader's reflection on the differences between the oral and literate media. One of these is mentioned by Ong: 'Oral communication unites people in groups. Writing and reading are solitary activities that throw the psyche back on itself' (69).

The attempt by Goytisolo to propose *Makbara* as a 'texto oral' and the claims that it should be read aloud are attempts to reverse the general reading customs occasioned by the introduction of writing and print. Goytisolo speaks of the reader having to possess an ear for the musicality of the text, and López-Baralt points to the oral qualities of the prose of the modern avant-garde writer.[42] But again, as Ong points out:

> Although Joyce's text is very oral in the sense that it reads well aloud, the voice and its hearer do not fit into any imaginable real-life setting, but only the imaginative setting of *Finnegans Wake*, which is imaginable only because of the writing which has gone before it. (103)

Likewise *Makbara* is a hybrid work. Its literate nature is incontestable but it relies perhaps less than previous novels on typography to work its effect on the reader, and the undoubted polyphony of voices within the text does develop a sense of a prosodic dimension; one can hear the multiple registers and intonations of the text. However, *Makbara* cannot recreate the oral situation that it so clearly evokes. The oral narrator created a situation in which the listener (or reader, if transcribed) could pretend to be one of the listening community.[43] Goytisolo does this at the end of the penultimate chapter—as readers we are located on the same level as the public of the *halaiquí*. Yet, in the last chapter, the narrator, though anonymous, evinces signs of being Western, literate and alien to the culture that he observes admiringly in the plaza. The references to the guidebooks suggest a European who has consulted such books only to dismiss that conventional approach to the foreign. The perspective is one of reluctantly detached observation: 'representación teatral' (203), 'viajero en un mundo móvil' (204), 'forastero' (215).

Whereas the narrative voice of the preceding chapters had had that mobile quality which allowed it to circulate among the different levels of the text, here the narrative is curiously anchored in a fixed point. As readers of the early chapters, we too circulated among the different levels, at once sharing the point of view of the Pariah, the pedestrians on a Parisian street, the narrator, and so on. In the last chapter we are located firmly with the writer as he observes or (re)creates in writing a utopian space. It is possible that Goytisolo means this as a passage of narratorless prose of the sort that he refers to in *Contracorrientes*;[44] however, as Culler has correctly pointed out,[45] in all situations the reader will inevitably create a narrator, and here the candidate appears as the writer confronted with the 'proverbial dificultad de enumerar lo que el espacio engendra' (206).

The final impression of the chapter is one of sadness, wistful contemplation of a happiness that cannot be grasped but must be aspired to on a daily basis.[46] However, this is not a failure of the text but rather an integral aspect of its subtle portrayal of the complexity of the utopian impulse. *Makbara* avoids a black-and-white vision. The world of the *zoco* is admired as a space of freedom and fraternity. But to the extent that the last chapter makes clear that this is an observed freedom by a Westerner, it partakes of the nature of myth, or illusion. The novel has already given signs of the possibility that this Arab realm is not quite so enticing for the Arabs themselves. The description on page 206 of the 'local comercial portátil' is an illustration of the novel's refusal to ignore this side of things, and conforms to Goytisolo's admission in *Crónicas sarracinas*:

> La 'Lectura del espacio en Xemaá-el-Fná' muy especialmente está construida sobre dicha antinomia: eludiendo a un tiempo la visión exclusivamente moral que rehúsa las virtudes anacrónicas, preindustriales del ocio, juego, espíritu de fiesta, etc., y la perspectiva exclusivamente hedonista, indiferente a la pirámide explotadora subyacente al espacio libre y plural de la plaza. Aceptar tan sólo la primera, sería condenarse a escribir un panfleto de crítica social; limitarse a la segunda, faltar gravemente al afecto y solidaridad humanos. (CS, 45)

To the extent that the chapter makes explicit its textual nature and the sense of its being a reading or a particular representation of a reality or even a subjective transfiguration of reality according to a particular ideal ('supervivencia del ideal nómada en términos de utopía' [205]), the text admits its status as art, as the liberated space of the non-real. This is reinforced by its theme being oral culture and the clear recognition by the text's contrast between narrator and *halaiquí* of the inaccessibility of the oral realm to the Western writer. Nonetheless, to the extent that the text can aspire to the artistic qualities of the oral ideal, it represents the potential of the utopian impulse for resisting the overarching power of repressive rationality.

The Text and the World

The novel includes within it a reflection on its own status as fiction. The revelation of the *halaiquí* at the end of the penultimate chapter foregrounds the fictionality of the narrative. The site of the storytelling is the plaza and this space is associated both metonymically and metaphorically with the activity of storytelling itself, with fiction (the last chapter weaves a link between the space of the plaza and the space of the text). The plaza and therefore the space of fiction is a 'minúsculo islote de libertad' within a miserable reality, 'un océano de iniquidad y pobreza' (200). The opposition established earlier between the reality of the protagonists and their dreams is here paralleled by the opposition between the plaza and the surrounding reality of Morocco (and the world), much as the old man praying draws a circle around himself (211). The reader is invited to see a similar parallel between the space of the text and extra-textual reality. Hence, the text, fiction, is the space of freedom, the space of utopia. However, it is of necessity limited, capable of providing an antidote to harsh reality and perhaps temporary escape, but incapable of eradicating reality, of direct effect on reality. The *halaiquí*'s arbitrary affixing of a happy ending emphasizes both the omnipotence and the impotence of the fictive process; all can be done in the story (on the page) but it is only because it has no direct influence on reality.

However, the relation between reality and the text is at the centre of the last chapter. Rather than abandoning any possibility of language being able to represent reality, the chapter actually attempts to do so. *Makbara* continues the trend of the previous novels of the trilogy in subverting the positivist notion of language's ability to represent reality objectively. Yet where the previous novels stressed the text's linguistic autonomy, its independence from the world and its operation according to its own set of rules, *Makbara* actually turns its attention to external reality in the form of the plaza. The text refuses to disguise its status as a version of that reality by drawing attention to unsuccessful attempts to capture it. Hence, the final section commences with a statement of the resistance of Moroccan reality to the discourse of the Western guidebooks.[47]

Goytisolo commences his description of the plaza with a statement of the resistance of the reality to representation:

> como una araña, como un pulpo, como un ciempiés que se desliza y escurre, bulle, forcejea, elude el abrazo, veda la posesión todas las guías mienten no hay por dónde cogerla ... (203)

The inevitable gap between language and lived reality is heightened by the suggestion of the gap, for the Westerner, between the reality of the Orient and the discourse of the West.[48]

However, paradoxically, this is merely a preface to Goytisolo's own attempt to capture that reality. He deliberately undercuts any pretence to authority or truth his account may have assumed before embarking on it. Even the title, 'Lectura del espacio en Xemaá-el-Fná', had also marked the account as a 'reading', that is, an individual perspective. This undermining of the representational authority of the account is compounded by the self-reflexive allusions to the writing process. The text presents itself as ambivalent, both a version of the reality of the plaza and at the same time a self-conscious fiction.

The last chapter then enters into a play of meanings. It seems to start as a demystified attempt to render Moroccan reality, free of Western prejudices, and yet reveals itself as fiction, that is, a form of mystification. Moreover, the reality described, the carnival space of the plaza, is also in the context of the novel projected as a utopia aspired to by the Pariah. The plaza as a utopian realm for the Pariah and for the *forastero* is a metaphor for the writing process itself, the text as carnivalesque literature.

There is no sense of the plaza constituting a real space of carnivalesque freedom for the indigenous Moroccan. Alongside the scenes of storytelling there are signs of the locals struggling hard to scrape a living, and the narrative specifies at one point how the atmosphere of the square 'predispone el ánimo del forastero al disfrute de un poco de libertad' (215). The utopian character of this experience is dependent on its radical difference from the reality of the West:

> impotencia, inutilidad de bocinas y máquinas : desquite de lo espontáneo, abigarrado, prolífero contra la universal regulación clasista ... (205)

Or again:

> lejos del orden molecular, irreductible de la gran urbe europea industrializada : agresión del reloj, apresuramiento, horas punta, infinita soledad compartida parachoques contra parachoques : separación celular en núcleos infusibles, apretujado aislamiento : herramienta robot cifra máquina : incorporeidad, distanciamiento, transparencia, ataraxia en los antípodas de la dulce familiaridad sin fronteras ... (215)

Similarly, as we have noted throughout, the novel's vision of reality and the utopian impulse and the working of its subversive effect depend for their success on the existence of the opposite. *Makbara* more than previous novels incorporates that opposite within its own vision.

Hence the chapter mixes apparent observation (206) with dreamlike fantasies (e.g. 216). *Makbara*, for all its play with myths, ideology and levels of reality, never loses sight of the 'strategic location' of the Westerner in relation to the East, hence again the complex vision of the novel. While encouraging us to establish links between the textual and the extra-textual, as parallel and even interwoven semiotic systems, to be perceived, interpreted and experienced as a realm of free-floating signs, mobile, anarchic, playful, sensuous, the narrative undermines the 'reality' of the extra-textual by implying that it is another myth, a part of the Western intellectual's privileged, if sympathetic, perspective on the East, another example of Orientalist mythology recognized by Goytisolo:

> Toda la literatura europea que aborda el mundo árabe o islámico subraya – independientemente de la simpatía o afinidad personal de algunos autores con él—su carácter ajeno, extraño e irreductible, de simple objeto creado por y para la mirada del hombre occidental. (CS, 30)

In another section the text highlights the difficulty of realistically representing external reality in words, the futility of trying to rival the photograph. The text actually tries to give a meticulously realistic description of the plaza and undercuts the account by the reference to

Prévert's poem, thus simultaneously undermining realistic description (labelling it an 'inventory'), bringing out the inevitably Western literary tradition the writer belongs to, and reintroducing the stock theme of the text's unavoidable intertextual links with other texts. There is a to and fro between text and world, with the text at first drawing attention to itself—'proverbial dificultad de enumerar lo que el espacio engendra' (206)—only, once again, to go on to make the effort:

> trastos, útiles, cachivaches arrastrados desde bocacalles y arterias por impetuoso maelstrón infinidad de objetos de toda laya donde quiera se pose la vista ... (206)

The last phrase points us to a phenomenological context of individual consciousness ('posar la vista') and external world ('objetos'). The text then proceeds to refer to the problem of representation:

> alinear pacientemente nombre, adjetivos, términos en lucha desigual con la perfecta simultaneidad de la fotografía : correr en vano tras ella, como viajero que pierde el tren y resuella grotesco por el andén hasta perder el aliento ... (207)

This admission of the futility of mimetic representation is merely a prelude to an attempt to record the contents of the square—'pirámides de almendras y nueces, hojas secas de alheña, pinchos morunos, calderos humeantes de harira, sacos de habas ...' (207)—only, as was said, to end with a reference to a poem by Prévert, 'Le Raton Laveur', which undermines the whole passage's aim to represent. A further point to note about this passage is the typographic detail of the layout on page 207 which, in its suggestion of a separate block of prose, symbolizes the essential solidity and materiality of the reality alluded to and contrasts with the 'poetic' layout of the final five lines on page 208, in the reference to Prévert, thus clearly suggesting a poetic (typographical, textual) tradition.

This to-ing and fro-ing highlights both the irretrievable gap between the real and the linguistic and, at the same time, a constant interaction between the two which suggests a desire on the part of the author to establish contact with that reality. However, the issue is further complicated by the suggestion, pointed out earlier, of the ambiguous nature of that reality. On the one hand, it is a subjective 'reading' of a 'real' space in Morocco, its features dependent on the foreignness of the spectator. On the other hand it is an idealized image coloured by a literary tradition, the mythic Arabia of the Arabian Nights. And on yet another reading it is merely an exercise in writing, seen as a utopian activity for which the plaza serves as a mere literary metaphor. These are just some of the ambiguities provided by the text, ensuring its 'palimpsestic' quality, for each new reading uncovers new or previous readings without being able to unify them into a single coherent account.

The attention to a reality and its attempted description, then, is a sign of the desire on the part of the author to link the aesthetic activity with lived experience, the extra-textual realm, a desire to show how the text *Makbara* is, like the faculty of imagination, like the interpersonal activity of the oral storyteller, a relevant and necessary part of human experience. This desire to show the human value of the aesthetic process is clear from the thematic significance awarded to the motifs of love and fraternity.

The depth of *Makbara* lies in the way it can contain contradiction, deconstruct its own propositions, undermine their authority, yet leave them intact to work their powerful effect on the reader. On page 220 there is a view of the oral storyteller as professional entertainer, 'vivir literalmente del cuento', to whose familiar stories the public is addicted. Here the oral narrative of the plaza comes across as evasion, temporary escape from harsh reality. The public is a 'cautivo feliz', the storyteller is a 'vendedor de sueños' and his tale is a 'cárcel verbal'. There is a sense of the story as merely a momentary release that contributes to the maintenance of the status quo. The storyteller is not liberator, but one of the exploiters—'vendedor'. There is a suggestion of the connection between discourse and power in the idea of the *halaiquí*'s superiority over others by virtue of his possession of the gift of the word. The fantasy of the dejected Pariah in 'Cementerio marino' was of the prestige and superiority that attached to the role of *halaiquí*, his ability to control others. It is as though the function takes on some of the wish-fulfilling element of the activity of fantasy, invention itself. The ideal constructed in fantasy is partly achieved by the fantasizing process itself.

This is followed by a virulent piece in which the radical, subversive, utopian, carnivalesque nature of the oral tradition, and of the novel, *Makbara*, is expounded:

> liberación del discurso, de todos los discursos opuestos a la normalidad dominante : abolición del silencio implacable infligido por leyes, super-sticiones, costumbres: en abrupta ruptura con dogmas y preceptos oficiales ... (221)

Here the narrator is arguing for, and creating as he does it, a discourse that partakes of the physicality of real experience, a language that not only expresses the body, as in carnivalesque literature, but which has a physicality to it:

> habla suelta, arrancada de la boca con violencia, como quien se saca una culebra tenazmente adherida a las vísceras : elástica, gutural, ronca, maleable : lengua que nace, brinca, se extiende, trepa, se ahíla ... (221)

This is variation on the constant theme of Goytisolo in which the body, the physical reality of the body, is recuperated as the repressed victim of the official ideology. The connection that was made in *Juan sin tierra* between writing and sexuality is here made between the text and the entire body:

> posibilidad de contar, mentir, fabular, verter lo que se guarda en el cerebro y el vientre, el corazón, vagina, testículos ... (221)

On one level the passage alludes to the carnivalesque tradition which gives voice to the elements of society unrepresented by official literature, satirizing the latter usually in terms of the grotesque. However, as we have noted, *Makbara* in important ways cannot repeat that tradition, a disjunction between itself and the oral tradition which the reference to 'analfabetos' serves to highlight.

The novel does achieve this in one respect: it focuses its attention on what Ong calls the 'human lifeworld'. This, he says, is a characteristic of the oral tradition, whereas 'writing fosters abstractions that disengage knowledge from the arena where human beings struggle with one another' (43–44). Oral narrative is 'empathetic and participatory rather than objectively distanced' (45). As opposed to *Juan sin tierra* and *Don Julián* which were extremely self-absorbed, *Makbara* deals empathetically with the trials and tribulations of the Angel and the Pariah. This empathetic relationship between the narrator and his characters is one way of interpreting the *yo–tú–él* narrative technique.[49]

This narrative decentring of the subject may have its roots in the *Libro de Buen Amor* but its aim is still a contemporary one: it is to dispel that 'distanciamiento' (215) the author perceives in Western culture and foster a more fraternal feeling of human interaction, a characteristic of oral culture. However, this effect is suddenly undermined in the last chapter—paradoxically the chapter devoted to the space of utopia, where utopia is contemplated from a distance. Similarly, as we noted earlier, the text in its self-conscious characteristics acts to undermine empathy and to cultivate a critical distance in the reader. The effect is to leave the reader under no illusions about the unattainability of the ideals referred to while at the same time emphasizing the importance of the desire to make them come about.

Knowledge and Interpretation

Makbara's attack on the rationality of the West leads, within the metafictional nature of the novel, to the theme of interpretation, the Western attitude to meaning, knowledge, the reduction of reality to rational limits and control. The reference to the guidebooks in the last chapter of the novel was a part of this, and part of the utopian nature of the plaza was that it was able to resist this subjection to knowledge. In so far as the plaza was a metaphor for the space of the text, the chapter was a reflection on the utopian status of a writing that offered itself less for cognition than fruition. The affinity with the Arab poetic tradition was founded on the characteristic of that tradition of regarding language in terms of its musicality rather than its semantics. Arabic verse appealed as much to the ear as to the intellect. Hence Goytisolo's emphasis on the prosodic qualities of *Makbara*. Goytisolo made this point in *Crónicas sarracinas*:

> El discurso del trovador, sometido a las exigencias melódicas del texto, se dirige tanto al oído como al intelecto. El auditorio—ayer en los zocos y plazas que frecuentara el Arcipreste, hoy en Xemaá-el-Fná—educa allí su oído literario: acata la métrica y acentuación que le brinda el relato, distribuye las frases con arreglo a aquéllas, olvida la chata distribución 'normal'. (CS, 54)

López-Baralt takes up this point about the anti-Aristotelianism of Arabic oral literature, emphasizing the musicality of the language which means that recitals can stir an audience that only partially understands the 'meaning' of the text. Hence, for López-Baralt 'muchos pasajes de *Makbara* resultan breves unidades poéticas de gran impacto artístico, pero fundamentalmente independientes del relato como tal'.[50]

While it is undoubtedly true that *Makbara* manages to create a richly textured prose style and multivoicedness that favours a reading aloud, certain factors inevitably distinguish it from the oral tradition. First, in the oral tradition the rhythmical element has a largely mnemonic value and motivation. As Ong says, oral literature is 'highly rhythmic, for rhythm aids recall, even physiologically' (34). The Arabic language is musical because of its peculiar vowel system in which many words can share the same vowels. As Gibb says:

> Inevitably, therefore, rhyme and assonance play a very large part in Arabic literary style from the first, not only in poetry, but in prose as well, and alliteration and jeux de mots, far from being avoided are regarded as special ornaments in belles-lettres.[51]

Also of interest to the prose style of *Makbara* is Gibb's comment about Arabic sentence structure. Due to the peculiarities of the Arabic verb structure, with its limited number of tenses,

> the presentation of the sentence is jerky or 'lyrical'; the component parts are originally autonomous and seldom explicitly subordinated as in the ordered hierarchy of European syntax. (9–10)

This describes very well the sentence structures of Goytisolo's novels and may even explain the fondness for the use of the verb in the infinitive or the gerund form, forms which suggest rather than circum-scribing themselves to some specific action. Such incorporations from other traditions, then, obviously are not dictated by the desire to approximate to the original, bound by a very different set of contexts and motivations, but rather serve Goytisolo's own artistic ends, the construction of a discourse which differs from Western discourse and resists the cognitive strategies of the Western reader. In this case the musicality and rhythmic quality of the Arab oral tradition serve as a model for a discourse that has a physicality, an artistic correlative to the repressed body. Again one is reminded of the comment in *Disidencias*, 'las palabras muertas del diccionario cobran vida, se agrupan sensualmente delante de nosotros [...] se transmutan en "cuerpo" como en la poesía árabe' (D. 263).

This opposition to a rational tradition has interesting implications for the subject of interpretation of text, since, much as was the case with Joyce, as Ong pointed out, *Makbara* for all its invocation of the oral tradition is very much a work of literature, and shares closer links to the literary corpus of Western literature than to the literature of the Arabic oral tradition.

As is customary with Goytisolo's metafiction, the text contains within it indicators as to the way it should be read. Various sections of the novel serve as self-referential *mises-en-abîme*. The chapter 'Hipótesis sobre un avernícola' is an example. In this chapter the Pariah, having been discovered in the catacombs with the Angel, is brought to the Cathedral of Learning of the University of Pittsburgh and exhibited before an audience and a panel of academics specializing in different disciplines who each attempt to 'explain' his identity and the reasons for his presence:

> preguntas sin respuesta, hipótesis o comentarios en voz baja del gentío que atesta la sala y comienza a manifestar su impaciencia en espera del panel de sabios y especialistas, la opinión autorizada, el dictamen, la conclusión promulgada con fuerza de ley, la justa e inapelable sentencia
> de dónde procede?
> qué idioma habla?
> cómo ha llegado hasta aquí?
> cuánto tiempo lleva en las catacumbas?
> por qué ha elegido vivir entre ratas? (164–65)

The interpretations of the academics show a greater concern with the intellectual authority of their respective disciplines than with the human predicament of the Pariah. Such an attitude, according to Said, was characteristic of the whole field of Orientalism, where the actual human reality of the Orient was secondary to the West's discourse on it.[52] At the same time, the scene serves as a *mise-en-abîme* of the novel itself and its relation to the public, in particular the academic critic. The academic tries to 'solve' the riddle of the Moroccan's presence, rather than attempt to communicate with him. The academic discourse of the

West is shown to value the coherence of its own system rather than a humane understanding of or sympathy with the subject in question.

In interiorizing the question of interpretation in this way, Goytisolo is making a comment on the intellectual institutions of Western society.[53] The scene not only parodies that attitude but manifests the inability of these disciplines to find the key to the Moroccan's presence. The importance of finding such a key dissolves at the end in the joyful scene of fraternal reunion. On a thematic level, the chapter undermines the authoritative status of these disciplines, revealing them less as sources of truth than discourses, different ways of structuring reality to make it more tractable. On a self-conscious level it can be read as a sign of *Makbara*'s aim to resist recuperation by a particular interpretive strategy.

Another example is the chapter 'Noticias del más allá'. Here the Angel has been recaptured by her co-religionists and transported back to Paradise and forced to make a confession, a written act of self-criticism in which she repents of her sins and returns to the fold. In face of her compatriots' prurient interest in the details of her relationship with the Pariah, she comments:

> inútil hacerles entender que no sabía quién eras : que ignorabas o habías olvidado su nombre y su traza : que mi amor era único y tu cuerpo, figura, apostura, atributos imperceptiblemente cambiaban ... (192)

The doubts which the reader of the novel had in trying to decipher the details of the various accounts of the Angel's relationship with the Pariah turn out to be shared by the Angel herself; the confusing portrayal turns out to be not something to be deciphered, interpreted, explained rationally but simply the defining characteristics of the relationship itself. The Angel here puts herself on to our level to implicitly tell us that we ought not to attempt to disentangle the multiple fluctuations of the text, but accept them as they are and take our interpretive process from there. This may seem an obvious point, but that is to underestimate the ingrained tendency in most readers, even those accustomed to postmodernist texts, to try to establish meaning in conventional terms, identifying characters as stable fictional personae who represent some stable set of values and locating characters' actions within some recognizable fictional world.

In despair at being forced to do the impossible—represent in writing her experience—the Angel devises a ploy to confuse her captors:

> mejor escribir, manchar el papel, sacar ozono del recuerdo,
> inventar, para confundirlas, algún burlón juego de palabras
>   marruecos, patria(s) de adopción en el doble
>   sentido del término : combados, fulgurantes,
>   ubérrimos, poderosos imanes : reserva ina-
>   gotable de divinas sorpresas!

rompecabezas?
y otra cosa mejor!
quien lo(s) cató que me entienda! (195)

The piece is a comic parody of the style of *Makbara* itself, with its typographical layout, punctuation, references to double meanings, baroque vocabulary and accumulation of adjectives. As parody it both points to and exaggerates the technique of *Makbara*. The Angel, as we have noted before, is a *mise-en-abîme* of the novelist himself. Her position is that of the Western dissident and her retraction here in writing corresponds with the author's position vis-à-vis *Makbara*, the production via writing of a text that will consternate, confuse and alienate the system and place her beyond the pale. The 'rompecabezas' implies a subversive strategy which aims at resisting the cognitive strategies that characterize the system and reflects by implication the aesthetic strategy of *Makbara*, its cultivation of enigma to oblige the reader to work at understanding the text. There follows then an ironic letter of self-criticism in which the Angel invites her expulsion on the grounds that she is undermining the system. The reaction this receives is again, one recognizes, that which *Makbara* implicitly aims for:

> sorpresa, asombro, estupefacción, cólera, repugnancia se pintaba sucesiva-mente en el rostro de los lectores ávidos de la carta ... (198)

Makbara does try to evade the normal interpretive strategies of the reader, as we have seen, both by contravening the conventions of the traditional novel and by introducing elements of a literary tradition, the Arabic oral tradition, alien to a Western reader. The aim is to endow the text with the same effect on the reader as the Moor has on the crowd in the first chapter, the generation of both repulsion and fascination, disquiet and curiosity. The text is generated by a decentring force. The narrative voice circulates among the protagonists, the spectators, the reader, and itself, like the *bululú*, like the Arcipreste. The effect is to create a de-hierarchized polyphony of narrative voices which the reader has little difficulty in understanding but finds problems in organizing into an ordered, logical narration, so that he gives himself to the play of voices and ends up, like the visitor to the plaza, 'inmerso en el vasto recinto establecido para solaz y gloria de los sentidos' (215).

As with Bakhtin's concept of the carnivalesque, this is a purely literary, textual experience. Hence again Goytisolo's carnivalized vision is not representational but utopian, as he himself says, quoting Bakhtin's analysis of Rabelais: 'preserva una brecha alegre en un futuro más lejano' (CS, 45). The space of the text becomes the counter-part of the plaza, that 'punto de convergencia de cuanto no era oficial [...] de extraterritorialidad en el mundo del orden y las ideologías oficiales', where 'el pueblo tenía siempre la última palabra' (CS, 53).

'Lectura del espacio en Xemaá-el-Fná' can be 'read' as an encouragement to an 'active' approach to the sign, a liberated and liberating method of reading, free of the quest for a transcendent, fixed meaning. The text is dominated by the principle of movement, the 'forastero' is moving through the square, not simply observing the activities and the people but 'reading' them:

> reino de aventuras y encuentros, lenguaje de caderas, telegrafía de gestos, semierecciones festivas : incitaciones visuales y acústicas al tanteo y exploración, al ejercicio de la caza furtiva, al magreo de la mano inconexa (215–16)

The references to the square as a semiological system of gestures, movements, body signals, which the spectator reads in the sense of sensuously perceiving them, draws attention to the text itself which calls out to be read in the same way:

> mercadillo de oferta y demanda donde el trato se cierra con sonrisas y señas y, peritos en el arte de una semiología espontánea, los trajinantes descifran deseos e impulsos mediante la lectura al trasluz de sus prendas ... (208)[54]

The text ends with an invitation to a 'lectura en palimpsesto' of the square and of the text itself. The square, the story, the text, are all examples of the 'ingrávido edificio sonoro en de(con)strucción perpetua'. The square is emptied daily and fills up the following day, the stories told one day are repeated the next. And the text? The text is the source of multiple, different readings, a 'precaria combinación de signos de mensaje incierto'. Or is it? Sceptical critics, such as Gil Casado, may refuse to accept this:

> *Makbara* no es un libro abierto con 'infinitas posibilidades', pues ni se transforma, ni se reinicia, ni se reelabora, por la simple razón de que los signos son inequívocos, el mensaje es cierto.[55]

Gil Casado may be underestimating the lengths to which Goytisolo successfully goes in making the language of the novel extremely ambiguous, disorienting the reader so that the message is far from certain or simply parodying that very urge to certainty which characterizes Gil Casado's style, the desire to reduce the novel to a fixity that allows him to proclaim that '*Makbara* no representa innovación alguna' (225). But he does have a point. As Ong points out, print 'encourages a sense of closure, a sense that what is found in a text has been finalized, has reached a state of completion' (132). However, this is part of the contradiction observed earlier, which far from invalidating the literary endeavour, enriches it. The novel constitutes an attempt to escape the limits of language, seen as integral to the urge to escape restrictions on all levels. The words on the page are final, but by playing with multiple points of view, merging temporal and spatial planes and confusing characters and narrative voices, the text ensures that it resists easy exegesis. The ambiguity of the text, its need of multiple readings before meaning can begin to be discerned and the uncertain nature of that meaning justify its call for a 'lectura en palimpsesto' (222).

Conclusion

Makbara continues the Goytisolan technique of an engagement with reality through its discursive practices. Within the context of a new discursive practice which attempts to enact in aesthetic terms the values and principles of movement (evasion of repressive authority), egalitarianism (non-hierarchical) and libidinal gratification (text which resists the cognitive urge in order to appeal to the acoustic, sensual urge), it seeks to parody the discourses of the contemporary hi-tech society that prevails in the West and to subvert the 'naturalness' of that ethos by opposing it to a counter-discourse represented by the Arabic oral tradition as well as the dissident discourse of the Angel.

However, none of these discourses is denied, defeated or condemned to failure. Rather they are all held in place by the text. In this way the text does not make any extravagant claims for its ability to dispense with the criticized reality, but at the same time by containing all the discourses in a non-hierarchical polyphony of voices makes its own plea for the value of heterogeneity, the right to difference.

This represents a more nuanced view of the power of the text than that of the previous novels. *Makbara* manages both to suggest the importance of literature while at the same time recognizing the limits of its influence. Hence the novel thematizes the relationship between reality and utopia and suggests how literature participates in the utopian impulse. *Makbara* as literature is, like fantasy, an integral part of the contestation of reality, and within that broad function of literature, *Makbara* belongs to the anti-official strand of literary history, along with the early oral literature of the *juglar* and the modern-day public storyteller, all those who participate in the Bakhtinian genre of carnival. The contradictions which characterize the novel point to *Makbara*'s more postmodernist rendering of the carnival theme, in which the carnival nature of the novel itself is put under examination. Above all, the contradiction between orality and literacy underlines the specifically textual nature of *Makbara*'s critique.

This is a constant theme in Goytisolo's work and present in *Juan sin tierra*. *Makbara*, however, differs from the latter both in the degree of success in achieving the effect and in the moral colouring it assumes. For if *Juan sin tierra* managed to create a text that, on a linguistic level, was rich, complex and semantically dense, the thematic undercurrent was so lucid and logical in its intention that it militated against the novel's claims to a subversion of all the reader's certainties. *Makbara*, on the other hand, comes closer in its integration of the principle of ambiguity and necessary contradiction. The novel has a much more successfully interrogative nature.

On a moral level, *Makbara*'s expansion of the theme of individual libidinal gratification beyond the solipsism of the onanistic theme of *Juan sin tierra* towards a view which, while still basically individualistic, is incorporated within a communal vision of fraternity and human interaction, advances Goytisolo's stance beyond the purely oppositional towards a properly positive utopian vision. This is important because it suggests Goytisolo has managed to eliminate a weakness in his approach hitherto, which was the contradictory pull between, on the one hand, the desire to shock and subvert, and on the other, the need to persuade. *Don Julián* and *Juan sin tierra* were masterpieces of narrative polemic which could not fail to provoke the reader. *Makbara*, on the other hand, is a work which manages to fill the moral void created by the destructive tactics of the previous two novels and it does so partly by an appeal to a pre-technological ideal of human community and fraternity, which, it is implied, still exists in the Moroccan plaza. An element of primitivism is common to all utopian projects; such speculations on the past serve to 'raise the question of the future by showing the mutable nature of past and present. They therefore strike at all ideological attempts to eternalize the present.'[56] However, it is in the contextualizing of the aesthetic process that *Makbara* makes its contribution to an evolving radical aesthetic in that it clarifies the role of literature in the utopian project and guards against making overreaching claims for it.

By 'contextualizing the aesthetic process' is meant that in the intricate network of motifs and textual paralleling, *Makbara* establishes the similarities and differences between the writing process and the lived experiences of fantasy and the alternative literary tradition of oral narrative. Whereas in *Don Julián* the situation was much more ambiguous, the text hovering in the limbo between representation and narrative autism, between the belief that art and imagination have no effect whatsoever on external reality and a sense of their devastatingly destructive and subversive powers, and *Juan sin tierra* on the other hand argued for the limitlessness of the powers of writing which were necessarily predicated on the non-real, literary status of the text, *Makbara*, still sharing the fundamental principles of these previous texts, manages to weave together more skilfully the different areas involved. The text presents the unattainability of utopia except in the form of the unquenchable desire for that utopia. Seen in this light, paradoxically, the Angel and the Pariah do emerge triumphant in their unending quest for fulfilment, the *halaiquí* with his determination to return the following day and the writer's look towards the 'infinitas posibilidades de juego' of the white page and his exhortation to the reader to undertake a 'lectura en palimpsesto'.

NOTES

1 J. Ríos (ed.), *Juan Goytisolo* (Madrid: Fundamentos, 1975), 128–29.

2 Pablo Gil Casado, '*Makbara* es un cementerio', *Cuadernos Americanos* XL(6) (1981), 217–26; Kessel Schwartz, '*Makbara*—Metaphysical Metaphor or Goytisolian World Revisited?', *Hispania* LXVII (1984), 36–42.

3 Goytisolo had said of *Juan sin tierra*: 'concibo *Juan sin tierra* como una obra última, el finis terrae de mi propia escritura en términos de comunicación, de coloquio. O, si prefieres, de "discurso" tal y como lo concibe Benveniste.' *Disidencias* (Barcelona: Seix Barral, 1977), 317

4 Juan Goytisolo, 'Sobre literatura y vida literaria', *Quimera* XXIII (1982), 21.

5 In a private interview Goytisolo commented that his interest in the prosodic quality of prose dates from 1974.

6 Bakhtin's own theory is open to similar criticism. Peter Stallybrass and Allon White, in their book *The Politics and Poetics of Transgression* (London: Methuen, 1986), note critics such as Terry Eagleton's questioning of the impact of carnival, seeing it as a form of 'licensed release' which 'therefore serves the interests of that very official culture which it apparently opposes' (13).

7 Katerina Clark and Michael Holquist, *Mikhail Bakhtin* (London: Harvard University Press, 1984), 304.

8 *En los reinos de taifa* (Barcelona: Seix Barral, 1986), 113.

9 Linda Hutcheon, *A Poetics of Postmodernism: History, Theory, Fiction* (London: Routledge, 1988), 206.

10 See Carlos Blanco Aguinaga, 'Sobre la *Reivindicación del conde don Julián*: la ficción y la historia', in *De mitólogos y novelistas* (Madrid: Turner, 1975), 51–71; Claudia Schaefer-Rodriguez, *Juan Goytisolo: del 'realismo crítico' a la utopía* (Madrid: Porrúa Turanzas, 1984); Michael Ugarte, *Trilogy of Treason: An Intertextual Study of Juan Goytisolo* (Columbia, MO, and London: University of Missouri Press, 1982); Jo Labanyi, *Myth and History in the Contemporary Spanish Novel* (Cambridge: Cambridge University Press, 1989).

11 Luce López-Baralt, *Huellas del islam en la literatura española: De Juan Ruiz a Juan Goytisolo* (Madrid: Hiperión, 1985), 205.

12 Gil Casado, '*Makbara* es un cementerio', 224–25. Levine's comments on fellatio and Lázaro's attitude to the sexual relations depicted in the novel reveal the same literal reading. 'Mientras que por un lado, se puede interpretar este culto al falo como componente esencial de la sátira que hace Goytisolo de la visión occidental del moro como símbolo de la sexualidad y la lujuria, por otro, al presentar esta sátira a través del ángel caído, símbolo de la rebelión contra dicha represión, Goytisolo reduce la carga de la crítica y nos deja con lo que parece ser una auténtica adoración del falo.' Linda Gould Levine, '*Makbara*: entre la espada y la pared—¿política marxista o política sexual?', *Revista Iberoamericana* CXVI–CXVII (1981), 103–04. Jesús Lázaro also simplifies the message of the novel when he comments, 'A través del falo y la felación, se recupera la verdadera dignidad de la palabra plena, la palabra de amor'. Jesús Lázaro, *La novelística de Juan Goytisolo* (Madrid: Alhambra, 1984), 250.

13 Brad Epps, *Significant Violence: Oppression and Resistance in the Narratives of Juan Goytisolo, 1970–1990* (Oxford: Clarendon Press, 1996), 246.

14 Gonzalo Sobejano, 'Valores figurativos y compositivos de la soledad en la novela de Juan Goytisolo', *Voces* I (1981), 30.

15 Edward Said, *Orientalism* (London: Routledge, 1978), 3. Said, in turn, has spoken of 'the imaginative works of Juan Goytisolo and Salman Rushdie, whose fictions and criticisms are self-consciously written against the cultural stereotypes and representations commanding the field [of Orientalism].' Said, 'Orientalism Reconsidered', in *Literature, Politics and Theory: Papers from the Essex Conference 1976–84*, ed. F. Barker *et al.* (London: Methuen, 1986), 227.

16 Uta Liebmann Schaub, 'Foucault's Oriental Subtext', *PMLA* CIII(3) (1989), 306.

17 Foucault, in the Preface to *Folie et Déraison*, quoted in Liebmann Schaub, 'Foucault's Oriental Subtext', 308.

18 Rana Kabbani, *Europe's Myths of Orient* (London: Pandora, 1988), 31–32.

19 Luce López-Baralt, '*Makbara:* Juan Goytisolo's fictionalized version of Orientalism', *The Review of Contemporary Fiction* IV(2) (1984), 138–45.

20 Liebmann Schaub, 'Foucault's Oriental Subtext', 308.

21 It is interesting in this connection, especially given Marcuse's influence on Goytisolo, to note Vincent Geoghegan's remarks about the relation between art and imagination in the theory of Marcuse: 'Imagination is an integral part of the "perverse" revolt against the unfree organization of sexuality in modern society and it prefigures the libidinal freedom of future rational society. In art, also, the "return of the repressed" is manifest—its imaginative structures make liberation a temporary reality and a possible goal.' Vincent Geoghegan, *Utopianism and Marxism* (London: Methuen, 1987), 100.

22 Memory too is an important part of this utopian impulse: 'For Marcuse, memory is the means to recapture earlier experiences of freedom and happiness. It is a way of thwarting any attempt to eternalize existing unhappiness. By showing that happiness once obtained, it also raises the possibility of, and the desire for, future satisfaction.' Geoghegan, *Utopianism and Marxism*, 101.

23 Antonio Bolívar Botia explains 'sedentary thinking' as that which defends 'el orden, la autoridad, los buenos modales o las instituciones' and defines the Deleuzian concept of 'pensée nomade' as that in which 'no se da una supuesta unidad de lo real, sino más bien se muestra su anarquía, su dispersión y su diferencia, del mismo modo que una tribu nómada se dispersa en un territorio sin distribuirlo entre sus componentes. No hay principio supremo, fundamento último o instancia ante la que apelar para decidir la esencia de las cosas.' Antonio Bolívar Botia, *El estructuralismo: de Lévi-Strauss a Derrida* (Madrid: Cincel, 1985), 160–61.

24 The fact that her sexual awakening takes the form of rape alerts us to the ambiguous, problematic nature of her condition.

25 Silvia Truxa, 'El "mito árabe" en las últimas novelas de Juan Goytisolo', *Iberoromania* June 1980, 104–05. See also Walter Ong, *Orality and Literacy: The Technologizing of the Word* (London: Methuen, 1982), 70.

26 In 'Presentación crítica' Goytisolo wrote: 'la esclerosis del marxismo en los países del bloque soviético ha facilitado la promoción de una poderosa casta burocrática investida de poderes casi sacerdotales, con sus obispos cuadros, sus comités-curias y sus omnímodos pontífice-secretarios generales' (54).

27 See Goytisolo's account of his personal view in *Contracorrientes* (Barcelona: Montesinos, 1985), 230–31.

28 *Contracorrientes*, 233.

29 This doubtless refers to the film *Morocco* with Marlene Dietrich and Gary Cooper. See *Crónicas sarracinas* (Paris: Ruedo Ibérico, 1981), 164.

30 José Miguel Ullán, 'Arabesco para la transparencia', *Voces* I (1981), 22.

31 Evelyne García, untitled article on *Makbara* in *Juan Goytisolo*, ed. J. Lázaro (Madrid: Ministerio de Cultura, 1982), 141.

32 There is an interesting parallel in the theory of Marcuse, whose vision of the utopian future was framed partly in terms of a regression to a precivilized, childish past. As Geoghegan says, 'this is not simple revivalism. Marcuse is not envisaging a total return to the past but rather an enrichment from the past on the basis of all that is best in modernity.' *Utopianism and Marxism*, 104.

33 Mikhail Bakhtin, *Problems of Dostoevsky's Poetics*, trans. R. W. Rostel (Ann Arbor, MI: Ardis, 1973), 108.

34 'El visitante o asiduo a Xemaá-el-Fná disfruta en verdad de una prerrogativa singular: la de zambullirse, en las postrimerías del milenio, en un mundo extinguido entre nosotros desde hace varios siglos; un mundo en el que el hombre medieval, tanto en el ámbito cristiano como el islámico, disponía soberanamente de su tiempo, se abandonaba a sus instintos de juego y aficiones al espectáculo, acudía al círculo abierto y fraterno de los narradores públicos, absorbía incansablemente sus historias, edificaba con éstas los rudimentos de su propia sociabilidad' (CS, 53).

35 López-Baralt, *Huellas del islam en la literatura española*, 184.

36 Arcipreste de Hita, *Libro de Buen Amor*, Verse 13 (Barcelona: Bruguera, 1977), 77.

37 Ong, *Orality and Literacy*, 29.

38 See *Crónicas sarracinas*, 44–45.

39 See Hutcheon, *The Poetics of Postmodernism*, Chapter IV, 'Decentering the Postmodern: The Ex-Centric', 57–73.

40 Gonzalo Sobejano, 'Valores figurativos y compositivos', 31. Similarly the technique was used by the Arcipreste, as Raymond Willis has noted: 'The structure of the poem may seem random and disjointed, but not if we see the work as originally an organic poetic whole whose texture is the quintessence of fluidity and mutability: every passage flows into the next, poetically if not logically; everything can be transformed into something else [...] The Archpriest himself tells us so, for scarcely had he started his Book, dialoguing in the first person with his readers, when, bewilderingly, the word yo, which up to st. 69 has designated the author of the book, turns into the book itself, the book with all its songs [...] This same yo, on another occasion, turns into Don Melón de la Huerta.' Raymond Willis, Introduction to *The Book of Good Love* (Princeton, NJ: Princeton University Press, 1971), xlvi.

41 Luce López-Baralt affirms that 'Lo primero que salta a la vista es la oralidad del relato. *Makbara*, como las grandes novelas del autor, pero aún en mayor medida, debe ser leída en voz alta'. López-Baralt, *Huellas del islam en la literatura española*, 194. Abigail Lee Six claims that '*Makbara* reveals itself to be a wholly spoken text'. Abigail Lee Six, *Juan Goytisolo: The Case for Chaos* (London: Yale University Press, 1990), 193. Annie Perrin, in '*Makbara* ou la voix retrouvée' (*Association des Publications de Clermont* II [1982]), focuses on the utopian effect of orality in a culture of the written word: 'Il y a dans *Makbara* un écho de l'utopie rousseauiste—rêve d'une parole libérée du dangereux supplément de l'écriture' (148). José Manuel Martín Morán, in 'La oralidad en las novelas de Juan Goytisolo' (*Antipodas; Journal of Hispanic Studies* VIII–IX [1996–97]), examines the concept across a range of texts, claiming rather straightforwardly 'en la obra de Goytisolo una serie de textos huye de las normas de la escritura, de los condicionantes propios de la tecnología de la imprenta y recupera elementos de la narrativa oral' (156). One of the most interesting and fullest treatments is that of Marta Gómez Mata in *Oralidad y polifonía en la obra de Juan Goytisolo* (Madrid: Ensayos Júcar, 1994). However, again the tendency is to centre on orality's capacity for channelling his 'denuncia y malestar frente a los omnipotentes medios de comunicación modernos' (64), and Gómez Mata even

suggests that 'Makbara pretende la constatación de que voz y escritura no tienen por qué ser elementos opuestos' (50).

42 'Existe un oído literario, como existe un oído musical. La lectura ideal de Makbara es una lectura en voz alta.' Goytisolo, 'Sobre literatura y vida literaria', Quimera XXIII (1982), 21. See also López-Baralt, Huellas del islam en la literature española, 194.

43 Ong, Orality and Literacy, 103.

44 'Como han probado lingüistas de la talla de una Kate Hamburger o un Yuki Kuroda hay ocasiones en que el lenguaje puede ser utilizado fuera de toda situación comunicacional real o imaginaria, es decir, en los que no hay donante o narrador', Contracorrientes, 54.

45 Jonathan Culler, Structuralist Poetics: Structuralism, Linguistics and the Study of Literature (London: Routledge, 1975), 200.

46 As Sobejano says: 'La obra que anuncia o parece anunciar esa liberación erótica y anárquica, desemboca en la página a mi entender más perfecta jamás escrita por Juan Goytisolo: "Lectura del espacio en Xemaá-el-Fná". Final que va de la euforia del día (clímax) a la melancolía. nocturna (anticlímax): exaltación de las gentes, de las cosas, de los espectáculos, del contacto humano, seguida de una reflexión literaria y solitaria. Lectura del espacio y de la alegría de la fraternidad, pero de una fraternidad contemplada'. Sobejano, 'Valores figurativos y compositivos', 31.

47 There is an echo of the Barthes of Mythologies in the reference to the Blue Guide. Barthes' essay on the Guide Bleu had attempted to demystify the bourgeois discourse of the travel book (and bourgeois discourse in general) as ideology masquerading as objective descriptiveness: 'Generally speaking, the Blue Guide testifies to the futility of all analytical descriptions, those which reject both explanations and phenomenology: it answers in fact none of the questions which a modern traveller can ask himself while crossing a countryside which is real and which exists in time.' Roland Barthes, Mythologies (London: Paladin, 1973), 76.

48 See Kabbani, Europe's Myths of Orient, 10 and Said, Orientalism, 22.

49 Ong, Orality and Literacy, 46.

50 López-Baralt, Huellas del islam en la literatura española, 195–96.

51 H. A. R. Gibb, Arabic Literature: An Introduction (London: Oxford University Press, 1974), 8.

52 Said, Orientalism, 20–21.

53 Linda Hutcheon sees this as a characteristic of postmodernism: 'Its [post-modernism's] institutional critique involves a challenging of those institutionalized discourse boundaries (history, literature, theory, philosophy, sociology) whose academic entrenchment has meant the privileging or trivializing of certain discursive practices.' Hutcheon, The Poetics of Postmodernism, 213.

54 Ong identified this as a true characteristic of this type of oral society: 'In primary oral cultures, even business is not business: it is fundamentally rhetoric. Purchasing something at a Middle East souk or bazaar is not a simple economic transaction [...] as a high-technology culture is likely to presume it would be in the nature of things. Rather, it is a series of verbal (and somatic) maneuvers, a polite duel, a contest of wits, an operation in oral agonistic.' Ong, Orality and Literacy, 68.

55 Gil Casado, 'Makbara es un cementerio', 223.

56 Geoghegan, Utopianism and Marxism, Chapter IV, 'Golden Ages and Myths', 67.

CHAPTER SIX

Conclusion: After *Makbara*

After publishing *Makbara* in 1981, Goytisolo published one more novel, *Paisajes después de la batalla*, in 1982 and then had an autobiographical break, 'un paréntesis en mi obra narrativa' as he termed it,[1] in which he produced his two volumes of memoirs, *Coto vedado* in 1985 and *En los reinos de taifa* in 1986. After this he resumed his novelistic career with *Las virtudes del pájaro solitario* in 1988. Since then he has produced four more novels, *La cuarentena* in 1991, *La saga de los Marx* in 1993, *El sitio de los sitios* in 1995 and, most recently, *Las semanas del jardín* in 1997. Some critics have chosen to see a change of direction in Goytisolo's writing and to talk of a new phase.[2] While it is true that his novels do incorporate new elements, these are no more than has always been the case even with the novels of the trilogy.[3] The fundamental concerns remain the same because they are, by this stage, established points of moral and aesthetic principle. Given the amount of writing which Goytisolo has produced since the trilogy and *Makbara*, which are the principal objects of study here, it would be unfeasible to attempt a detailed study of all of these works. They are too complex to reward anything other than an extended analysis and they merit a study apart. What we can do, however, is to look at the way Goytisolo's writing has developed in the light of what has been said about the earlier novels in order to examine how the novels fit in broadly to the pattern outlined.

Two broad characteristics of the novels in the 1980s and 1990s stand out. They are, on the one hand, a pronounced development of the postmodernist nature of the writing and, on the other, an equally noticeable spiritual turn.[4] These twin trends seem on first sight to be incompatible but, as we will see, that need not necessarily be the case. The spiritual turn in Goytisolo's recent fiction can be seen as perfectly consistent with his attacks on the negative impact of modernity and indeed with a broader postmodernist outlook characterized by a 'disenchantment with modernity':

> The resurrection of the 'sacred' as a sphere of experience pertinent to modern forms of life, as a counter to the nihilism of the modern world ... certainly constitutes a part of what has been described as the postmodern condition.[5]

Paisajes después de la batalla

Paisajes is highly postmodernist in that it is ironic, highly self-referential, parodic, fragmented, self-subverting. Yet at the same time, in this novel Goytisolo for the first time introduces the theme of the wandering dervish as his literary ideal,[6] and one of the intertextual elements is a reference to the poetry of the Persian mystic Rumi. The link between the apparently incompatible strands of Sufi mysticism and postmodernism is not immediately obvious. The former, of course, is important to Goytisolo less as a theology than as a poetic tradition (and as such links in with his admiration for San Juan de la Cruz), and in literary terms there are certain parallels between the two doctrines of mysticism and postmodernism. One of these is that they are both in their own ways antithetical to certain well-established Western concepts of a stable self.[7] While the mystic's dissolving of the Self fits in with a postmodernist, Foucauldian subversion of the subject, the appeal to oneness with a Godhead or single Truth does seem incompatible with the postmodernist antilogocentric impulse. Mysticism and postmodernism also share, in different but not unrelated ways, a critical posture towards the prevailing Western ideology of rationalist materialism. This begins a theme that will form the centre of almost all the following novels, according to which poetry, but by extension literature as a whole, is the only possible antidote and subversive force left to combat the prevailing Western doctrine of scientific rationalism.[8] In addition, Goytisolo's attraction to the Sufi mystics as to San Juan is clearly related to their essential unorthodoxy and non-conformity.

One thing that could be said, especially in the light of the 'autobiographical parenthesis' referred to, is that the nature of the novels' treatment of the autobiographical element has altered slightly. This is not surprising. This study has emphasized the importance of the autobiographical strand as a fundamental characteristic of the post-*Señas* period, and the authenticity that it lends to the writing is essential to the radical significance of the narrative dislocations that occur and which evidence the transgressive nature of the writing process. In one sense, in the post-memoirs phase of Goytisolo's writing, the authorial angst detectable certainly in *Juan sin tierra* and even to a lesser degree in *Makbara* has largely disappeared, but the autobiographical continues to subtend almost all the novels and certainly resurfaces in an obscure and complex but very powerful way in the last two novels, *El sitio de los sitios* and *Las semanas del jardín*. However, there is less a sense of the writer battling through writing with his own demons than one of an author drawing on the well of personal experience in his literary battle with social injustice. What is interesting is the way the novels use the authorial question (or questioning of authorship) as the principal site for their subversion of the reading process.

Paisajes centres on the self of the author to an extreme and grotesque extent.[9] Epps cleverly notes how *Paisajes* and *Las virtudes* 'push at the borders between the self, life and writing (auto-bio-graphy)'.[10] The protagonist shares Goytisolo's Parisian home, his district the Sentier and is even referred to as 'ese goytisolo'. The novel deliberately plays on the author figure in order to subvert the reader's normal habits of naturalization. We are encouraged on the one hand to treat it as autobiography,[11] only to have that interpretation disrupted by outrageously implausible details and elements of farcical self-parody. The reader's values are shaken by the removal of a stable viewpoint through which to assess the concepts that are in play, and this is done principally by playing with the notion of authorship. The novel can be seen to carry on a process of epistemological subversion characteristic of Goytisolo's mature period as a whole by deliberately seeking to undermine the conventional sense of the self as located in a stable narrating persona. Most critics have stressed the autobiographi-cal element as a predominant feature of the novel. Claudia Schaefer-Rodríguez focuses on the autobiographical theme, suggesting that Goytisolo adopts the appearance of autobiography in order to parody it, allowing 'for the questioning and dethroning of authorship and the authority of the textual voice as originator or creator as well as historical being outside the artistic creation'.[12]

Whereas in the previous novels, including *Makbara*, the issue of authorship was questioned, we could always identify certain stable positions, even if the novels achieved their ultimately unsettling effect by preserving an unresolved tension, for example, between the anony-mous, Western, literate voice of the last chapter of *Makbara* and the *halaiquí nesrani*. With *Paisajes* the process of naturalization is thrown even further into doubt, not by the removal of the narrative voice (that, we have seen, could not be done),[13] but by its explicit problematiza-tion.[14] The novels from *Makbara* onwards have eschewed the attempt to do away entirely with *énoncé* in favour of a more radical disturbing of narrative levels.[15]

Curiously, the opening pages introduce a Joycean echo which immediately initiates the debate. The text opens with a scene of a socio-linguistic disaster in Paris, a 'postmodern hecatomb'[16] in which the street signs have all been turned into Arabic, much to the dismay of the native Parisians. In the second section we meet the 'autor de la tropelía', and the use of the term 'autor' is deliberate. From now on the narrator, who in this highly self-conscious narrative reveals himself to be one and the same with the protagonist, will struggle in mock-fashion to find words to describe the protagonist, 'héroe', 'sujeto del relato' etc., and they will always underline the fictional status of the account. This narrator reveals his alter ego as an apparently indolent, indifferent and sexually perverse inhabitant of a Parisian flat (not dissimilar to that of Goytisolo himself on the Rue Poissonnière) whose main distractions from writing are relieving himself in the washhand basin and filing his nails (PDLB, 17–18). The latter curious detail cannot but recall the reference in Joyce's *Portrait of the Artist as a Young Man* in which Stephen Dedalus discusses his artistic principles with his friend, Lynch:

> The personality of the artist, at first a cry or a cadence or a mood and then a fluid and lambent narrative, finally refines itself out of existence, impersonalizes itself, so to speak. The esthetic image in the dramatic form is life purified in and re-projected from the human imagination. The mystery of the esthetic, like that of material creation, is accomplished. The artist, like the God of creation, remains within or behind or beyond or above his handiwork, invisible, refined out of existence, indifferent, paring his fingernails.[17]

The attitude of indifference of Goytisolo's 'hero'—'el espacio material de su desaguisado había dejado de interesarle después de la alevosa perpetración [...] la hecatombe se producía a un centenar de metros de allí [...] pero él [...] como si nada' (16–17)—and the idiosyncratic detail of the nail-filing make the Joycean connection irresistible, and yet what is its significance? Goytisolo's novel displays completely the opposite approach, an author who, far from refined out of existence, is ubiquitously present and visible. A further detail from the Joyce text seems to confirm the intertextual allusion. Dedalus's friend Lynch responds to his aesthetic disquisition in dyspeptic terms: 'What do you mean, Lynch asked surlily, by prating about beauty and the imagination in this miserable Godforsaken island?' (215). Stephen's aesthetic theories are not to be taken at face value, and certainly not as representative of Joyce's own. As Keith Booker has noted, Stephen's remarks can be read as an 'expression of the attitude of ahistorical aesthetic distance that is often associated with certain models of literary modernism'. Goytisolo's narrator deliberately undercuts such an approach to literature in a typical piece of postmodernist pastiche which presents the author as directly involved not only in the action of the text but, by implication, in the political and historical issues to which the text alludes.[18]

The tension between artistic activity and social responsibility is a recurrent theme of *Paisajes*. In many ways, the novel can be read as a postmodernist reworking of *Señas de identidad*.[19] The links with *Señas* are numerous, from the references to the exiled Spaniards discussing and plotting the downfall of the regime to the detail of the musician who refuses to compose until the death of the dictator (SI, 257; PDLB,

64–65). Most telling are the references to the narrator-protagonist's sense of guilt at his artistic vocation and his abandoning of direct political struggle. The guilty self-accusations and questions in *Señas*—

> Te fuiste de España (abandonando a tus amigos en medio de una lucha política difícil e incierta) ... y en estos dos años de bohemio parisiense, ¿qué has hecho? ... ¿qué eres? (SI, 377)

—find their echo in the passage in *Paisajes*:

> y tú ¿qué?; los americanos han llegado a la luna, y tú ¿qué?; están sacando petróleo del Sáhara, y tú ¿qué?; ya hay guerrilla urbana en Segovia, y tú ¿qué? (PDLB, 144)

One noticeable change, of course, is the broadening (and mock-narrowing) of the political concerns that fuel the author's guilt.

Hence the issue of social transformation and artistic commitment is at the heart of this novel, and in line with what we noticed in *Makbara*, in *Paisajes* Goytisolo combines satire of social issues with a metafictional reflection on the role of the artist which both insists that formal, aesthetic revolt is the only option open to the writer and at the same time puts the effectiveness of that process in doubt. The concentrated play on the author–narrator–reader relationship is such as to remove any possible certainty about the precise ideological content of the novel or the effectiveness of its textual strategy. While, on the one hand, we can recognize the broad strategy of the novel's self-reflexiveness as part of the attack on 'the sense of oppression by endless systems and structures of present-day society—with its technologies, bureaucracies, ideologies, institutions and traditions'[20] evident in scenes like that in the Préfecture where French administration's Kafkaesque bureaucracy leading to violent oppression of foreigners is parodied (PDLB, 119–23), the novel also leads the reader to wonder about the ultimate effect of this strategy. As Linda Hutcheon comments:

> Textual self-consciousness certainly can be (and has been) used as a deliberate stategy to 'provoke readers to critically examine all cultural codes and established patterns of thought', but must it necessarily do so? Could it not, instead [...] be a form of solipsistic navel-gazing and empty ludic game-playing?[21]

For Hutcheon, the positive interpretation takes its inspiration from a Marcusian belief in the beneficially liberational effects of self-conscious art. As she says, 'the underlying belief here is clearly that self-awareness combats self-delusion [...] and that (even in textualized form) it can be a form of resistance to the power of homogenizing mass culture and of traditional strategies of representation'.[22] If Goytisolo does escape the accusations of ludism and narrative navel-gazing it is because in true postmodern fashion he is aware of the risks and thematizes them within the narrative. In the last section he states wearily: 'Por favor, nada de

"experimentación", "sintagma verbal", "niveles de lectura", "propósito lúdico"' (193). And in the narrator-protagonist's case the problem
is not navel-gazing but urine-scrutinizing:

> un paseíto al baño a acarciarse los cañones de la barba ante el espejo,
> apretarse una espinilla en la aleta de la nariz [...] mear directamente en el
> lavabo; un viejo hábito contraído hace años, después del lancinante dolor
> causado por los cálculos renales ... (17)

The novel ends with the narrator-protagonist repeating exactly the
same process. The circularity could appear fatalistic and pessimistic and
Goytisolo has met with that charge. Referring to the next novel, *Las
virtudes del pájaro solitario*, for example, Brad Epps accuses Goytisolo
of 'an abdication of hope and a slide into despair'[23] because the novel's
end implies that 'transcendence is not, narratively speaking, realized in
the text'.[24] The same might be said for *Paisajes* but I would question
whether true transcendence is what is sought. What the novels do aim
for is a reading process which is both liberating and subversive and
might possibly stand as the prelude to transcendence in terms of
freedom from extratextual oppression.[25] The end of *Paisajes* sends
the reader back to the beginning in the same way that we had seen in
Don Julián, and the implication is that we are dealing with a novel as
process not product. The narrator explicitly states his literary strategy
as the novel as puzzle:

> componer un libro abierto al conjunto de voces y experiencias, construido
> como un rompecabezas que sólo un lector paciente, con gustos de aventurero
> y etnólogo, sería capaz de armar ... (188)

The book is a textual analogue of the city and the author's writing
process is a textual 'callejeo', a familiar Goytisolan image of freedom
in movement. For the reader, too, it must be a similarly liberating
experience:

> el tiempo ya no apremia su tiranía ha cesado; puedes callejear escribir
> extraviarte en el doble espacio de la cives y el libro inventar trayectos
> laberínticos desorientar desorientarte ... (192)

The ideological debates underlying the novel are not always easily
resolvable, and that is how it should be. The novel does not offer
answers but poses questions. It is, as it states, a 'fábula sin ninguna
moralidad' (193), though not amoral.[26] However, its insistent advocacy
of freedom from oppression and its espousal of heterogeneity and the
right to be different is quite unmistakable. This makes it surprising that
it can be taken to task by Epps for its sexual politics. For no matter
what the ambiguities and possible inconsistencies in Goytisolo's sexual
politics, and Epps analyses these exhaustively, if not dispassionately,[27] it
would seem clear that the parody of the militant homosexuals, the
Maricas Rojos, is, on one level, not an attack on homosexuals but on a

particular sect within that social grouping, but more important is its function on a literary level. Rather than 'destroying' the text as Epps suggests,[28] they actually want to 'secure' it, to pin it down and fix its meaning on their own terms. Far from being the agents of 'parodic fragmentation', the fragmentation is the outcome of the failure of their project. The attackers enter the narrator's home intent on securing an interpretation of his work. The episode is an extremely funny but crucial fragment of the jigsaw of the text. Essentially the intruders represent the radically reductionist and repressive wings of the critical establishment. They are a jibe at the excesses of queer, Marxist, psychoanalytic, Lacanian theory intent on imposing their interpretations on the text. The parody is of the ruthlessly desperate academic faced with the textual *rompecabezas* which is *Paisajes* and who wants to find a key to its meaning in the author himself. Hence his files, his personal documentation, his home is ransacked for clues. Their solution is to attach an exploding device to his chest and force him to confess. The scene echoes those in *Makbara*, both 'Hipótesis sobre un averní-cola' and 'Noticias del más allá', where the subversiveness of the text provokes either academic attempts to fix meaning by application of a method or a forced 'auto-crítica' by the author himself. The tactic there was 'inventar, para confundirlas, algún burlón juego de palabras' (M, 195), and here the approach is similar:

> Cuidado lector: el narrador no es fiable [. . .] no deja de engañarte un instante. Su estrategia defensiva, destinada a envolverte en una nube de tinta, multiplica las presuntas confesiones para ocultar lo esencial . . . (177)

The central strategy of confusing the reader in order to liberate the reading is finally achieved when the device explodes, in a typically ambiguous way—was it the bomb on his chest or the effect of the telegram received from the 'individuo moreno' in the Place du Caire (191), itself a fulfilled prediction of the African hermit (167)?

Here the evolution from *Juan sin tierra* can be seen. From the radical but ultimately rather sterile threat of withdrawal of communication, we have progressed to a complication of communication in such a way as to open the way to multiple readings (both in the sense of re-readings and of various non-linear readings within the novel as one section projects ahead and back to others, in a form of narrative achrony). This is summed up in the last section where the narrator seizes on a mathematical principle, the Commutative Law, which states that the factors of a product can be interchanged without altering the result.[29] This is a direct contravention of one of the basic principles of narrative identified by Todorov in a quote from Lev Vygotski's *Psychologie de l'art*:

> Nous savons déjà que la base de la mélodie est la corrélation dynamique des sons qui la constituent. Il en est exactement de même quant au vers qui n'est

pas la simple somme des sons qui le constituent mais leur succession dynamique, une certaine corrélation [...] Ainsi les sons a, b, c, ou les mots a, b, c, ou les événements a, b, c, changent totalement de sens et de signification émotionnelle, si nous les mettons, disons, dans l'ordre suivant: b, c, a; b, a, c.[30]

In this way, the novel tries to set itself apart from and in direct opposition to the normal reading process, seen as an imposition of the author's meaning on the reader. The text, true to its postmodern principles, sets out to induce an alert, actively sceptical attitude in the reader.[31]

Las virtudes del pájaro solitario

Las virtudes del pájaro solitario is one of the most radically unsettling of Goytisolo's novels. The author dissolves his position into a shifting narrative of multiple anonymous voices and an endlessly changing perspective. Yet even here, elusive and allusive autobiographical references to a homosexual history and the impact of AIDS[32] are incorporated to develop the idea of contamination associated with the writing process (San Juan, the forbidden library, the text we are reading), all combined in an attack on society's attempts to control and repress difference. The novel develops the theme of the search for a supreme sense of inner oneness as experienced by the Sufic mystics and, in Goytisolo's interpretation, San Juan de la Cruz. As a result, it appears to mark the beginning of a new cycle in this author's development: a new development characterized nonetheless by a return to, and intensification of, the complex aesthetic characteristics of the novels of the Trilogy and Makbara, suggesting that the aim to disconcert and challenge the reader on an artistic level remains a priority in Goytisolo's literary project. The aim in the previous novels to resist straightforward naturalization on the part of the reader is carried on into this novel. In a clear allusion to the poetry of San Juan and, by implication, his own novel, the narrator rejects the possibility of 'descifrar las oscuridades del texto, hallar una clave explicativa unívoca', and says:

> no sería mejor anegarse de una vez en la infinitud del poema, aceptar la impenetrabilidad de sus misterios y opacidades, liberar tu propio lenguaje de grillos racionales...? (LVPS, 59)

Abigail Lee Six notes that Las virtudes goes further than the previous novels in the disorienting effect of a polyphony of narrative voices which the reader is unable to identify, and concludes that 'this can be regarded as the outcome of Goytisolo's aspirations to a state of ultimate fluidity; gone are the spectacular metamorphoses from one fixed narrator-identity to another, and instead we have only total freedom of movement of the narrative voice because it has no identity from which to depart or metamorphose'.[33]

Hence, in spite of the autobiographical parenthesis, *Las virtudes* in its assumption of a much more anonymous author-narrator, splintered into a variety of voices, clearly follows on from the preceding novel, *Paisajes*. Similarly, as with all the previous novels, the novel combines three levels of narrative self-reflexiveness, intertextual dialogue and allusion to the 'real' world.

One of the most important examples of the text's reflection on its own processes occurs in the fifth part of the second section: 'no sería mejor anegarse de una vez en la infinitud del poema...' (59). This is in the context of an intertextual dialogue with the work of San Juan de la Cruz. The narrator identifies himself with the tortured poet and assumes for his own text the mysterious, disorientating characteristics of the mystic's verse:

> aceptar la impenetrabilidad de sus misterios y opacidades, liberar tu propio lenguaje de grillos racionales, abandonarlo al campo magnético de sus imantanciones secretas ... (59)

The final part reveals a further intertextual partner in the creative process as the long mystical poem, *The Conference* or *Language of the Birds (Manteq at-Tair)* written in the twelfth century by the Persian Sufi Farid ud-Din Attar. This is a long allegorical poem, known as *mathnavis*,[34] recounting how a group of birds, led by a hoopoe, go in search of a mythical creature, also in the form of a bird, the Simorgh, who represents 'Reality' or 'God'.[35] The birds make their various excuses for not being able to undertake the arduous journey and the hoopoe counters all their excuses with reasons for going. In the end, thirty set off on a journey that is an allegory for the Sufi path 'through the Seven Valleys of Seeking, Love, Gnosis, Self-reliance, Acknowledgment of One-ness, Uncertainty, and, lastly, Destitution and Death to Self. In the end they discover the Simurgh, and in so doing discover themselves.'[36]

Goytisolo's dialogue with Attar's work is complex and operates on several levels, but as with San Juan, one of the most important is the specifically literary, and in addition, the way in which the literary work achieves a social impact. Dick Davis explains how a prominent feature is the author's resort to paradox, either due to the genuinely inexpressible nature of their ideas or to avoid orthodox reprisal.[37] In Goytisolo's case the same characteristic has as its aim the deliberate disorientation of the reader and combating of rational thinking (LVPS, 59). But this intentional obscurity has a similar motivation in both. As Davis says, 'the reader is being asked to look at some problem in an unfamiliar way, and logic is often deliberately flouted so that we are, as it were, teased or goaded—rather than logically led—into understanding' (17). The two authors, and this is no doubt part of the appeal for Goytisolo in the Persian's work, share the wish, as Davis puts it, speaking of Attar, to 'insist that "normal" apprehensions and expectations are questionable, to turn them inside out' (20). Furthermore, Attar's work hinges on two central Sufi beliefs: the need to destroy the Self and the importance of passionate love. The latter is 'always a love that flies in the face of either social or sexual or religious convention ... it is very commonly homosexual love' and 'is seen by the world as scandalous'.[38] Hence the interconnections between Goytisolo's text and its Persian precursor extend to the theme of homosexuality which is contained within the polysemy of *pájaro*.[39]

The relationship developing between Goytisolo and the mystical writers and poets in this period of his writing is a complex one. I have alluded in the first chapter to the ideas expressed in his latest books of essays, in particular *El bosque de las letras* and *Cogitus interruptus*, in which the mystical poets and their contemporary allies such as José Angel Valente and Lezama Lima are enlisted in the battle against an oppressively reifying materialism. Society's faith in science and rationality and the erasure of a spiritual dimension are the principal threats seen by Goytisolo, and poetry, literature and mystical thinking are the primary weapons in the intellectual's armoury. Goytisolo's actual attachment to the religious sentiments is more doubtful. He is not nor has he ever hinted at becoming a religious believer.[40] It seems clear, then, that Goytisolo's interest is literary and social.[41] The authors he enlists intertextually serve him in his literary treatment of social concerns. Hence, where San Juan's use of language might aim at capturing and conveying the mystical experience, Goytisolo mimics the techniques for the purpose of confounding and convincing the reader. It is what he described in another context, referring to Cervantes, as the art of 'seculariz[ar] [...] el poder suasorio del discurso religioso, de la palabra revelada a los profetas, transmutando la literatura en una especie de religión laica, de creación puramente humana, aunque dotada de una transcendencia próxima a la de aquélla'.[42] For the mystic to achieve the experience of union with God, it was necessary to abandon worldly values, and principal among these was the rational, logical frame of mind. On a different level, Goytisolo's novels have had the same aim: the capturing for the writer himself and, by implication, for the reader of an ideal state of freedom, liberated from the shackles of conventional attitudes and modes of thinking. In this endeavour, the writing process has always been more than a mere vehicle of description. It has been characterized by a more performative intention. Writing has been for the author and the reader the very means of attaining that desired state.

One can see from the outline given above that Attar's allegory has a high degree of self-reflexiveness about it. The actual account of the journey is for the reader the journey or process of self-discovery itself.

Hence the dénouement is a linguistic one, a play on words. Luce López-Baralt summarizes the allegory thus:

> numerosos pájaros vuelan en busca de su Rey o Simurg hasta que los treinta pájaros (si-murgh) que logran sobrevivir el arduo vuelo milenario descubren que ellos mismos son el Simurg o Pájaro-Rey que procuraban encontrar. Es obvio que la leyenda alude al encuentro de los pájaros con ellos mismos y con su propia identidad atormentada, que es más hermosa de lo que pensaban.[43]

The last chapter of *Las virtudes* similarly deals with a moment of self-discovery:

> quién y cómo era yo?
> entre columpios, troncos, bejucos, ramas y otros instrumentos de diversión, advertí la existencia de un diminuto espejo y me planté frente a él de una volada me reconocí ... (168)

Given the homosexual connotation of *pájaro* in the text, the scene could refer to a final moment of acceptance of his condition. Given also that the *pájaro*, through the link with San Juan and the homosexual community, has also represented all persecuted individuals, in particular dissident writers, the allegory can apply also to the writer and the writing of the text *Las virtudes* itself, an unconventional, maligned form which incurs the opprobrium of the orthodox majority. Yet it is precisely the text's unconventional nature and the rejection it provokes that seals the writer's release from society, as prefigured in *Paisajes* (PDLB, 183–84). Like the legend of the Simorgh, the text that starts off as the expression of the writer's experience of alienation and persecution is, in the end, the very vehicle of his release. Similarly for the reader, as for the birds on their journey, the rigours of the reading process produce the transformative effect. The coincidence between the possible meanings of the legend and the textual process itself is suggested in the final words: 'antes de volar con las demás aves y cerrar definitivamente las páginas del libro ya compuesto' (170).

Critics such as Epps and Linda Gould Levine have questioned what I have maintained in this study to be the crucial feature of Goytisolo's writing, i.e. the interface between the aesthetic and the social, between text and world. As with previous novels, Goytisolo focuses on worldly issues (here it is AIDS, Cuba's repression of homosexuals, etc.) and binds their treatment up with the literary project (through the allegiance of the author-narrator to San Juan de la Cruz and the Sufi mystics). Epps and Levine differ in their approaches and the former takes the latter (and Goytisolo) to task for the manner in which the two are connected. For Epps the social issue, AIDS and the homosexuals' plight, is paramount and he ultimately criticizes Goytisolo for refusing to write a more specifically sympathetic novel in relation to this historical issue.[44] He criticizes Levine for daring to attempt a positive reading of the AIDS metaphor,[45] an interpretation which in his view elides the reality of the homosexual issue as tragically and irrevocably negative.

Powerful and passionately argued as Epps' case is, it cannot avoid the overpowering fact that Goytisolo's text steadfastly refuses reduction to a gay aesthetic.[46] Indeed, one is tempted to imagine that accusations of political incorrectness would be most pleasing to the author.[47] The ambiguous siting of the AIDS question is part and parcel of Goytisolo's aim to shake all our convictions.

Epps rightly refers to a rather glib tendency of readers of Goytisolo to see the texts as contaminatory without looking at the exact process of contamination. For Epps, Goytisolo exploits the AIDS metaphor in a negative way (from a homosexual point of view) by seeing it as a positive form of contagion—when in fact it is a killer for the homosexual community, precisely the sort of community that Goytisolo claims to defend. Similarly he criticizes Goytisolo and interpreters like Levine for transforming it into a positive and denaturalizing its gay content. Epps takes Goytisolo's postmodernist perspective to task in that, by fostering ambiguity, plurality and heterogeneity, he is actually playing down difference and supporting an 'anything goes' policy. In addition, Epps hints at what he sees as an abdication of responsibility by Goytisolo in his turn away to spirituality. The liberation of the body is abandoned in return for a mystico-textual surrogate.

For Epps, then, by making *Las virtudes* a textual revolt against a historical reality, Goytisolo (and with him critics like Levine) evades the challenge to make novels historically accountable. For this reason, Epps sees the novel as sliding into despair and resignation (431) because the transcendence cannot be achieved in the text; it occurs only after the text is finished. The implication is that utopia remains elusive to the artist and his textual process is a failure. This, of course, goes to the crux of our debate. Epps essentially takes Goytisolo to task for making his utopian endeavour a purely or merely textual one.[48] This, he claims, is also Levine's flaw.

The use made by Goytisolo of the AIDS image is a highly ambiguous one and goes to the heart of the novel in terms of its narrative strategy. However, unlike Epps, I would not interpret AIDS as being the theme of the novel. Levine's article does dissect the AIDS metaphor very skilfully and her use of Susan Sontag's text, *Aids and its Metaphors*, is justified. Where I would depart from Levine is not only in her actual interpretation of the motif of the 'jayanes' (LVPS, 44), but also in her apparent distinction between (fictive) reality and the reality of the text. She extrapolates a fictional world from the text within which the author-narrator hankers nostalgically after sexual union but finds in this post-AIDS climate that such real physical gratification is inaccessible. There are only substitutes:

La unión no puede realizarse en el cuerpo del amado, pero sí puede ocurrir en el cuerpo del texto. El abrazo con los jayanes viriles será imposible, pero no la caricia de la mística sufí.[49]

Thus, it is suggested, textual fulfilment compensates for impossible fulfilment in the realm of history. This leads her to suggest that the last pages of the penultimate section involving the apparent death of the sanjuanesque narrator in his cell can be interpreted as involving a positive view of AIDS—though on a metaphorical rather than real level —in that it is accepted by the narrator as a 'gift' from the beloved, here the poet Ibn al-Farid, the mingling of their poetry being interpreted as a symbolic copulation. This, says Levine, could be an example of a compensatory mythology for AIDS which Sontag thought impossible because 'AIDS, like cancer, does not allow romanticizing or sentimentalizing, perhaps because its association with death is too powerful'.[50] The exact nature of this compensatory mythology[51] is not clear from what Levine says, but with qualifications it could provide a valuable clue to the implications of the text. What is less satisfying is Levine's suggestion of the text as consolation for a failed utopia.

A more fruitful and coherent approach might be to recognize more fully the novel's explicitly metafictional and essentially postmodern character. This would see the relationship between the text and 'history-in-the-text', i.e. the way the 'real' is alluded to in the text, as a more symbiotic and fluid one. Rather than the surrogacy argument of Levine whereby utopia is posited, then seen as unattainable but a textual surrogate offered as consolation,[52] or Epps' criticism of the text for not submitting fully to the complexities of the real, we would have a concept of the text as contagion (a biological metaphor for subversion that dates back to *Don Julián*'s use of the motif of syphilis) as a possible (no more than that) effect of the text on society. This may be a weak interpretation of artistic effectiveness but it is the most convincing in practice, and therein may lie its strength.[53] It emphasizes, on the one hand, postmodernism's essential 'realism' and also its profound actuality, its concern with the here-and-now. As Hutcheon claims:

> The postmodern ... shares none of the avant-garde's Utopian orientation towards the future, despite its propensity for revolutionary rhetoric, at times. It has little faith in art's ability to change society directly, though it does believe that questioning and problematizing may set up the conditions for possible change.[54]

The scene Levine refers to (LVPS, 163–64) can be read metaphorically as alluding to the infection of San Juan's literature with Islamic influences, as in the thesis of Luce López-Baralt,[55] and hence the death of the narrator coincides with the birth of his nearly completed text, a possible (re)creation of the lost *Tratado* of San Juan which would presumably have displayed to the full these foreign influences.[56] Hence the positive reading of the AIDS motif is not in the explicit sense of the disease, though Goytisolo does play with elements of that, but with the more general and ambiguous significance that Goytisolo had given the term from the start and which Levine sensitively outlines at the start of her article; it is the 'sentido menos convencional'[57] referred to here, where the image 'deviene en metáfora por excelencia para connotar la contaminación', contamination in the (positive) sense of contamination of conventional society by intellectual dissidents. Sontag's book emphasized how the AIDS epidemic had the effect, apart from ravaging its victims, of casting into relief the attitude of the guardians of conservative, conventional thinking.[58] Goytisolo's 'unconventional' siding with AIDS as a narrative motif is due to its power to unsettle and provoke established society. This is the positive side of the image of AIDS in the novel, but it can only be understood as such if AIDS is interpreted metonymically, and ambivalently, as part of the wider notion of contamination, rather than, and this is Epps' approach, as the dominant image in its own right. As a result, Epps finds it difficult to accept Levine's otherwise legitimate reading and he sees *Las virtudes* as, in an important sense, a (failed) novel about AIDS.

If we examine the end of the novel, I would argue, *contra* Epps, that this is one of the clearest indications of the (hope in the) utopian potential of the text, for the suggestion is not that the transcendence lies beyond the text but that it is synonymous with it. Hence the metaphor of the Simorgh—a group of birds who quest after the ideal only to discover they are the ideal—suggests a text about liberation which turns out to be the liberation process itself. The reader is liberated at the end of the reading process, although here not by being thrown back at the text for an essential *relectura*. The text here hints at the end that the author-protagonist-reader '[cierran] definitivamente las páginas del libro, ya compuesto' (LVPS, 170). Where a circular reading (similar to that in *Don Julián*) might lay itself open to the accusation of a fatalistic textual hermeticism, the ending of *Las virtudes* points rather optimistically to the reading process, the text, art as our freedom or source of freedom, 'setting up the conditions for possible change'. Goytisolo dissolves the history/art gap by making art historical, showing its integral role in life.

The text carries within it a discussion of art and its role in historical issues. In this case an important one is the AIDS epidemic. Goytisolo exaggerates for ironic effect the way the disease (or infection) is presented in society and does so by taking the example of Cuba where the suggestions of the more fanatical and not so fanatical elements of Western liberal democracies were put into practice and AIDS sufferers actually herded into concentration camps (UMAPS).[59] By conflating the AIDS sufferer with San Juan, Goytisolo inextricably links the victim of

AIDS with the victim of an intolerant society in general (on the literary and religious levels in the case of San Juan and the literary and political levels in the case of writers in the Soviet Union).[60]

The AIDS sufferers (by extension writers: Jorge Ronet, San Juan, Russian dissidents) are seen in the early part to be confined to an unreal setting (modelled on the Russian spa in *En los reinos de taifa*, itself a model of an artificially state-controlled society). Their attitude symbolizes an essentially conformist view of art (i.e. art as compensation, consolation—essentially the accusation that Epps ultimately levels at Goytisolo): 'nos aferrábamos como actrices novatas al texto de la representación cotidiana' (20).[61] This unwillingness to engage with the real means that 'nos aterraba la idea de dejar el lugar, transgredir los límites' (20). The concept of a sterile art which is not transgressive and ultimately artificially conventional can be both applied to the artificial ineffectiveness of 1950s social realism and to an uncommitted modernism, what Hutcheon refers to as 'the modernist (humanist) premises of art's apolitical autonomy'.[62] Similarly, Lyotard has spoken of 'a modern aesthetics of the sublime', i.e. a nostalgic one offering the reader 'matter for solace and pleasure'.[63]

Epps accuses Goytisolo's text of precisely this[64] when he says that in *Las virtudes* Goytisolo is 'offering a consolatory message'.[65] The novel is surrounded by a 'cloud of resignation ... steeped in nostalgia'.[66] Epps, however, overlooks the novel's subversiveness. He and Smith,[67] for example, criticize the scene where the other guests or patients 'enjoy' the spectacle of the death of the Seminarista (clearly an AIDS sufferer[68]). But far from a Baudrillardian enjoyment of catastrophe at a safe distance, this is a scene where the patients are clearly seen negatively and criticized for their passive *Schadenfreude*. These are gays who renege on their past ('arrepentidas' [38]) in the light of present suffering. Once again Goytisolo tackles the issue by critiquing the conventional view of AIDS as a just punishment for past sins.

It is noticeable that the characters, with whom we are tempted to identify, only to reject such identification, are highly conventional in their faith in science and religion. They think that AIDS/death has been 'vencida por la ciencia, exorcisada por la religión, arrojada a los dominios de Plutón' (39). This attitude assumes ridiculous proportions when they think that the ageing process has been reversed (37) and this is made explicit a few pages later: 'la situación era irreal pero nos sentíamos confortadas' (39). This escapist Christian response to AIDS/death is contrasted with the narrator's suffering of it and apparent embrace of it as a sign of love and fulfilment (163–64). A link is made between eroticism and escape from a stifling family atmosphere: 'episodios rancios y enmohecidos [...] con prismáticos contemplas [...] media docena de jayanes de cuerpo oleoso (44). This 'ideal de la sexualidad masculina' which Levine claims is sought by Goytisolo in text after text and now perceived from a perspective of nostalgia[69] is a recurrent image throughout the text and I would suggest stands rather like the union of the Bride and the Beloved in the *Cántico* reset in a homosexual context. The element of the vision that marks it out as non-nostalgic but utopian and AIDS-conscious is the sensuous, non-penetrative nature of the fantasy ('*parecen* copular' [44]—my emphasis). In a manner worthy of San Juan, the vision is described in terms which mingle inextricably the (homo)erotic, the mystical and the textual:

> aspirar el aroma feroz de su aceite, absorberte en la sinuosa trabazón de las presas, admirar su textura corporal, obtener la gracia de su sonrisa ... (44)

> anhelo de posesión compartida, lenitiva fricción del tórax maltrecho con aceite vertido por los alcuceros, difusa quietud transmutada en dicha, alquimia, dilatación, calor, goce, luz, anonadamiento ... (61)

The earlier quest of the novels for purely sexual liberation is no longer the ideal, not due simply to the existence of AIDS, but to the emergence of a new ideal in response to changed historical circumstances. In an era of crass materialism, spiritual fulfilment is seen as superior to the earlier purely physical ideal. AIDS, rather than being the main subject and seen as provoking an escape into mysticism, is rather merely part of a broader contemporary panorama which leads to a preference for a more spiritual remedy. This move to spirituality does not eschew the physical, hence its literary manifestation is the deeply erotic format of the verses of Rumi and San Juan de la Cruz.

Rather than a negative, evasive or despairing book, *Las virtudes* is one which enacts the escape from the failures of the past towards the potential fulfilment of the future in the writing process. Hence the terrace scene (at times likened to the author-narrator's post-Civil War childhood) is one of stasis, artificiality and nostalgia for past harmony and acting out or repetition of roles. It suggests an artistic approach of escape, art as solace, nostalgia for the past. The alternative scenario is the narrator's identification with San Juan, one of illness, suffering, persecution and the ravages of illness (dissidence) due to the practice of subversive literature. The narrator chooses the latter:

> los personajes sentados en semicírculo intentan disuadirte con gestos indicativos de peligro pero caminarás sin hacerles caso a la gloria de tu palenque o tálamo bañado en la impregnadora luminosidad del día [...] el ave sutil e incolora, perfilada con inocente esbeltez en el cielo, parece volar sin dejar des estar inmóvil, suspendida con graciosa ingravidez sobre el himeneo en donde aguardan sonrientes los luchadores ...[70]

The desire is for escape in the sense of transcendence, self-fulfilment. This appears to be the situation at the end but could be a dream, illusion on the very verge of death or expression of dissidence in artistic form.

The narrator dies of AIDS in the penultimate section, but this is a prelude to a mystical rebirth. The book becomes his self and the channel of immortality as contaminating force. Hence the appropriateness of the metaphor of 'the language of the birds'. Fulfilment is found in language. The end echoes that of *Don Julián*, *Juan sin tierra*, *Makbara*: infinite subversion through the existence of the text. The evidence of the subversiveness of books is conveyed through the allusions to inquisitorial book-burnings (139), the imprisonment of writers and the swallowing of offensive texts to avoid repercussions, libraries of prohibited books (105).

Clearly Goytisolo's identification with San Juan, as with the Sufi mystics, is primarily a literary one. In *Las virtudes* the author identifies with San Juan but in a characteristically ambiguous way. The central motif of the *pájaro* is used both in its mystical sense of the soul questing for union with God and as the word for homosexual in Cuban slang. Goytisolo plays throughout the novel on this ambiguity, comparing the persecution of San Juan and other unorthodox figures by the officials of the Church with the contemporary persecution of homosexuals. The predominant characteristic of the novel is its susceptibility to a plurality of interpretations. Following the lead set by San Juan, the author creates a text that is infinitely suggestive and irresolvably ambiguous. In order to do so he has gone further than before in the removal of reference points with which the reader can naturalize the text. Goytisolo has even commented that 'en el libro hay zonas oscuras, incluso para mí'.[71] The essential mystery of the verses of San Juan, and by implication the text of Goytisolo, creates a deliberately unsettling effect:

> el lenguaje multiforme e infinitas posibilidades significativas de sus versos les tiene perplejos, la confusión de espacios, tiempos, temas y personajes les envuelve en un sueño despierto del que inútilmente intentan zafarse ... (84)

Hence in line with what we have observed in previous novels, *Las virtudes* continues the theme of the subversive nature of books. The whole of Chapter IV centres on a library of forbidden books, a 'reino de pensamiento erróneo [...] adonde van a parar las ideas potencialmente contaminadoras' (105–06). However, as I have stressed throughout, here, too, the ultimate subversion resides less in subversive ideas than in a language and form that resists interpretation. Hence the importance of the intertextual dialogue with San Juan, whose work according to Goytisolo is characterized by 'la radicalidad del misterio'.[72] San Juan belonged to the 'místicos que desasosegaban y subvertían' (116) and did so through the creation of 'unos versos necesariamente ambiguos y grávidos de misterio, unas metáforas omnivalentes, reacias a toda interpretación restrictiva y dogmática' (86). Colin Thompson, whose book on San Juan Goytisolo acknowledges in the 'Reconocimientos' section of *Las virtudes* (171), has summed up the *Cántico* as follows:

> Many of the images in the poem do not have a single interpretation [...] The onus of perceiving their significance rests on the reader [...] As such, the reader is freed from the tyranny of forcing [the image] to stand for one particular [...] thing, and it opens out before him, waiting for him to enter into its profundity.[73]

Las virtudes' debt to San Juan is at the formal, literary level of a technique which resists recuperation, and Goytisolo applies this technique on behalf of his customary social and political concerns.

La cuarentena

Published in 1991, *La cuarentena* operates on several levels. The social themes of *Las virtudes*, such as AIDS, nuclear holocaust and ecological destruction, are here condensed into a recognizable historical reality, the Gulf War of January 1991, which encapsulates within the novel man's capacity for cruelty and self-destruction. The mystical theme is continued in a narrator-protagonist whose aim seems to be a quietistic withdrawal from the world in search of inner harmony and oneness. The novel also displays many of the formal postmodernist features—narrative disunity and dispersal, undermining a stable narratorial persona, deliberate fostering of narrative undecidability and unresolvability—that have come to characterize Goytisolo's novels in this period. Where previous novels developed an intertextual dialogue with San Juan or the Arcipreste, here the inspiration is the *Guía espiritual* of the seventeenth-century Spanish Quietist Miguel de Molinos, the Islamic mystic Ibn Arabi and Dante.

At the beginning of *La cuarentena* the narrator tells us of his plan to write a text about death and the afterlife. He is inspired both on a literary level, by the work of poets and mystics such as Dante, Ibn Arabi and Molinos, but also, on a personal level, by the death of a close friend 'y el afán de reanudar en la escritura mi delicada relación con ella' (9).[74] Thus in the novel the narrator undergoes an imaginary 'death' and descent into the *barzakh*.[75] The writing also coincides with the outbreak of the Gulf War. Hence the introductory chapter links three elements: the preoccupation with death, the tragedy of the Gulf War and the desire to deal with these issues in the writing process. The theme of the Gulf War is crucial to the novel as it enables Goytisolo to criticize aspects of modern society. In his view, the war was a perfect illustration of 'el totalitarismo de la ciencia o, dicho de otra forma, el fundamentalismo tecnocientífico que se traduce en una modernidad incontrolada que está destruyendo el planeta'.[76] The theme of the Gulf War also serves, appropriately, to allude to a postmodern debate about the role of the media in contemporary society.[77]

As we have noted with the other works, *La cuarentena* attempts to enact its social critique through the literary process, once again seen as a process of contamination of the reader. At one point the narrator refers to his own novelistic technique:

> reunir los elementos del texto en un ámbito impreciso e informe, establecer entre ellos una fina telaraña de relaciones, tejer una red de significaciones por encima del espacio y el tiempo, ignorar las leyes de verosimilitud, desechar las nociones caducas de personaje y trama, abolir las fronteras de realidad y sueño, desestabilizar al lector multiplicando los niveles de interpretación y registros de voces, apropiarse de los acontecimientos históricos y utilizarlos de combustible al servicio de su proyecto ... (85)

The use of a metafictional style, the blurring of epistemological and ontological boundaries within the text, the incorporation of historical reality into the narrative, mark *La cuarentena* as a form of what Linda Hutcheon calls 'historiographical metafiction', which incorporates history into the fictional process, acknowledges its existence in order to question our perception of it.[78] As is customary in Goytisolo's fiction, the social critique is carried out less at the level of rational argument than at the more formal level, through a subversion of the reading process.[79]

> ¡Cuarentena del autor, cuarentena del lector, cuarentena del libro, indispensables a la acción energética, transformativa de la palabra escrita! (86)

La cuarentena's deliberate blurring of the boundaries between the text and the real, or even, within the text, between the fictional real and the realms of dream, imagination or spirit, serves to foster a radical uncertainty in the reader.[80] The style and the form of the novel are designed deliberately to bar the reader's access to a stable reality (or 'truth'). Such typically postmodernist play exposes Goytisolo's novel to the accusation, frequently levelled at the postmodernist movement, that it is a pessimistic philosophy condemned to passivity.[81]

Television and video play a central role in the narrative. The presentation of the 'reality' of the Gulf War is synonymous with its media representation, mainly on television, video or in the press. The primary source of reference for the narrator is the television. When faced with scenes of devastation in his wanderings through the *barzakh*, he says 'no he visto nada de eso con mis ojos ni siquiera en los programas del Circuito Televisivo' (16). Television is the archetypal postmodern medium and here it channels the narrator's oneiric visions, the scenes of the war and even his experience of the past (18).[82] However, more striking than the pre-eminence that the novel affords this medium is the narrator's seeming complicity with it. Rather than denouncing the role of the media, the novel seems actively to embrace it. Rather than rejecting the postmodern view of the mediatized nature of reality, in *La cuarentena* it is assumed and thematized. As a result, the novel is less 'about' the Gulf War itself than a reworking in fictional form of the media representation of the war.[83]

The novel's foregrounding of the medium over the event reproduces a narrative world very similar to Baudrillard's vision of society where the media reduce everything, especially 'hot' events such as wars, to 'cool' events. Douglas Kellner sums up Baudrillard's theory thus:

> all the media of information and communication neutralize meaning, and involve the audience in a flat, one-dimensional media experience, which he defines in terms of a passive absorption of images or resistance to meaning, rather than an active processing or production of meaning.[84]

But whereas Baudrillard's view is essentially pessimistic in that change or transformation seem out of the question,[85] Goytisolo's treatment of the discourses of postmodern society holds out the possibility of a solution.

The narrator's experience in the *barzakh* seems inextricable from the images on an all-pervasive TV screen (35). The end of the war is experienced in a hotel 'en torno al televisor' (81). The principal frame of reference for the novel is the simultaneity of the events of the war, transmitted by television, and the writing of the novel. The one recognizable 'reality', i.e. the war, is relayed by the television and 'reworked' by the author in the context of a self-conscious narrative. To this extent *La cuarentena* presents a classically postmodernist view of reality: there is no 'raw' experience of reality but only mediated versions. However, the novel's radical play with narrative (ontological) levels provides scope for a disruptive strategy.

At times the *barzakh* seems to serve as a comment on the nature of contemporary reality, while on other occasions the distinction between the imaginary world of the *barzakh* and the 'real' world is drawn:

> El tiempo no corre aquí como antes. Por eso no verás relojes ni nada parecido. Allí hablan de días, meses y años; pero una pausa puede eternizarse entre nosotros en medio del interrogatorio. ¡Basta con que conecten el vídeo y revivan para ti episodios y escenas de tu pasado! (18)

Like the *barzakh*, video constitutes a realm where the normal rules of time and space do not apply. The *barzakh* is also a quarantine which is that of the novel, too, both as a writing and reading process. The novel, like the *barzakh*, is a realm apart, 'por encima del espacio y el tiempo' (85), like the world of dream or imagination, distinct from, yet integral to, real life. So video, the *barzakh* and the text are presented as *alternative* realms. But unlike the true intermediate realm of Islamic tradition from which there is no return, the experience of this narrative *barzakh* may serve as a corrective to events or behaviour in the real world.[86] Hence, the angels warn the narrator that 'ESTO SÓLO ES UNA VISIÓN. LE ESPERAMOS AQUÍ CUANDO FALLEZCA DE VERAS' (106).

At other times, the alternative status of TV and video is of a more passive, escapist nature. The narrator is settled in front of a screen by his companion and reminded of his power to control the medium: '¿Ves bien?, dice ella. Si la visión es confusa o emborronada, puedes ajustarla a distancia con el programador' (27). Watching the screen the narrator withdraws into a quietistic detachment which takes him out of space and time and makes him unconscious of 'reality': 'sin cuidar ni atender, conforme a la "Guía", a cosa de sensibilidad'. In this state, he watches passively the visions of war and devastation on the TV screen: 'recibes pasivamente la sucesión de imágenes crueles de la pantalla en el reposo y vacío de tu silencio'. His companion comfortingly informs him that he can adjust the image and even, 'si el tema te abruma o azora, dice ella, puedes cambiar de canal' (28). Here a mystical detachment is associated with the passive and equally detached viewing of a television screen.[87] And yet, at the same time, the medium is seen to be able to relay unpalatable images (so much so that the Dama de la Sombrilla complains and laments the absence of a satellite dish, presumably to allow her to channel-hop to more agreeable stations). However, the unsettling reporting function of television is undermined by the interruption of an advertising slot.

Television's ability equally and indiscriminately to project images of war and of hell (synonymous in the novel) and advertising displays the Baudrillardian capacity of the medium to accommodate disparate contents in such a way that meaning is neutralized. In his Gulf War essays Baudrillard notes that advertising 'competes victoriously with the war on our screens, both alternating in the same virtual credit of the image'.[88] In *La cuarentena* this feature is ironized; the film of the horrors of war or the suffering of the victims of hell, interrupted unexpectedly by a shampoo advert, prompts the narrator to make a humorous remark about the pervasive ubiquity of multinationals even in the *barzakh*. The narrator describes the girl in the advertisement in ironically overblown terms ('aclara su abundosa cabellera bajo la ducha, colmada de beatitud narcisista, casi orgasmática' [29]). This parodic treatment leaves the reader in no doubt about the absurd and insidiously exploitative eclecticism of the media. In this way, Goytisolo's novel can side with Baudrillard's analysis of the media while at the same time offering a critique of it. The meaning neutralized by television is restored through irony.

The novel implies the collusion between the world of advertising and the forces behind the war. The Dama de la Sombrilla hawks residential accommodation in Paradise; the narrator 'atraído como otras sombras errantes a la sala de proyecciones del holding' watches fascinated 'el vídeo de propaganda con versos de Dante e imágenes del paraíso grabadas por Doré' (66). In this scene, the propaganda effect of the video is totally subverted by an apparent technical hitch, resulting here in a different series of images of the horrors of war being shown to the assembled viewers:

> En vez de los planos del mundo sublunar y la visión beatífica, la pantalla reproduce imágenes de devastación y de ruina [...]
> (Voz en off: say hello to Allah!)
> ¡Alguien (¿un diablillo o genio?) ha sustituido el vídeocasete en el aparato lector unido al televisor de la Dama de la Sombrilla! (66)

The voice-over ('say hello to Allah!') implies that even with this new, unwelcome video we are still in the territory of the Western media, and this leads to a range of interesting suggestions. We are told that the Dama's paradisiacal accommodation is designed by 'los expertos del Alto Mando de la mundialmente célebre operación Tempestad en el Desierto', and this establishes a clear link between the technological advances underpinning consumer 'progress' in the West and the victory in the Gulf War. The implication is that consumer capitalism is predicated on the same technological base as the arms industry, merely another facet of Western domination. The video of the destruction of war participates in the same propagandistic function of TV and video as the advertising slot; the Western media's depiction of the war was brutally shocking but essentially aimed at defending the Western position.[89] The switching of the videos is seen as a a minor act of sabotage, a modest subversion by '¿un diablillo o genio?' who remains unknown. The importance of the scene lies in the fact that the mediatized representation of the real is susceptible only to such minor subversions, and this hints at the theme we have seen repeated insistently, the power and the limited scope of literature for transgression. Noticeably the subversion merely rearranges the order of media content rather than opposing it with something else, thus suggesting media's all-pervasiveness.[90]

La cuarentena does not demystify social reality in the traditional sense of stripping away, through satire, media myths and providing access to the 'truth'. The novel displays a more radical approach which both assumes a diagnostic of social reality (or hyperreality) akin to Baudrillard's and looks for ways of contesting it on its own terms. To do so the text draws attention explicitly or implicitly to its own status. In this way the technical hitches in the scenes referred to can be likened to the fly-squashing episode in Don Julián in that they point metaphorically to the textual process, which is the true site of subversion.

Part of that subversion is the confusion of ontological levels referred to above. Another is the novel's treatment of the author-narrator figure.

Despite the extreme self-consciousness of the novel, the reader is unable to identify a stable narrator figure. We have, on the one hand, the narrator who descends into the *barzakh*, and, on the other, the author who composes the text. The former is an essentially passive receptor of visions, images and dreams, and the latter is the active producer of the text. The distinction is not a stable one. At the beginning of the novel the narrator is an author speaking of the composition of a text only to reveal that at one point he 'died' and descended to the *barzakh*, thus becoming a protagonist in his own fiction. At other times this narrator-protagonist is seen re-emerging from the *barzakh* to converse with his wife, and returning, not to the *barzakh* but to his study where he is composing the novel about a voyage to that twilight zone. Occasionally he is revealed as unsure of exactly which state he is in:

> ¡Su mujer! ¿Será posible?
> ¿Había abandonado temporalmente, para saludarle, el reino de lo sensible o era él quien había dado el salto atrás, introduciéndose por fractura y escalo en un mundo ya extinto? (69)

The reader is tempted to identify with one or the other. Identification with the passive narrator encourages a sense of being prey to an enigmatic and unstable 'reality'. With the active 'author', the text holds out the hope of active engagement with that reality. But even the author's control over his own material is placed in doubt. Towards the end of the novel and referring to the end of the war, the narrator conjures up images of fleeing refugees and an analogy is drawn between the Gulf War and the Spanish Civil War, but note how all is still subordinate to the image of the television:

> Las imágenes reproducidas en el telediario, ¿correspondían a lo acaecido después de cuarenta días de infierno aéreo o exhumaban recuerdos sepultos en su memoria de la sombría guerra civil?
> Dudaba, dudaba todavía.
> Pues, ¿quién escribía de verdad aquella página? ¿El autor sesentón inclinado a su mesa de trabajo o el niño ignorante que asistía por vez primera en su vida al derrumbe de un sueño y el fin abrupto de una esperanza? (108)

Rather than contrasting memory of past experience with direct experience of present time, the author-narrator appears confronted by television images which blur the two and recall what Baudrillard termed the 'structural unreality of images and their proud indifference to the truth'.[91] The author uses the uncertainty surrounding television images to cast doubt on his own narration. There is a clear Borgesian echo in the narrator's hesitant opposition of writing as an expression of past experience and writing as an artificial, worked construct ('su mesa de trabajo').[92] At heart is the crux of the postmodern debate about the extent to which postmodernism translates into aesthetic terms an ethical wish to question dogma and repressive certainties. However, the radical and aggressive subversion of the reader seen in *Juan sin tierra* with its declared aim of 'enseñarle [al lector] a dudar' has evolved into a tone which is both gentler and more ambivalent. Here the author seems to share the doubt which he actively promotes in the reader. Both *Las virtudes* and *La cuarentena* try to unsettle the reader with the ultimate concern that not even the author is sure how the text should be interpreted.

In *La cuarentena* the treatment of reality and its representation by the media shows Goytisolo assuming the implications of a postmodern reality while avoiding the risk, so often levelled at Baudrillard, of a nihilistic acceptance of an unchangeable state of affairs. The novel falls into the category of those postmodern works which, according to Linda Hutcheon, 'contest the "simulacrization" process of mass culture—not by denying it or lamenting it—but by problematizing the entire notion of the representation of reality'.[93] It is precisely this 'positive' post-modern contestation of history that characterizes Goytisolo's next novel.

La saga de los Marx

La saga de los Marx is an unusual book and in many ways a departure for Goytisolo in so far as developing personal concerns is kept to a minimum and instead the novel concentrates more, on the one hand, on an external issue, the figure of Marx and the legacy of his philosophy, and, on the other, the function of the literary text. It bears a greater resemblance to *Juan sin terra* and *Paisajes después de la batalla* than to the preceding novels *Las virtudes* and *La cuarentena*. It incorporates a discussion of the novel which is very reminiscent of *Juan sin tierra* and makes a defence of the radically experimental text in the face of commercial or editorial demands; it also incorporates the idea of literature as contamination, when it speaks of the 'contaminación cervantina del espectador' (200). However, where the critique of the novel in *Juan sin tierra* was carried out for its own sake, i.e. the novel as a bourgeois genre dynamited from the inside, here there is more a sense of a postmodernist narrative technique as a superior way of understanding history, giving fresh insight into the past and the present.

In some ways, *La saga*, as its title suggests, could be considered an attempt at fictionalized biography. Goytisolo tries to uncover the true significance of the person of Marx, his relations with his family and the legacy of his philosophy. Randolph Pope sees it as different from previous novels in that 'there is less a search for a kindred exemplary figure and more a need to understand critically the roots of the present to shape the future better'.[94] Thematically the novel is close to *Paisajes* in that the collapse of communism which was presaged in that novel has now actually occurred.[95] This link finds mention in the novel itself:

> desde que el paisaje de ruinas ideológicas presentido hace una docena de años (cabeza intacta de Karl, escultura oxidada de Friedrich, perilla y un trozo de calva del ínclito Vladimir Ilich, desenterradas por equipos de eruditos y arqueólogos en busca de las bases, profecías y dogmas del materialismo dialéctico) es una realidad ... (198–99)

The framework of the novel is that of the narrator who has been commissioned by an editor, Mr Faulkner, to write a book on Marx.[96] The problem is that the writer is producing a postmodernist, Cervantes-inspired, self-reflexive fantasy on the German philosopher whereas his editor wants a more commercially viable biographical approach. Essentially the argument here parallels much of what we find in *Juan sin tierra* in the dialogue between the author-narrator and Vosk:

> su mayor deseo habría sido aprovechar la visita para felicitarle, celebrar sus bien probadas dotes de creador, decirle que su novela sobre Marx era realmente magnífica!, la había leído con atención extrema, sin perderse una tilde, con la esperanza de encontrar al fin un hilo conductor, ver surgir de sus páginas como personajes de carne y hueso a Moro y su familia [...] en suma, una novela real como la vida misma ... (82–83)

In one way it is rather disappointing that Goytisolo is seen here to be repeating an argument that one might consider already won in the earlier work, but clearly it can also be accepted that while the literary debate may have moved on, the reality of the publishing world is another matter. That Goytisolo is still preoccupied by this can be seen in the introduction to *El bosque de las letras*:

> Hoy el papel privilegiado del autor como guía e inspirador de multitudes subsiste tan sólo en las sociedades 'atrasadas'. El cine primero, la televisión y la informática después, han circunscrito el campo de la literatura y creado un nuevo tipo de lector para quien la palabra es mero acompañamiento o ilustración de la imagen. La victoria de ésta—desde la adaptación de novelas al cine a la fabricación de las mismas con miras a la pantalla—ha contribuido al actual proceso de instrumentalización del lenguaje y a una degradación casi general de la escritura. (110)

Faced with the demand for novels of the 'bestseller' type, which Goytisolo describes as 'la brevedad ruidosa y existencia efímera de la producción editorial de consumo instantáneo', the only respectable response is accepting 'el reto de la dificultad e incluso del hermetismo como una opción personal de resistencia' (EBDL, 11–12). This goes to the heart of the literary debate in *La saga*. The author-narrator's editor takes him to task for failing to observe the chronological and topographical niceties of the realist novel (84) as well as other off-putting effects:

por qué esos largos párrafos sin puntuación? te había dicho en otra
circunstancia, no veías acaso que desconcertaban al lector y lo alejaban del
libro? (81)

As with previous novels, Goytisolo frames the social issue in the context
of a literary debate in which, in true postmodernist fashion, the reader is
intimately implicated. The reader is faced with the writer's personal act
of resistance and invited to side with it, struggle with the difficulty and
hermeticism of the text, or reject it. Part of the success of *La saga* and
another feature it shares with *Paisajes* is that it has a lighter, more
humorous tone which maintains the challenge of the reading without
making it too forbidding. In addition, the reader is given the customary
clues in the shape of metafictional explanation. This comes in section
four in the scene involving the television programme, *La clave*, and its
screening of *La Baronne rouge*, a typical cinematic bio-pic on Marx's
wife, Jenny von Westphalen. The film represents precisely that trend in
contemporary culture referred to by Goytisolo in the quote above, and
which elsewhere he has called 'la sustitución de la ideología por el
espectáculo'.[97] During the discussion of the film, in which the author-
narrator is an invited guest, there is explicit reference to the novel itself
and its ongoing process of writing. The author is introduced by the
programme's presenter:

> finalmente, a mi derecha, el autor de la novela que están ustedes leyendo,
> precisamente en la página
> tú: ciento ochenta y cuatro
> realizador (jovial): ya lo han oído Vds., ciento ochenta y cuatro! una cifra
> bastante respetable que, gracias a la colaboración de todos nosotros se
> acrecentará a lo largo de este programa y le permitirá completar la cuarta
> parte de su 'mamotreto', como cariñosamente le llama! (184)

This is the Cervantine element of the novel, involving the deliberate and
explicit flouting of the narrative boundaries between author and
fictional world. The interruption of the action between pages 198 and
201 is not only akin to Sterne's in *Tristram Shandy*, as the text itself
admits ('tu imperdonable descuido, como el del desdichado Sterne al
olvidar al personaje de la fisgona con la cara pegada al ojo de la
cerradura por espacio de casi doscientas páginas' [200]) but also recalls
Cervantes, who in the first part of *Don Quijote* interrupts the account of
the battle between Quixote and the Biscayan because the 'first author',
i.e. the Moor, Cide Hamete Benengeli, has lost the relevant part of the
manuscript. As Robert Spires notes, the effect of this is to challenge 'the
assumption of authorship established in the prologue'. He goes on to
explain how the episode (and Cervantes' novel in general) complicates
the problem of narrative authority further:

> Since the 'second author' in effect is only an author when he narrates the
> search and otherwise is only a transcriber, and Cide Hamete as historian is

supposedly also on a combination translator-transcriber, and the anonymous author may in fact be a community of authors, none seems to qualify as the 'I' of the narrating act.[98]

This questioning of authorship through the figure of the transcriber had been a central feature already of *Paisajes*, and the notion of the community of authors anticipates Goytisolo's latest novel, *Las semanas del jardín*. The link between the literary debate and the topic of Marx is established in this 'freeze-frame' in the narrative. Marx, from his poster overlooking the television set, exhorts the author-narrator, 'en lugar de ocuparse tanto en mí y mis ideas haría mejor en explicar a los lectores el propósito y estructura de su novela!' (199). The author agrees and explains how, in his view,

> la obra comprometida con tu editor, como todas las de tema biográfico-realista aclamadas por público y crítica, no corre el riesgo de dejar inexpresadas las premisas del juego al escamotear los métodos conforme a los cuales una propaganda insidiosa configura la mente de los lectores que arriman al texto? (199–200)

Once again, Goytisolo reveals his aim, consistent with that stated at the very beginning in *El furgón de cola*, of criticizing the real by attacking the discourses of that society. Is it the case that the novelist has moved on very little? Not quite. Goytisolo's work combines consistency with evolution. His critique of society, influenced explicitly from the start by thinkers such as Barthes, and more implicitly by Foucault, has been consistently one of demystification. The play with the novel form has been dictated by a resistance to discursive conventions (in this case, narrative) which refuse to challenge the reader's perceptions:

> en una sociedad uniformada por el imperio de la imagen, qué valor literario y moral tendría poner la pluma al servicio de ésta y trazar relatos históricos como esas escenas reconstituidas en estudio de acontecimientos y crímenes sórdidos?

What has evolved is the analysis of the nature of those discursive conventions and the novelistic technique that engages with them. *La saga* shares the postmodernist perspective of the previous novel, *La cuarentena*, in the novel's engagement with the role of the media, principally television, in fabricating a version of history for ideological purposes. Particularly noticeable is the novel's acceptance of the inevitability of mediatization of reality by a variety of discourses and the increasing influence of technology:

> no sería más incitativo y fecundo desenmascarar los mitos e instancias intermedias que operan entre el gran público y Marx, integrando en la obra los filtros a través de los que percibimos su elusiva y contradictoria personalidad? (200)

This integration of the means of mediatization within the novel is an extension of the purely narrative self-consciousness of previous novels (though it was glimpsed in *Makbara* with the pastiche of TV advertisements and sensationalist reporting) to include other types of discourse, but in particular the archetypal postmodernist media of television and cinema.[99] In *La saga* Goytisolo suggests that the all-pervasive nature of the media has led to a blurring of boundaries in real life (he cites indirectly the example of the Dan Quayle/Murphy Brown incident)[100] and that the aim of the novelist should be to play on that confusion with a view to 'contaminating' the reader:

> en vez de resignarse a aceptar la escritura como sierva de la tecnología por qué no introducir los estereotipos y mediatizaciones de aquella en el ámbito de la novela, invirtiendo los papeles y subordinando las cotidianas irrupciones televisivas y sus mensajes subliminales a las reglas del campo de maniobras abierto por Cervantes? el rasgo de genio de ese anodino vicepresidente norteamericano de polemizar con el personaje de la madre soltera de una popular serie televisiva, no era la prueba concluyente de la interacción entre realidad y ficción, de la contaminación cervantina del espectador ... (200)

Central to the critique of television and to the novel in general is the question of truth. The above passage continues:

> del camino a seguir para calar en las capas de nuestra aprehensión de lo real, más allá de la lisura mendaz de su fotografía? (200)

The principal criticism of television seems to be that it does not capture the truth of reality but rather is governed by other motives. In his book, Pope, for example, refers to the way television puts the enjoyment of the spectator before compassion for Jenny's life.[101] Jenny herself in her conversation with the narrator notes how the series they are making about her is all about money and little about capturing the suffering of her life:

> qué saben esas damas del mundo editorial y la prensa que ahora proyectan una serie televisiva sobre mí a cambio, cómo no, de unas cantidades de dinero con las que hubiéramos podido vivir siete vidas lo que fue la muerte de mi pequeña Franziska? (119–120)

Both in its treatment of the media and the approach to truth and its elusiveness, the novel displays a clear postmodernist approach that has been developing since *Makbara* but which is here placed thematically centre-stage. In one of his early comments on the novel, Goytisolo mentions how his Cervantine approach aimed at viewing events relativistically with 'una mirada poliédrica y con voces polifónicas'[102] was encouraged by some readings in quantum theory:

> Curiosamente, cuando estaba elaborando esto, leí unos ensayos sobre teoría cuántica, que sostienen que la naturaleza tiene lados distintos y que son recíprocamente incompatibles. Una vez que se llega a este relativismo se puede acabar con la tiranía de la racionalidad científica.[103]

Goytisolo does not specify the essays, but such ideas form the basis of Jean-François Lyotard's *The Postmodern Condition: A Report on Knowledge*, published first in 1979. Lyotard uses insights gained from recent discoveries in quantum mechanics and chaos theory to formulate a theory of 'postmodern science as the search for instabilities'.[104] It is not possible here to explore the arguments surrounding Lyotard's views nor the validity of postmodern science,[105] but it is easy to see how Goytisolo's work shares Lyotard's anti-authoritarianism and his distrust of system. In a famous quotation, Lyotard defined postmodernism as 'an incredulity towards metanarratives'. For Lyotard a 'metanarrative' or a 'grand narrative' is an over-arching, universalizing system that seeks to impose its truth on the world. One of the primary metanarratives rejected by Lyotard and other postmodernists is that of Marx,[106] whose totalizing theory, in their view, seeks to provide explanations for all aspects of social experience.[107] In *La saga*, Goytisolo accepts this diagnosis of Marx but attempts, on the one hand, to rescue the thinker by presenting his case in a series of interlocking 'small narratives'[108]— Marx seen from the perspective of his wife, his daughters, Lenchen, his critics, his supporters, alternative accounts of the consequences of his theory, etc.; on the other hand, the novel suggests that a new metanarrative has taken over, the 'dura lex, sed lex del monetarismo y la libre empresa' (118).

Goytisolo couches this complex debate within the framework of a literary debate conducted at the level of text, in which the reader is inextricably involved, and this, once again, is how he attempts to extend his treatment of the issue beyond mere analysis. At the centre of this debate is the conflict between the model of the novel demanded by Mr Faulkner and the novel that the narrator wants to write. The aim of the former is commercial success. It is likened to the film, *La Baronne rouge*, when the author, asked for his opinion on the film says, 'el modelo a imitar según mi editor!' (185). So the chain of association links the commercial novel, the TV film and the prevailing system of global capitalism. The author-narrator's novel has the aim of showing how 'la desaparición del sistema marxista como forma de gobierno, no auguraba a la vez la necesidad irrebatible de un nuevo Marx?' (118). Faulkner and his like are portrayed as laying claim to truth. He demands from the author a 'novela real como la vida misma' (83) and Gradgrindian 'facts':

> lo que exigen nuestras lectoras y lectores son Hechos! déjese usted de elucubraciones y visiones oníricas inútiles para el público ... aténgase estrictamente a los Hechos!

The novel incorporates an ironic allusion to its postmodernist pretensions when the editor explicitly warns the author off association with certain 'trendy' theorists and techniques ('manda a paseo a los eruditos y profesores que hablan de Baudrillard y Bajtín y celebran tus cronotopos!' [108]).

The novel aims at undermining what it sees as the prevailing mentality, and one way is by casting doubt on the basis of 'facts', underlining how facts are often distorted for other purposes. For example, spurred on by the necessity of pleasing his editor, the author resorts to transcribing historical documents to provide a 'realistic' portrayal of Marx. On one occasion he includes a letter only to doubt its veracity as it had been used by Karl Vogt to defame Marx (94–95). This campaign of defamation is referred to by Nico-laievsky and Maenchen-Helfen, in their book (used by Goytisolo) *Karl Marx: Man and Fighter*, and that campaign itself consisted of 'allega-tions [...] woven into such a highly ingenious web of lies, with truth and known fact so skilfully blended with half-truths and impudent fabrications, that some of the insinuations were bound to stick in the minds of those not fully acquainted with the facts of "emigrant" history'.[109]

Mr Faulkner is such a one, and while doubting the letter, the author mimics his editor saying: 'en cualquier caso, como diría Thomas Gradgrind, era un Hecho!', and his subsequent extrapolation that the letter proves the link between Marx's authoritarian nature and the evils of Communist regimes is a parody of how Marx's reputation has been distorted.

On another occasion, Goytisolo, seeking a Balzacian account of Marx, reproduces another document, a report sent by a spy working for the Prussian government. This is contained in Robert Payne's biography (another source used for the novel), and Payne notes how 'unlike most reports by police spies, it is written with warm humanity and sym-pathy'.[110] Interestingly, although Goytisolo in his novel says nothing, Payne goes on to point out the historical inaccuracies of Stieber's report.[111]

Goytisolo has often declared the sources that inspire and inter-connect with his work, but whereas in works like *Las virtudes* and *La cuarentena* the purpose has been intertextual dialogue, in *La saga* the aim is more one of exploring the interface between fiction and fact, questioning the basis of historical knowledge, revealing its essential relativism. Hence the truth beneath the surface of myths and images is not a stable, single truth, a hidden telos, but rather an awareness and acceptance of the multifaceted, often conflicting nature of truth and the need to adopt a sceptical stance. However, Goytisolo manages to skirt the charge of radical scepticism frequently levelled at postmodernism by, on the one hand, conveying a sense of warmth and sympathy towards Marx and his critique of capitalism and a sense of outrage at monetarism's monopoly, while at the same time removing the reader's natural epistemological footholds, usually found in the guiding voice of a stable narrator always ready to set matters in context.

The end of the novel delivers a typically ambiguous verdict on the 'poderes de la escritura' (200). On the surface the novel is, like Marx's theories, consigned to the dustbin, yet on the other hand the reader is the proof that the book was indeed published and read. The last statement of the narrator fits exactly into the theme emphasized throughout of incompatible statements: 'nunca escribirías *La saga de los Marx*!' (222).

El sitio de los sitios and *Las semanas del jardín*

The dilemma of the power of the writer and the limits of that power continues to underscore Goytisolo's next novel (his penultimate to date), *El sitio de los sitios*, published in 1995. The novel deals with the Bosnian war, a political and humanitarian issue which absorbed Goytisolo for the duration of the conflict.[112] The novel develops out of this increasing concern with what he calls 'un empobrecimiento generalizado de la cultura, una imposición de modas y una invasión audiovisual que hace que todo se trivialice y uniforme'.[113] Sarajevo was seen by Goytisolo as a political failure and a humanitarian disaster, but it was also a critical test for writers and intellectuals. While some were silent, others 'han proseguido su labor cultural bajo las bombas, resistiendo, escribiendo textos hermosísmos'.[114] Clearly for Goytisolo the aim was, as in *La saga*, to challenge history through the powers of fiction. *El sitio*, he says, is 'una novela que opone la verdad de la ficción a la historia oficial'.[115] 'Truth' in this context is less a specific content than a process, commencing with the act of honesty of the work's admitting to its fictive status, 'Todo aquí es escritura!' (30), and within that, deliberately blurring the ontological bounds by using the figure of the real author described in the third person in the opening section. The subsequent 'death' of this character and the ensuing convolutions of the story, taking their lead from Cervantes once again, but also from Borges, claim for literature the power, 'el poder mirífico de la literatura' (155), to combat the cynical, instrumental and manipulative use of language by losing the 'victim' in the web of language.

> Habíamos extraviado al representante del mando multinacional, cuyo doble lenguaje y cinismo contribuyen a perpetuar nuestra desdicha, en el laberinto o jardín de los textos que se bifurcan y ramifican hasta tejer un bosque. (155)

The result for the victim is a loss of reason, 'perder el juicio y dejar de actuar', and the implication is that the reader experiences something similar, a radical subversion of the rational ability to understand the text. For the visitor to the labyrinth, the novelist provides clues but also false trails, and like the labyrinth, the novel has as its purpose not resolution, but rather the essence of the disorienting process itself.

The following novel, Goytisolo's last to date, *Las semanas del jardín*, published in 1997, grows out of *El sitio*, although the central theme is different. Here there is a return to a Spanish context, specifically the Civil War, and the central figure is Eusebio, a disgraced member of an upright right-wing family mentioned in the preceding novel (ESDS, 169).[116] *Las semanas del jardín* revolves around this mysterious poet-character, forgotten member of the 27 Generation, seemingly hounded by the victorious regime for his political beliefs and, especially, his homosexuality. This central theme of conflict between a typically marginal figure and the repressive forces and discourses of the Franco regime is subjected to a characteristically complex formal treatment. Once again the notion of authorship, both in the narrato-logical sense of 'Author' and in the 'real' sense of novelist (LSDJ, 12–13) is eschewed, and in the novelist's place the text posits a community of writers all from different backgrounds with different literary tastes and political affiliations. The idea of a community of authors harks back to the group of researchers in *Las virtudes* occupied with the work of San Juan, and it also identifies the novel with a pre-modern tradition when collective authorship was the norm:

> La poesía sufí, como el Romancero de su país, es fruto en gran parte de una elaboración colectiva. Las casidas de Sidi Abderrahmán Al Maxdub pertenecen hoy a la totalidad del pueblo que las recita ... (LSDJ, 28–29)

As with *Paisajes*, the figure of the 'transcriber' is invoked to disclaim any 'authority'. Indeed, he informs the reader in the first section that this constitutes a deliberately anti-authoritarian gesture. The notion of the author is synonymous with the oppressiveness of single meanings and the supplanting of the novelist is a 'liberating' act. The decision of the community at the end of the novel to 'invent' an author, who turns out to be a certain Juan Goytisolo whose biographical data just happen to coincide, as does the photograph (supposedly a 'rostro [compuesto de] distintas imágenes en un astuto montaje' [174]), with the details of the real author Goytisolo, is another example of the clear dependence on existing conventions for the purposes of subversion.

At the end of the novel the reader is no closer to a clear picture of who Eusebio is nor to the 'truth' of his life-story, merely experiencing a confused sense of multiple possibilities and the intriguing temptation to re-read the text (not necessarily in linear fashion—the narrator of the first section refers to the work as a 'hypertext') to attempt to link the numerous interconnecting, often contradictory versions, and establish a pattern, if only a fluctuating one. At the end of the day, the 'hero' of the novel, and he merits that title, is Eusebio, who resists the interpretation to which he is subjected by the 28 'colectores' of the novel, much as we hope he did manage to resist the 're-education' process of the Francoist system.

> Pero esta vez no me enfrentaba a enfermeros ni siquiatras, sino a un monstruo de repulsivas cabezas: tantas como colectores del Círculo. Me sentía observado desde mil ángulos y facetas, acosado por una mirada prismática, un ojo múltiple, poliédrico. (171)

The fact that the novel posits irresolvably the two 'hypotheses' of succumbing to the 'siquiatras eugenistas del Movimiento' or the 'supuesta huida y las huellas confusas de su vida ulterior' (13) is entirely in keeping with the trend in all of Goytisolo's novels, but especially of this latter period, to offer the possibility of utopian escape, to work assiduously on the reader through the formal process to encourage that liberation, but to admit to the limitations of literature's impact on the real.

El sitio ends on a seemingly despairing 'Nota del autor':

> el escritor [...] tuvo que recurrir a la ficción para huir y curarse de las imágenes que a su vez le asediaban. Tal es el poder de la literatura. (ESDS, 182)

At the same time, Goytisolo tells us that 'El sitio continúa ... sin ninguna posibilidad de huida ni curación a la vista. Tal es el límite final de la literatura.'

This afterword raises the troubling spectre that has haunted us throughout this study, of literature, but in particular the radically self-conscious, postmodern literature which Goytisolo has practised in greater or lesser measure since *Señas de identidad*, just being a temporary refuge, an 'islote de libertad y fiesta en un océano de iniquidad y pobreza', as *Makbara*'s *halaiquí* phrased it, with no effect on the real world of historical events. However, the constant and radical engagement of the novels, not merely cognitively but almost viscerally, with the reader, the politicization of an active reading process, ensures that neither for writer nor reader is the textual process an isolated or isolating experience. Speaking of *El sitio*, Goytisolo expressed the hope that the book is 'una cura, o por lo menos un contagio al lector de la sensación del asedio'.[117] In his narratives Goytisolo, in the words of David Herzberger, 'opens up to scrutiny the sign systems by which we live, and offers creative fictions that oppose publicly accepted histories',[118] but unlike Herzberger I would not despair of the redemptive potential of the novels.[119] The reader is the first and most important beneficiary of this 'political act of dissent' which is Goytisolo's fiction and the key, ultimately, to its utopian impulse and performative potential.

NOTES

1 Miguel Riera, 'Regreso al origen: entrevista', *Quimera* LXXIII (1988), 36.

2 Javier Escudero, 'La preocupación ante la muerte en el último Juan Goytisolo: *La cuarentena*', *La Torre* VIII(3) (1994), 207.

3 José Manuel Martín Morán, 'Los espejos del pájaro solitario', *RLit* LII(104) (1990), 535.

4 Cf. Escudero, 'La preocupación ante la muerte', 207. Epps concurs with Escudero (*Eros, mística y muerte en Juan Goytisolo (1982–1992)* [Almería: Instituto de Estudios Almerienses, 1994], that '*Paisajes* is not simply a sequel to what precedes it, but is also an opening onto the enigma of spirituality'. Brad Epps, *Significant Violence: Oppression and Resistance in the Narratives of Juan Goytisolo, 1970–1990* (Oxford: Clarendon Press, 1996), 7.

5 Barry Smart, *Postmodernity* (London: Routledge, 1993), 89. See also John O'Neill, 'Religion and Postmodernism: The Durkheimian Bond in Bell and Jameson— With an Allegory of the Body Politic', in *Postmodernism/Jameson/Critique*, ed. Douglas Kellner (Washington, DC: Maisonneuve Press, 1989), 139–61.

6 In *El bosque de las letras*, Goytisolo tells us that the real-life model he had in mind was Jean Genet, who emerges again as one of the inspirations for the Eusebio figure in *Las semanas del jardín*. Goytisolo, *El bosque de las letras* (Madrid: Anagrama, 1995), 96, 101.

7 'Man's duty is to wear away the body, "to die to self," in order that the spark within him may be united, and remain permanently with, the One Reality or Truth. This is the basic assumption of Sufi mysticism.' Reuben Levy, *An Introduction to Persian Literature* (New York: Columbia University Press, 1969), 95.

8 'Cuando la ciencia contemporánea, con su descubrimiento de lo infinito material, despoja al universo de su metafísica y simbología, el corpus visionario de los místicos y doctrinarios chiís nos recuerda la dimensión espiritual e imaginativa del ser humano, en la que el fulgor del verbo, como la palabra poética, rescata aquél de su mutilación, empobrecimiento y desdicha.' *El bosque de las letras*, 143.

9 Goytisolo himself has insisted that *Paisajes* is closely linked to his previous novels, especially the trilogy. He also remarks, echoing the text itself, that 'es también una recapitulación más amarga e irónica, es una autobiografía grotesca con una voluntad denunciadora de los lugares comunes de la época'. J. M. Plaza, 'Juan Goytisolo: "Mis novelas comienzan a valorarse con el paso del tiempo"', *Disidencias: Suplemento cultural de 'Diario'* CXCII(2) (1984), viii.

10 Epps, *Significant Violence*, 7.

11 The number of truly autobiographical details is considerable. There are references to the narrator's birth on 5 January (102) and again to the chalet in Bonanova (169). Details such as his aversion to nature and museums (PDLB, 56 and 69 respectively) find support in the memoirs; cf. *En los reinos de taifa*, 262 and *Contracorrientes*, 149. In the latter there is even a degree of coincidence in wording which proves an extension of the motif of the relation between the narrative and the 'fantasías científicas' of 'Juan Goytisolo'.

12 C. Schaefer-Rodríguez, 'Goytisolo through the Looking-Glass: *Paisajes después de la batalla*, Autobiography and Parody', *Journal of Mid-Western Modern Language Association* XIX(2) (1986), 16.

13 This, in spite of what Goytisolo may have advocated and aspired to (see *Contracorrientes*, 54) and, possibly, even thought he had achieved in 'Lectura del espacio en Xemaá-El-Fna'. The reader will always strive to create a narratorial voice of some sort.

14 Sean Burke has noted how the author 'is neither a locus of forces nor a

psychobiographical site, but a metaphor for the text operating at the most consistent and plausible level of interpretation, a purely formal principle of the determinacy of textual knowledge'. Sean Burke, *The Death and Return of the Author: Criticism and Subjectivity in Barthes, Foucault and Derrida* (Edinburgh: Edinburgh University Press, 1992), 109.

15 For this reason Brian McHale identifies the dominant of postmodernist fiction as ontological subversion (contrasting with the epistemological subversion of modernism). Brian McHale, *Postmodernist Fiction* (London: Methuen, 1987), 9–11. From *Makbara* onwards, Goytisolo's play with the narrative levels is so fluctuating and unstable as to keep the reader in a permanent state of questioning. *El sitio de los sitios* is a good example of the constant creation and subversion of fictional levels.

16 Epps, *Significant Violence*, 8.

17 James Joyce, *Portrait of the Artist as a Young Man* (London: Penguin, 1975), 214–15.

18 M. Keith Booker, *Joyce, Bakhtin and the Literary Tradition: Toward a Comparative Cultural Poetics* (Ann Arbor, MI: University of Michigan, 1995), 126.

19 In a private interview with Goytisolo in Paris on 27 August 1985 he commented: 'También hay un paralelo entre *Paisajes* y *Señas*. En *Paisajes* he logrado todos los distintos planos que yo quería conjugar en *Señas*, y que ahí no dominaba la forma, y en *Paisajes* sí que los he logrado. Es decir, el juego entre el escritor, digamos Juan Goytisolo, el escritor que no el mismo … bueno, la persona, el escritor, el protagonista, el lector, todo, hacer jugar todo esto … pues en *Señas*, está hecho con mucha torpeza, claro.'

20 Patricia Waugh, *Metafiction: The Theory and Practice of Self-Conscious Fiction* (London: Methuen, 1984), 38.

21 Linda Hutcheon, *A Poetics of Postmodernism: History, Theory, Fiction* (London: Routledge, 1988), 206. The quotation included is from Larry McCaffery, *The Metafictional Muse* (Pittsburgh, PA: University of Pittsburgh Press, 1982), 14.

22 Hutcheon, *A Poetics of Postmodernism*, 206. Her allusion is to Herbert Marcuse, *The Aesthetic Dimension: Towards a Critique of Marxist Aesthetics* (London: Macmillan, 1979).

23 Epps, *Significant Violence*, 431.

24 Epps, *Significant Violence*, 416.

25 'Art's separation from the process of material production has enabled it to demystify the reality reproduced in this process. Art challenges the monopoly of the established reality to determine what is "real" and it does so by creating a fictitious world which is nevertheless "more real than reality itself".' Marcuse, *The Aesthetic Dimension*, 22.

26 Randall Stevenson notes 'it may be that the most moral sort of text is one which leaves readers free to determine morality for themselves'. Randall Stevenson, *Modernist Fiction: An Introduction* (London: Prentice Hall, 1998), 222.

27 See Epps, *Significant Violence*, 370ff.

28 Epps, *Significant Violence*, 363.

29 W. Gellert *et al.*, *The VNR Concise Encyclopedia of Mathematics* (New York: VNR, 2nd edition, 1989), 22. Goytisolo has given an amusing alternative insight into this section as an illustration of how chance can intervene in the creative process: 'Recuerdo que estaba escribiendo las páginas finales y no encontraba el párrafo, cuando ya, más o menos, había rizado el rizo del texto. Me daba cuenta de que faltaba algo y, sobre todo, un título. Mientras estaba escribiendo yo había esperado una carta urgente que había pedido a la portera de mi casa, una española que llevaba un montón de años viviendo en Francia y que [...] hablaba un idioma bastante confuso [...] entonces le pregunté si había llegado esta carta, me dijo que no y me trajo el correo ordinario.

Aquella carta no había llegado. Al cabo de dos horas, mientras yo estaba trabajando, llaman al timbre y me dice: "Aquí está la carta, es que los factores—les facteurs—han llegado en orden distinto". Entonces, le contesté inmediatamente: "El orden de los factores no altera el producto" y éste fue el título de la última secuencia de *Paisajes después de la batalla*. O sea que ahí intervino también un elemento sorpresa, un elemento ajeno que, en ocasiones, te da la clave'. *Juan Goytisolo: semana del autor*, ed. Manuel Ruiz Lagos (Madrid: Ediciones de Cultura Hispánica, 1991), 68.

30 Tzvetan Todorov, 'Les catégories du récit littéraire', in *Communications*, VIII (Paris: Ecole Pratique des Hautes Etudes, 1966), 139

31 Randall Stevenson speaks of 'a wider postmodern challenge to all theories, explanations or versions of life—part of a widespread contemporary scepticism of all constructions of reality'. He sees such scepticism as 'appropriate to an era [...] in which it is more than ever essential to see language and image not as innocent means of representing a world, but as inevitably bound up with intentions to control it.' Stevenson, *Modernist Fiction*, 202.

32 The play with Goytisolo's autobiography in this novel is so pervasive but enigmatically indirect that it tempts treatment as a sort of *roman à clef*. The most detailed treatment of this is Manuel Ruiz Lagos's article 'Pájaros en vuelo a Simorg: transferencias y metamorfósis textual en un relato de Juan Goytisolo: *Las virtudes del pájaro solitario*', in *Escritos sobre Juan Goytisolo: coloquio en torno a la obra de Juan Goytisolo* (Almería: Instituto de Estudios Almerienses, 1988).

33 Abigail Lee Six, *Juan Goytisolo: The Case for Chaos* (London: Yale University Press, 1990), 199–203. This effect can be seen to be inspired by San Juan. Colin Thompson has noted of the *Cántico*'s beginning: 'a bewildering array of images [...] causes the reader to lose his way almost at once. Rarely is it clear who is addressing whom, and about what.' Colin Thompson, *The Poet and the Mystic: A Study of the Cántico Espiritual of San Juan de la Cruz* (Oxford: Oxford University Press, 1977), 84.

34 Levy, *An Introduction to Persian Literature*, 98.

35 Levy, *An Introduction to Persian Literature*, 98

36 Levy, *An Introduction to Persian Literature*, 99.

37 Dick Davis, 'Introduction', *The Conference of the Birds* by Farid ud-Din Attar (London: Penguin, 1984), 11. Davis's spelling of the name differs from Levy's. Goytisolo in *Las virtudes* refers to the author merely as Al Attar (LVPS, 171).

38 Davis, 'Introduction', *The Conference of the Birds*, 19–20.

39 *Pájaro* is Cuban slang for homosexual.

40 In an interview from the late 1970s he states quite categorically: 'No soy religioso, soy agnóstico', and to the question of whether he is comforted by or needs the idea of God, he adds equally firmly: 'No; pero en cualquier caso, preferiría la religión musulmana a la católica'. María Mérida, *Los triunfadores: treinta y seis entrevistas a otros tantos personajes importantes* (Barcelona: Plaza y Janés, 1980), 168.

41 Epps speaks of a 'move in Goytisolo's writing from a rejection to an acceptance of the rhetoric, if not the "reality", of spirituality'. Epps, *Significant Violence*, 450–51.

42 *El bosque de las letras*, 213.

43 Luce López-Baralt, 'Inesperado encuentro', *Quimera* LXXIII (1988), 55–60. This is an excellent introductory article on *Las virtudes del pájaro solitario*. Also note Davis's explanation: 'The moment depends on a pun—only thirty (*si*) birds (*morgh*) are left at the end of the Way, and the *si morgh* meet the Simorgh, the goal of their quest'. Davis, 'Introduction', *The Conference of the Birds*, 16.

44 That for Goytisolo, at least, AIDS in this novel is not intended to have such a specific significance is seen in his comment: 'A las personas que se salen de la norma como los locos o los homosexuales se les trata de enfermos [...] Por eso la enfermedad,

en mi novela, funciona como metáfora, como demostración de que la llamada normalidad se consigue a fuerza de sacrificar las formas de pensamiento independientes.' Interview with Benjamín Prado, *Diario 16*, 26 January 1988.

45 'Levine assures us that AIDS, as metaphor, can cease being "malevolent" and can occupy another space in "our" bodies and minds.' Epps, *Significant Violence*, 440.

46 This does not prevent an intelligent reading of the novels in terms of the theme of homosexuality, as in Paul Julian Smith's 'Homosexual Desire in Goytisolo's Trilogy of Treason', in *Laws of Desire: Questions of Homosexuality in Spanish Writing and Film, 1960–1990* (Oxford: Clarendon Press, 1992).

47 Levine in other contexts has taken Goytisolo to task for his ambiguous and potentially unsympathetic stance towards women (cf. '*Makbara*: entre la espada y la pared—¿política marxista o política sexual?', *Revista Iberoamericana* CXVI–CXVII [1981]) and Goytisolo has—in a private conversation with this author—commented on the 'problem' with Levine's constant reduction of issues to the feminist perspective. This may explain the possible appearance of Levine herself in parodic form in the figure of Ms Lewin-Strauss. Epps, too, suspects this (*Significant Violence*, 439 n. 68).

48 Epps, *Significant Violence*, 438–39.

49 Levine, '*Makbara*: entre la espada y la pared', 234.

50 Susan Sontag, *Aids and its Metaphors* (London: Penguin, 1989), 23–24.

51 If Levine intends it in the way Sontag talks of the nineteenth-century notion of feverish creativity induced by syphilis (*Aids and its Metaphors*, 22–23), then that would seem an intolerably positive reading of AIDS.

52 The paradoxical effect being, of course, to heighten and underline the pain of unattainability.

53 Also, in line with our metafictional approach in which the texts suggest their own reading, the text as 'infecting' the reader is increasingly the claim that the texts and Goytisolo make for the 'poderes de la escritura'. Although, naturally, it is not a guarantee of their effectiveness.

54 Hutcheon, *A Poetics of Postmodernism*, 218. She also cites earlier E. L. Doctorow's comment that 'a book can affect consciousness—affect the way people think and therefore the way they act. Books create constituencies that have their own effect on history' (200).

55 Luce López-Baralt, *San Juan de la Cruz y el Islam (Estudio de las filiaciones semíticas de su literatura mística)* (Mexico: El Colegio de Mexico, 1985).

56 López-Baralt emphasizes this aspect of homage-cum-recreation: 'descubrimos maravillados que el *Tratado del pájaro solitario*, ese texto perdido que tanto se evoca en la novela [...] ha sido metafóricamente devuelto a la literatura española [...] Quien hubiera dicho al atormentado engullidor de papeles que fue San Juan de la Cruz que en los albores del segundo milenio otro compatriota descastado iba a re-crear—con una creatividad pasmosa y arriesgadísima—su *Pájaro solitario* y a devolverlo simbólicamente a las letras hispanas.' López-Baralt, 'Inesperado encuentro', 59.

57 Levine, 'El papel paradójico del "Sida" en *Las virtudes del pájaro solitario*', in *Escritos sobre Juan Goytisolo: II Seminario Internacional sobre 'Las virtudes del pájaro solitario'*, ed. Manuel Ruiz Lagos (Almería: Instituto de Estudios Almerienses, 1989), 228.

58 Sontag, *Aids and its Metaphors*, 60–61. Note, too: 'The behaviour AIDS is stimulating is part of a larger grateful return to what is perceived as "conventions", like the return to figure and landscape, tonality and melody, plot and character, and other much vaunted repudiations of difficult modernism in the arts' (78).

59 'Epidemics of particularly dreaded illnesses always provoke an outcry against leniency or tolerance [...] Demands are made to subject people to "tests", to isolate the ill and those suspected of being ill [...] or to erect barriers [...] Societies already

administered as garrisons, like China [...] and Cuba [...] are responding more rapidly and peremptorily.' Sontag, *Aids and its Metaphors*, 80–81.

60   The setting of the first section of the novel, the 'jardín de reposo', has clear echoes of the Russian visit evoked in Goytisolo's memoirs. In *En los reinos de taifa*, 277–78, Goytisolo refers to his trip to the Soviet Union in July 1965 and the visit to the 'residencia veraniega de escritores' where he and his companion, Monique Lange, were met by employees dressed as nurses. He describes the setting at one point as 'aquel amable decorado teatral de Chejov' (278). In *Las virtudes* the narrator says 'todo era decorado y cartón' (21).

61   This may also refer to the Goytisolo of 1950s social realism.

62   Hutcheon, *A Poetics of Postmodernism*, 230. Of course, not all modernist art is necessarily apolitical, but modernist aesthetics often is, and political implications tend to be much more indirect than with postmodernism. See Stevenson, *Modernist Fiction*, 208–28.

63   Jean-François Lyotard, *The Postmodern Condition: A Report on Knowledge* (Manchester: Manchester University Press, 1986), 81.

64   Paul Julian Smith says something similar when he suggests that *Las virtudes* 'would thus offer (HIV negative) readers a vicarious pleasure similar to that of the television viewer watching acts of terror from the safety of a favorite armchair'. Paul Julian Smith, 'Juan Goytisolo and Jean Baudrillard: The Mirror of Production and the Death of Symbolic Exchange', *Revista de Estudios Hispánicos* XXIV (1990), 53.

65   Epps, *Significant Violence*, 443, with regard to AIDS, i.e. by avoiding AIDS and focusing on mysticism.

66   Epps, *Significant Violence*, 431.

67   Smith says that the novel 'stages an apparently gratuitous return to the "spectacle of death" generally repressed in modern societies' ('Juan Goytisolo and Jean Baudrillard', 54).

68   See Ruiz Lagos' footnote in his article 'Sobre *La Cuarentena*. El maestro Ibn Arabi amonesta a Dante Alighieri', in Juan Goytisolo, *La Cuarentena* (Barcelona: Círculo de Lectores, 1991), 165: 'murió recientemente de sida en Barcelona'.

69   Levine, 'El papel paradójico del "Sida"', 233. Smith, too, interprets the vision as nostalgic ('Juan Goytisolo and Jean Baudrillard', 56).

70   Unlike the opposition suggested by Smith between 'the "almost extinct and impossible love" of the wrestlers' and the 'effortless *jouissance* of the mystic bird', this passage actually seems to establish the intimate connection between the two, the wrestlers as an image of mystical union. Cf. Smith, 'Juan Goytisolo and Jean Baudrillard', 56.

71   Riera, 'Regreso al origen', 40. Such a remark appears as a deliberate piece of added obfuscation on the part of the author that matches San Juan's attempt in the *Glosas* to 'adensar y profundizar al extremo el enigma de sus versos ciñéndolos en un halo de ambigüedad y misterio imposible de traspasar' (LVPS, 151). Goytisolo in the same interview with Riera (38) comments approvingly on San Juan's tendency in the Commentaries on his poetry to add to the ambiguity of the text rather than dispel it by fixing a single interpretation. This Goytisolo compares to the practice of the Sufi mystics.

72   Riera, 'Regreso al origen', 37.

73   Thompson, *The Poet and the Mystic*, 97.

74   Miguel Dalmau's recent biography of the Goytisolo brothers reveals her identity as that of Joelle Auerbach. Miguel Dalmau, *Los Goytisolo* (Barcelona: Anagrama, 1999), 548–53.

75   'In eschatology, the word *barzakh* is used to describe the boundary of the world of human beings [...] and its separation from the world of pure spirits and God [...] the

Sufis use this term in the sense of the space between the material world and that of the pure spirits.' H. A. R. Gibb and J. H. Kramers, *A Shorter Encylopaedia of Islam* (London: Luzak, 1961), 59. Goytisolo's admired Ibn Arabi defines the *barzakh* as a 'world of imagination': 'A *barzakh* is an intermediate reality that both separates and comprehends what lies on either side. It is a name given to the "world of suspended images" (Suhrawardi) or the "world of the imagination" (Ibn Arabi), the intermediate ontological realms that separate the ocean of the spirits from that of the corporeal bodies.' William C. Chittick, 'Eschatology', in *Islamic Spirituality: Foundations*, ed. Seyyed Hossein Nasr (New York: Crossroad, 1987), 390.

76 Interview with María Luisa Blanco, 'En Marrakech puedo escribir y vivir', *Cambio 16*, 20 April 1992, 78. Cf. *El bosque de las letras*, 299–300.

77 An example of this was the controversy over Jean Baudrillard's deliberately provocative articles on the Gulf War which seemed to argue that the conflict would not and did not take place, and attracted much criticism as an example of postmodernist excess, implying that reality is unknowable behind a surface of conflicting discourses. For Baudrillard, the predominance of the media in contemporary society meant the substitution of a 'realistic war' by a 'virtual war' in which 'everything which is turned into information becomes the object of endless speculation, the site of total uncertainty'. 'The Gulf War: is it really taking place?', in *The Gulf War did not take Place* (Bloomington, IN: Indiana University Press, 1995), 41. For a critical account of the controversy, see C. Norris, *Uncritical Theory: Postmodernism, Intellectuals and the Gulf War* (London: Lawrence and Wishart, 1992).

78 Hutcheon, *A Poetics of Postmodernism*, 92–93.

79 In an excellent article, Linda Gould Levine talks of the novel's aim of 'transmisión del virus al lector mismo' and speaks of how Goytisolo's technique 'intensifica el deseo del lector externo de distanciarse del primero y de abrir su sistema inmune al germen que acecha en el libro'. 'La escritura infecciosa de Juan Goytisolo: contaminación y cuarentena', *Revista de Estudios Hispánicos* XXVIII (1994), 104. But she does not explain exactly how this contagion works, though the suggestion is that it is at the level of ideas, Goytisolo winning over the reader by the emotional force of his argument. She says: 'La lógica interior que los textos de Goytisolo comunican últimamente al lector es tan irresistible que termina por alterar nuestro sistema inmune y penetrar el centro mismo de nuestro pensamiento' (106).

80 Certainly *La cuarentena* does strive for textual undecidability. One critic has already noted the novel's penchant for the interrogative. Antonio Candau, 'Sobre el autor y la muerte: Juan Goytisolo, *La cuarentena* y la retórica de la interrogación', *Revista Canadiense de Estudios Hispánicos* XIX(2) (1995), 263–79.

81 'Baudrillard's postmodernism is [...] a culture of passivity [...] All boundaries have been abolished, reality has "imploded" and the traditional sociological notion of the social has disappeared [...] Postmodern culture abhors active agents for the individual is no longer an actor but rather "a terminal of multiple networks" including television, computers, telephones, micro-satellites.' Alan Swingewood, *Cultural Theory and the Problem of Modernity* (London: Macmillan, 1998), 171–72.

82 Marc O'Day has noted that 'Television is arguably the postmodern medium *par excellence*', in 'Postmodernism and Television', *The Icon Critical Dictionary of Postmodern Thought*, ed. Stuart Sim (Duxford: Icon Books, 1998), 112; cf. 154.

83 Philip M. Taylor notes that 'it is important to stress right at the outset that there were essentially two wars going on: the war itself, fought by the coalition's combined military forces against the regime of Saddam Hussein, and the war as portrayed by the media. The latter did not necessarily reflect the reality of the former.' Philip M. Taylor, *War and the Media: Propaganda and Persuasion in the Gulf War* (Manchester: Manchester University Press, 1998 [1993]), 8.

84 Douglas Kellner, *Jean Baudrillard: From Marxism to Postmodernism and Beyond* (Cambridge: Polity Press, 1989), 70.

85 'It is useless to dream of a revolution through content or through form, since the medium and the real are now in a single nebulous state whose truth is undecipherable.' Jean Baudrillard, *In the Shadow of the Silent Majorities*, quoted in Kellner, *Jean Baudrillard*, 69.

86 'In verse 100 of Sura xxiii, the godless beg to be allowed to return to earth to accomplish the good they have left undone during their lives; but there is a barzakh in front of them barring their way.' Gibb and Kramers, *Shorter Encyclopaedia of Islam*, 59.

87 This conjures up a negatively passive image of the postmodern media consumer akin to what Marc O'Day has termed the 'postmodern hedonist': 'the archetypal decentred subject with a maximum attention span of three minutes. Living in a world of schizophrenically fragmented instants, she cruises the surfeit of channels available to her, zapping her remote control and hopping between channels and programmes unconnected by time, space or genre' ('Postmodernism and Television', 116).

88 Baudrillard, 'The Gulf War: is it really taking place?', 31. Kellner explains that for Baudrillard 'one of the fundamental processes of the contemporary age involves the absorption of all modes of expression by that of advertising [...] Consistent with his media theory in which "the medium is the message", it is the form of advertising, its ubiquity, its saturation and neutralization of all possible meanings which is significant for Baudrillard.' Kellner, *Jean Baudrillard*, 98.

89 'Moreover, the idea that "the media are American", that Anglo-American news organizations dominate the flow of news to the detriment of the Third World, had not only found substantiating support in the war, it had even been underlined by the coalition's media arrangements, with their Anglo-American emphasis [...] The ability of the American-led coalition to drive its military message home and abroad by superior technology and by controlling international communications systems and news organizations had demonstrated for such people that the New World Order and the New World Information Order had merged into one.' Taylor, *War and the Media*, 266.

90 For Hutcheon, postmodernism 'does not pretend to operate outside the system, for it knows it cannot; it therefore overtly acknowledges its complicity, only to work covertly to subvert the system's values from within'. Hutcheon, *A Poetics of Postmodernism*, 224.

91 Baudrillard, 'The Gulf War: is it really taking place?', 46–47.

92 Borges, in 'Borges y yo', has the narrator query: 'No sé cual de los dos escribe esta página'. Jorge Luis Borges, *El hacedor* (Madrid: Alianza, 1998), 62.

93 Hutcheon, *A Poetics of Postmodernism*, 223.

94 Randolph Pope, *Understanding Juan Goytisolo* (Columbia, SC: University of South Carolina Press), 154. Pope considers *La saga* one of Goytisolo's best novels.

95 Goytisolo has said: 'Lo que allí es como una profecía—el personaje camina en un paisaje de ruinas ideológicas—en *La saga* [...] se ha cumplido. Es una realidad.' Rosa Mora, 'Marx, a partir de Cervantes: Juan Goytisolo publica *La saga de los Marx*', 'Babelia', *El País*, 11 December 1993, 14.

96 There may be some significance in the choice of the surname for the editor. The American Nobel laureate William Faulkner, a serious modernist writer, also worked as a Hollywood scriptwriter in order to solve his financial problems. His biographer, Richard Gray, reports that he once confided to his publisher: 'I have realised lately how much trash and junk writing for movies corrupted into my writing'. Richard Gray, *The Life of William Faulkner: A Critical Biography* (Oxford: Blackwell, 1994), 289.

97 'Juan Goytisolo: una guerra interminable', interview with César Alonso de los Ríos, *El Semanal*, 28 January 1996, 27.

98 Robert Spires, *Beyond the Metafictional Mode: Directions in the Modern Spanish Novel* (Lexington, KY: University Press of Kentucky, 1984), p.19.

99 Steven Connor has pointed out how TV, video and the cinema are not only classically representative of contemporary society but they also provide scope for critique and subversion of that very society: 'It is the very familiarity of TV, and the global spread of TV expertise, both in production and consumption, that make this question of transgression and incorporation recur with such violent persistence.' Steven Connor, *Postmodern Culture: An Introduction to Theories of the Contemporary* (Oxford: Blackwell, 1997), 182.

100 During the American Presidential election campaign in May 1992, the Republican Vice-President Dan Quayle attacked Murphy Brown, a popular TV sitcom character on CBS, played by Candice Bergen. For Quayle the programme's lead character, a single mother, undermined family values by 'mocking the importance of fathers, by bearing a child alone and calling it just another lifestyle choice'. This led to an interesting blurring of the fact/fiction boundary as subsequent episodes made reference to Quayle.

101 Pope, *Understanding Juan Goytisolo*, 155.

102 The idea finds its way, too, into the most recent novel, *Las semanas del jardín* (Madrid: Alfaguara, 1997), 171.

103 Mora, 'Marx, a partir de Cervantes', 14. Robert Spires, in *Post-Totalitarian Spanish Fiction* (Columbia, MO, and London: University of Missouri Press, 1996), notes quantum theory's links with literary postmodernism (23–29).

104 Lyotard, *The Postmodern Condition*, 53ff.

105 Alan Sokal and Jean Bricmont, in their polemical work *Intellectual Impostures: Postmodern Philosophers' Abuse of Science* (London: Profile Books, 1998), have already tried from the position of classical scientists to debunk the scientific basis of Lyotard's and others' thinking. See 125–28.

106 Lyotard, *The Postmodern Condition*, 36–37.

107 As Stuart Sim notes: 'Take away the element of universality and Marxism is no longer really Marxism to its adherents; the theory's claim to ultimate authority is not an optional extra but a defining characteristic.' Stuart Sim, *Jean-François Lyotard* (London: Prentice Hall/Harvester Wheatsheaf, 1995), 37.

108 Lyotard, *The Postmodern Condition*, 60. Goytisolo himself has said that 'tal como están las cosas, nuestra única forma de defendernos es la diseminación de verdades parciales. Yo vengo a señalar la complejidad de la realidad, y la imposibilidad de dar una única versión oficial. Este era ya el tema de *La saga de los Marx*. El editor encarga una novela histórica que es imposible.' Alonso de los Ríos, 'Juan Goytisolo: una guerra interminable'.

109 B. Nicolaievsky and O. Maenchen-Helfen, *Karl Marx: Man and Fighter* (London: Allen Lane, 1973), 266.

110 Robert Payne, *Marx* (London: W. H. Allen, 1968), 251.

111 'It was not true, for example, that Jenny accustomed herself to a bohemian existence and felt at home in her poverty. Nor were Marx's eyes black—they were brown.' Payne, *Marx*, 252.

112 Goytisolo travelled to Sarajevo in 1993 and in the same year published his reports for *El País* in the book of reportage, *Cuaderno de Sarajevo*.

113 Emma Rodríguez, ' "La literatura es nuestra última resistencia": Juan Goytisolo publica *El sitio de los sitios*, una novela sobre Sarajevo', *El Mundo*, 18 November 1995.

114 Rodríguez, ' "La literatura es nuestra última resistencia" '.

115 Rodríguez, ' "La literatura es nuestra última resistencia" '.

116 The background of the *comandante* as described in this section (ESDS, 167–

75) can be read as a variation on Goytisolo's own, and Eusebio has elements of his uncle, Ramón Vives, a figure who lurks behind the 'señor mayor' of *Las virtudes*, and for whom Goytisolo feels a deep affinity and guilt-ridden debt. See *Coto vedado* (Barcelona: Seix Barral, 1985), 31–33. The name is also associated with Eusebio Borrell, the husband of Juan's favoured Aunt Consuelo, Ramón Vives' sister. Dalmau notes that 'compartía los mismos gustos que ella y también cultivaba la poesía'. Dalmau, *Los Goytisolo*, 105. The name in the Goytisolo family is also associated with contagion as Juan's father shunned Uncle Eusebio, suspecting him of infecting Aunt Consuelo with tuberculosis. *Coto vedado*, 34.

117 Yolanda Aguilar, 'EE UU tiene más presos políticos que Marruecos', *Cambio 16*, 27 November 1995, 102.

118 David Herzberger, *Narrating the Past: Fiction and Historiography in Postwar Spain* (Durham, NC, and London: Duke University Press, 1995), 143.

119 Herzberger, *Narrating the Past*, 140.

Bibliography

Works by Juan Goytisolo

NOVELS

Señas de identidad (México City: Joaquín Mortiz, 1966; Barcelona: Seix Barral, 1976).
Reivindicación del conde don Julián (México City: Joaquín Mortiz, 1970; Barcelona: Seix Barral, 1976).
Reivindicación del conde don Julián, ed. Linda Gould Levine (Madrid: Cátedra, 1985).
Juan sin tierra (Barcelona: Seix Barral, 1975).
Makbara (Barcelona: Seix Barral, 1980).
Paisajes después de la batalla (Barcelona: Montesinos, 1982).
Paisajes después de la batalla, ed. Andrés Sánchez Robayna (Madrid: Austral, 1990).
Las virtudes del pájaro solitario (Barcelona: Seix Barral, 1988).
La cuarentena (Madrid: Mondadori, 1991).
La saga de los Marx (Barcelona: Mondadori, 1993).
El sitio de los sitios (Madrid: Alfaguara, 1995).
Las semanas del jardín: Un círculo de lectores (Madrid: Alfaguara, 1997).

COLLECTIONS OF ESSAYS

Problemas de la novela (Barcelona: Seix Barral, 1959).
El furgón de cola (Paris: Ruedo Ibérico, 1967; Barcelona: Seix Barral, 1976).
Disidencias (Barcelona: Seix Barral, 1977).
Libertad, libertad, libertad (Barcelona: Anagrama, 1978).
El problema del Sáhara (Barcelona: Anagrama, 1979).
España y los españoles (Barcelona: Editorial Lumen, 1979).
Crónicas sarracinas (Paris: Ruedo Ibérico, 1981; Barcelona: Ruedo Ibérico, 1982).
Contracorrientes (Barcelona: Montesinos, 1985).
Aproximaciones a Gaudí en Capadocia (Madrid: Mondadori, 1990).
El bosque de la letras (Madrid: Anagrama, 1995).
Cogitus interruptus (Barcelona: Seix Barral, 1999).

MEMOIRS

Coto vedado (Barcelona: Seix Barral, 1985).
En los reinos de taifa (Barcelona: Seix Barral, 1986).

OTHER WRITINGS

'Para una literatura nacional popular', *Insula* CXLVI (1959), 6, 11.
'Writing in an Occupied Language', *The New York Times Book Review*, 31 March 1974, 47.
'Presentación crítica de José María Blanco White', in *Obra inglesa de D. José María Blanco White* (Buenos Aires: Formentor, 1972; Barcelona: Seix Barral, 1974).

'Telediario 1984', *El País*, 15 December 1981, 15.
'Novela, crítica y creación', *Revista Iberoamericana* CXVI–CXVII (1981), 23–32.
'Sobre literatura y vida literaria', *Quimera* XXIII (1982), 16–21.
'Los derviches giróvagos', *El País Semanal* CDLXI (9 February 1986), 22–31.
'El Cairo. La Ciudad de los Muertos', *El País Semanal* DXIII (8 February 1987), 30–37, 60–64.
'El árbol de la literatura', *Quimera* LXXIII (1988), 41–44.

INTERVIEWS AND ARTICLES IN THE PRESS

Aguilar, Yolanda, 'EE UU tiene más presos políticos que Marruecos,' *Cambio 16*, 27 November 1995, 102–04.
Alonso de los Ríos, C., 'Juan Goytisolo sin tierra', *Triunfo*, Madrid, XXX(673) (1975), 26–28.
—— 'Juan Goytisolo: una guerra interminable', *El Semanal*, 28 January 1996, 24–30.
Black, Stanley, Interview, Paris, 25 August 1985 (unpublished).
Blanco, María Luisa, 'En Marrakech puedo escribir y vivir', *Cambio 16*, 20 April 1992, 76–79.
González Ruano, Mauro, 'Entrevista: Una literatura total', *Ozono* XI (1976), 57–61.
Hernández, José A., 'Juan Goytisolo—1975', *Modern Language Notes* XCI (1976), 337–55.
Isasi Angulo, A.C., 'La novelística de Juan Goytisolo (Entrevista con el autor)', *Papeles de Son Armadans* LXXVI(226) (1975), 65–87.
Juristo, Juan Angel, 'Goytisolo se desmarca de la narrativa española', *El Independiente*, 30 January 1988, 33–34.
Kohut, Karl, 'Entrevista', in *Escribir en París* (Barcelona: Hogar del Libro, 1983), 77–103.
Lázaro, Jesús, 'Fragmentos de una charla con Juan Goytisolo', in *Juan Goytisolo*, ed. J. Lázaro, Serie España, Escribir Hoy, 11 (Madrid: Ministerio de Cultura, 1982), 151–55.
Loubet, Enrique, 'Goytisolo vs. el mito español', *Excelsior*, México, 20 February 1970, 16A–17A.
Mérida, María, 'Juan Goytisolo: la resaca del pasado', in *Los triunfadores: treinta y seis entrevistas a otros tantos personajes importantes* (Barcelona: Plaza y Janés, 1980).
Molina, C.A. and Luis Suñén, 'Entrevista: Juan Goytisolo o la heterodoxia consciente', *Insula*, CCCLXVII (1977), 4.
Mora, Rosa, 'Marx, a partir de Cervantes: Juan Goytisolo publica *La saga de los Marx*', 'Babelia', *El País*, 11 December 1993, 14–15.
Ortega, Julio, 'Entrevistas a Juan Goytisolo', in *Disidencias*, 289–325.
Plaza, J.M., 'Juan Goytisolo: "Mis novelas comienzan a valorarse con el paso del tiempo"', *Disidencias, Suplemento cultural de 'Diario 16'* CXCII (2 September 1984).
Riera, Miguel, 'Regreso al origen', *Quimera* LXXIII (1988), 36–40.
Ríos, J., 'Desde *Juan sin Tierra*', in *Juan sin Tierra* (Madrid: Editorial Fundamentos, 1978), 9–25.
Rodríguez, Emma, '"La literatura es nuestra última resistencia": Juan Goytisolo publica *El sitio de los sitios*, una novela sobre Sarajevo', *El Mundo*, 18 November 1995.
Rodríguez Monegal, E., 'Destrucción de la España sagrada: diálogo con Juan Goytisolo', *Mundo Nuevo* XII (1967), 44–60.
Sánchez Arnosi, M., 'Juan Goytisolo: "la creación literaria como liberación"', *Insula* CDXXVI (1982), 4.

Sanz, Luis, 'Entrevista con Juan Goytisolo', *Camp de l'Arp* XLIII–XLIV (1977), 17–19.
Trenas, Pilar, 'Juan Goytisolo, ahora sin amargura ni rencor', *ABC*, 7 June 1981, 36–37.
Tuñón, Amparo, 'Juan Goytisolo: Una tierra propia', *Camp de l'Arp* XLVIII–XLIX (1978), 75–79.
White, Edmund, 'Holy War in the Tenth Arrondissement', *New Statesman*, 16 October 1987, 28–30.

SECONDARY WORKS

Albert Robatto, M., *La creación literaria de Juan Goytisolo* (Barcelona: Planeta, 1977).
Anderson, Reed, '*Señas de identidad*: Chronicle of Rebellion', *Journal of Spanish Studies* II (1974), 3–19.
Arcipreste de Hita, *Libro de Buen Amor* (Barcelona: Bruguera, 1977).
Attar, Farid ud-Din, *The Conference of the Birds*, Introduction by Dick Davis (London: Penguin, 1984).
Bakhtin, Mikhail, *La cultura popular en la Edad Media y en el Renacimiento: El contexto de François Rabelais* (Madrid: Alianza, 1987).
—— *Problems of Dostoevsky's Poetics*, trans. R.W. Rotsel (Ann Arbor, MI: Ardis, 1973).
Barthes, Roland, 'La faz barroca', in Severo Sarduy, *De donde son los cantantes* (Barcelona: Seix Barral, 1980), 3–6.
—— *Image–Music–Text*, ed. Stephen Heath (London: Fontana, 1984).
—— *Mythologies* (London: Paladin, 1973).
—— *The Pleasure of the Text* (London: Jonathan Cape, 1976).
—— *Sade, Fourier, Loyola* (Paris: Seuil, 1971).
—— 'To Write: An Intransitive Verb?', in *The Languages of Criticism and the Sciences of Man*, ed. R. Macksey and E. Donato (Baltimore, MD: Johns Hopkins University Press, 1970), 134–45.
—— *Writing Degree Zero* (New York: Hill and Wang, 1968).
Baudrillard, Jean, *The Gulf War did not Take Place* (Bloomington, IN: Indiana University Press, 1995; French original 1991).
Beck, M., *The Analysis of Hispanic Texts: Current Trends in Methodology* (New York: Bilingual Press, 1976).
Belsey, Catherine, *Critical Practice* (London: Methuen, 1980).
Benveniste, Emile, *Problèmes de linguistique générale* (Paris: Gallimard, 1966).
Berki, R.N., *Socialism* (London: Dent, 1975).
Berns, G., 'El retorno simbólico en *Señas de identidad* de Juan Goytisolo', in *The Analysis of Hispanic Texts: Current Trends in Methodology*, ed. M. Beck et al., First York College Colloquium (New York: Bilingual Press, 1976), 49–56.
Bernstein, J.S., 'Body, Language and Divinity in Goytisolo's *Juan sin Tierra*', in *The Analysis of Hispanic Texts: Current Trends in Methodology*, ed. L. Davis and I. Tarán, Second York College Colloquium (New York: Bilingual Press, 1976).
—— 'Reivindicación del conde don Julián y su discurso eliminado', *Voces* I (1981), 55–66.
Best, Steven and Douglas Kellner, *Postmodern Theory: Critical Interrogations* (London: Macmillan, 1991).
Beyrie, Jacques et al., *Deux romans de la rupture? 'Tiempo de silencio' et 'Señas de identidad'* (Toulouse: Université de Toulouse-Le Mirail, 1980).
Bieder, Mary Ellen, 'La cárcel verbal: Narrative Discourse in *Makbara*', *Review of Contemporary Fiction* IV(2) (1984), 120–27.
—— 'A Case of Altered Identity: Two Editions of Juan Goytisolo's *Señas de identidad*', *Modern Language Notes*, LXXXIX (1974), 298–310.

—— 'De *Señas de identidad* a *Makbara*: estrategia narrativa en las novelas de Juan Goytisolo', *Revista Ibero-americana* CXVI–CXVII (1981), 89–96.

Black, Stanley, 'Autobiography and Intertextuality in *Carajicomedia* by Juan Goytisolo', *NUI Maynooth Papers in Spanish, Portuguese and Latin American Studies* II (2001), 1–32.

—— 'Mysticism, Postmodernism and Transgression in *La Cuarentena* by Juan Goytisolo', *Bulletin of Hispanic Studies*, University of Glasgow LXXVIII (2001), 241–57.

—— 'Orality in *Makbara*: A Postmodern Paradox?', *Neophilologus* LXXIX (1995), 93–106.

—— 'Señas de identidad by Juan Goytisolo: A Metafictional Reading', *Journal of Hispanic Research* III (1994–95), 291–305.

Blanco Aguinaga, C., 'Sobre la *Reivindicación del conde don Julián*: la ficción y la historia', in *De mitólogos y novelistas* (Madrid: Turner, 1975), 51–71.

Blasco, F.J., 'El palimpsesto urbano de *Paisajes después de la batalla*', *Anales de Literatura Española Contemporánea* X (1985), 11–30.

Bolívar Botia, A., *El estructuralismo: de Lévi-Strauss a Derrida* (Madrid: Cincel, 1985).

Booker, M. Keith, *Joyce, Bakhtin, and the Literary Tradition: Toward a Comparative Cultural Poetics* (Ann Arbor, MI: University of Michigan, 1995).

Booth, Wayne, C., *The Rhetoric of Fiction* (Chicago, IL: University of Chicago Press, 1961).

Borges, Jorge Luis, *El hacedor* (Madrid: Alianza, 1998).

Bowie, Malcolm, 'Jacques Lacan', in John Sturruck (ed.), *Structuralism and Since* (Oxford: Oxford University Press, 1982).

Braun, L.V., 'The "Intertextualization" of Unamuno and Juan Goytisolo's *Reivindicación del conde don Julián*', *Hispanófila* LXXXIX (1987), 39–56.

Brown, Norman O., *Life Against Death: The Psychoanalytical Meaning of History* (London: Sphere, 1970).

Buckley, Ramón, *Problemas formales en la novela española contemporánea* (Barcelona: Península, 1973).

Burke, Sean, *The Death and Return of the Author: Criticism and Subjectivity in Barthes, Foucault and Derrida* (Edinburgh: Edinburgh University Press, 1992).

Burns, E. and T. Burns (eds), *Sociology of Literature and Drama* (London: Penguin, 1973).

Butler, Christopher, *After the Wake: An Essay in the Contemporary Avant-Garde* (Oxford: Oxford University Press, 1980).

Butt, John, *Writers and Politics in Modern Spain* (London: Hodder and Stoughton, 1978).

Cabrera, Vicente, 'Movilidad y repetición narrativas en *Juan sin tierra*', *The American Hispanist* I(11) (1976), 7–9.

Candau, Antonio, 'Sobre el autor y la muerte: Juan Goytisolo, *La cuarentena* y la retórica de la interrogación', *Revista Canadiense de Estudios Hispánicos* XIX(2) (1995), 263–79.

Cardaillac, D., 'Algunos problemas de enunciación en *Señas de identidad*', *Les Langues Neo-Latines* LXXIV(234) (1980), 48–56.

Carenas, F., 'Juan Goytisolo: otra concepción de la moralidad y el arte', *Cuadernos Americanos* XL(5) (1981), 107–14.

—— 'La razón de ser del último lenguaje de Juan Goytisolo', *Cuadernos Americanos* CXCII (1974), 116–23.

Carrasquer, F., 'Una subida más de Juan Goytisolo', *Insula* CDXCVII (1988), 13.

Castellet, J.M., *La hora del lector* (Barcelona: Seix Barral, 1957).

—— 'Juan Goytisolo contra la España Sagrada', in *Literatura, ideología y política* (Barcelona: Anagrama, 1976), 82–95.

Chittick, William C. 'Eschatology', in Seyyed Hossein Nasr (ed.), *Islamic Spirituality: Foundations* (New York: Crossroad, 1987), 378–409.

Cirre, J.F., 'Novela e ideología en Juan Goytisolo', *Insula* CCXXX (1966), 1–2.

Clark, Katerina, and M. Holquist, *Mikhail Bakhtin* (London: Harvard University Press, 1984).

Cohan, Steve, and Linda M. Shires, *Telling Stories: A Theoretical Analysis of Narrative Fiction* (London: Routledge, 1988).

Connor, Steve, *Postmodern Culture: An Introduction to Theories of the Contemporary* (Oxford: Blackwell, 1997).

Conte, Rafael, 'Juan Goytisolo, Don Julián y la destrucción', *Informaciones*, Madrid, 24 June 1971, 12.

—— 'Narrativa española: *Juan sin Tierra* de Juan Goytisolo: la destrucción y sus límites', *Insula* CCCXLIX (1975), 5.

Corrales Egea, J., 'Cambio de ritmo de *Señas de identidad* a la *Reivindicación del Conde don Julián*', *Norte (Revista Hispánica de Amsterdam)* XIII(4–6) (1972), 114–18.

Culler, Jonathan, *Barthes* (London: Fontana, 1983).

—— *Structuralist Poetics: Structuralism, Linguistics and the Study of Literature* (London: Routledge, 1975).

Currie, Mark, *Postmodern Narrative Theory* (London: Macmillan, 1998).

Dalmau, Miguel, *Los Goytisolo* (Barcelona: Anagrama, 1999).

DeGeorge, Richard, and M. Fernande, *The Structuralists: From Marx to Lévi-Strauss* (New York: Anchor Books, 1972).

Derrida, Jacques, *L'écriture et la différence* (Paris: Editions du Seuil, 1967).

Díaz, Elías, *Pensamiento español 1939–1975* (Madrid: EDICUSA, 1978).

Díaz, Janet W., 'Origins, Aesthetics and the "nueva novela española"', *Hispania* LIX (1976), 109–17.

Diaz-Migoyo, G., 'Juan Goytisolo's Novel Trilogy: A Reader's Personal Memory', *Review of Contemporary Fiction* IV(2) (1984), 76–80.

Doblado, Gloria, *España en tres novelas de Juan Goytisolo* (Madrid: Playor, 1988).

Dolgin, Stacey, *La novela desmiticadora española (1961–1982)* (Barcelona: Anthropos Editorial del Hombre, Ambito Literarios/Ensayo, 1991).

Durán, Manuel, 'Vindicación de Juan Goytisolo: *Reivindicación del conde don Julián*', *Insula* CCXC (1971), 1–4.

Durán, Manuel, 'El lenguaje de Juan Goytisolo', in J. Ríos (ed.), *Juan Goytisolo* (Madrid: Fundamentos, 1975), 53–70.

—— 'Perspectivas críticas. Horizontes infinitos. Un orden desordenado: la estructura de *Juan sin Tierra*', *Anales de la Novela de Posguerra*, Kansas, III (1978), 75–88.

Eagleton, Terry, *Literary Theory: An Introduction* (London: Blackwell, 1983).

Easthope, Antony, *Poetry as Discourse* (London: Methuen, 1983).

Eco, Umberto, *The Open Work*, trans. Anna Cancogni, introduction by David Robey (London: Hutchinson Radius, 1989).

Embarec, M.J., 'Lectura marroquí de *Makbara*', *Voces* I (1981), 83–86.

Epps, Brad, 'The Politics of Ventriloquism: Cava, Revolution and Sexual Discourse in *Conde Julián*', *Modern Language Notes* CVII (1992), 274–97.

—— *Significant Violence: Oppression and Resistance in the Narratives of Juan Goytisolo, 1970–1990* (Oxford: Clarendon Press, 1996).

Escarpit, Robert, ' "Creative Treason" as a Key to Literature', in Elizabeth Burns and Tom Burns (eds), *Sociology of Literature and Drama* (London: Penguin, 1973), 359–67.

Escudero, Javier, *Eros, mística y muerte in Juan Goytisolo (1982–1992)* (Almería: Instituto de Estudios Almerienses, 1994).

—— 'La preocupación ante la muerte en el último Juan Goytisolo: *La cuarentena*', *La Torre* VIII(30) (1994), 207–16.

Ferreras, J.I., *La novela en el siglo XX (desde 1939)* (Madrid: Taurus, 1988).

Flaubert, Gustave, *Bouvard and Pécuchet*, trans. A.J. Krailsheimer (London: Penguin, 1976).

Forrest, G.S., 'La destrucción del mito por medio del mito. Dos "Prometeos" de la nueva novela española', *Modern Language Notes* XCIII (1978), 297–309.

Frank, Joseph, 'Spatial Form in Modern Literature', in Mark Schorer, J. Miles and G. McKenzie (eds), *Criticism: The Foundations of Modern Literary Judgement* (New York: Harcourt, Brace, 1958).

Freud, Sigmund, *Jokes and their Relation to the Unconscious* (London: Penguin, 1976).

—— *Two Short Accounts of Psycho-Analysis* (London: Penguin, 1962).

Fuentes, Carlos, 'Entre Forster y Batjin', *El País*, 4 January 1989, 28.

—— 'Juan Goytisolo: la lengua común', in *La nueva novela hispanoamericana* (Mexico City: Joaquín Mortiz, 1969), 78–84

—— 'Juan Goytisolo or the Novel as Exile', *The Review of Contemporary Fiction* IV(2) (1984), 72–75.

—— 'Juan Goytisolo y el honor de la novela', *El País*, 3 January 1989, 28.

Gallego, André, and Henri Guerreiro, 'Pour une chronogénèse de *Señas de identidad*. Temps escamoté, temps anéanti, temps dominé', in Jacques Beyrie et al. (eds), *Deux romans de la rupture?*, Table ronde organisée par l'UER d'Etudes Hispaniques et Hispano-Américaines, Toulouse, 28–29 February 1980, Travaux de l'Université de Toulouse–Le Mireil, Tome XIII (Toulouse: Université de Toulouse–Le Mireil, 1980), 123–41.

García, Evelyne, untitled article on *Makbara*, in J. Lázaro (ed.), *Juan Goytisolo*, Serie España, Escribir Hoy, 11 (Madrid: Ministerio de Cultura, 1982), 139–51.

Garraleta Taberna, M. 'Las primeras obras de Juan Goytisolo: praxis y teoría', *Notas y Estudios Filológicos* (1984), 43–63.

Gellert, W., et al., *The VNR Concise Encyclopedia of Mathematics* (New York: VNR, 2nd edn, 1989).

Genette, Gérard, *Figures of Literary Discourse* (Oxford: Blackwell, 1982).

—— *Narrative Discourse* (Ithaca NY: Cornell University Press, 1980).

Geoghegan, Vincent, *Utopianism and Marxism* (London: Methuen, 1987).

Gibb, H.A.R., *Arabic Literature: An Introduction* (London: Oxford University Press, 1974).

Gibb, H.A.R., and J.H. Kramers, *Shorter Encyclopaedia of Islam* (London: Luzac, 1961).

Gil Casado, Pablo, '*Makbara* es un cementerio', *Cuadernos Americanos* XL(6) (1981), 217–26.

Gimferrer, Pere, 'Riesgo y ventura de Juan Goytisolo', prologue to *Obras completas* (Madrid: Aguilar, 1977), 9–64.

Gómez Mata, Marta (with César Silió Cervera), *Oralidad y polifonía en la obra de Juan Goytisolo* (Madrid: Ensayos Júcar, 1994).

Góngora, Luis de, *Soledades*, ed. John Beverley (Madrid: Cátedra, 1980).

González, B.A. 'The Evolution of Juan Goytisolo's Narrative Technique: Time, Character and Point of View', PhD thesis, University of California, Berkeley, 1979.

——, 'Language and Referentiality in *Señas de identidad*', *Revista Canadiense de Estudios Hispánicos* XI(3) (1987), 611–21.

—— 'Mimesis and Narrative Discourse: Goytisolo's Search for Immediacy', *The Review of Contemporary Fiction* IV(2) (1984), 80–88.

Gray, Richard, *The Life of William Faulkner: A Critical Biography* (Oxford: Blackwell, 1994).

Harris, Derek, *Luis Cernuda: A Study of the Poetry* (London: Tamesis Books, 1973).

Hawkes, Terence, *Structuralism and Semiotics* (London: Methuen, 1977).

Heath, Stephen, *The Nouveau Roman: A Study in the Practice of Writing* (London: Elek, 1972).

Herpoel, Sonja, 'Presencia de la utopía en *Juan sin Tierra*: la auténtica, subversiva revolución', *Revue Belge de Philologie et d'Histoire* LXII(3) (1984), 521–29.

Herzberger, David, 'History, Apocalypse, and the Triumph of Fiction in the Post-War Spanish Novel', *Revista Hispánica Moderna* XLIV (1991), 247–73.

—— 'Literature on Literature: Four Theoretical Views of the Contemporary Spanish Novel', *Journal of Spanish Studies* VII(1) (1979), 41–62.

—— *Narrating the Past: Fiction and Historiography in Postwar Spain* (Durham, NC, and London: Duke University Press, 1995).

—— 'An Overview of Postwar Novel Criticism of the 1970s', *Anales de la Narrativa Española Contemporánea* V (1980), 27–39.

—— 'Split Referentiality and the Making of Character in Recent Spanish Metafiction', *Modern Language Notes* CIII(2) (1988), 419–35.

—— 'Theoretical Approaches to the Spanish New Novel: Juan Benet and Juan Goytisolo', *The Review of Contemporary Fiction* XIV(2) (1980), 3–17.

—— 'The Theoretical Disparity of Contemporary Spanish Narrative', *Symposium* XXXIII (1979), 215–22.

—— 'Toward the Word/World Conflict: The Evolution of Juan Goytisolo's Novelistic Theory', in *Perspectivas de la novela. Ensayos sobre la novela española de los ss.XIX y XX de distintos autores y con una nota introductoria de Alva V. Ebersole* (Madrid: Ediciones Albatros Hispanófila, 1979), 103–13.

Hossein Nasr, S. (ed.), *Islamic Spirituality: Foundations* (New York: Crossroad, 1987).

Hutcheon, Linda, *Narcissistic Narrative: The Metafictional Paradox* (London: Methuen, 1984).

—— *A Poetics of Postmodernism: History, Theory, Fiction* (London: Routledge, 1988).

Jackson, Rosemary, *Fantasy: The Literature of Subversion* (London: Methuen, 1981).

Jakobson, Roman, 'Linguistics and Poetics', in R. and F. de George (eds), *The Structuralists: From Marx to Lévi-Strauss* (New York: Anchor Books, 1972), 84–122.

Jameson, Fredric, 'The Ideology of the Text', *Salmagundi* XXXI–XXXII (1975–76), 204–46.

—— *The Prison-House of Language: A Critical Account of Structuralism and Russian Formalism* (Princeton, NJ, and London: Princeton University Press, 1974).

Jefferson, Ann, *The Nouveau Roman and the Poetics of Fiction* (London: Cambridge University Press, 1980).

Jiménez, Pedro, 'Notas sobre *Reivindicación del conde don Julián* de Juan Goytisolo', *Revue des langues vivantes* XL (1974), 177–83.

Jones, R. O., *Poems of Góngora* (Cambridge: Cambridge University Press, 1966).

Jordan, Paul, 'Goytisolo's *Juan sin Tierra*: A Dialogue in the Spanish Tradition', *Modern Language Review* LXXXIV (1989), 846–59.

Joyce, James, *Portrait of the Artist as a Young Man* (London: Penguin, 1975 [1916]).

Juin, Hubert, 'Les sentiers de Juan Goytisolo', *Le Monde*, 2 August 1985, 11.

Kabbani, Rana, *Europe's Myths of Orient* (London: Pandora, 1988).

Kamen, Henry, *The Spanish Inquisition: An Historical Revision* (London: Phoenix, 1997).

Katz, Barry, *Herbert Marcuse and the Art of Liberation: An Intellectual Biography* (London: Verso, 1982).

Kellman, Steven G., *The Self-Begetting Novel* (New York: Columbia University Press, 1980).

Kellner, Douglas (ed.), *Jean Baudrillard: From Marxism to Postmodernism and Beyond* (Cambridge: Polity Press, 1989).

—— *Postmodernism/Jameson/Critique* (Washington, DC: Maisonneuve Press, 1989).

Kennedy, Alison Margaret, 'Dissidence and the Spanish Literary Tradition in the Later Novels of Juan Goytisolo', unpublished DPhil thesis, University of Oxford, 1996.

Kermode, Frank, *Essays on Fiction: 1971–82* (London: Routledge, 1983).

Kristeva, J. et al., *Langue, discours, société: pour Emile Benveniste* (Paris: Seuil, 1975).

Kronik, John, Review of *Formalist Elements in the Novels of Juan Goytisolo* by Género J. Pérez, *Modern Language Notes* XCVI(2) (1981), 462–68.

La Rosa, J.M. de, 'Juan Goytisolo o la destrucción de las raíces', *Cuadernos Hispanoamericanos* CCXXXVII (1969), 779–84.

Labanyi, Jo, 'The Construction/Deconstruction of the Self in the Autobiographies of Pablo Neruda and Juan Goytisolo', *Forum for Modern Language Studies* XXVI(3) (1990), 212–21.

—— *Myth and History in the Contemporary Spanish Novel* (Cambridge: Cambridge University Press, 1989).

Laing, R.D., *The Divided Self* (London: Pelican, 1965).

Larrain, Jorge, *The Concept of Ideology* (London: Hutchinson, 1979).

Lautréamont, Comte de, *Maldoror*, trans. Paul Knight (Harmondsworth: Penguin, 1978).

Lawrence, T.E., *Seven Pillars of Wisdom* (London: Jonathan Cape, 1942).

Lázaro, Jesús, *La novelística de Juan Goytisolo* (Madrid: Alhambra, 1984).

—— (ed.), *Juan Goytisolo*, Serie España, Escribir hoy, 11 (Madrid: Ministerio de Cultura, 1982).

Ledford-Miller, L., 'History as Myth, Myth as History: Juan Goytisolo's *Count Julián*', *Revista Canadiense de Estudios Hispánicos* VIII (1983), 21–30.

Lee Six, Abigail, *Juan Goytisolo: The Case for Chaos* (London: Yale University Press, 1990).

—— 'La paradigmática historia de Caperucita y el lobo feroz: Juan Goytisolo's Use of Little Red Riding Hood in *Reivindicación del conde don Julián*', *Bulletin of Hispanic Studies* LXV (1988), 141–51.

—— 'Sterne's Legacy to Juan Goytisolo: A Shandyian Reading of Juan Goytisolo', *Modern Language Review* LXXXIV (1989), 351–57.

Leiris, Michel, *L'Age d'homme*, Précédé de 'De la littérature considérée comme une tauromachie' (Paris: Gallimard, 1939).

Lentricchia, Frank, *After the New Criticism* (London: Methuen, 1983).

Levine, Linda G., 'La aniquilación del catolicismo en *Reivindicación del conde don Julián*', *Norte* IV–VI (1972), 133–141.

—— '*Don Julián*: una "galería de espejos" literarios', *Cuadernos Americanos* CLXXXVIII(3) (1973), 218–30.

—— 'La escritura infecciosa de Juan Goytisolo: contaminación y cuarentena', *Revista de Estudios Hispánicos* 28 (1994), 95–110.

—— *Juan Goytisolo: la destrucción creadora* (Mexico City: Joaquín Mortiz, 1976).

—— '*Makbara*: entre la espada y la pared—¿política marxista o política sexual?', *Revista Iberoamericana* CXVI–CXVII (1981), 97–106.

—— 'La odisea por el sexo en *Reivindicación del conde don Julián*', in *The Analysis of Hispanic Texts: Current Trends in Methodology* (New York: Bilingual Press, 1976), 90–108.

—— 'El papel paradójico del "Sida" en *Las virtudes del pájaro solitario*', in *Escritos sobre Juan Goytisolo: II Seminario Internacional sobre 'Las virtudes del pájaro solitario*', ed. Manuel Ruiz Lagos (Almería: Instituto de Estudios Almerienses, 1989), 227–36.

—— (ed.) *Reivindicación del conde don Julián*, by Juan Goytisolo, Letras Hispánicas 220 (Madrid: Cátedra, 1985).

Levine, Susan F., ' "Cuerpo" y "no-cuerpo": una conjunción entre Juan Goytisolo y Octavio Paz', *Journal of Spanish Studies. Twentieth Century* V(2) (1977), 123–35.

—— 'The Lesson of the *Quijote* in the Works of Carlos Fuentes and Juan Goytisolo', *Journal of Spanish Studies. Twentieth Century* VII (1979), 173–85.

Levy, Reuben, *An Introduction to Persian Literature* (New York: Columbia University Press, 1969).

Liebmann Schaub, Uta, 'Foucault's Oriental Subtext', *PMLA* CIV(3) (1989), 306–16.

Lodge, David (ed.), *Modern Criticism and Theory: A Reader* (London: Longman, 1988).

López, J., 'La obsesión metalingüística en Juan Goytisolo: a propósito de *Juan sin Tierra*', *Cuadernos Hispano-americanos* CXVII–CXVIII(351) (1979), 621–26.

López-Baralt, Luce, 'Hacia una lectura mudéjar de *Makbara*', in *Huellas del Islam en la literatura española: de Juan Ruiz a Juan Goytisolo* (Madrid: Hiperión, 1985), 181–209.

—— 'Inesperado encuentro', *Quimera* LXXIII (1988), 55–60.

—— 'Juan Goytisolo aprende a reír: los contextos caribeños de *Makbara* y *Paisajes después de la batalla*', *Insula* CDLXVIII (1985), 3–4.

—— '*Makbara*: Juan Goytisolo's fictionalized version of Orientalism', *The Review of Contemporary Fiction* IV(2) (1984), 138–45.

—— *San Juan de la Cruz y el Islam* (Estudio sobre las filiaciones semíticas de su literatura mística) (Mexico: El Colegio de Mexico, 1985).

Lorda Alaiz, F.M., 'Materiales e idea, tema y técnica en *Señas de identidad*', *Norte* XIII(4–6) (1972), 107–13.

Lotman, Yuri M., *The Structure of the Artistic Text* (Ann Arbor, MI: University of Michigan, 1977).

Loupias, Bernard, 'Importance et signification du lexique d'origine arabe dans le *Don Julián* de Juan Goytisolo', *Bulletin Hispanique* LXXX (1978), 229–62.

Lyon, J.E., 'The Structure of Juan Goytisolo's *Señas de identidad*', *Quinquereme* I(2) (1978), 249–57.

Lyotard, Jean-François, *The Postmodern Condition: A Report on Knowledge* (Manchester: Manchester University Press, 1992 [1986]).

MacCabe, Colin, *James Joyce and the Revolution of the Word* (London: Macmillan, 1978).

McCaffery, Larry, *The Metafictional Muse* (Pittsburgh, PA: University of Pittsburgh Press, 1982).

McHale, Brian, *Postmodernist Fiction* (London: Methuen, 1987).

Macherey, Pierre, *A Theory of Literary Production* (London: Routledge, 1978).

Mainer, José Carlos, 'Letras sin tierra: Juan Goytisolo', *Camp de l'Arpa* XXIII–XXIV (1975), 8–11.

Marcuse, Herbert, *The Aesthetic Dimension: Towards a Critique of Marxist Aesthetics* (London: Macmillan, 1979).

—— *Eros and Civilization* (London: Abacus, 1973).

Martin, G.D., 'Structure in Space: An Account of *Tel Quel*'s Attitude to Meaning', *New Blackfriars* (1971), 541–52.

Martín Morán, J.M., 'Los espejos del pájaro solitario', *RLit* LII(104) (1990), 527–35.

—— 'La escritura mística de Juan Goytisolo', *La Torre* VIII(29) (1994), 25–49.

—— 'La oralidad en las novelas de Juan Goytisolo', *Antipodas: Journal of Hispanic Studies*, University of Auckland, VIII–IX (1996–97), 155–72.

——— 'La palabra creadora. Estructura comunicativa de *Reivindicación del conde don Julián*', in *Revindicación del conde don Julián*, critical edition of L. Gould Levine (Madrid: Cátedra, 1985), 309–52.

——— *Semiótica de una traición recuperada: génesis poética de 'Reivindicación del conde don Julián'* (Barcelona: Anthropos, 1992).

Martínez Cachero, J.M., 'El novelista Juan Goytisolo', *Papeles de Son Armadans* XXXII (1964), 124–60.

Martínez-Tolentino, Jaime, *La cronología de 'Señas de identidad' de Juan Goytisolo*, Problemata Literaria 13 (Kassel: Edition Reichenberger, 1992).

Meerts, Christian, 'El espejo', in J. Ríos (ed.), *Juan Goytisolo* (Madrid: Fundamentos, 1975), 93–108.

——— *Technique et vision dans 'Señas de identidad' de Juan Goytisolo* (Frankfurt: Vittorio Klostermann, 1972).

Milner, Andrew, *Contemporary Cultural Theory: An Introduction* (London: UCL Press, 1994).

Molho, Maurice, *Sémantique et Poétique: A propos des 'Solitudes' de Góngora* (Bordeaux: Editions Ducros, 1969).

Morán, Fernando, *Novela y Semidesarrollo* (Madrid: Taurus, 1971).

More, Thomas, *Utopia* (London: Penguin, 1974).

Morrissette, B., 'Narrative "You" in Contemporary Literature', *Comparative Literature Studies* II (1965), 1–24.

Moylan, Tom, *Demand the Impossible: Science Fiction and the Utopian Imagination* (London: Methuen, 1987).

Navajas, Gonzalo, *La novela de Juan Goytisolo* (Madrid: SGEL, 1979).

——— *Teoría y práctica de la novela española posmoderna* (Barcelona: Ediciones del Mall, 1987).

Nelson, E.W., 'The Self-Conscious Narrator in Goytisolo's *Juan sin Tierra*', *Symposium*, XXXV (1981), 251–66.

Nicolaievsky, Boris, and O. Maenchen-Helfen, *Karl Marx: Man and Fighter* (London: Allen Lane, 1973).

Norris, Christopher, *Deconstruction: Theory and Practice* (London: Methuen, 1982).

——— *Derrida* (London: Fontana, 1987).

——— *Uncritical Theory: Postmodernism, Intellectuals and the Gulf War* (London: Lawrence and Wishart, 1992).

O'Neill, John, 'Religion and Postmodernism: The Durkheimian Bond in Bell and Jameson—With an Allegory of the Body Politic', in Kellner (ed.), *Postmodernism/Jameson/Critique*, 139–61.

Ong, Walter J., *Orality and Literacy: The Technologizing of the Word* (London: Methuen, 1982).

Ortega, José, 'Aproximación estructural a *Reivindicación del conde don Julián* de Juan Goytisolo', *Explicación de Textos Literarios* III(1) (1974), 45–50.

——— 'Estilo y nueva narrativa española', in *Actas del Sexto Congreso Internacional de Hispanistas* (Toronto: University of Toronto, 1980), 547–51.

——— *Juan Goytisolo: Alienación y agresión en 'Señas de identidad' y 'Reivindicación del conde don Julián'* (New York: Torres, 1972).

Ortega, Julio, 'Entrevista con Juan Goytisolo', in J. Ríos (ed.), *Juan Goytisolo* (Madrid: Fundamentos, 1975), 121–36.

Oviedo, J. Miguel, 'La escisión total de Juan Goytisolo: hacia un encuentro con lo hispano-americano', in J. Ríos (ed.), *Juan sin Tierra* (Madrid: Fundamentos, 1977), 95–105.

Payne, Robert, *Marx* (London: W.H. Allen, 1968).

Pellón, Gustavo, 'Juan Goytisolo y Severo Sarduy: discurso e ideología', *Hispanic Review* LVI (1988), 483–92.

Perez, Genaro J., *Formalist Elements in the Novels of Juan Goytisolo*, Studia Humanitatis (Madrid: Porrúa Turanzas, 1979).

—— 'Some leitmotifs and bridges in the sonata form structure of Juan Goytisolo's *Reivindicación del Conde don Julián*', *Hispanófila* I(66) (1979), 41–52.

Perez Silvestre, J.C., *La trayectoria novelística de Juan Goytisolo. (El autor y sus obsesiones)* (Barcelona: Oroel Eds., 1984).

Perrin, A., 'Dans la peau de l'autre ou le travestissement dans *Makbara* de Juan Goytisolo', in *Actes du Colloque de Pontgibaub* (Clermond-Ferrand: Association des publications Clermont II, 1982), 149–72.

—— '*Makbara*: The Space of Phantasm', *Review of Contemporary Fiction* IV(2) (1984), 157–76.

—— 'Pour une écriture-lecture-audition *Makbara* ou la voix retrouvée', *Association des Publications de Clermont II* (1982), 139–52.

Piedrahita Rook, C., 'La "toma" de la palabra por Juan Goytisolo en *Don Julián*', *Hispanófila* LXXXIV (1985), 43–50.

Plaza, Sixto, 'Los elementos epifóricos y diafóricos de *Makbara*', in *Prosa Hispánica de Vanguardia*, ed. Fernando Burgos (Madrid: Orígenes, 1986), 255–59.

Pope, Randolph D., *Understanding Juan Goytisolo* (Columbia, SC: University of South Carolina Press, 1995).

Quiñonero, P. J., 'Ante la aparición de *Juan sin Tierra*. Los últimos rumbos de Juan Goytisolo', *Informaciones*, Madrid, 12 June 1975, 5.

Raban, Jonathan, *Arabia Through the Looking Glass* (London: Fontana, 1983).

Rabinow, Paul (ed.), *The Foucault Reader: An Introduction to Foucault's Thought* (London: Penguin, 1984).

Ramos, A., 'La anti-España de Juan Goytisolo', *Explicación de Textos Literarios* X(2) (1982), 15–32.

—— 'Defensa del erotismo en *Don Julián*', *Iris* III (1982), 159–74.

—— 'El marco espacio-temporal en *Don Julián*', *Letras de Deusto* XVI(36) (1986), 25–36.

—— 'La polifacética figura de Isabel la Católica en *Reivindicación del conde don Julián*', *Insula* CDLXIV–CDLXV (1985), 20.

—— 'Texto y contexto en *Reivindicación del Conde Don Julián* de Juan Goytisolo', *Insula* CCCXCVI–CCCXCVII (1979), 19.

Rimmon-Kenan, S., 'A Comprehensive Theory of Narrative: Genette's *Figures III* and the Structuralist Study of Fiction', *PTL: A Journal for Descriptive Poetics and Theory of Literature* I (1976), 33–62.

—— *Narrative Fiction: Contemporary Poetics* (London: Methuen, 1983).

Ríos, Julián, 'The Apocalypse according to Juan Goytisolo', *The Review of Contemporary Fiction* IV(2) (1984), 127–38.

—— 'Ficcionario de tópicos', *Quimera* LXXIII (1988), 45.

—— (ed.), *Juan Goytisolo* (Madrid: Fundamentos, 1975).

—— (ed.), *Juan sin tierra* (Madrid: Fundamentos, 1978).

Rogmann, H., 'El contradictorio Juan Goytisolo', *Insula* CCCLIX (1976), 1, 12.

Romero, Héctor, 'La evolución crítico-literaria de Juan Goytisolo', *Revista de Estudios Hispánicos* VIII(3) (1974), 323–43.

—— *La evolución literaria de Juan Goytisolo* (Miami, FL: Ediciones Universal, 1979).

—— '*Señas de identidad*: una nueva etapa en la novelística de Juan Goytisolo', *Hispanófila* I(53) (1975), 61–71.

Ruiz Lagos, Manuel, 'Pájaros en vuelo a Simorg: transferencias y metamorfósis textual en un relato de Juan Goytisolo: *Las virtudes del pájaro solitario*', *Escritos sobre*

Juan Goytisolo: coloquio en torno a la obra de Juan Goytisolo (Almería: Instituto de Estudios Almerienses, 1988), 171–228.

—— 'Sobre *La Cuarentena*. El maestro Ibn Arabi amonesta a Dante Alighieri', in Juan Goytisolo, *La Cuarentena* (Barcelona: Circulo de Lectores, 1991), 143–70.

—— 'Un viaje errático', *Quimera* LXXIII (1988), 46–50.

—— (ed.) *Juan Goytisolo: semana de autor* (Madrid: Ediciones de Cultura Hispánica, 1991).

Russell, Charles, 'Individual Voice in the Collective Discourse. Literary Innovation in Postmodern American Fiction', *Substance* XXVII (1980), 29–39.

Said, Edward W., *Orientalism* (London: Routledge, 1978).

—— 'Orientalism Reconsidered', in F. Barker et al. (eds), *Literature, Politics and Theory. Papers from the Essex Conference 1976–84* (London: Methuen, 1986), 210–29.

Salgarello, A., 'Estructura de la novela contemporánea: el ejemplo de Goytisolo en *Reivindicación del conde don Julián*', *Hispanófila* LIII (1975), 25–39.

Sanz, Santos, *Lectura de Juan Goytisolo* (Barcelona: Pozanco, 1977).

Sarduy, Severo, *De donde son los cantantes* (Barcelona: Seix Barral, 1980).

Sartre, Jean-Paul, *Qu'est-ce que la littérature?* (Paris: Gallimard, 1948).

Schaefer-Rodríguez, C., 'Goytisolo through the Looking-Glass: *Paisajes después de la batalla*, Autobiography and Parody', *Journal of Mid-West Modern Language Association* XIX(2) (1986), 13–29.

—— *Juan Goytisolo: del 'realismo crítico' a la utopía* (Madrid: Porrúa Turanzas, 1984).

Scholes, Robert, *Structuralism in Literature: An Introduction* (London: Yale University Press, 1974).

Schulman, Aline, 'Luis Cernuda et Juan Goytisolo, Filiation et dissidence', in Jacques Beyrie (ed.), *Deux romans de la rupture?*, 67–75.

Schulman, Aline, '*Marks of Identity*: Identity and Discourse', *The Review of Contemporary Fiction* IV(2) (1984), 145–57.

Schwartz, Kessel, *Juan Goytisolo* (New York: Twayne, 1970).

—— 'Juan Goytisolo: Ambivalent Artist in Search of his Soul', *Journal of Spanish Studies* III (1975), 187–97.

—— 'Juan Goytisolo: las coacciones culturales y la *Reivindicación del conde Don Julián*', in Ríos (ed.), *Juan Goytisolo*, 151–67.

—— 'Juan Goytisolo: Cultural Constraints and the Historical Vindication of Count Julián', *Hispania* LIV (1971), 960–66.

—— 'Juan Goytisolo, *Juan sin Tierra* and the Anal Aesthetic', *Hispania* LXII (1979), 9–19.

—— 'Juan Goytisolo's Non-Fiction Views on "La España Sagrada"', *Revista de Estudios Hispánicos* XVI (1982), 323–32.

—— '*Makbara*—Metaphysical Metaphor or Goytisolian World Revisited?', *Hispania* LXVII (1984), 36–42.

—— 'Themes, "Ecriture" and Authorship in *Paisajes después de la batalla*', *Hispanic Review* LII (1984), 477–90.

—— 'Women in the Novels of Juan Goytisolo', *Symposium* XXXI(4) (1977), 357–67.

Senabre, Ricardo, 'Evolución de la novela de Juan Goytisolo', *Reseña*, January 1971, 3–12.

Sieburth, Stephanie, 'Reading and Alienation in Goytisolo's *Reivindicación del Conde don Julián*', *Anales de la Literatura Española Contemporánea* VIII (1983), 83–93.

Silió Cervera, César (with Marta Gómez Mata), *Oralidad y polifonía en la obra de Juan Goytisolo* (Madrid: Ensayos Júcar, 1994).

Sim, Stuart *The Icon Critical Dictionary of Postmodern Thought* (Duxford: Icon Books, 1998).

—— (ed.), *Jean-François Lyotard* (London: Prentice Hall/Harvester Wheatsheaf, 1995).

Smart, Barry, *Postmodernity* (London: Routledge, 1993).

Smith, Paul Julian, 'Juan Goytisolo and Jean Baudrillard: The Mirror of Production and the Death of Symbolic Exchange', *Revista de Estudios Hispánicos* XXIV (1990), 37–61.

—— *Laws of Desire: Questions of Homosexuality in Spanish Writing and Film 1960–1990* (Oxford: Clarendon Press, 1992).

Sobejano, Gonzalo, 'Ante la novela de los años setenta', *Insula* CCCXCVI–CCCXCVII (1979), 1, 22.

—— 'Don Julián, iconoclasta de la literatura patria', *Camp de l'Arpa* XLIII–XLIV (1977), 7–14.

—— *Novela española de nuestro tiempo (En busca del pueblo perdido)* (Madrid: Editorial Prensa Española, 1970).

—— review of *Radicalidades* by P. Gimferrer, *Hispanic Review* XLVII (1979), 549–51.

—— 'Valores figurativos y compositivos de la soledad en la novela de Juan Goytisolo', *Voces* I (1981), 23–33.

Sokal, Alan, and Jean Bricmont, *Intellectual Impostures: Postmodern Philosophers' Abuse of Science* (London: Profile Books, 1998).

Sontag, Susan, *Aids and its Metaphors* (Harmondsworth: Penguin, 1989).

Sotomayor, Carmen, *Una lectura orientalista de Juan Goytisolo* (Madrid: Espiral Hispano Americana, 1990).

Spires, Robert C., 'La autodestrucción creativa en *Reivindicación del Conde don Julián*', *Journal of Spanish Studies. Twentieth Century* IV (1976), 191–202.

—— *Beyond the Metafictional Mode: Directions in the Modern Spanish Novel* (Lexington, KY: University Press of Kentucky, 1984).

—— 'From Neorealism and the New Novel to the Self-Referential Novel: Juan Goytisolo's *Juan sin Tierra*', *Anales de la Narrativa Española Contemporánea* V (1980), 73–82.

—— 'Latrines, Whirlpools and Voids: The Metafictional Mode of *Juan sin Tierra*', *Hispanic Review* XLVIII (1980), 151–69.

—— 'The Metafictional Codes of *Don Julián* versus the Metafictional Mode of *El cuarto de atrás*', *Revista Canadiense de Estudios Hispánicos* VII(2) (1983), 306–09.

—— 'Modos narrativos y búsqueda de identidad en *Señas de identidad*', *Anales de la novela de posguerra* II (1977), 55–72.

—— *La novela española de posguerra: creación artística y experiencia personal* (Madrid: Cupsa, 1978).

—— 'El nuevo lenguaje de la nueva novela', *Insula* CCCXCVI–CCCXCVII (1979), 6–7.

—— *Post-Totalitarian Spanish Fiction* (Columbia, MO, and London: University of Missouri Press, 1996).

Stallybrass, Peter, and Allon White, *The Politics and Poetics of Transgression* (London: Methuen, 1986).

Stevenson, Randall, *Modernist Fiction: An Introduction* (Hemel Hempstead: Prentice Hall, 1998).

Sturrock, John, *Structuralism* (London: Paladin, 1986).

Suleiman, Susan R., *Authoritarian Fictions: The Ideological Novel as a Literary Genre* (New York: Columbia University Press, 1983).

Suñen, L., 'Juan Goytisolo: punto y seguido', *El País*, Libros, 5 December 1982, 5.

—— '*Makbara* de Juan Goytisolo', *Insula* CDII (1980), 5–6.

Swingewood, Alan, *Cultural Theory and the Problem of Modernity* (London: Macmillan, 1998).

Taylor, Philip M., *War and Media: Propaganda and Persuasion in the Gulf War* (Manchester: Manchester University Press, 1998).

Thompson, Colin P., *The Poet and the Mystic: A Study of the Cántico Espiritual of San Juan de la Cruz* (Oxford: Oxford University Press, 1977).

Todorov, Tzvetan, 'Les catégories du récit littéraire', in *Communications*, VIII (Paris: Ecole Pratique des Hautes Etudes, 1966), 125–51.

—— *Introduction to Poetics* (Brighton: Harvester Wheatsheaf, 1981).

Truxa, Silvia, 'El "mito árabe" en las últimas novelas de Juan Goytisolo', *Ibero-romania*, June 1980, 96–112.

Ugarte, Michael, 'Juan Goytisolo: Unruly Disciple of Américo Castro', *Journal of Spanish Studies. Twentieth Century* VII (1979), 353–64.

—— *The Poetics of Prose* (Oxford: Basil Blackwell, 1977).

—— *Trilogy of Treason: An Intertextual Study of Juan Goytisolo* (Columbia, MO, and London: University of Missouri Press, 1982).

Ullán, José Miguel, 'Arabesco para la transparencia', *Voces* I (1981), 15–22.

Valente, J.M., 'Lo demás es silencio', *Insula* XXIV (1969), 15.

Vazquez Montalbán, M., 'Juan Goytisolo o la reivindicación de Boabdil el chico', *Triunfo* CDLI (23 January 1971), 62, 64.

Vegas Gonzalez, S., 'La función terrorista del lenguaje', *Cuadernos Hispano-Americanos* CCCXXXV(111–12) (1978), 190–212.

Waugh, Patricia, *Metafiction: The Theory and Practice of Self-Conscious Fiction* (London: Methuen, 1984).

—— *Practising Postmodernism/Reading Modernism* (London: Edward Arnold, 1992).

Williams, Raymond, *Keywords: A Vocabulary of Culture and Society* (London: Fontana, 1976).

Willis, Raymond S. (ed.), *Libro de Buen Amor* (Princeton, NJ: Princeton University Press, 1971).

Woodcock, George, *Anarchism* (London: Pelican, 1977).

Yerro, Tomás, *Aspectos técnicos y estructurales de la novela española actual* (Madrid: Eunsa, 1977).

Ynduráin, F., 'La novela desde la segunda persona', in G. and A. Gullón, *Teoría de la novela* (Madrid: Taurus, 1974), 159–82.

Index